The High
Summits
of Wales

The High Summits of Wales
A Guide to Walking the Welsh Hewitts

by

Graham Uney

Logaston Press

LOGASTON PRESS
Little Logaston, Logaston,
Woonton, Almeley, Herefordshire HR3 6QH

First published by Logaston Press 1999
Copyright © Graham Uney 1999

ISBN 1 873827 65 2

Set in Times & Lucida by Logaston Press
and printed in Great Britain by
MFP Design & Print, Manchester

Front Cover: Approaching Trum y Ddysgl on the Nantlle ridge
Rear Cover: The author on Tal y Fan, on completion of his circuit of
the Welsh Hewitts in 1998

Contents

PART TWO - TRAVELOGUE OF A WELSH HEWITTEER

ACKNOWLEDGEMENTS

First and foremost, I would like to thank my long-suffering partner Rachel, for her encouragement, opinions, understanding and support. Acknowledgement and thanks is also due to my parents, to Irene and the boys, and also to Andy for sharing many great mountain days with me.

My Welsh Hewitt expedition of 1998 would not have been possible without the support of a number of different sponsors, and to the following I am grateful and in debt:- The Brasher Boot Company through Christa Johnson of The Face, Saunders, Weatherstop, Global Mobility, Bestfoods Ltd (Knorr), Aiguille Alpine Equipment, Novartis Nutrition UK Ltd (Ovaltine), Porvair, and The Red Lion Inn of Llanafan-fawr. I must also thank Mountain Range for providing me with equipment at wholesale prices.

Others whom I should also thank are The Climbers' Club for allowing me to quote from their series of guidebooks, and Alan Dawson, Dave Hewitt and John and Anne Nuttall for their advice and encouragement.

I also wish to thank the Tate Gallery, London, for allowing reproduction of the painting of Cadair Idris on p.119, the Fitzwilliam Museum, Cambridge, for that of Dolgelly on p.100, and especially Brian Byron for drawing all the maps.

FOREWORD

I am delighted to respond to a request for a Foreword to this book on the Welsh Hewitts and I do so with enthusiasm. While I was born on Ynys Mon, I was brought up in Colwyn Bay with the privilege of access to Snowdonia where the variety of rugged country still manages to surprise and delight the experienced walker. Living in South Wales, I have come to revel in the Brecon Beacons, the less accessible joys of Bannau Sir Gar and the neglected challenge of the Black Mountains. I have a soft spot for the Berwyns, but it is fitting that the brooding challenge of Cadair ldris in mid Wales has been represented as the symbol of the Welsh mountains in a new sculpture outside Cardiff Station.

One of the poems inscribed on that sculpture suggests that it is possible to reflect the peace of the mountains on the streets of the city:

> *Mae enaid angen munud - o afael*
> *Y dref, ac mae gwynfyd*
> *Fry yn bell o ferw'n byd*
> *Yn hedd mynydd am ennyd*   *Rhys Dafis*

Certainly, there is a sense of scale in the mountains, which helps put our day to day concerns into perspective:

> *And you shall listen then to the silence*
> *That is not silence, to the murmur*
> *Of the uneasy centuries among the ancient hills and valleys*
> *As here you stand with the mountain breeze on your brow.*   *ldris Davies*

The new sculpture at the heart of our capital city does a great service by celebrating the Welsh mountains and stressing their personality. For too long we have been apologetic for much about Wales. Certainly the height of our mountains is less than those of Scotland and Switzerland. But they provided the thrill and the challenge needed by those who conquered Mount Everest. They offer a personal challenge and thrill to youngsters from every part of the principality and from visitors from outside.

I am delighted to commend the publication of this book and the establishment of the Welsh Hewitts Club. In the past I have responded to the challenge of the cross Wales walk, planned by the West Midlands YJ group, which involves 45 miles and includes Plynlimon. For those, like me, who need a specific challenge to rouse us from laziness the challenge to get to know every one of the Hewitts is a fresh dose of medicine. I hope it is the medicine that proves catching in this case!

Alun Michael
Secretary of State for Wales

INTRODUCTION

Although on a world-wide scale our mountains and hills cannot boast wonderfully great altitudes, silvery sweeps of curving, rubble-strewn glaciers or mile-high rock faces, our greatest asset is a hugely diverse scenery providing a rich habitat for some of the most endearing animals and plants on the face of the earth. This, coupled with a long standing tradition of land management even in our wildest, most desolate and lonely places, whether managed as a vast expanse of heathery grouse moorland, or controversially planted with regimented rows of Sitka spruce by the Forestry Commission, has ensured that access to our high hills for the lover of real wildness has, by-and-large, been freely granted. Over the years this freedom to roam has not always been so forthcoming from either the small-time dale-head farmer, or the vast estates of Highland Scotland. Hillgoers do well to remember that what we use freely as our weekend playground is worked by people who have to make a living from the land. The truth is that all land in our glorious island is owned and managed by somebody.

Few areas of Britain could really lay claim to being 'wilderness' if the definition is taken as 'untamed by man'. Even the highest reaches of the Scottish glens often have evidence of past dwellings. Ruined crofts and shielings dot the flat parts of any 'wild' corrie. The empty wastes of the Pennines and parts of Mid and South Wales are ideal sheep farming country and, if heather is predominant, will most likely be managed as a game-bird moorland. What we find when we trudge up into these hidden corners of our countryside is an immense sense of 'wildness' rather than 'wilderness'.

The very fact that thousands of walkers, cyclists, climbers and others venture into these wild corners throughout the year, in search of the bliss of solitude, means that in reality it is very difficult to spend even a short length of time in our mountains without coming across fellow hillgoers.

The Munros and the Wainwrights (see the following section for definitions) have become increasingly popular with hillgoers over the past couple of decades, along with a handful of well-known hills within our various national parks. Hills such as Kinder Scout in the Peak District have begun to suffer from over-popularity, its vast expanses of delicate peat moorland, ringed with rough edges of gritstone becoming eroded into wide, muddy paths by countless passing feet. We are, of course, all as guilty as the next eager walker, returning time and again to our favourite mountains and fells, and each time adding to the damage. The real pity of it is that in this country we have a plethora of lesser-known peaks, admittedly of lesser height than the more frequented ones, but certainly offering as great a challenge to the walker as any of our highest mountains. One of these groups of challenging peaks is the hills of Wales over 2000'. These 'Welsh Hewitts' are what this work is concerned with.

While mighty **Snowdon** takes the strain of thousands of walkers and train travellers on her various ridges and flanks every weekend in summer, countless other summits of Snowdonia receive little more than half a dozen. Obviously **Snowdon** is bound by height alone to be very popular, and it has to be said that it really is a beautiful mountain. But then again so is **Rhobell Fawr**, **Plynlimon** or **Moel Ysgafarnogod**, each in its own very different way.

I am a strong believer in mountain exploration, rather than just following a tourist track to the summit. I love spending hours searching through hidden cwms and scrambling over quiet ridges; exploring ruins of copper mines or navigating off the beaten track in a dense conifer plantation. Witnessing a soaring red kite or a herd of red deer go towards making a perfect mountain day just as much as reaching an over-crowded summit. Through the two parts of this book I hope to encourage the reader to venture off the main paths; to look at our mountains from all sides; to struggle to the summits in all weathers, not just on an August bank holiday weekend; and to devise their own way of reaching a summit. The first part should give enthusiastic walkers a taste of what is on offer, and hopefully help them to enjoy our mountains to the full. Although a number of guidebooks have already appeared on the mountains of Wales, to my knowledge none deal with the mountains in this way, certainly not as a definitive guide to all of the Hewitts of Wales.

Obviously one of the best ways to fully explore the mountains, even from the comfort of your own home, is with the aid of an Ordnance Survey map. To me this is indispensable. Many people rely too much on guidebooks, following their each and every step to gain their particular summit. I often wonder what happens to these people when the hills are covered in fog and they find themselves off the path with no real idea of how the terrain around them fits into the pages of the book. They could be just 100 yards to one side of the path described in the book but, unable to see through the mist, would be to all intents and purposes, very much lost. If you don't know where you are, then a guide book becomes useless, but a map can be used to relocate yourself and get your-self back on the right track. For that very reason, Part One should be used alongside the relevant Ordnance Survey map, as listed in Appendix 4. I have included some basic navigation notes in Appendix 2, to give some idea of how to find your way in the mountains. Using Part One in conjunction with a map will also further encourage you to get away from the beaten tracks and to explore the mountains to the full.

Part One introduces the Hewitts of Wales by groups of each individual range of hills, whereas Part Two, as a travelogue of my walk to climb all of the Welsh Hewitts, is aimed at encouraging people to plan and undertake their own long-distance backpacking trips. The intention isn't so much to encourage walkers to follow in my footsteps—rather to go and discover the Hewitts of Wales for themselves.

THE WELSH HEWITTS CLUB

Working on this book stimulated the idea of forming a Welsh Hewitt Club. There is some terrific countryside across Wales in which these 137 hills lie, and it seemed worthwhile to promote them as an alternative to the Scottish Munros, albeit that the latter top out at over 3,000' as opposed to the 2,000' of the Hewitts.

However, it would have been no more than an idea unless organisations had come forward to help fund the establishment of the club. In this particular thanks are due to Alun Michael, MP, and The Welsh Tourist Board for seeing the potential for Wales, to the counties of Conwy, Ceredigion and Powys for both moral and financial support, and to Gwynedd for the former; and also to the Brasher Boot Company for generous support in addition to that provided to Graham Uney during his exploration of all the hills.

The Club is established with the aim of promoting the 20 groups of hills across Wales in which the 137 Hewitts lie as areas to walk, climb, or explore, whilst retaining their natural and wild environment as far as possible. The Club will maintain a list of those who climb all 137 summits, publish newsletters and, hopefully, undertake activities within the groups of hills from time to time.

Membership will be open to anyone who has the best interests of the hills in mind.

An initial address for the club is given in the appendices, and those buying the book will find a membership application form enclosed with it. This will contain the latest details of the Club for it is hoped that the Club will eventually find a home within Wales. Initially, it is important to have as its co-ordinator someone who knows all the Hewitts well, and who perhaps better, therefore, than Graham Uney himself.

PART ONE

THE WELSH HEWITTS

The Concept of the Welsh Hewitts

Over the years it has become popular, in a very British sort of way almost verging on fanaticism, for hillgoers to make it their ambition to achieve every mountain objective on a given list. I say 'hillgoer' because the word 'hillwalker' would have brought to mind the most obvious group of people who head for the hills each weekend—the Munroists. These thousands of people have chosen as their particular ambition the challenge to climb every Scottish hill above 3000' (the Munros). At the moment there are probably around 1,000 on the list who have completed the challenge, some of whom have in fact climbed the Munros more than once. Hamish Brown, a well-known Scottish mountaineer and writer is said to have climbed them all something like eight times, making at least two different rounds of Munros with two of his dogs, and one with the pupils of a school he once taught at! As I said, fanaticism, although I'm sure Hamish would deny it. To be fair, it is not only walkers who go to these extremes, hence the use of the word 'hillgoers'. I know of a number of rock climbers who are avidly ticking lists of climbs published in the highly successful trilogy of books Classic Rock, Hard Rock and Extreme Rock, in fact one of them nearly wept when he read that a cliff in the Lake District which took the line of a climb in Hard Rock had actually fallen down, and now lays scattered around the hillside at the back of the Langdale Pikes. He had been planning to visit just a week later, but now alas, he, like many others ticking Hard Rock, will be unable to achieve their ambition. Snow and ice climbers have their own particular 'bible'. Cold Climbs details the classic winter climbs in Britain, many of which, due to our frequently fickle conditions, have to wait years before seeing a successful ascent. Of course, many climbers attack all four of these lists in one fell swoop.

The Munros, listed in Munros Tables, are not the only list to attract the attention of the hillwalker. In Scotland alone there are also the Corbetts—hills above 2500', but below 3000', not as popular as the Munros, but for that very reason often regarded by the more discerning walker as the better challenge. The Corbetts also have a much greater geographical spread than the Munros and so get the walker into even further flung corners of Scotland.

Between 2000' and 2500' are the Grahams. This is a particularly unpopular group, mainly because they are largely over-shadowed by the Munros and Corbetts, but also because there is a lack of good paths leading to the summits, some of which are given over to agricultural land so increasing access difficulties. It is very likely that the list of Grahams has not been completed in total by anyone. In the Scottish Southern Uplands there are the New Donalds, also above 2000' high but with a different definition of what constitutes a separate peak. Four lists of hills, and that's just in Scotland.

To add to the confusion we also find ourselves beset by the names Murdo and Marilyn. The list of Murdos came about due to the lack of a definite criteria for Scottish 3000'ers in Munros Tables. When Sir Hugh Munro first surveyed the Scottish 3000'ers he didn't decide on what height gain or loss between neighbouring hills made them into separate summits. The original Tables seem to have been drawn up on a bit of a whim. In fact what many so-called Munroists go out of their way to achieve today is actually a much-revised list bearing little resemblance to Sir Hugh's original. In Alan Dawson's list of the Murdos, which have a definite drop on each side of 30 metres, there are actually twice the number of Munros—surely a much more worthy challenge? As for a Marilyn? This is a hill anywhere in the British Isles, regardless of height, with at least 150 metres drop on each side. It would appear that this is quite possibly the hardest list to bag for there are 1,549 Marilyns in Britain with a further 455 in Ireland. So far no one has managed them all, although Rowland and Anne Bowker of Portinscale near Keswick, are both pretty close.

In England by far the most popular grouping of hills is the Wainwrights. These hills and mountains of the Lake District became very popular after the series of seven Pictorial Guides written by Alfred Wainwright in the 1950s and '60s. Even today, the Wainwrights rival the Munros for popularity, and being anything over 1000' high, are for the most part much easier to achieve. The Wainwrights in particular give a good example of how a guidebook author can bend his own rules to suit himself. Wainwright decided to concentrate on hills above 1000' but made an exception for little Castle Crag in the 'Jaws of Borrowdale'. He freely admits in the guide that surveys have proven that the summit must be below 1000', but he includes it regardless. Conversely, on the side of Pillar Mountain overlooking the heavily wooded valley of Ennerdale stands the proud pinnacle of Pillar Rock. It is admittedly very much attached to the parent mountain, but to all those who walk and climb among the fells of Lakeland, Pillar Rock is definitely a separate summit. So why did Wainwright conveniently ignore its obvious challenge? Pillar Rock is in many respects similar to the famous Inaccessible Pinnacle on the Cuillin Ridge of the Isle of Skye. The 'In Pin' is the only Munro which requires the skills of a rock climber to reach its lofty top, and likewise the ropes, harnesses and heavy ironmongery of the modern climber come into play for an ascent of Pillar Rock. Wainwright could by no stretch of the imagination be said to have been comfortable on the crags and rocks of his beloved mountains, and so he chose to convince himself that Pillar Rock was no more than just another Lakeland crag, rather than an independent summit. Most convenient! There are other parallels between Munro and Wainwright. The Inaccessible Pinnacle was one of the only two mountains on Munro's list that he failed to climb, and likewise, Pillar Rock never saw an ascent by the indefatigable Alfred Wainwright.

For the rest of England, Wales and Ireland the walker in search of a challenge has had to rely on a number of lists compiled over a period of time, none of which have ever been given a particular group name. During the late 1980s the husband and wife team, John and Anne Nuttall surveyed the various ranges of England and Wales and published a two volume guide detailing every hill above 2000'. This was certainly a step in the right direction. Many hillwalkers welcomed the new lists and went about the rather enjoyable business of bagging them all. Since then, however, the more discerning hillwalker has come to realise that a number of the hills in the Nuttalls' books are actually nothing more than boring bumps on a subsidiary ridge of the parent mountain. Even today, as each hill becomes more and more trodden by the thousands of pairs of feet climbing to these summits, other surveyors among them have continued the Nuttalls' work and discovered other grassy knolls which just about struggle above the height of 2000'. Thus the list grows from year to year. Not particularly worrying as the list of Munros either grows or shrinks with every new addition of the Munros Tables. The problem with the Nuttalls' list is that to qualify as a separate hill worthy of climbing in it's own right, a summit need only rise 50' above an intervening col before the next hill. On our metric maps where contours are spaced 10 metres apart, 50' is quite a small margin and is somewhere between one and two contour lines. Therefore a single ring contour anywhere above 2000' is a contender for a 'new' Nuttall. Of course the whole situation is made all the more preposterous by the simple fact that the Ordnance Survey quite rightly use metres to measure all heights and distances on their maps, but hillwalkers still prefer to deal in feet and miles, making conversion from one to the other necessary. You may even find yourself using both, side-by-side, whilst out on the hill. Very confusing!

3

In terms of defining a 'sensible' list of the High Summits of Wales the choice was clearly between 1000', 2000' and 3000'. The former would be nigh on impossible to list as there must be countless thousands of grassy little bumps that would top out at over 1000', many of them hardly counting as 'high summits' when dwarfed by their neighbours. Conversely selecting 3000' would only provide 15 peaks, not fulfilling the aim of encouraging exploration of a wider range of Welsh countryside. 2000' was the clear choice, but how to overcome the Nuttall problem? That's where the Hewitts came in. The list of Welsh Hewitts (**H**ills of **E**ngland, **W**ales and **I**reland above **T**wo **T**housand feet) by Alan Dawson contains 137 2000'ers in Wales. The main difference between the Hewitts and the lists drawn up by the Nuttalls is that the Hewitts use 100' of height gain or loss to define separate summits. This ensures that the Welsh Hewitts are very much more independent of each other than are the Nuttalls, and few walkers would deny that each Hewitt is a very separate summit. Together they provide a breadth of scenery and history covering a wealth of the land of Wales.

SNOWDON

Yr Wyddfa, the highest and probably most popular mountain in England and Wales is known to everyone simply as **Snowdon**. Yr Wyddfa, the Welsh name, refers to a 'burial ground' and is apt for the summit rocks itself, for legend has it that King Arthur slew a fierce giant called Rhita Gawr, and had a great cairn thrown over him on the highest mountain in Eryri. Unfortunately there is no archaeological evidence to back up this story behind the huge cairn at the top of **Snowdon**. Yet King Arthur himself is supposed to be asleep in a cave on **Y Lliwedd** with his knights, whilst there used to be an old cairn known as Carnedd Arthur at Bwlch y Saethau, the pass of the arrows, between **Snowdon** and **Y Lliwedd**. Alas, it is no longer there.

But **Snowdon** is much more than being the highest mountain south of the Scottish border. In all, eight summits in the range rise above 2000 feet as Hewitts, and three of those are 3000 footers. All of them are very different from each other, and all are worthy of the hill walker's attention.

The wooded valley of the Nant Gwynant forms the border to the south, with its twin lakes of Llyn Gwynant and Llyn Dinas, its tiny hamlet of Bethania, a Youth Hostel and a camp site, and of course, the busy A498. At the western end of this road lies the village of Beddgelert from where the popular approach to the **Moel Hebog** range starts. At Beddgelert the roads divide, one heading south for the Aberglaslyn Pass and Porthmadog, while the other heads north up the Nant Colwyn and over to Rhyd Ddu, down beside Llyn Cwellyn and on to Waun Fawr. It is this latter road, the A4085 that forms the western boundary of the Snowdon massif. Heading east up Nant Gwynant the A498 climbs to a pass above the head of the cwm, and continues beyond a junction to Capel Curig. At this junction stands the proud Hotel of the Pen-y-Gwryd, one of the main centres for early explorations of Snowdonia. It is from here that the A4086 winds a torturous way up to the narrow col between the **Snowdon** group and the Glyders, at the top of which stands the well known Pen-y-Pass Youth Hostel, the Snowdonia National Park Ranger Information Centre, a café and a large car park. Heading north down the other side of 'the pass', as it is invariably named by all 'in the know', the road loses height quickly and drops beneath towering cliffs festooned with colourful climbers, and on to the popular hot spot of Llanberis. Only to the north does the **Snowdon** range lack a definite boundary, as the terrain just falls gently away from **Moel Eilio**, the north-ernmost peak of the group, to Bangor, Caernarfon, the Menai Strait and the island of Anglesey.

The group as a whole is fairly compact, although it can be conveniently divided into two distinct areas for the purpose of description. From Llyn Cwellyn in the west, the now-famous path, 'the Snowdon Ranger' climbs easily in long zig-zags around the open, grassy slopes of **Moel Cynghorion**. Above a little lake on the right, Llyn Ffynnon-y-gwas, the path climbs up to an obvious col, Bwlch Cwm Brwynog. To the south of this col lie the rugged heights of the main **Snowdon** ridges, while to the north, the hills become grassier, and more dome-like. This is the **Moel Eilio** section of the group, and for the purposes of keeping this chapter manageable, I will describe these hills separately.

A track heads uphill from the turn off for the Youth Hostel in Llanberis and winds its way up, out of the town to the Bwlch-y-groes. From here an obvious path heads south over an eroded moor of grass and bilberry, climbs a stile high up and brings the walker out onto the flat, grassy summit plateau of **Moel Eilio**, 'the supporting bare hill', at 2382'. W.P. Haskett Smith tells us in *Climbing in the British Isles*, that it is often spelt 'Aeliau', which of course it may have been when his book was first published in 1895, though nowadays the hill's name is always written as 'Eilio'.

If the day is clear, the views from the summit plateau will be tremendous, taking in the whole of Anglesey to the north, the open sea out to the west, with the small hills of 'The Rivals', Yr Eifl, silhouetted against the sparkling waters. Nearer at hand, the **Moel Hebog** range looks spectacular, particularly the 'elephant mountain', **Mynydd Mawr**, just across the defile of Nant-y-Betws, although it is necessary to walk westwards from the summit cairn to see these latter hills to full effect, due to the convex nature of the plateau. It is, however, the high ridges of **Snowdon** itself that domi-nate the view across the intervening hills of mat-grass to the south.

A deep cwm is gouged out of the hills to the east, above Llanberis, and contains the quiet waters of Llyn Dwythwch. In fact, for the whole of this section of the Snowdon range, it is invariably the eastern flanks that throw down broken rocks and scree into the valley. The western slopes are predominantly grass-covered, as are the summits. The ridges forming the two sides of this cwm can be climbed to form an alternative and very enjoy-able approach to **Moel Eilio** from Llanberis.

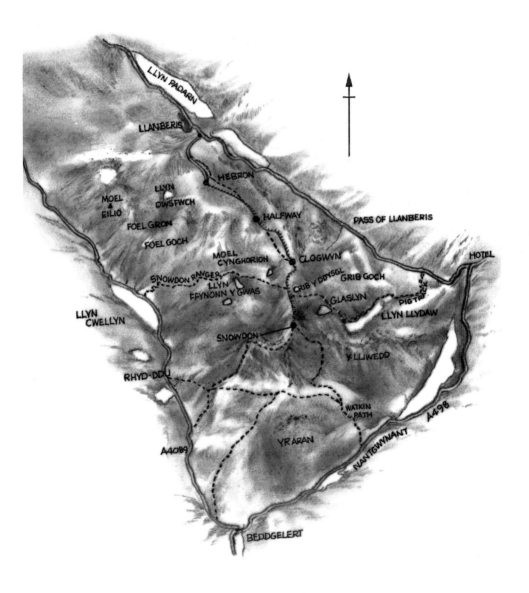

The steep, vegetated shoulders to the west are not really ideal for an ascent from Betws Garmon, although it is possible to gain the Bwlch-y-groes via a track from Waunfawr, just to the north, and follow the path to the summit as described above.

South of **Moel Eilio**, the path climbs a stile and descends to the twin cols of Bwlch Gwyn and Bwlch Cwm Cesig, before the short stroll to the top of **Foel Gron**, 'the round bare hill', at 2064'. This Hewitt is particularly unremarkable however, and is never climbed for its own sake. Indeed it would seem that the only way to reach its top without reverting to climbing stone walls and trespassing is to take this ridge walk over from **Moel Eilio** to Foel Goch as described, or vice-versa.

South-east of **Foel Gron**, the ridge bends around to the minor top of Foel Goch, with a stile just short of the summit. The way leads alongside the fence on a good path down to Bwlch Maesgwm, just above the zig-zags of the 'Snowdon Ranger' track up **Snowdon** itself. It is possible to gain the path along the Eilio ridge direct from there by simply ascending the grassy tongue, but few would want to miss out on the easy stroll over **Moel Cynghorion**.

At Bwlch Maesgwm, a gate leads through a wall and the two tracks diverge. The one heading downhill will soon pick up the zig-zags and have the walker back at the Snowdon Ranger Youth Hostel beside Llyn Cwellyn in no time, while the one to the left climbs quite steeply up short grass beside a fence. Soon however, the ridge levels out, and the walking becomes very easy to the top of **Moel Cynghorion**, 'bare hill of the councillors', at 2211'. Cliffs plunge down from the very top, beyond a feeble fence and this is one of the very best places in the area to relax and admire the view. Across the wild wastes of Cwm Brwynog, you can see the tiny train labouring under its load of passengers towards the Clogwyn Station above Llechog.

500 feet downhill to the south-east is the Bwlch Cwm Brwynog and the continuation up **Snowdon**, but for many walkers, this straightforward ridge traverse will be enough for one day.

For those wishing to return to Llanberis a good way down from the summit of **Moel Cynghorion** is the very steep north ridge. This leads down to Helfa, and across the Afon Arddu to Hebron Station and the Llanberis Path up **Snowdon**. Another possibility is to return to Bwlch Maesgwm and pick up a good track down the valley of Maesgwm, which heads north below the steep screes and broken crags of Foel Goch.

South of Bwlch Cwm Brwynog the moorgrass slopes rise higher and higher, passing broken crags, scree and boulders to Yr Wyddfa. You either love or hate **Snowdon**. Few English people feel the urge to make the pilgrimage to Scafell Pike's top, highest point in England, but this cannot be said for **Snowdon**. For many people it is the only mountain they will ever climb in their lives, and for a large percentage of those who do scale its rough flanks, the Snowdon Ranger Path provides one of the easiest ways to the top. It is very probable that it is also the oldest track to the summit and was used by all the early travellers.

In 1770 Joseph Cradock wrote in *Letters from Snowdon* of the inn from which all ascents of **Snowdon** were made at that time, 'we found shelter in a small thatched hut at the foot of the mountain, near a lake which they call Cychwhechlyn [Cwellyn] which I leave you to pronounce as well as you are able... We were determined to amuse ourselves as well as we could in this dreary situation. For this purpose we sent for a poor blind harper and procured a number of blooming country girls to divert us with their music and dancing.'

By 1854, when that great tourist in the classic mould, George Borrow, journeyed through Wild Wales, the 'small thatched hut' had become the centre for personally conducted ascents of **Snowdon**. In his book *Wild Wales*, Borrow mentions an interview with a father and son-in-law by the side of the road. After questioning the pair about the lake, Llyn Cwellyn, Borrow made the mistake of assuming the older man to be a fisherman.

"'Fisherman!" said the elderly man contemptuously, "not I. I am the Snowdon Ranger."

"And what is that?"' asked Borrow.

The younger man felt inclined to answer for the older, who had 'tossed his head proudly and made no reply' to the question.

"'A ranger means a guide, sir. My father-in-law is generally termed the Snowdon Ranger because he is a tip-top guide, and he has named the house after him the Snowdon Ranger. He entertains gentlemen in it who put themselves under his guidance in order to ascend **Snowdon** and see the country."'

It is also recorded that early accounts often spoke of the place as Bronyfedw, a name which is still given to the cluster of farmhouses just south of what is now the Snowdon Ranger Youth Hostel.

There is a car park by the shores of Llyn Cwellyn near the Hostel, from where the Snowdon Ranger Path begins. Across the A4085 the path climbs steeply to the left of the Hostel and begins a series of zigzags. This soon becomes easier as it nears the southern flanks of **Moel Cynghorion** and enters the grassy, northern slopes of Cwm Treweunydd. The track continues along its obvious course, contouring for a while before climbing towards the col of

Snowdonia from Capel Curig, from an old engraving

Bwlch Cwm Brwynog. It is as well to remember that the track does not actually gain this col, but climbs steeply up the slopes just to the south. The way is obvious, but in mist it could be confusing if you had it in mind that you were going to come to a col. The lapping waters of Llyn Ffynnon-y-gwas lie down the slope to the right as you climb, and underfoot more zigzags make the gradient easier to handle. As height is slowly gained it becomes more obvious that you are climbing a long, fairly narrow ridge, with the flanks falling away as grass and scree to the south-west into the tarn riddled openness of Cwm Clogwyn, and the precipitous crags of Clogwyn Du'r Arddu plunging into the abysmal depths of upper Cwm Brwynyog to the north. Hidden in this latter is the barren, boulder strewn banks of Llyn Du'r Arddu.

Actual details of Clogwyn Du'r Arddu, The Black Cliff, known universally as 'Cloggy', cannot be grasped from the ridge above, but the undoubted magnificent splendour of the place is apparent to all who wander slightly off the main track to peer into the depths from the cliff edge.

Cloggy has always been a crag for the hard men of rock climbing, and is often revered by the Welsh climbing fraternity as the Mecca of British Climbing. This is of course, highly controversial, as each of the mountain districts of Britain have devotees who would all claim a similar title for their favourite high mountain crag. Lakeland habitués would say the same for Scafell, climbers from the west coast of Scotland would name Ben Nevis as the Shrine of British Climbing, and those from the east coast would say that Lochnagar or Creagan Dubh Loch deserve that title. The truth is that there has always been a degree of competitiveness between the habitués of each area, and though climbers in general are happy to climb in a variety of different locations, they always feel compelled to return time and again to their particular region. Thus names such as Menlove Edwards, Joe Brown and Pete Crew will always be linked with Welsh rock climbing, even though they all climbed extensively throughout Britain, and likewise, the Abraham Brothers, Jim Birkett and Bill Peascod will always be known as Lakeland climbers, whilst Harold Raeburn, Jim Bell, Jimmy Marshall and Tom Patey will always be remembered as Scottish climbers.

However you look at it though, you have simply got to admit that Cloggy is a wonderfully atmospheric place, and few could deny that the Black Cliff does have one of the largest concentrations of hard rock climbs on any cliff in Britain.

Climbing on Cloggy began as early as 1798, although this was in the name of botany rather than that of mountaineering. The Reverends P. Williams and W. Bingley ascended the Eastern Terrace of Clogwyn Du'r Arddu in search of alpine plants. The account by Bingley is as gripping to read as that of any of the more recent climbing adventures and tales of daring-do. He tells how 'the steep section immediately above us was the only one that presented any material danger. Mr Williams, having a pair of strong shoes with nails in them, which would hold their footing better than mine, requested to make the first attempt, and after some difficulty he succeeded ... When he had fixed himself securely to a part of the rock, he took off his belt, and holding it firmly by one end, gave the other to me: I laid hold, and, with a little aid from the stones, fairly pulled myself up it.' Impressive stuff for the times. He goes on, 'After this we got on pretty well, and in about an hour and a quarter from the commencement of our labour, we found ourselves on the brow of this dreadful precipice, and in possession of all the plants we expected to find.' Today, the Eastern Terrace, along with that of its neighbour, the Western Terrace, provide the only relatively easy ways up the cliff, being more of a scruffy scramble than a climb. This does not however, imply that they should be attempted by the ill-equipped hillwalker.

The first actual rock climbs on Cloggy took place in 1905, the East Wall Climb falling to the Abraham brothers—George Dixon and Ashley Perry, and Deep Chimney seeing an ascent by Mr P.S. Thompson and party. From then onwards the list of first ascentionists on the cliff reads like a who's who of British rock climbing: Herbert Carr, Frank Smythe, A.S. Pigott, and Jack Longland were all very active in these early years. Smythe and Longland went on to much greater things. Smythe led a successful expedition to Kamet (25,447') in the Indian Himalaya in 1931, and took the glory for bagging the highest summit ever climbed at that time. Longland reached 27,400' on Everest in 1933, but is also well known as being the founder of White Hall Outdoor Pursuits Centre near Buxton in Derbyshire, the first ever local authority centre in Britain. He was knighted in 1970.

In the 1930s climbing on Cloggy, and indeed on many other mountain crags throughout the British Isles, was dominated by Colin Kirkus, Maurice Linnell, Menlove Edwards and G.G. Macphee. Kirkus, a Liverpool lad, was a shy, retiring type, who incredibly became a tiger on the rocks. Apart from playing a significant part in opening up the bold slab routes on Cloggy, he made the first climb on the daunting East Buttress of Scafell in the Lake District (Mickledore Grooves in 1930), and was one of the leading activists on many other Welsh mountain crags at that time. Kirkus died in war-torn Germany when his plane was shot down.

Maurice Linnell likewise was a leading player in the game, climbing many routes on Cloggy. He was killed in a climbing accident on Ben Nevis in 1934, an accident which also seriously injured Kirkus, his partner at the time. This accident almost saw Kirkus give up climbing for good.

John Menlove Edwards, another Liverpool rock climber, is widely considered the best climber of the 1930s. He was strictly a habitué of the mountain crags of North Wales and opened up countless crags and hard climbs. Increasing disappointment over his work as a psychiatrist led to his suicide in 1958.

George Graham Macphee was another good all-rounder, climbing throughout Britain, but making a real impact on Welsh climbing by bagging the first ascent of the Great Slab of Cloggy with Kirkus in 1930. A Scottish doctor, his must have been a life of almost continuous travelling if his exploits on Welsh, Lakeland and Scottish rock are anything to go by, unusual for the 1930s, although of course his affluence as a doctor meant he could afford his own car. Macphee is credited with first coining the name 'Cloggy'.

There were many other prominent names in Welsh rock climbing during this period, but these four are perhaps the most significant. Other famous names followed including the legendary members of the Rock and Ice Club in 1951. For the next eight years the names of Joe Brown, Don Whillans, Nat Allen, Slim Sorrell and others of the club dominate the list of first ascentionists. The climbs these working class heroes were pulling off on Cloggy were way ahead of anything that had been attempted before, earning members of the club, and the climbs they ascended, a notable degree of respect from other climbers of the time, and to a certain extent, right up to the present day. Perhaps a short quote from the log of the climber's hut, Ynys Ettws, down in the Llanberis Pass is all that needs to be said, 'Spent hours trying to do Pinnacle Flake, one of Mr Joe Brown's easier climbs, and were quite unable to leave the ground.'

That other climbers held the routes of Brown and Whillans in awe is apparent, though slowly, through the late fifties and early sixties, other parties began having a degree of success on these test-pieces. Inevitably, once a climber had managed to struggle up a Rock and Ice route or two, his confidence in his own ability would greatly improve, and soon, by the early to mid sixties, Martin Boysen, Pete Crew, Bas Ingle and Jack Soper joined the higher ranks of leading rock climbers of the day, having achieved success on these desperate Rock and Ice routes.

Grades on Cloggy by this time were pretty advanced in comparison to other mountain crags of Britain, but as elsewhere, they were to come on in leaps and bounds over the next few decades. Controversial tactics were often employed in an effort to further the possibilities on this grim cliff. In 1980, John Redhead tried desperately to force a line up a fearfully blank section of the East Buttress of Cloggy. The current guide says of Master's

Snowdon from Capel Curig by John Varley (1778-1842)
This pencil and watercolour sketch was probably made during a tour of Snowdonia in 1802, a year in which the inn at Capel Curig would have hosted many a watercolour artist

Wall, as it was to become, 'An intimidating route, audacious in concept, strenuous in execution and making grave demands on mind and body.' He finally achieved a high point at around 80 feet and placed a bolt, from which his partner lowered him off. This is just a simple builder's expansion bolt, placed in a pre-drilled hole in the rock and used as protection from a ground fall by clipping the rope through it via a snap-link or karabiner. Although these tactics had been used to some extent in the past, the practise was generally felt to be unacceptable by a large part of the climbing fraternity. Those placing bolts usually feel that this is the only way forward, whilst those who are against, feel that it is denuding the rock of its natural qualities, and that these hard lines should be left clean for a future generation to attempt. Only three years later, that future generation arrived at Cloggy. Jerry Moffatt inspected the wall by abseil from above, chopped the bolt out, and climbed the pitch and its continuation line. Master's Wall is graded as Extreme Severe Class 7 (E7 to those in the know). There are few climbers in the world who currently climb at this grade on this type of route. But that isn't the end of it. There are six other E7 routes on Cloggy, and amazingly, one E9! This is considered to be the hardest grade at the moment, although the climbing magazines often report of new climbs that 'This could be the first E10 on British rock'. As the system is open-ended to take account of rising standards, both physically and mentally, it is only a matter of time before our guidebooks are graced with climbs graded E11 and E12.

On October 4th, 1986 a young climber of exceptional ability, Johnny Dawes climbed what is described in the guide as, 'An incredibly "necky" lead requiring total commitment. Probably the most serious route in Britain ...' This is the Indian Face—Cloggy's E9!

So, as you stand on the bouldery top of Cloggy, watching the tiny train across the wide cwm to the east, struggling uphill with its convoy of carriages strung out in front, try to imagine the historical significance of this wonderful crag beneath your feet, the Black Cliff, hallowed ground to the rock climber.

Above the cliff edge of Clogwyn Du'r Arddu, the terrain eases in gradient and the whole flank of this part of **Snowdon** opens out. The path gains the railway tracks, of which, more shortly, and brings the walker to a small standing stone which marks the top of the Pig Track at Bwlch Glas.

Crossing the railway tracks, the path is still very obvious, and skirts the edge of the Clogwyn y Garnedd cliffs, falling steeply into the delightful tarn of Glaslyn to the east.

On this approach to **Snowdon**, the short platform for the railway is soon underfoot, beyond which to the south is the Snowdon Hotel, not a hotel as

The summit of Snowdon as depicted on a postcard of the 1930s

such, being more of a tourist-style gift shop full of 'I've Climbed Snowdon' T-shirts and the like, and a cafe. This is the regrettable side of **Snowdon**, the crowds, rubbish and general holiday atmosphere. There is a history of selling refreshments to walkers on the summit of **Snowdon**, however, dating as far back as 1838. In 1845 a licence was granted to sell intoxicating liquor, and the café-cum-bar has seen a steady trade in beer since the railway was constructed in 1896, bringing tourists from Llanberis to the summit, without the inconvenience of having to actually walk.

As already mentioned, the summit itself is believed to be the resting place of a giant, Rhita Gawr, who was slain by King Arthur. The huge cairn is unmistakable and stands at 3560' above the sea, just to the east of the station. An O.S. trig pillar graces the top.

As you would expect, the views are astounding, reaching as far as Northern Ireland, Snaefell on the Isle of Man and Scafell Pike in Lakeland, although you will need to wait until the day is crisp and clear to see that far.

This ascent via the Snowdon Ranger Path is only one aspect of **Snowdon**. The summit itself is like the hub of a wheel, the six ridges thrown down in all directions being the spokes. Perhaps the best way to describe these ridges, and the delightful cwms which separate them, is to follow the wheel round clockwise, from the Snowdon Ranger Path, describing each in turn.

From the Snowdon Ranger Path the train can be seen chugging up a long ridge across the cwm to the east. This is also the ridge taken by the popular Llanberis Path.

The village of Llanberis, boasting a population of only around 2,000, though this increases during the tourist season when almost half a million people visit, has long been the main settlement of the valley. At Dinas Ty Du, 1076' above sea level and one mile west of the present day village, the remains of an iron age fort have been found. Hut circles behind the fort can also be traced.

By the mid-6th century Christianity had begun to spread through Wales and St. Peris, a Cardinal and son of Helig ap Glannog founded a religious centre at Nant Peris, just up the valley from Llanberis.

Perhaps the most obvious sign of past settlers in the area today is the vast spoil heaps from the slate quarries which tower over the village from across Llyn Padarn and Llyn Peris to the east. These were originally worked by small groups of men working independently, and as far back as 1772 there were five quarries above Llyn Padarn, and three above Llyn Peris. The quarried stone was dressed, then taken down to the shore of the lake by horse-drawn sledges. It was then taken down the lake by boat, and on to Caernarfon by cart. The land on which these quarries were being worked was owned by the huge Vaynol Estate and leased to the quarrymen, but when the lease expired in 1828, the estate joined into a partnership with the workers, and organised the quarrying to be a more profitable business. In its heyday, around the 1870s, the quarry partnership employed 3,000 men, but by 1969 the slate was becoming uneconomical to mine, and with a work force of only 300, it closed down.

But slate quarrying was by no means the only source of employment in Llanberis. The Snowdon massif is good quality farmland for livestock, and sheep farming has been carried out for generations.

Nowadays however, the main industry is undoubtedly tourism. Every other building on the main street seems to be a Hotel or B&B. There are cafés galore, book shops, outdoor equipment shops, and across the main road, Electric Mountain. This exhibition centre is focused around explaining to visitors the ins and outs of Hydro Power, via a drive-through-the-mountain-display.

Without a doubt, the most popular tourist attraction in Llanberis is the Snowdon Mountain Railway. This was opened in March 1896, after only 72 days work on laying the track. This was supplied by a British company, Messrs. Richard Cammell & Co. but the locomotives and rolling stock were manufactured by a Swiss engineering company.

On Easter Monday the first train made the ascent. All went well to the summit, but disaster was to strike on the descent. Subsidence had slightly buckled the line above Clogwyn Station, and as the train made its return journey to Llanberis, it left the tracks and automatically uncoupled itself from the coaches. The automatic hand brakes on the coaches averted further disaster, but the locomotive plunged down a ravine to become a total wreck. The two crew—driver and fireman—were lucky to escape uninjured, but two panicking passengers had jumped from the coaches, and one died from his injuries. Since that fateful day, a day that should have been a grand opening, but ended in tragedy, there have been no other major accidents.

There are five stations on the line; Llanberis, Hebron, Halfway, Clogwyn and the Summit.

The Snowdon Mountain Railway is not the only narrow gauge railway plying its trade in Llanberis. In 1824 the Dinorwic Quarry owners built a railway from Allt Ddu, near Deiniolen, along the north bank of Llyn Padarn to Port Dinorwic to transport the slate to the ships. However, like the other quarries in the area, it officially closed down in 1969. Within three years the locomotives and rolling stock had been purchased, and the then unemployed quarrymen were taken on to rebuild the section of track beside the lake. In 1972, when the Padarn Railway began operating as a tourist attraction, these same quarrymen were employed to run the line.

Other tourist facilities in the Llanberis area include a wealth of museums, craft workshops, and of course, outdoor pursuits.

It probably goes without saying that no self respecting hillwalker would stoop to the level of the average tourist, and take a ride on the Snowdon Mountain Railway.

Dolbadarn Castle by Llyn Peris, from a drawing on stone by H. Waldon from a sketch by H.L. Jones

For those based in Llanberis that want to climb **Snowdon** from there, there is an easy path which for the most part follows the railway tracks. The gradient all the way up is pretty constant, and once the upper mountain is gained, beyond the Halfway Station, the views begin to open up across the yawning gulf of the Pass of Llanberis to the left.

Mid-way between Halfway and Clogwyn Stations, the railway track swings off to the left, whereas the footpath continues more or less dead-ahead. A good view can be had of 'The Pass' if you follow the line of the railway instead, and take the stroll over to the top of the little knoll known as Llechog.

As the railway passes Clogwyn Station, the footpath crosses from the western side and runs almost parallel to it, to the summit of **Snowdon**.

Back down in Llanberis, the clockwise exploration of the range is continued by heading up The Pass, through Nant Peris and on, along the A4086, beneath the many buttresses which line both sides of the road. The road over the pass itself, opened in 1818, did a great deal to lessen the crowds of tourists attempting an ascent of Snowdon from Llanberis, for from Gorphwysfa, the old inn at the summit of Pen-y-Pass, there are a choice of four very different ways up the mountain, suitable for day-tripper and hardened mountaineer alike.

But before Pen-y-Pass Youth Hostel, the old Gorphwysfa, is reached a deep cwm opens up on the northern side of the **Crib y Ddysgl - Crib Goch** ridge, and is a good way for the fell-wanderer to see a quieter side of these mountains. At the point were the road crosses the Afon Nant Peris, a bridge called Pont-y-Gromlech, a way can be made up the rocky slopes into Cwm Glas, not to be confused with the upper part of Cwm Dyli over **Crib y Ddysgl** to the south, where the lake is called Glaslyn.

A rocky ridge is thrown down into the upper reaches of Cwm Glas, effec-tively slicing the cwm in two. The right-hand, western most cwm provides the only easy continuation onto the main ridge for the walker, passing the tiny Llyn Bach, and gaining the Llanberis Path just slightly higher than Clogwyn Station. The left-hand, easternmost cwm is Cwm Uchaf, with the marked nick of Bwlch Coch at its top. Bwlch Coch is the col between **Crib y Ddysgl** and **Crib Goch**. The rocky ridge separating the two upper cwms is the Clogwyn y Person Arête, or the Parson's Nose. This gives a wonderful, easy way onto the tops for the rock climber or bold scrambler and was first ascended in 1884 by A.H. Stocker. The rock scenery all around is superb and full of mountaineering history. Again, many of the earliest pioneers climbed here, though more often than not, climbing on our mountain crags in the nineteenth and early twentieth centuries was seen purely as training for ascending the much higher peaks in the Alps, Caucasus and Greater Ranges. Many climbs were done throughout Britain in the name of 'training', but it wasn't until Walter Parry Haskett Smith climbed the Napes Ridge and Napes Needle on Great Gable in the Lake District in 1886, that the sport of British rock climbing in its own right began.

There are many other good climbs and scrambles in Cwm Glas, but this book is aimed chiefly at the hill walker, not the rock climber.

From the car park at the top of Pen-y-Pass, four delightful ways to the summit of **Snowdon** are open to the walker, and even the hardest of these, the traverse of **Crib Goch** and **Crib y Ddysgl**, which takes in some seriously exposed scrambling, is a possibility for those with a head for heights.

A good track leaves the car park at its top, westernmost corner and begins contouring around the craggy slopes of a minor summit at 609 metres. After a fairly gentle climb, way above the tiny cars whizzing along the road in The Pass to the north, an obvious col is reached below the towering mass of **Crib Goch**, bristling with red slabs and broken scree. This is Bwlch y Moch, the pass of the pigs. It is amusing to note how this track, which contours from the col around the southern side of **Crib Goch**, and is known as The Pig Track, has over the years become known as The Pyg Track, P-Y-G being the often abbreviated term for the Pen-y-Gwryd Hotel to the east of Pen-y-Pass. Of course, many of the early walkers would have come this way from their lodgings at Pen-y-Gwryd, and perhaps that is how the name of the path had come to change. However, many writers of walking and climbing in Snowdonia have realised this mistake, and slowly the walking public are coming round to the using the proper name,'The Pig Track'.

The Pig Track contours around the southern slopes of **Crib Goch**, and gives an easy way up to Bwlch Glas, high up on Snowdon where the Llanberis Path begins its final climb to the top. However, the traverse of the crenellated crest of **Crib Goch** and **Crib y Ddysgl**, is incredible, and not to be missed by the more energetic and robust walker. From Bwlch y Moch a path ascends steeply to the base of shattered slabs. These can be climbed at a number of places and the general way is obvious, although care should be taken not to knock loose stones down on those coming up behind you, for this traverse is one of the most popular easy mountaineering expeditions in the British Isles, and there will be other walkers aplenty. Soon the slabs close in, and the path reaches a prominent pointy top, from where the crest of **Crib Goch** stretches out westwards in a sharp edge of impeccable rock. Do not be misled, this is a way for walkers, but do not expect to be striding

19

out on grass or heather. For the most part the terrain underfoot is good, solid rock and you should expect to make use of your hands at least half as much as your feet to further any progress. However, if tackled with a cool head, conscientiously and with an amount of awareness for what those around you are doing, even the timidest walker should have little problem completing the traverse. The confident walker will be happy to tackle this level crest with hands-in-pockets and feet firmly placed on the very top of the rib, though most people find it is easier to shuffle along on the western face, using the abundant ledges as footholds and the crest itself as a handrail. Some of course tackle the whole ridge on their bums!

At the end of the ragged knife-edge ridge, the way becomes easier and a prominent cairn marks the top of **Crib Goch**, 'the red ridge', at 3028'. Beyond this point a wild cluster of high pinnacles, including one featured in one of the Abraham brothers' classic photographs, the Crazy Pinnacle, rise out of the deep cwms at either side, totally blocking the way along the ridge. For many walkers this is the most nerve-wracking part of the whole ridge, but in actual fact the scrambling here is easier than that up the slabs to gain the crest above Bwlch y Moch. The first two pinnacles are outflanked on the south side to a windy notch. Passing through the notch and following a series of exposed ledges on the north side of the third pinnacle, its summit is eventually reached. An easy gully leads down to Bwlch Coch, and the hard part of the famous **Snowdon** Horseshoe is over. This is the classic traverse of the four Hewitts hemming in Cwm Dyli to the south of the **Crib Goch** ridge, and is arguably the best ridge crossing outside of the Isle of Skye on Scotland's western seaboard. Only there, on the serious, black gabbro of the Cuillin can a more satisfying day be had, although of course, the Cuillin Traverse is reserved strictly for the mountaineer.

The second Hewitt of the Horseshoe, **Crib y Ddysgl**, rises quite gently at first from Bwlch Coch, although a high broken step in the ridge adds a challenging scramble to those wanting more of the same after **Crib Goch**. There is a path which outflanks this step on the left, but for the best enjoyment, a series of chimneys, blocks and short walls can be ascended nearer to the crest until the terrain levels off, and sections of walking with just the odd bit of scrambling lead up to the trig pillar at the summit of **Crib y Ddysgl**, probably meaning 'ridge of the dish' at 3494'. However, W.P. Haskett Smith wrote in *Climbing in the British Isles* in 1895 that, 'the common derivation of the name is from "destillare" - i.e. "dripping ridge". The climate of Wales, however, is not such as to make any ridge remarkable merely because it drips ... Attempts to derive the name from "disgl" ("dish") seem equally futile. Possibly the explanation may be found in the word "dysgwyl" ("watch", "expect") ... which would make it parallel to names like Lookingstead, etc.' Whatever the true meaning of the name, that of 'ridge of the dish' seems to now be universally accepted. To confuse matters even more, the actual summit area is called Garnedd Ugain, which strangely means 'cairn of twenty'.

From **Crib y Ddysgl** it is a short, easy descent to Bwlch Glas at the top of the Snowdon Ranger Path, where the railway tracks are joined, along with the Llanberis Path, and the Miner's and Pig Tracks which climb out of Cwm Dyli to the east. The standing stone mentioned above marks the top of this important col, and the last leg of the journey to the summit of **Snowdon** begins and is shared by all of the routes.

Back on the Bwlch y Moch, below the east ridge of **Crib Goch**, there is usually a small crowd of walkers daring themselves to commit the day to having a bash at the ridge described above. For many, the sight of the bare-looking slabs leading to the ridge is enough to put them off. If you are among these doubtful walkers, do not worry, a grand day can still be had by continuing along the Pig Track. This is easy to follow, and gives good views down into the bottom of the cwm, where lie the blue waters of Llyn Llydaw. Further along, as you contour beneath Bwlch Coch on its southern side, the upper cwm containing Glaslyn rises up above Llyn Llydaw, and soon the Miner's track climbs from the northern shores of the former to join the Pig Track just before the final steep ascent, made slightly easier by a constructed zigzagging path, to the standing stone at Bwlch Glas, and so to the summit.

The Miner's Track leaves the car park at Pen-y-Pass from its lower, southern end, and follows a good stone track around the rush filled tarn of Llyn Teyrn to cross a causeway over Llyn Llydaw. Only a huge diameter water pipe line flowing from Llyn Llydaw spoils what is a wonderful view of **Snowdon** and its Clogwyn y Garnedd face at the head of the cwm. This huge rambling face, which falls direct from the summit to the very shores of Glaslyn is one of the climbers main winter playgrounds. Here there is a good selection of classic winter climbs in the medium grades, often following gully lines, and usually in climbable condition for the best part of the winter. The climbs are very popular, particularly the Trinity Routes and the Great Gully, but there is an ever present danger of cornice collapse and avalanche risks. Being generally loose and vegetated, Clogwyn y Garnedd is no place for the climber in summer.

Across Llyn Llydaw, the impressive north face crags of **Y Lliwedd** plunge from the very summit of the mountain, but more on that Hewitt in a while.

Pont-y-Garth and Snowdon, from Illustrations of the Natural Scenery of
the Snowdonian Mountains, *1829*

There is much evidence of mining beside the two lakes in Cwm Dyli, but
nothing has been mined there for some time. In the early part of the nineteenth century, copper was mined in the cwm, and due to a lack of good road
access, had to be taken up, over Bwlch Glas, and down the other side of
Snowdon to the road near Rhyd Ddu. When the road was made over the
Llanberis Pass, the dressed ore could be carried over the Bwlch y Moch and
was stored in a warehouse at Pen-y-Pass until it could be moved on.
However, in 1856 the Miner's Track was constructed, and horses could be
used to cart the ore more easily. The only obstacle was Llyn Llydaw, which
was initially crossed by raft. An accident occurred which brought about the
building of the causeway that is still used today. These mines, collectively
known as the Britannia Copper Mine, closed down in 1926.

Once the track has climbed up to Glaslyn, there is often some confusion
as to the correct way to take. The path goes on around the shores of the lake
and begins to climb up beside a stream. This however, becomes quite
desperate, and many a walker has come to the conclusion that they have
taken the wrong turning. The correct path climbs up a scree slope, soon after
gaining the shores of Glaslyn, beside a collection of dilapidated mine buildings. Once up the scree, the Pig Track comes in from the right, and the way
up to the standing stone at Bwlch Glas, and so the summit, is obvious.

Glaslyn is said to be the haunt of an improbable monster, an 'afangc' which once inhabited a deep pool on the Afon Conwy near Betws-y-Coed. From time to time it would emerge and cause various troubles to the local people, as monsters are want to do. One of its main sources of amusement seems to be that of causing frequent floods in the valley. In a show of neighbourly love, the people of Betws-y-Coed decided to drag the monster from the pool and across the watershed into the next valley, thereby leaving the problem for the people there to worry about. Of course the afangc had to be tempted out of the water by a beautiful maiden (it must have been quite tiring being a beautiful maiden in those days!), and was captured and fastened to a pair of oxen with chains, dragged over a shoulder of **Moel Siabod** and down into the head of Nantgwynant. To make sure the beast didn't return, they made a point of dragging him as far up into the head of the cwm as they could get him. After a lengthy struggle, they made the enclosed upper cwm of **Snowdon** which holds Llyn Ffynnon Las, the green fountain—the old name of Glaslyn—and released him into its tranquil waters. It can only be assumed that the afangc still lives there, as this part of **Snowdon** is widely held to be the wettest corner of Britain.

South-east from the summit of **Snowdon** rises a magnificent peak of sweeping crags beneath another knife edge ridge, mirroring **Crib Goch** across Cwm Dyli. This is **Y Lliwedd**, 'the hue' at 2946', the mountain which forms the southern wall of Cwm Dyli and the last Hewitt on the classic **Snowdon** Horseshoe round.

Y Lliwedd can be ascended from a number of starting points, but the usual one begins along the Miner's Track from Pen-y-Pass. Just before the causeway crossing Llyn Llydaw, a path turns off left towards the towering cliffs falling from the summit, and also called Lliwedd. The path is good underfoot, and soon after crossing the natural outflow of the Afon Glaslyn, begins the steady ascent up the north-east ridge of **Y Lliwedd**.

The crags themselves are among the most historical of Welsh cliffs. Quite apart from the history of mountaineering, Lliwedd is linked with Arthurian Legend. It is widely believed that King Arthur's last battle took place on Bwlch y Saethau, the col between **Y Lliwedd** and **Snowdon**, the translation of the name being 'pass of the arrows', throwing some credence on this theory. It is also said that King Arthur rests with his knights in a gully on the cliffs, an honour that has been bestowed upon the dark recesses of Slanting Gully. That these tales have passed on down the years to become the legends that are still told today, is evident in an early account by Sir Thomas Malory (*c*.1470) who wrote that 'King Arthur yoed up to the creste of the cragge, and then he comforted himself with the colde winde.'

As far as mountaineering history is concerned, the first ascent of Lliwedd is credited to A.H Stocker and T.W. Wall. This, a dramatic ascent of the West Buttress on 4th January 1883 heralded the start of much exploration by many famous names over the years. That this first ascent was dramatic is evident by the fact that many other worthy parties had attempted to climb the grim slabs of this face of **Y Lliwedd**, and up until then all had met with defeat. Many considered this northern face of the mountain to be impregnable. The actual line taken on that day is not now known, the details having been lost in time, and even the redoubtable Archer Thomson, who's name would ever after be linked with Lliwedd, admitted only a decade after that first ascent that he could not identify some of the major obstacles of the route as described by Wall in the *Alpine Journal*.

James Merriman Archer Thomson began his climbing career in Deep Ghyll on Scafell in the Lake District, but 1894 saw his first ascent of Bilberry Terrace Route on Lliwedd. By 1896, Thomson had made 14 new climbs in Snowdonia. Prior to that there had only been 12 recorded climbs in the whole of North Wales. Archer Thomson went on to produce a total of 19 first ascents on this, the dank north face of **Y Lliwedd**. He died in 1912.

Other names linked with the exploration of Lliwedd include that of Oscar Eckenstein, a great Himalayan explorer of the late nineteenth century. He went to the Karakorum with Conway in 1892, organised his own expeditions to K2 and climbed among the volcanoes of Mexico making an early ascent of Popacatapetl. Eckenstein partnered Thomson on a number of first ascents on Lliwedd. Martin Conway, later to become Lord Conway of Allington, was one of the great mountain explorers of the nineteenth century. He made the first traverse of the Karakorum via a route up the Hispar Glacier, down the Biafo and then up the Baltaro. This opened up some of the greatest mountains in the world. The role call of climbers on Lliwedd includes the Abraham brothers, Winthrop Young, Jack Longland, Menlove Edwards, Wilfred Noyce, Harold Drasdo, Tony Moulam and Hugh Banner.

However, perhaps the most notable name to leave his mark on Lliwedd, is that of George Herbert Leigh Mallory. Mallory hailed from Cheshire and was first introduced to climbing in the Alps by Andrew Comyn Irvine. Lliwedd is one of the few European cliffs to be graced with first ascents by Mallory, his real passion being Everest. He was on the first three Everest expeditions and was among the party that was the first to see the North Face and to reach the North Col. Mallory was last seen by Noel Odell, as he reached the first step on the North-East Ridge with Irvine in 1924. In 1933 an ice-axe was found at 27,600', but at the time it was widely believed that the pair did not reach the summit. This of course will never be known for sure, but over the last few years there has been much renewed controversy over the matter, and some now believe that it is quite possible that Mallory and Irvine reached the summit of Everest before perishing. This would pre-date Hillary and Tensing's ascent by 29 years, and would re-write mountaineering history.

Lliwedd is an unpopular cliff for climbers these days, mainly because of the lack of hard climbs that appeal more to the modern climber. However, for those in search of long, mountaineering style routes away from the crowds, Lliwedd is a fantastic place to climb.

The path up **Y Lliwedd** climbs up the ridge to the left of these crags, soon leaving them well below to the north, although a number of deep-cut gullies or couloirs split the mountain, effectively forming three separate peaks. Although the walking is easy all the way, the steep drop to the north is ever obvious. The actual summit at 2946' is the one furthest west, and is unmarked by a cairn, but cannot be mistaken, as it is a prominent pointy top in the classic mould.

Heading north-west the way drops steeply down to a small col, Bwlch Ciliau, and the walker has a choice of either following the path slightly to the left, or to scramble down the rough rocks which rim the edge of the cliff. Great care must be taken if following this latter course, although the scrambling is nowhere hard.

Once down at the col, a number of rocky bluffs lead over to the bigger col of Bwlch y Saethau, and a wide path climbs up out of the valley from the south. This is the Watkin Path up **Snowdon**, but more of this shortly.

Just before reaching Bwlch y Saethau, a broad, rocky arête is thrown down to the north and forms the ridge which separates Glaslyn and Llyn Llydaw in Cwm Dyli. This provides a different approach to **Snowdon** and **Y Lliwedd** from above Llyn Llydaw, but is only for the scrambler. The way is obvious throughout, and the confident can more or less pick their own line up to the col.

The ascent to **Snowdon** from Bwlch y Saethau winds a perfect way across scree and broken rocks to the west, away from the fairly obvious crest which is the East Ridge, and only for scramblers. You should keep this crest well on your right, heading further away from it as you climb. The path climbs steeply up to the main ridge coming up from the south, and falls short of the summit of **Snowdon** by only a couple of hundred metres. If walking in the other direction, perhaps as part of the **Snowdon** Horseshoe, it is well to remember that the descent to Bwlch y Saethau is marked by a large standing stone.

The Watkin Path up **Snowdon** starts down in Nantgwynant to the south, between the twin lakes of Llyn Gwynant and Llyn Dinas, and provides a very different way onto the tops. The path is named after its creator, Sir Edward Watkin, who was famous for doing everything on a grand scale. He began work on an early channel tunnel, drilling from both sides of the channel until the government thwarted his attempts, but not before a mile of tunnel has been constructed from both the English and Continental sides. At the age of 70 he retired to Nantgwynant and built himself a chalet. He constructed the Watkin Path, as we know it today, so as to have a way to the summit of **Snowdon** from his own front door! It was opened by the then Prime Minister, William Gladstone in 1892, himself aged 83. Gladstone was a personal friend of Watkin, and a boulder set high up in Cwm Llan commemorates the opening of the path and is known as the Gladstone Rock.

A car park beside the A498, just north of Bethania is the starting point for the Watkin Path. It heads easily up the western, true right bank of the Afon Cwm Llan until a point is reached near the sheep folds of Plascwmllan. A path heads due west for the high col between **Yr Aran** and Allt Maenderyn, but the Watkin Path continues up the bottom of the cwm, crossing to the other side of the stream. As the cwm turns northwards and takes the name Cwm Tregalan, the path begins its steep climb up onto the rocky flanks of **Y Lliwedd**'s western face. The rocks here though are nowhere continuous, and much grass is in evidence. The path climbs abruptly through this to Bwlch y Saethau and on to the summit of **Snowdon** as described above.

Yr Aran is a wonderful peak that suffers greatly from being in such close proximity to much greater heights. It can be climbed from Cwm Llan by aiming for the col mentioned above and the way is easy with a rough path to follow. From the col, Bwlch Cwm Llan, a stone wall heads south and has a vague path of sorts running alongside. The wall vanishes as it makes a contouring way across the north-east slopes of the hill, but the path is still evident. Soon, however, another wall is seen coming up much more directly from the lower parts of Cwm Llan. This follows a little-known ridge above the broken crags of Clogwyn Brith. Whichever of these ways you choose to gain the ridge higher up, a stile gains a good path and leads quickly up to the summit of **Yr Aran**, 'the mountain', at 2451'. Its summit stands atop a rocky rib and is obvious.

From Bwlch Cwm Llan, the wonderful south ridge of **Snowdon** follows a good line over the intervening top of Allt Maenderyn and gives a good way of ascending the mountain from either Nantgwynant or Beddgelert.

Some rough ground rises immediately above the col, but a wide, stony path is soon underfoot, and climbs above the very edge of the plunging void of Cwm Tregalan to the east. Away to the west the Hebog ridges rise above the forests of Beddgelert. The way is good throughout, with just a bit of mild scrambling to keep the interest up, but it is as the path gains height and the Llechog ridge comes in from the west, taking the Rhyd Ddu Path, that the ridge becomes narrower and more of a sharp crest. Still, it is a case of good hillwalking rather than scrambling and soon a high col, marked on the map as Bwlch Main, passes by before the final gradient to the top of **Snowdon**.

The Beddgelert Path up **Snowdon** is hard to follow these days, and is not actually marked on the map as a right of way. It leaves the Rhyd Ddu road about half a mile out of the village of Beddgelert, and passes through the farm of Wernlas-deg before gaining height and contouring around the northern side of a long ridge coming down from **Yr Aran** towards Beddgelert. The path shown on the map continues contouring to the old slate mines just below the western crest of the Bwlch Cwm Llan, but it is also possible to gain the ridge to the east, taking in the minor summit of Craig Wen, following the ridge to **Yr Aran**, and dropping down to the Bwlch from there.

The same mines below the Bwlch can also be gained from Rhyd Ddu further north along the A4085. A car park at the southern end of the village has a track leaving from it which is well marked as the Rhyd Ddu Path up **Snowdon**. For the first part it is a good farm track throughout and seems to aim directly form Bwlch Cwm Llan. The bull-dozed track does in fact do just that, and gives the option of climbing the Allt Maenderyn ridge from Rhyd Ddu. However, just through a gate near Pen ar Lon, a bridleway crosses the track, coming in from Ffridd Uchaf farm about mid-way between Rhyd Ddu and Beddgelert, and heading off up the broad slopes of Rhos Boeth over a stile. This is the way of the Rhyd Ddu Path. It soon begins to climb, and within a mile of leaving the bull-dozed track, it brings you out onto the rim of the wild cirque of Cwm Clogwyn. The Snowdon Ranger Path can be seen climbing the ridge across the cwm, and four llyns dot the rugged grandeur of the wet cwm bottom at your feet. Only the little frequented crags of Llechog bar the way from the walker wishing to explore that quiet corrie. However, few would come this way to drop back down into the cwm. The way turns right along the rim and climbs via a few zigzags to join the path over Allt Maenderyn near Bwlch Main.

Although the legends of King Arthur in Snowdonia have been dated back as far as the sixth century, a site on this ridge known as Mur Murianau

27

dates from before the year One. A few piles of stones, a crude wall and a flat area mark what historians and antiquarians believe to be the site of one of the most sacred Druid temples in Britain. Little is known of the place except that the name, Mur Murianau is the old Welsh equivalent of the term 'Holy of Holies'.

And so ends a clockwise exploration of this unique range of mountains. I hope that through these pages, you will gain a feel of the greatness of the Snowdon massif, and rather than put it down as an over-rated, over-populated tourist trap, will be tempted into pulling on your walking boots and exploring the quieter side of Snowdon. There are beauties aplenty to discover, and the rewards are great.

Just prior to publication of this book, there was much speculation as to the future of **Snowdon** as an open paradise for walkers and climbers. The owner of the vast Hafod-y-Llan and Gelli Iago Estate which, apart from owning much land on Anglesey, also included about a third of **Snowdon**, together with a part of the actual summit, put the **Snowdon** side of his estate up for sale. For £3 million the eventual buyer was to become the owner of **Lliwedd** and **Cnicht** as well as the southern section of **Snowdon**. Depending on who this owner was to be, the deal had great potential to cause untold access problems for the outdoor lover. The owner, Mr Richard Williams sold up despite the land being in his family for over 300 years. He inherited the land from his grandfather in 1988, but felt that his resources would be better put towards his Anglesey estate. It was reported that initial enquiries regarding buying the estate had been forthcoming from around the globe.

The Chris Brasher Trust, which raises money through sales of products under the Brasher Boot Company name, immediately issued a challenge to hillgoers. In an interview with the British Mountaineering Council, Chris Brasher, one time Olympic runner and well travelled mountaineer, said, 'Rally your members in defence of Snowdon. For every pound you contribute we will add a further pound,' and began by laying down £200,000. The appeal to save Snowdon from becoming owned by an absentee landlord, as has recently happened with many of the grand estates of Highland Scotland, was launched under the wing of the already existing National Trust Snowdonia Appeal, whose president is the actor Sir Anthony Hopkins. Sir Anthony began the appeal by donating £1 million. The appeal proved a success and the land is now in the care of the National Trust.

GLYDERAU

Apart from the Snowdon range itself, the Glyders, which lie just to the east of that range, must surely rank as the most popular mountain group in Wales. In all, the nine Hewitts of the Glyders form a compact, curving range, with huge armchair-like corries forming the eastern and northern walls, while the sides which face west and south are more rounded, gentle and grassy, offering much less of interest to the hillwalker.

These southern and western sides have as their boundary the busy A4086 which follows the valley bottom from Llanberis, up to the top of Pen-y-Pass and eastwards to Capel Curig via the Dyffryn Mymbyr. While there are one or two routes onto the tops from this side, these are inferior to the approaches from the north, following steep rocky slopes of mat grass and scree.

The northern side of the group couldn't be more different. Huge ridges of shattered rock fall into the valleys of the Afon Llugwy and the Nant Ffrancon, each one forming distinct cwms of the utmost grandeur and beauty, whilst retaining an essential element of ruggedness and a distinct air of wildness. The valley on this side is served by the A5 trunk road, and on any sunny day in summer, literally thousands of cars line the roadside as people make for the heights and crags of the Ogwen Valley.

Geologically, these northern cwms of the range are unique to the mountains of North Wales as a whole, and yet so alike to each other within the group. Nowhere else is there such a uniformity in the weathering and glaciation over the centuries than is to be found here, and it is no coincidence that it is only the north-eastern sides of the Glyders that have had corries gouged out of their flanks. As is the case today, the prevailing winds during the ice age were south-westerly. These would have deposited snow on the leeward side of the Glyder range, in shallow hollows that lay high up on what was then a broad, open plateau. As this snow turned to ice, it began to move in a rotatory motion, grinding and gouging material out of these shallow hollows, and collecting rocks and other debris from the sides and backwall. In turn these aided the process further by grinding even deeper into the growing basin. The only exception to this obvious north-east facing formation in the Glyder range is that of the Marchlyn Mawr which faces north-west. This was formed by an identical series of actions to the other corries of the range, but as a deep valley, that of the Afon Dudodyn, falls to the south-west—into the prevailing winds—this would have acted as a funnel, directing the wind-driven snow over the col which lies at the head of the Marchlyn Mawr corrie. Not that this type of glaciation is unique to the Glyders—in fact pretty much the same was happening everywhere—but there is an incredible sameness to each of the Glyder's corries. It is suggested that this was caused by the supposed uniformity of the then bare plateau, and the open way up the Nantgwynant and Aberglaslyn, which let the wind through from the south-west without deviation. This has left us with the Glyders as they are today, possibly the best example of glaciation in the mountains of Wales, and one of the grandest mountain playgrounds in Britain.

The Glyders range can be split into two fairly convenient halves, and indeed, many people look at the two halves as separate mountain groups, which they aren't. A low col is often used as a pass from Nant Peris in the west to Ogwen Cottage in the east and has a wild, grass-ringed tarn at its top. This is Llyn y Cwn, Lake of the Dogs. North of this tarn rise the four Hewitts of the Elidirs, the northern half of the Glyders, whilst curving around to the east are the two highest Glyders—**Glyder Fawr** and **Glyder Fach**—**Tryfan** and the two moorland tops of **Y Foel Goch** and **Gallt yr Ogof** above Capel Curig. These five Hewitts are usually known collectively as the Glyders.

The northernmost Hewitt of the range is **Carnedd y Filiast**, 'cairn of the greyhound bitch', at 2694'. The whole eastern façade of this mountain mass is made up of immense slabs of rock, falling in an almost uniform gradient to the depths of wild Cwm Graianiog. This is the gently undulating expanse of Atlantic Slab, nestling at the back of this quiet corrie, and providing the rock climber with an element of solitude and seriousness not often found on crags in the British Isles. The right-hand, northernmost ridge of the cwm, separating it from the next corrie along towards Bethesda, Cwm Ceunant, can be ascended by the energetic walker from the delightful pastures of the middle Nant Ffrancon. The way is obvious over short-copped grass, and if the edge of the slab is kept in sight, the ridge leads directly to the cairn atop a long, low rib of outcropping rock.

To the west, the slopes of **Carnedd y Filiast** fall in a convex nature to the once wild shores of Marchlyn Mawr. However, this reservoir is now much despoiled by slate quarrying, and the dammed water is often horribly low and forms a hideous sight beneath such noble mountains. It is possible to climb **Carnedd y Filiast** from Marchlyn Mawr, but I can hardly recom-

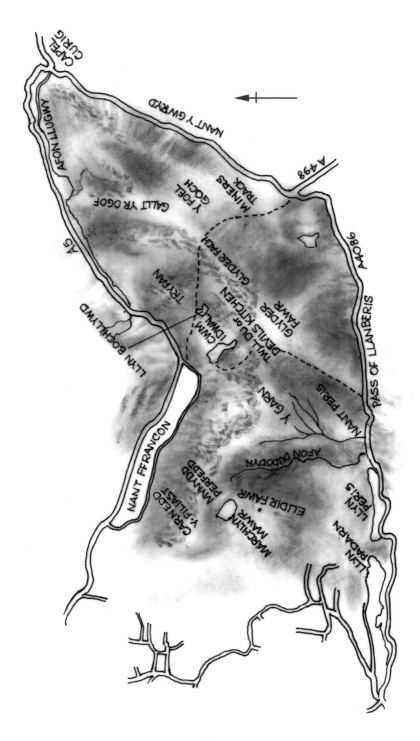

mend it. Much better to either climb up from Nant Ffrancon, or visit this summit on a traverse of the other Hewitts in the Elidir range.

Half a mile south of **Carnedd y Filiast** rises a gentle dome, topped by a substantial cairn amid much wet bog grass and sedge. This is a minor top called Mynydd Perfedd, meaning 'middle mountain', a summit which forms the point where the ridge containing **Elidir Fawr**, abuts onto the main north-south ridge of the range.

Elidir Fawr is unlike the other summits of the Glyders, and indeed also the other high summits of Snowdonia, in that it is formed chiefly of Cambrian rocks, that is sandstones, shales and slates. Throughout the rest of Snowdonia, with the exception of the Rhinog range far to the south, this Cambrian strata lies deep beneath the much harder rocks of the Ordovician series. Only in the Rhinog range, on **Elidir Fawr**, and to a lesser extent on nearby **Carnedd y Filiast** do those sandstones and shales outcrop at the summits. This is also one of the main reasons that there is much slate quarrying in evidence on the slopes of **Elidir Fawr**, indeed, if you have followed the suggested paths on the Snowdon range in the previous chapter, you cannot fail to have noticed the huge quarried scars which fall from the slopes of **Elidir Fawr** right down to the shores of Llyn Padarn and Llyn Peris. This Caernarfonshire Slate-Belt, as it is known, actually contains the largest slate quarries in the world.

Apart from the obvious approach to the summit of **Elidir Fawr** from Marchlyn Mawr in the north, there are a number of ways, more suitable for the walker, to gain the top. But first, the cwm holding Marchlyn Mawr itself.

High above the trapped waters lies Craig Cwrwgl or 'Coracle Crag', a face that would be rarely visited if it were not for an impressive, almost impregnable looking pinnacle, completely detached from this, the northern flank of **Elidir Fawr**, its parent mountain. This is The Pillar of Elidir, a much coveted prize amongst rock climbers, despite its out of the way position. The classic rock climber's route of the whole mountain is undoubtedly 'Corrugated Cracks', a tough 'Hard Severe' which was first ascended in July of 1937. It is by no means the earliest climb to be done on Craig Cwrwgl though. That redoubtable pioneer, Archer Thomson climbed a few lines here in the early part of this century.

This Pillar really is the only point of interest on the northern side of **Elidir Fawr**, and indeed the whole of its western flank is also devoid of interest to the hillgoer, being taken up with the vast slate quarries mentioned above.

To the south of the summit, the deep, boggy valley of the Afon Dudodyn gives about the best means of approach from the west side of the range. A farm track leads past the camp site in Nant Peris, and on towards the few scattered cottages and farm buildings at Fron, cowering beneath the spoil and screes of the abandoned works. A well sign-posted public footpath leads up into the corrie, and soon drops beside the rushing brown waters of Afon Dudodyn. A bridge crosses the stream after a few hundred yards, and some suggest that you are better climbing directly up the open south ridge of the mountain to the summit from there. The way is steep but straight forward, but I always prefer following the rough course of the tumbling waters on its northerly bank, right up the valley to its very head. The way underfoot is often boggy, but sheep tracks can be found contouring above the worst of this bog grass and hard rush obstacle. Just below the prominent col between **Elidir Fawr** and Mynydd Perfedd, marked on the 1:25000 map as Bwlch y Marchlyn, the stream takes a sharp turn to the north and makes directly for the col. As you near what is a fairly sharp crest at the col, the sweeping screes and broken crags to the north take the eye down to the shores of Marchlyn Mawr. A good path traverses this crest, and can be followed easily westwards to the top of **Elidir Fawr**, a rough jumble of small boulders, at 3031'.

Back at Bwlch y Marchlyn, a rocky rib rims the edge of the cwm to the north, but soon becomes easy grass and leads to Mynydd Perfedd, but the path traverses around the southern side of this minor hill, and takes the walker to Bwlch y Brecan, a broad col at the head of the Afon Dudodyn to the south-west and Cwm Perfedd to the north-east.

The easy dome of **Foel-goch**, 'red bare hill', at 2726', takes the Hewitt-bagger away from the main path, which contours around the hill to the west. Heading south up **Foel-goch** from the col, the way is steep but short up red screes of shale, and runs beside a fence to the summit, marked by a ladder stile leading over the fence to a small cairn of stones.

The O.S. map shows a public footpath climbing up beside the Afon Gafr from Nant Peris, almost to the very summit of **Foel-goch**, but this is very hard to follow on the ground, and it is better to pick a way up the Afon Dudodyn as described.

To the east, two remarkably rocky ridges are thrown down to the Nant Ffrancon, and both give excellent scrambles to the summit for those without an aversion to steep ground. These two ridges, Yr Esgair and Y Llymllwyd are both suitable for the hardier hillwalker, although the former has much rotten rock and requires great care. They can be used to give a good, short outing from the Ogwen Valley, using one in ascent and the other in descent. Y Llymllwyd is perhaps the easiest to locate in descent and is somewhat wider throughout. It falls into Cwm Cywion, 'valley of the chickens', to the south-east of the summit and leads quickly back to Blaen-y-nant, 'head of the valley', in Nant Ffrancon. It is not known if Cwm Cywion's name actually refers to chickens of the farmyard type, or the old Welsh name for the red grouse 'iar y mynydd', which translates as 'hen of the mountain', although the latter is probably the case. It is perhaps worth mentioning that Yr Esgair is listed in the current scramblers guide as a grade three scramble, equating it to a low grade rock climb, so bare this in mind if you have no rock climbing ability.

A mile south of **Foel-goch** towers the highest of the Elidir group, with the straightforward name of **Y Garn**, 'the cairn' at 3107'. As with the rest of the group, its western slopes can only be termed 'boring', offering nothing of interest to excite the exploratory instinct of the hill wanderer. There is one path, mentioned earlier, climbing up Cwm Cneifio from a point just south of Nant Peris. This gains the broad, grassy col near Llyn y Cwn, from where twin paths up boulder scree lead northwards to the cairn at the top of the mountain.

Although quite a few do climb **Y Garn** along that route, the more discerning walker would always start the ascent from the east and the Ogwen Valley.

Ogwen Cottage has long been the centre of the valley as far as mountain exploration is concerned. It was once a humble, and if the early accounts are anything to go by, somewhat seedy inn. Through the ages every major name in mountaineering has stayed there, and even the early travellers used it as basic accommodation. Even Charles Kingsley is said to have stayed at the Cottage and fished from a rowing boat on Llyn Ogwen. The original building no longer exists, though a huge Local Authority Mountain Centre has been built on the site.

Next door is Idwal Cottage, the very first Youth Hostel in Britain, and is still popular with tourists today. It was the favourite haunt of many of the top climbers of the thirties. In fact, Colin Kirkus is said to have written much of his early instructional book, *Let's Go Climbing!* there. Idwal Cottage also figures in Elizabeth Coxhead's novel, *One Green Bottle*.

The early explorers in the Ogwen Valley were botanists, and it is no coincidence that the area above the Rhaeadr Ogwen saw many of them collecting plant specimens among the dank recesses of the cliffs which ring the cwm around Llyn Idwal.

The lake which feeds Rhaeadr Ogwen, Llyn Ogwen, is in itself of great interest to those who study the formation of valleys. At one time it flowed eastwards, down the Afon Llugwy, through Capel Curig and Betws-y-Coed to the sea via the Afon Conwy, but as time has passed, the waters at the head

What was that sudden apparition me, seen for a moment dim and gigantic through the mist, hid the next in darkness? The next flash showed him a line of obelisks, like giants crouching side by side, staring down on him from the clouds. Another five minutes, he was at their feet, & past them; to see above them again another line of awful watchers through the storms and rains of many a thousand years, waiting, grim and silent, like those doomed senators in the Capitol of Rome, till their own turn should come, and the last lightning stroke hurl them too down, to lie for ever by their fallen brothers, whose mighty bones bestrewed the screes below.

He groped his way between them; saw some fifty yards beyond a higher peak; gained it by fierce struggles and many falls; saw another beyond that; and, rushing down and up two slopes of moss, reached a region where the upright lava-ledges had been split asunder into chasms, crushed together again into caves, toppled over each other, hurled up into spires, in such chaotic confusion that progress seemed impossible.

A flash of lightning revealed a lofty cairn above his head. There was yet, then, a higher point! He would reach it, if he broke every limb in the attempt! and madly he hurried on feeling his way from ledge to ledge, squeezing himself through crannies, crawling on hands and knees along the sharp chines of the rocks, till he reached the foot of the cairn; climbed it, and threw himself at full length on the summit of the Glyder Fawr.

An episode on Glyder Fawr from Two Years Ago
by Charles Kingsley, 1857

of the stream have gouged out a rocky passage westwards, eventually opening up the spectacular falls of the Rhaeadr Ogwen and redirecting the stream down into the Nant Ffrancon, running northwards to enter the Menai Strait near Bangor. At the present time, Llyn Ogwen is in the process of being split into two separate lakes by a continuous flow of silt deposits being washed down from Llyn Bochlwyd, 800' above. It is this same process that formed the two separate lakes of Llyn Padarn and Llyn Peris at Llanberis to the west of the Glyders. Silt from Llyn Dwythwch, beneath the eastern face of Moel Eilio, was washed down to form a bank across what was then a single lake.

It was Cwm Idwal that drew many of the early botanists and geologists, and many famous names have recorded their finds in the locality, including Lhuyd, Pennant, Darwin and Ramsey. Llyn Idwal and its environs are now protected as a National Nature Reserve, the first to be declared as such in Wales. Its plant species include many not often found in mountain districts, though some are endemic to this part of Snowdonia. A lime-rich soil base accounts for some of these rarities—the calcicoles.

From a mountaineering point of view, the cliffs at the back of the Cwm have always been important. The savage cleft of Twll Du, 'The Black Pit', although these days invariably named the Devil's Kitchen, saw much interest from the early walkers and climbers who visited Ogwen. Indeed, in those days it was considered something of a feat merely to ascend **Glyder Fawr** via the path which leads up and across the base of the chasm.

However, on 3rd March 1895 J.M. Archer Thomson, without doubt then the most accomplished pioneer in Wales, along with H. Hughes, 'surreptitiously appropriated the hatchet from Mrs Jones's coal-cellar at Ogwen Cottage', and started out on an attempt to scale the inner depths of the Devil's Kitchen for the first time. Water flow was frozen into an immobile state at the end of what must have been a harsh winter, and the pair approached the cleft via a casual stroll across Llyn Idwal, which was frozen to a depth of 7 or 8 inches. The climb itself was found to be quite easy up to a point, as the whole chasm was banked out with snow. Near the top the hatchet came into play, used to hew steps out of the steep ice which cloaked the walls, and so to clear a capstone which blocked the upper pitches of the gully. It is reported that 'the rate of progress up the icy upper section was about five feet an hour and they finally reached the top at 7.15 p.m.'

Most of the walking routes in the area had been popular for a good while prior to this remarkable achievement, indeed, many of the early travellers including Lhuyd and Pennant made ascents of a number of notable peaks in the Glyder range as part of their tour. One or two rock climbs had also been done on the nearby crags, but this first ascent of the Devil's Kitchen must surely rank as one of the earliest examples of hard ice climbing in Wales, if not in the whole of the British Isles. Even today, when the waterfall through the cleft freezes at all, it gives a good, classic winter climb of grade IV.

A good path leaves the car parks at Ogwen and Idwal Cottages, near the foot of Llyn Ogwen, and heads south-west into Cwm Idwal. Within just a few easy minutes walking Llyn Idwal comes into view and the path divides, passing around either side of this beautiful stretch of crag enclosed water. When these two paths join up at the other end of Llyn Idwal, just before the last steep climb across the base of the Devil's Kitchen, you can follow either. Personally I prefer the one along the south shore, purely because of the wonderful close-up views of the Idwal Slabs that you get from this side.

The Idwal Slabs are another dramatic natural rock feature, covered by a host of excellent easy to middle grade rock climbs. Like most of the other crags in this area, the emphasis here is on tradition, many of the climbs dated back to the late 1800s and early 1900s, to the very start of British rock climbing.

The path up into Twll Du is obvious and in places has been well graded with steps of slabby rock and boulders to make walking easier and reduce erosion. Soon the dark cleft that is Twll Du, the Devil's Kitchen, rises up in the dank right wall, a seething mass of spray clinging to the moss-covered walls of the inner chasm, but don't be tempted to enter this inner sanctuary, as the going is hard, and even in summer conditions, the way up, out of the top of the close gully, provides a wet and often desperate Very Difficult rock climb.

Above the opening to the Devil's Kitchen, the terrain seems to become easier, and soon the broad col holding the clear waters of Llyn y Cwn is underfoot. The way up **Y Garn** from the col is pretty straightforward up the scree paths to the right.

To the south, further scree slopes fall down shattered gullies and broken crags from the eerie summit plateau of **Glyder Fawr**. The path starts up a well worn gully, but soon spills out of its top onto the broader slopes above. Here weird blocks and boulders shoot into the sky forming rough spikes and clusters of embedded spears. The whole plateau is liberally covered with these clumps of rock. Cairns seem to lead the way, but if you have a look around you, you will see others, well off the path, leading to nowhere in particular.

Shortly after, the plateau begins to flatten out, a cluster of solid stone blocks looms up and is noticeably higher than the others here abouts. A short easy clamber up from the east side and the summit of **Glyder Fawr**, 'the large mound of stones', at 3279' has been reached.

The rough south ridge of **Glyder Fawr**, sweeping down a long line of scree, grass and short outcrops, gives one of the few reasonable ways onto the summits of the range from that side. A public footpath leads through the garden of the Pen-y-Pass Youth Hostel, to the north of the main Hostel building, and climbs onto the rocky ridge behind. There are good views of Llyn Cwmffynnon down on the right as you gain this ridge, while across the pass to the left, the towering pinnacles of the **Crib Goch** ridge stand out as etched castle turrets against the sky. The path gains craggy slopes, and zigzags to make some headway up the steep flank of the mountain. A promi-

The way lies beneath that vast precipice, Castell y Geifr, or The Castle of the Goats. In some distant age, the ruins of a rocky mountain formed a road by a mighty lapse. A stream of stones, each of monstrous size, points towards the Cwm; and are to be clambered over by those only, who possess a degree of bodily activity, as well as strength of head to bear the sight of the dreadful hollows frequent beneath them.

Observe, on the right, a stupendous roche fendue, or split rock, called Twll-Du, and The Devil's Kitchen. It is a horrible gap, in the centre of a great black precipice, extending in length about a hundred and fifty yards; in depth about a hundred; and only six wide; perpendicularly open to the surface of the mountain. On surmounting all my difficulties, and taking a little breath, I ventured to look down this dreadful aperture, and found its horrors far from being lessened in my exalted situation; for to it were added the waters of Llyn y Cwn, impetuously rushing through its bottom.

Reach the Glyder Fawr .... The prospect from this mountain is very noble. Snowdon is seen to great advantage; the deep vale of Llanberis and its lakes, Nant Francon, and variety of other singular views. The plain which forms the top is strangely covered with loose stones like the beach of the sea; in many places crossing one another in all directions, and entirely naked. Numerous groupes of stones are placed almost erect, sharp pointed, and in sheafs: all are weather-beaten, time-eaten, and honey-combed, and of a venerable grey-colour. The elements seem to have warred against this mountain: rains have lashed it, and the winds made it the constant object of their fury. The shepherds make it the residence of storms, and style a part of it Carnedd y Gwynt, or the Eminence of Tempests.

From a Tour in Wales by Thomas Pennant, 1781

nent knoll at 646 metres gives some respite from the endlessly abrupt gradient, and also affords a good place to sit and admire the view, particularly as this is one place in the Glyders that you are more than likely to be alone. Above the knoll, the climb resumes with more steep ground, but all in all, the ascent from Pen-y-Pass is less technically difficult than any other way up the mountain, even if it does lack that definite charm that is bestowed upon the routes from the north. At last the slope eases in angle, and the bouldery terrain of the summit plateau is soon underfoot.

Possibly the best way of ascent for the ordinary walker who wishes to climb **Glyder Fawr** without taking in **Glyder Fach** *en route*, is to make for the prominent ridge of Y Gribin above Llyn Ogwen. Y Gribin actually separates the two main cwms of this northern side of the range, Cwm Idwal to the west and Cwm Bochlwyd to the east, and form a delightful rocky way to the col between the two Glyders, Bwlch y Ddwy Glyder, from which either **Glyder Fawr** or **Fach** can ascended.

Initially the way is very good, and the path climbs gently above the dramatic cwms. However, higher up, the ridge narrows and the path veers off slightly to the right to take to a scree-filled gully. If you ignore the path and take to the sharp-edged ridge above instead, you will be in for some wonderfully airy scrambling. Nowhere is it difficult, as huge bucket-holds abound, but there is some loose rock, so care should be taken.

The top of Y Gribin is marked by a cairn and is amazingly grassy and knoll-like after so much rock. The way to **Glyder Fawr** is easy, and a path of sorts leads off to the west to the summit.

Glyder Fach is the lesser of the two height-wise, but is a much more popular summit as far as walkers go. From Bwlch y Ddwy Glyder at the top of Y Gribin, a path heads first south-east, around some huge stone spears embedded in the mountainside known as Castell y Gwynt, 'Castle of the Winds', an eerie place in mist, then turns off to the east, picking a way over more rocky ground to the boulder strewn summit of the mountain. The actual top stands at the highest point of a pile of massive blocks, many the size of houses, and requires some scrambling of an easy nature to attain. The old O.S. 1:25000 map shows a trig pillar at the highest point at 3261', but there is no sign of it today. In fact it is hard to imagine how there would be room for a pillar on the little rocky perch that is the summit.

100 yards east of the summit stands, or should I say lays, the well known landmark of the Cantilever Stone. This huge flagstone rests atop a jumble of boulders and is described by Thomas Pennant in his 'Tour' as 'The tops are frequently crowned in the strangest manner with other stones lying on them horizontally. One was about twenty-five feet long and six broad. I climbed up, and on stamping it with my foot felt a strong tremulous motion from end to end.' Pennant climbed **Glyder Fach** in 1781, but even today, few walkers ascend the mountain without also clambering onto the Cantilever Stone and having a good old jump about for the benefit of the cameras.

The Cantilever Stone on Glyder Fach, from Pennant's Tour in Wales, 1781

Another track coming up from the south is the Miner's Track from the Pen-y-Gwryd Hotel. The way, though obvious, is uninteresting throughout, and only those with a need to cross the range on foot as quickly as possible should go to the trouble. There are far finer ways onto the Glyders.

Llyn Bochlwyd nestles in the corner formed by the north face of **Glyder Fach**, and the rambling west face of **Tryfan**. A number of different paths leave the A5 in the Ogwen Valley and make for this wonderful little tarn. However, once there, they all converge and make for the stony col between **Glyder Fach** and **Tryfan**—Bwlch Tryfan with its seemingly out of place stone wall, traversing the ridge.

The **Glyder Fach** side of the col has a path up a scree shoot which gives fairly easy access to the summit plateau, but over the wall (on the Cwm Bochlwyd side), a turreted rib of rock is thrown down right to the col. This is Bristly Ridge, a superb, easy scramble. The rock is marvellous throughout, though is now becoming polished through over-use, and the top of the ridge is within a few minutes walk of the summit of **Glyder Fach** and the Cantilever Stone.

The only other recognised walking route to the summit of **Glyder Fach** is the long, undulating east ridge. It is this ridge that is crossed by the Miner's Track mentioned above. The whole, broad ridge offers a predominantly moorland walk over much bog grass and heath, and takes in two minor Hewitts before descending to Capel Curig. However, before considering this open, vegetated ridge, the jewel of the Glyders calls for our attention to the north-east—**Tryfan**.

Ask a child to draw a mountain, and those tiny hands will create a scene of steep slopes, leading to a pointed summit amid a blaze of rough ridges and a simplistic outline. That mountain is **Tryfan**.

Driving west up the Ogwen Valley from Capel Curig, even those with the most modest of hillwalking ambitions, indeed even those with none at all, cannot fail to notice this splendid trinity of buttresses, each cut off from its neighbour by dark, recessed gullies, and each with a jagged col of exposed rock falling between the heights. Just as it should be, the highest point of this grand mountain stands aloft above the open crags and slabs of the central mass, the centre of the trinity. The summit itself is a wonderfully airy spot, with huge gulfs slumping into the depths of the cwm to the east, right from the very edge of the summit blocks. And of these summit blocks themselves; two huge bosses of rock, almost identical, stand alert at the very highest point like ancient pillars at the entrance to some druidical stone circle. These are Adam and Eve, and it is the tradition that anyone who can make the jump from one to the other becomes a freeman of Tryfan. This may not sound particularly harrowing, but when you consider that they stand perhaps thirty inches apart, and the penalty for a misplaced foot is a long fall of almost two thousand feet into the void of Cwm Tryfan, many people are understandably put off by this.

But first—the summit slopes. From Bwlch Tryfan the blocky South Ridge is perhaps the only suitable way for the walker, although even here it is necessary to make use of hands almost as much as feet. Many revel in the exquisite scrambling to be found on the very crest of the ridge, but something of a path winds a way up over the western side of this crest. It is fairly obvious underfoot, passing to the west of the top of the South Peak, and as the ridge narrows towards its top, there is simply nowhere else to go! Once at the summit, a few large boulders need to be climbed before you can relax and admire the view. Most people, however, spend much of their time on the summit trying to build up the courage to attempt the jump. Personally, I find it easier to scramble up the block which is furthest north, (nobody seems certain which is Adam and which is Eve) then jump to the southern one, although the climb down from that, is harder than climbing down from the other. Have a good look and do it the way that seems best for you, but watch your footing!

It is worth noting that in addition to the way up Cwm Bochlwyd to the stone wall at Bwlch Tryfan mentioned above, a delightful path climbs steadily up the eastern face of **Tryfan**, known simply as the Heather Terrace, from the farmstead of Gwern Gof Uchaf, meaning 'the upper swamp near the cave', beside the A5. The way initially is well marked, passing beneath the tilted slab of Tryfan Bach, and once the Terrace has been gained becomes obvious, traversing below the rocky ribs and gullies taken by the rock climbs on the east face. The way onto the Terrace has to be looked for carefully, however, as the path leads away onto the North Ridge.

The summit stands at 3002' and as such, **Tryfan** is the smallest of the Welsh 3000'ers. The name itself is widely taken as meaning 'three tops' which is of course evident from both east and west, and entirely plausible. However, W.P. Haskett Smith wrote that 'The Welsh dictionaries give a word "tryfan" with the sense of "anything spotted through" and, whether or not this has anything to do with the origin of the name, the component rocks certainly are quartz-speckled in a most extraordinary manner.'

The other recognised way for the hillwalker, although for the most part involving much easy scrambling, is the long North Ridge. This drops down to within a few hundred feet of the busy A5, and as such is very popular. Although the scrambling is slightly harder than that to be found on the South Ridge, it is not difficult in summer conditions and provides the best way to the top, and combined with a descent of the South Ridge achieves a complete traverse of the mountain.

Other ways there are aplenty, but these are reserved strictly for the rock climber and more accomplished scrambler. Many classic rock routes follow lines up the three main buttresses of the East Face, mainly in the lower grades, and as on the other high mountain crags of Snowdonia, are steeped in mountaineering history. Along with the many other famous climbing names already mentioned in this book, there is that of O.G. Jones linked with the early exploration of the crags of **Tryfan**, and indeed the other cliffs of the Glyders. Owen Glynne Jones (often referring to himself as the Only Genuine Jones) was one of the foremost pioneers of rock climbing in Britain, having first come to the sport after seeing one of the photographs taken by the Abraham brothers of the Napes Needle in a shop window in The Strand, London. After beginning his mountaineering career on **Cadair Idris**, he climbed extensively throughout Europe, and made many first ascents in the Lake District and Wales. He should be remembered as establishing the first system of grading climbs in rock climbing guidebooks, a classification still used to group together climbs of the same difficulty. Jones died in 1899 whilst trying to climb the Ferpècle Arête on the Dent Blanche in the European Alps. His guide, Furrer, took a fall and pulled off Jones together with a second guide, Vuignier, who was also on the rope. Incredibly, the fourth person on the rope, Hill, survived when it broke, and he was left to find his own way off the route.

Eastwards from the main, higher Glyders, a long undulating ridge of cotton and bog grass moorland runs over the last two Hewitts of the group, eventually descending via a delightful, low-level route to the little village of Capel Curig. The first of these Hewitts when following the ridge from **Glyder Fawr**, is **Y Foel Goch**, the 'bare red hill', at 2641'. The way is less interesting than the paths to be found on the higher mountains, but does have a certain charm of its own. From the crossing of the Miner's Track over the ridge from Pen-y-Gwryd in the south to Cwm Tryfan in the north, a vague path leads eastwards over the bogs, passing the tiny tarn of Llyn Caseg-fraith, 'lake of the dappled mare'. The going is very easy underfoot, apart from having to dodge the marshy bits, and soon the gentle climb up to the summit is underway. These slopes are often grazed by herds of feral goats, well-known for their rock climbing antics on nearby **Tryfan**. There are very few of these once-domesticated animals roaming the mountains of Snowdonia, the only other recorded herds being on Cadair Idris, the Arenigs and Rhinogs, although personally, I have only seen them in the latter range.

The summit area of **Y Foel Goch** has a couple of grassy little knolls scattered about its top, but the small cairn to the left of the path marks the highest point.

Slightly further east, but off the main path, lies **Gallt yr Ogof**, 'cliff of the cave', at 2503'. Again, this has little to offer those in search of ruggedness, although the spur which falls down to the A5 to the north-east ends in a tumbling, vegetated cliff, hosting a number of not-so-popular rock climbs.

The way up from Capel Curig starts up the farm track by the side of Joe Brown's outdoor shop. At the cluster of farm buildings known as Gelli, the open hillside should be gained and soon an obvious path follows the long ridge of Cefn y Capel over much boggy ground before a wall is climbed via a stile. Above the stile the way becomes steeper, and soon the path passes within a few hundred yards of the small summit knoll of **Gallt yr Ogof**. A cairn marks the top of this unremarkable little hill.

CARNEDDAU

The Carnedds, or Carneddau to give them their proper title, are a vast range of high mountains and subsidiary hills. The main trend of the highest mountains in the range follows a general north-east to south-west ridge, with the lesser hills connected to this ridge by high cols, abutting onto the main ridge from all angles. In all, there are 16 Hewitts in the group, seven of which rise above 3000', thereby forming the largest single high mountain mass in Britain south of the Scottish border. The range as a whole is strictly three sided, the long eastern edge being formed by the defile of the Dyffryn Conwy, with its rail and road links from the coast running southwards into the very heart of Snowdonia. The North Wales coast and the busy A55 form the northern border, and the A5 running up through the Nant Ffrancon Valley, Ogwen Valley and alongside the Afon Llugwy from Bangor to Betws-y-Coed mark the western and southern extremes of the range.

A glance at the map will reveal that there is no particular pattern to the range as a whole, other than that already pointed out, that the highest summits form a long, fairly straight chain running south-west to north-east. Perhaps the best way to describe such a confused country is to begin where most hillwalkers also start their explorations, in the Ogwen Valley to the south.

Pen yr Ole Wen translates beautifully as 'top of the white light', and is often the first mountain climbed on any day trip into the Carneddau's wild, remote interior. The direct way from Ogwen Cottage looks far from inviting as broken slopes of scree intertwine with dense heather on the steep flank, and the odd outcropping of rock and boulder seem to bar the way for the ordinary walker. However, this, the south ridge of the mountain is just about the quickest way onto the tops, and if a steady pace is set, the gradient is never too taxing. From the car parks near Ogwen Cottage, head off down the Nant Ffrancon road for a couple of hundred metres, until a gap in the wall on the right leads over to an easy crossing of the stream below the Rhaeadr Ogwen. A bit of a path is soon underfoot, and continues winding a torturous way up through the shattered flanks of the ridge. Higher up a choice of ways up open gullies full of scree lead to a final bouldery easing before the stony top is reached. The cairn sits at 3209' on the brink of Cwm Lloer immediately to the north.

The broad ridge forming the southern rib of this cwm, and falling away to the east of the summit provides an alternative means of climbing **Pen yr Ole Wen**. At the eastern end of Llyn Ogwen lie the buildings of Glan Dena surrounded by pines. A path picks an obvious way up through the bouldery hillside, passing to the right of Glan Dena before following the banks of the Afon Lloer up to the wedged in tarn of Ffynnon Lloer up in the base of the cwm. The east ridge of **Pen yr Ole Wen** rises up on the left as you approach the tarn and is followed easily up to the summit.

Following the rim of the cwm around to the north, the terrain becomes more ridge-like and passes by the cairn at Carnedd Fach before a gentle but stony rise up to **Carnedd Dafydd**, 'David's cairn', at 3425'. Northwards the eye sweeps across the head of Cwm Pen-llafar to the heights of **Yr Elen** and **Carnedd Llewelyn**, but steep crags fall away immediately in that direction, and the walker must head east to continue along the ridge.

The whole of the western face of **Carnedd Dafydd** drops into a wide, undistinguished defile taking the Afon Berthen down into the Nant Ffrancon valley at Ty'n-y-maes, but generally does not provide a good ascent. The exception to this is the well defined ridge of Mynydd Du which forms a separating hog's back between this defile and the much deeper Cwm Pen-llafar. This ridge can be reached from Bethesda by heading south-eastwards to Gwaun-y-gwiail along a minor road named Braichmelyn, then continuing on a public footpath which leads into the very depths of the cwm head. This path provides the usual approach to climbers intent on scaling the wild heights of Ysgolion Duon, 'The Black Ladders', a highly respected preserve of the winter climber, although some excellent rock climbs have been done here in summer too. W.P. Haskett Smith notes in his *Climbing in the British Isles* that the old name is Cefnysgolion Duon (it should be noted that the ridge above the cliff is still known as Cefn Ysgolion Duon) which 'might be forced into meaning "The Black Schools," and this sense greatly bewildered a learned native, who observes, "It is impossible to imagine a spot less suited to the operations of a school master."' Probably the best known climb on the cliff is the Western Gully, described in the Climbers' Club guide to the Carneddau as 'One of the great Welsh Classics ... sustained at a high standard with an inescapable line.' The climb is given the grade of Severe in summer, and V in winter, so although it was first ascended in 1901, it still cannot be considered easy by anyone's standards. The Black Ladders are among the few great climbing crags of the Carneddau, indeed the only other cliff that could be

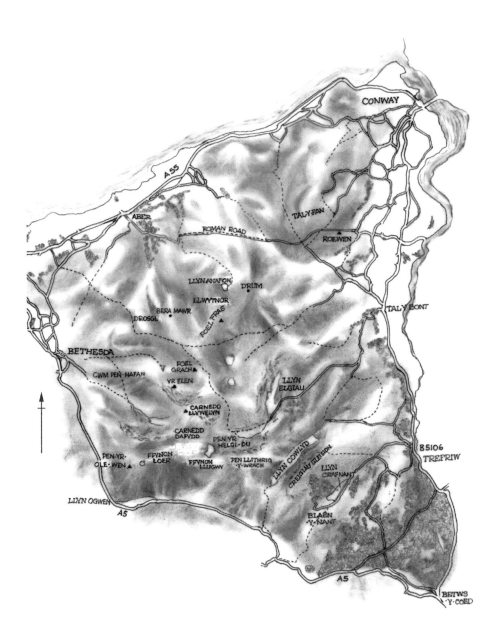

considered important is Craig yr Ysfa further east, but that shall be detailed shortly. For those intent on ascending **Carnedd Dafydd** on foot, the ridge of Mynydd Du should be gained soon after passing through the intake wall, near a collection of sheepfolds, rather than continuing all the way up into the cwm. If, however, you aspire to easy climbing, the wonderful ridge of Crib Lem gives a brilliant scramble all the way to the very summit. Huge piles of boulders lie beneath the steep walls of Llech Du, a real hard man's crag, slightly lower down the valley than Ysgolion Duon. A way can be found around Llech Du on its right, and onto the ridge of Crib Lem, bordering the small hanging valley of Cwmglas Bach to the east. The way is easy, and follows a series of delightful steps up this promontory in a really wild environment.

The origin of the name **Carnedd Dafydd** and that of its higher twin to the north-east, **Carnedd Llewelyn** has never been made certain. The two most likely candidates for the honour of having such marvellous mountains named after them are either Llewelyn the Great (1194-1240) who is known to have had a fortification on **Carnedd Llewelyn** (it is likely that the ancient cairns passed on the way over from **Pen yr Ole Wen**, and that at the summit of **Carnedd Dafydd** are remains of the fortified observation posts which once lined the whole of the ridge), and his successor Dafydd. The other oft quoted origin of the names is that of the last of the Welsh princes Llywelyn ap Gruffydd (Llewelyn Griffith) and his brother Dafydd. Whoever are the correct owners of the names associated with these mountains will probably never be determined, but to the hillwalker, that hardly seems important, both alternatives provide a wonderful link with the past.

The way on to **Carnedd Llewelyn** from **Carnedd Dafydd** is again stony, and follows the rim of the corrie around to the east, along what is marked on most maps as Cefn Ysgolion Duon. Slight confusion can be experienced at a point one mile from **Carnedd Dafydd** where the ridge splits into two. In mist the obvious continuation seems to be down a long south-easterly ridge which runs down to Ffynnon Llugwy, and only a careful check with the compass will put the walker back onto the right course, a less obvious ridge running northwards over the high col of Bwlch Cyfryw-drum and on to the much broader slopes of **Carnedd Llewelyn**.

Another ancient cairn, made into a windbreak, marks the top of Llewelyn's Cairn, at 3491' the highest mountain in the whole range. This, the central part of the Carneddau forms the shape of a large cross when looked at on the map. Roughly northwards lie the many smaller hills of the Northern Carneddau, while to the immediate west, the solitary summit of **Yr Elen** forms a ridge between Cwm Pen-llafar and Cwm Caseg. The

*From an old engraving looking towards Llyn Ogwen from **Carnedd Dafydd**. **Tryfan** and **Glyder Fawr** in the Glydderau are on the left, with Y Garn and the slopes of **Pen yr Ole Wen** on the right*

eastern arm of this cross takes in **Pen yr Helgi Du**, and **Pen Llithrig y Wrach** before dropping down to the shores of the Llyn Cowlyd Reservoir. Even then, this long eastern ridge doesn't end. Beyond Llyn Cowlyd a rocky smaller ridge throws up the delightful summits of **Creigiau Gleision**.

At the risk of causing confusion, I will detail the ascent of **Yr Elen**, then continue describing the main ridge northwards to its termination at lowly **Tal y Fan**, before returning to take a look at this subsidiary eastern ridge and its summits.

Rough, featureless slopes of stone and mat grass lead down to a narrow col above the tiny Ffynnon Caseg, 'the mare's fountain', before a good path is gained climbing easily up to the summit of **Yr Elen**. It is widely believed that this name means 'hill of the fawn' but I think it likely that it derives from the old Welsh 'y leng' meaning 'the legion'. If this is the case **Yr Elen** would mean 'hill of the legion', quite possible considering that the Roman road, Sarn Helen, 'road of the legion', passes close by to the east. The top of **Yr Elen** is crowned by a small cairn at 3156', while another cairn to the west gives good views over Anglesey and beyond. The north-west ridge of **Yr**

Elen gives a good though steep descent to Gwaun-y-gwiail near Bethesda, providing an excellent day traversing Cwm Pen-llafar, if the Crib Lem ridge of **Carnedd Dafydd** is climbed earlier to gain the high tops and ridges.

North of **Carnedd Llewelyn** the terrain becomes kinder on the legs and feet, although still maintains a proud height of over 3000 feet. The path from the summit heads just slightly east of north, and after a fairly gentle mile, rises to the stony summit of **Foel Grach**, 'scabby bare hill', at 3202'. A small cairn marks the highest point, while to the north-east of the top, tucked in behind a short bouldery outcrop, a small refuge provides welcome reprise from the elements on the foulest of days. A broad ridge heads off to the south-east, forming the southern wall of the cwm holding the twin lakes of Melynllyn and Llyn Dulyn. Climbing onto the Carneddau from the east via these two lakes gives an altogether quieter experience than approaches from either the north or the south. Cars can be parked at Trasbwll below Llyn Eigiau Reservoir, which in turn can be reached from Tal-y-Bont on the west side of the Conwy Valley.

North again from **Foel Grach**, the rocky little summit of **Garnedd Uchaf**, 'highest cairn' at 3038' lies amid a wash of grassy expanses fringed with warty tors. A mad plateau-land stretches away to the north-west, and two of the rocky tors in that direction are sufficiently elevated above their surroundings to be included in the list of Hewitts.

Nant Ffrancon, which marks the western edge of the Carneddau,
as seen on an old postcard

Leaving the summit of **Garnedd Uchaf** behind, the path crosses much boggy ground on its way over to **Drosgl** and the Beras, passing the spiky outcrops at Yr Aryg on the way. Just over a mile to the north-west, a compact jumble of boulders and slabs juts out of the grassy moorland. This is Bera Bach, the 'little hayricks', not quite big enough to be a Hewitt, but nevertheless a good enough viewpoint from which to take in the splendour of these desolate northern moors. **Drosgl** lies to the west of this point, while **Bera Mawr** lies to the north-east.

Drosgl has a good network of paths and sheep tracks which rise from the foothills to the north and west. Indeed, one of my favourite approaches to these hills is to climb the small dome of Moel Wnion from near Bont Newydd, just south of Abergwyngregyn on the A55. As you crest the top of the neat little hill the whole of the western Carneddau rise high above in the wild heartland of these expansive wastes. A broad col, with the tiny knoll of Gyrn to the west, separates Moel Wnion from the higher **Drosgl**. I once came this way in the bleakest of winters. Winds howling spindrift across the open slopes blurred all vision, and I hardly dared stop at all during a gruelling seven hour day for fear of losing too much body heat. As I pulled up the final stony slope of **Drosgl**, a couple of ponies loomed out of the whiteness, and obviously not being too happy with their lot, decided to follow me. Unfortunately for them, it was early on in the day, and it took them a good hour or so to realise that I wasn't about to lead them to shelter immediately. With a few wild-eyed snorts, they eventually cantered off at the head of the Afon Goch away to the east.

Drosgl, 'rough ground' lies at 2487', but in all but the mildest of weather, feels a good deal higher. Its summit is very dome-like and is marked by a good solid cairn, and a number of confusing smaller ones. It can be reached from Bethesda by following a path along the north side of the Afon Caseg, and up over the ridge of Gyrn Wigau.

Bera Mawr, 'big hayricks' at 2605' to the east of **Drosgl**, is a much better hill, its summit being composed of a number of blocks and boulders, thrown together into a huge pile. From **Drosgl** it is easily possible to traverse the bouldery northern flank of Bera Bach to gain this Hewitt. Similarly, easy though stony ground separates **Bera Mawr** from **Garnedd Uchaf** to the south. Easy scrambling or more adventurous 'boulder problems' lead to the sharp little summit.

The best way of climbing **Bera Mawr** is undoubtedly from the north. A car park at Bont Newydd has a wonderful track leaving the bridge on its eastern side. This passes through delightful woodland before emerging beneath the impressive Aber Falls. In rare harsh winters, this waterfall is often cloaked in a web of climbers' ropes and accoutrements. The main climbs follow excellent lines and have been given suitable names, such as 'Fountain of Youth', 'Well of Loneliness' and 'The Angel's Tears'. These are all quite hard challenges.

Nearer the falls the path zigzags up a scree slope on the left bank of the stream, then passes around a rocky step immediately above the falls themselves. Once above the falls the way is much more open and a scene of desolation sets in. **Bera Mawr** rises roughly on the right as you look up into the cwm, while **Llwytmor** lies less steeply and bracken covered on the left.

The four Hewitts of **Bera Mawr**, **Garnedd Uchaf**, **Foel-fras** and **Llwytmor** form the head of the cwm taking the Afon Goch over the Aber Falls. Back on **Garnedd Uchaf**'s summit, a path heads off north-eastwards, soon picking up a fence and wall which lead directly to the summit of **Foel-fras**. **Foel-fras** means 'prominent bare hill', which seems a bit grand for such a dull hill. Being 3091' above the sea helps to maintain its popularity, but really the only thing that is prominent about it is the fact that a six-foot high stone wall crosses its summit. Enclosures are rare in the Carneddau. It actually took me three visits before I realised that the stone wall is so high, the first two times it was all but buried beneath pristine snow drifts, only the top fourteen inches or so showing above the iron-hard crust! **Foel-fras** is also the place that I spent the last night of my Welsh Hewitt Traverse in 1998. I bivvied out by its summit cairn with my pal, Andy who had travelled down from Scotland for the weekend to do the last few hills of my walk with me.

It is also possible to climb **Foel-fras** from Llyn Dulyn, the way being steep but not too rough underfoot.

The main ridge continues in a north-easterly direction, but first a brief look at the final Hewitt of the Afon Goch quartet. **Llwytmor**, 'big grey hill', at 2785' forms a small, flat-topped hill to the north-west of the main ridge. From **Foel-fras** it is an easy matter to descend to the wide col which separates the two, from where a short ascent leads to the small summit cairn. Across the compact grassy plateau to the north, a bigger cairn has been hollowed out to form a windbreak, but this is lower than the one to the south.

Another way of climbing **Llwytmor** is from the Aber Falls as mentioned above. Once the open cwm has been reach above the falls, short grass, bracken and occasional heather clumps cover the north-west ridge over Llwytmor Bach. This provides a good climb if a round of the cwm is in mind. A sheepfold just above the falls provides some basic shelter if the weather turns nasty.

If you continue along the road over the bridge from the car park at Bont Newydd, it climbs steadily uphill to soon bring a good track underfoot. This runs along the bottom of the valley to the north and east of **Llwytmor**, beside the Afon Anafon. At its source, the sheltered tarn of Llyn Anafon nestles in the crook of the ridge rimmed by **Llwytmor**, **Foel-fras** and the smaller dome of **Drum**. Until my traverse of all the Welsh Hewitts in 1998 I had never climbed **Drum**, though since then I have twice been back to explore its environs. It's a fairly unassuming summit, marked by a large ancient cairn known as Carnedd Penyborth-goch, hollowed out to form a windbreak. Twice I have been chased around the grassy summit by swarms of wasps. The top itself stands at 2526', and translated into English means simply 'ridge'. It is easily possible to gain the wide col between **Drum**, and its higher neighbour **Foel-fras** from Llyn Anafon. A fence points the way to the summit.

A minor road heads up into the openness of the Northern Carneddau from the Conwy Valley in the east and gives a good, high level starting point for a number of hills in the area. The map shows a maze of roads climbing up through the village of Rowen, though in actual fact these are not really suitable for motors. A number of gates must be opened and closed, and the road itself is almost at the point of being taken over by the fume-stained grass which grows along the middle. The only decent road leaves the Dyffryn Conwy at Tal-y-Bont and passes through Llanbedr-y-cennin. This leads through many twists and turns to a roadside lay-by just south of **Tal y Fan**, and continues for a short way westwards to a car park near Bwlch y Ddeufaen, 'pass of the two stones', which still mark this Roman road, although it is likely that they pre-date the Roman occupation. Scores of standing stones, burial chambers, stone circles and even stone axe factories have been found in this area, dating back to Neolithic and Mesolithic man.

Along the track from the car park, passing between the stones at Bwlch y Ddeufaen, a path leaves the col and follows a wall to the south-west, up the ridge of Carnedd y Ddelw, cairn of the idol, known as Drosgl. The way is easy and well-worn, swinging left just before the top of Carnedd y Ddelw, a Nuttall but not a Hewitt. An ancient cairn marks the top as indeed they seem to on every hill in the area. The Roman road passes to the north of these hills, joining up with the minor road at Bont Newydd, and just to the north of Foel-ganol, another track leaves the main one to head south into the hills. It gains the ridge just to the south of Carnedd y Ddelw where it joins the path along the tops for the final short climb up **Drum**.

To the east of **Drum** is a rocky little knoll, known as Pen y Castell, 'top of the castle', again a Nuttall and not a Hewitt. This does, however, give a good ascent of **Drum** if a track is taken along the south side of the ridge running down to Llanbedr-y-cennin from Pen y Castell. It is then as easy matter to take in that little top before tackling the south-east ridge of **Drum**.

To the east of Bwlch y Ddeufaen lies the lowly little summit of **Tal y Fan**, appropriately meaning 'end peak'. Appropriately, this was the last peak of my Hewitt bagging trip in 1998. Though only 2001' high, it does provide some good walking over rocky knolls, replete with dense heather and bilberry, and as such is invariably popular. **Tal y Fan** can be, and usually is, ascended from the lay-by on the minor road mentioned above, near Cae Coch. A well signposted path leads up to a stile at a small col, just to the west of the summit. A wall is then followed to another stile with the summit trig pillar on the southern side. The views of the North Wales coast are spectacular, although the other Carneddau do not flaunt their best sides towards **Tal y Fan**. It is a lucky walker, or a very early riser who has the summit of **Tal y Fan** to himself on all but the bleakest of days.

Another route to the top, and preferable to that already mentioned, is to start at Bwlch y Ddeufaen. Follow the stone wall steeply uphill eastwards, turning left to take in the summit of Foel Lwyd. A path heads off through the heather down to the col on the previous route, and so to the summit. There are many public footpaths criss-crossing the moorland to the north, giving options for an ascent from Llanfairfechan or Conwy, although the Penmaenmawr Quarries on the northern edge of these moors detract from the experience.

As mentioned earlier, there is a long ridge running south-eastwards from the highest point of the Carneddau, **Carnedd Llewelyn**. This includes two Hewitts before Llyn Cowlyd Reservoir, and a further two across its barren waters to the east.

When descending the east ridge of **Carnedd Llewelyn** over Penywaun-wen, the ridge soon narrows, falling in precipitous slopes on both sides, though that to the north being more rocky and having huge gullies, and what is known to climbers as the Amphitheatre, cleaving the rangy buttresses. This is Craig yr Ysfa, probably the most important rock climbing crag of the whole Carneddau group. The Climbers' Club guide to the Carneddau attempts to throw some light onto the meaning of the name, stating that 'The word ysfa does translate to mean a craving or itching. However, a much more likely explanation is that our ysfa is derived from the old Welsh word hysfa. This was where a shepherd would collect his sheep from the high pastures.' They give the meaning therefore as 'cliff of the gathering', which is more than likely correct. However, that guide also points out that previous to it there had been a number of errors. 'One can enjoy', the Craig yr Ysfa chapter continues, 'such morsels of writing as ... "Experience, bitter experience, has proved that the simple literal translation of the name must be accepted."' It goes on to describe how a party had left Pen-y-Gwryd intent on scaling one of the gullies on the crag, 'Hardly had they roped up when they were attacked by myriads of small, but active and virulent gnats. The battle was fierce and long. No sooner had one cloud been added to the heap of slain that littered the bottom of the gully than other and still other clouds appeared .... clinging with one hand and with the other endeavouring to slay their ten thousands, the members of the expedition finally emerged into the upper world, but at what cost! They have however the satisfaction of knowing that they have torn from the dark recesses of these cliffs the fearful secret of their name.' This expedition took place in 1916, but warm sunny days of little breeze could equally be used to describe a typical gully climb on Craig yr Ysfa today.

Legend has it that Craig yr Ysfa was first discovered as a rock climbing ground by raiders from the Lake District. In the early years of British mountaineering it was usual for the majority of climbers to remain fairly loyal to one particular area. There was much competition between climbers in the Lakes and in Wales, and although each faction occasionally climbed in the other's area, it would never do for a party from the Lakes, say, to snatch a first ascent of a climb in Snowdonia, from beneath the very noses of the Welsh climbing community. That this did happen, and to a certain extent continues to happen is evident even today.

Craig yr Ysfa lay dormant until 1900. Cox and Kretschmer in the 1943 guidebook to the area noted that it had first come to the attention of climbers when a party having climbed a line on Scafell in the Lake District, spied the cliff through a telescope across the outer waters of Morecambe Bay. They wrote that, as a crag 'it relies too much on mere bulk and not enough on steepness.' This amply sums up Craig yr Ysfa, but these days steeper lines have been discovered and climbed, and there is plenty here for climbers of all grades. The most popular routes, however, are probably the famous Great Gully, climbed by Archer Thomson and party in 1900, and Amphitheatre Buttress climbed in 1905 by the redoubtable Abraham brothers of Keswick. Both climbs are today graded as Very Difficult, by today's standards not really that hard.

Below Craig yr Ysfa lie the headwaters of Llyn Eigiau Reservoir in Cwm Eigiau, a wild land of savagery and desolation.

Pen yr Helgi Du, 'head of the black hound', at 2733' is a pleasant little mountain. Descending from **Carnedd Llewelyn**, the path passes above

Craig yr Ysfa, then drops to a col above Ffynnon Llugwy Reservoir. An easy approach to these hills can be had by leaving the car at the road side down in the Ogwen Valley near Gwern Gof Isaf and taking the tarmac road which leaves the main A5 just to the east. The walking, as you would expect is very easy, but cars are not allowed to use this reservoir access road. From the reservoir the path becomes a bit vague at first, taking the right bank, before climbing in short zigzags up to the col. **Pen yr Helgi Du** is than tackled over a short, scrambly ridge to its summit to the east. The top is flat and grassy and has a small cairn at its highest point. There is another, well-built cairn further east at a lower level.

Another path climbs up from the Ogwen Valley near the Climbers' Club hut at Helyg. This small building has long been the traditional base for explorations on the crags of the valley. The path takes the well-defined south ridge of the hill leading directly to the summit.

A path descends the east ridge of **Pen yr Helgi Du** and gives the continuation onwards towards **Pen Llithrig y Wrach**, 'slippery hill of the witch', at 2621'. Between the two lies the small col of Bwlch y Tri Marchog, 'pass of the three knights'. Wonderful names of the past, who's stories are sadly no longer traceable, adorn these wild lands of the Carneddau.

Below **Pen Llithrig y Wrach**'s eastern face of scree and heather lies Snowdonia's longest lake, Llyn Cowlyd. A way to the top of the Hewitt can be followed from the southern end of this reservoir. Faint paths come and go through short heather, mat grass and bilberry, but soon the top is underfoot with its small cairn. The southern end of the reservoir can be reached from the A5 near Bron Heulog along an indistinct path which becomes very boggy closer to the lake. A public bridleway continues along the western shore to the dam at the northern end where cars can be parked, using access along a minor road heading westwards into the hills from Trefriw in the Conwy Valley.

East of Llyn Cowlyd lies a delightful switchback ridge taking in two more lesser Hewitts. The whole is known as **Creigiau Gleision**, that also being the name given to the highest summit, while the second Hewitt is merely called **Creigiau Gleision North Top**. **Creigiau Gleision** translates simply as 'blue rocks'. A traverse of this short ridge is one of my favourite low level outings in the whole of Wales taking in a number of other, smaller summits *en route*, each one having a character of its own, some being rocky little warts, others being merely heather capped.

The ridge can be gained from either the southern or northern end of Llyn Cowlyd, but the way is invariably boggy and heathery and so cannot be recommended in preference to a traverse from the Crafnant Valley.

*The Fairy Glen near Betws-y-Coed,
the town which marks the south-western
boundary of the Carneddau,
as shown on an old postcard*

Wedged into the corner formed by the A5 through the Llugwy Valley between Capel Curig and Betws-y-Coed and the B5106 which runs along the western side of the Conwy Valley, lies a wonderland of forests, lakes and rocks. The whole area is well worth exploring in its own right, and provides a good place to stretch the legs when wild weather limits the possibilities of going high. A minor road runs south-west into the area from Trefriw, taking the walker to car parks and picnic sites near Llyn Crafnant.

The area has a number of good crags and outcrops but could never be called popular with so many higher cliffs in the vicinity over in the Ogwen Valley and the Pass of Llanberis. The Mynydd Climbing Club have published their own guide to the area, and also own the cottage of Blaen-y-nant at the head of the valley.

From Blaen-y-nant a path climbs steadily up to a col to the south. This is an old pack horse route over to Capel Curig, from where an ascent can also be started from behind the Youth Hostel at Plas-Curig. This way follows the course of the Nant y Geuallt and is excellent throughout. Both routes meet at the col between the little heathery lumps of Clogwyn Mawr and Clogwyn Mannod (it should be noted that many of these names are not shown on the Landranger map, but are on the Outdoor Leisure).

The first little summit is Crimpiau and is gained by a good little path through the heather on the western side of the col. Beyond Crimpiau the way descends alongside a broken wall, crossing it at a col before a boggy climb up to Craig-wen and the start of the ridge proper.

Beyond Craig-wen lies another boggy col, Bwlch Mignog before the final short climb around the rocks and heather of Moel Defaid to Craiglwyn. The summit of **Creigiau Gleision** is just a short distance across the next broad col to the north, and a good path leads the way.

Creigiau Gleision, at 2224', is a wonderful rocky little summit, giving good views across Llyn Cowlyd to **Pen Llithrig y Wrach** and northwards to the Dyffryn Conwy flanks of the eastern Carneddau. More peaty ground leads across the short intervening ridge to **Creigiau Gleision North Top**, at 2080'. Just north-east of the **North Top**, a fence cuts across the ridge and can be followed northwards to the dam of Llyn Cowlyd, or around in an arc to the east. Heading eastwards, a dank forest down in the Crafnant Valley soon comes into view, and at a heathery col, a way can be forced through the pathless ground, following a line of fence posts, to the corner of the forest. A public footpath then leads via a series of firebreaks and forestry tracks to the cottage of Hendre near Blaen-y-nant at the end of a wonderful day among delightful hills.

THE MOELWYNS

On initial inspection, it is hard to find anything complementary to say about this much desecrated range. The township of Blaenau Ffestiniog lies at its heart, and it can be no surprise to anyone passing through to find that the area within a radius of about two miles of Blaenau has been excluded from the Snowdonia National Park. The Ordnance Survey maps clearly show a broad yellow band around the screes of slate spoil and sad remains of torn apart mountains. That there is beauty here after so much destruction is remarkable. There are areas of wildness, of remote corries, hidden tarns and delightful streams despite the fact that man has done much damage to this mountain range, and indeed, though to a lesser extent, continues to harm.

Natural borders are hard to define as the Hewitts of the range are scattered willy-nilly in a seemingly crazy pattern, but perhaps it is sufficient to say that the whole range stands between the valley of the Nantgwynant to the north-west, has Llyn Conwy and other tributaries of this river to the east and the Vale of Ffestiniog to the south.

In all, 12 of these hills are classified as Hewitts, and these can be split pretty easily into three obvious groups. Immediately east of Blaenau Ffestiniog lie the three summits of the Manods, while to the west rise the scattered ridges of the main Moelwyn chain, comprising eight Hewitts. Far to the north, though still connected to the main Moelwyns by a series of heathery knolls, subsidiary summits and sparkling tarns lies the solitary cone of **Moel Siabod**, just to the south of Capel Curig.

Moel Siabod, probably translating as 'bare hill of the abbot', rises 2861' above the sea. What is evident to all who climb it is that it once rose much higher than that. The whole of the eastern cwm holding Llyn y Foel is gouged out of the mountain of Ordovician rocks, but it is easy to imagine how the slope leading up to the corrie rim, would have continued higher before glaciation removed the uppermost segment of its top.

Few people climb **Moel Siabod** from the west, although it should be noted that that is not entirely out of the question, if one is prepared for endlessly rough ridges and many smaller tops. From **Ysgafell Wen** in the main Moelwyn range, a ridge heads off northwards to Llyn Edno, then a

Moel Siabod from the Bangor Road,
a watercolour by Paul Sandby Munn (1773-1845)

series of rugged little summits, beginning with Moel Meirch at 607 metres, curves round to eventually pick up the long western ridge of **Moel Siabod**, the ridge being known as Moel Gîd. The way is long and arduous, but takes the walker into delightful, little frequented hill country.

Moel Siabod is usually climbed from Capel Curig. One track leaves the valley at the western side of Plas y Brenin, the National Mountain Centre on the A4086. This is the old Capel Curig Inn, which in turn became the Royal Hotel and in 1955, an outdoor pursuits centre. It is now owned by the Mountain Leader Training Board and as such is the main centre for training for all aspirant mountaineering instructors in England and Wales. Scotland have their own centre at Glenmore Lodge in the Cairngorms.

The path crosses the Nantygwryd via a bridge, then climbs gently up through conifers to gain the open fellside, roughly to the north of the main summit ridge. A good path is underfoot throughout and the fit can gain the summit in little more than an hour from the valley. A bridge opposite the Clogwyn Café, near the Youth Hostel in Capel Curig, also leads out onto forestry tracks, and if the right branch is taken along a contouring track, the path mentioned above is gained just beyond an old derelict barn in the trees on the left.

CAPEL CURIG

A 4086

PONT CYFYNG

BETWS·Y·COED

CARNEDD MOEL SIABOD ▲

Y CRIBAU

DOLWYDDELAN

PENTRE BONT

LLYN GWYNANT

LLYN·YR·ARDDU

MOEL MEIRCH

MOEL DYRNOGYDD

A 470

LLYN EDNO

YSGAFELLWEN

A 498

MOEL PENAMNEN

MOEL DRUMAN

LLYN·YR ADAR

LLYN NEWYDD

LLYN BOWYDD

LLYN CONGLOG

ALLT FAWR

CNICHT

CWM CROESOR

LLYN CWMORTHIN

BLAENAU FFESTINIOG

TANYGRISIAU

LLYN·Y·MANOD

MOELWYN MAWR ▲

MANOD MAWR ▲

LLYNAU

MOELWYN BACH

FFESTINIOG

A4085

LLYN MAIR

On the south side, the view of the precipice from its brink, is enough to stupify the senses, and almost to petrify the whole animal system, so that I found it necessary to keep aloof. The wind blew fresh from the east ... I could distinctly make out the ridge of mountains in the vale of Clwyd, and others as far south as Cader Ferwin in Merionethshire. It was a grand and novel sight, the sun strongly shining upon those distant objects, and on most of the immediate varieties of hills, rocks, and water; with a dark cloud forming a gloomy canopy above me, throwing a shade and obscurity all around, which contrasted admirably with the splendour of the eastern distance. Snowdon itself was likewise involved in an almost impenetrable cloud, from the body of vapours that sluggishly moved along ... The sun was now sinking towards the horizon, and tinged the whole atmosphere with his setting colour. I anticipated the exhibition, and prolonged my departure from the mountain till his rays had lost their influence on our hemisphere. In about half an hour the whole had attained a depth of red, that must be incredible to any, but to those who have been eye-witnesses. Snowdon seemed a dreadful mass of fire, and the clouds which hovered upon his top, and about his base, the consequence of it: the utmost fury of the burning Etna (barring the ill effects of it), could never have displayed a scene more sublime. Glydar mountain on the right, and the other extremity of Moel-Siabod, being detached from Snowdon, received but a small degree of red, as if reflected from him: a circumstance which added greatly to the magnificence of the scene ...

Regardless of the distance to the inn, I remained till I could scarcely see my way through bogs and over precipices, and was soon left in total darkness ...

Sunset seen from Moel Siabod as described by Edward Pugh in Cambria Depicta, A Tour through North Wales illustrated with Picturesque Views by a Native Artist, 1813

The summit is a nice little jumble of boulders set well back from the lip of the eastern cwm, and is adorned with a trig pillar. A large cairn, hollowed out as a windbreak offers shelter from the elements and is marked on the map as Carnedd Moel Siabod. It is said that this once formed a pen for the ponies used to carry the early tourists up the mountain. As is usually the case with isolated mountains, **Moel Siabod** provides excellent views of most of the peaks of Snowdonia.

Perhaps the most popular way of ascending the mountain, and by far the best, is from Pont Cyfyng, 'the narrow bridge', about a mile east of Capel Curig on the A5. Again the way is obvious, heading initially for the abandoned Rhos Quarry. This ceased operations in 1972. A signposted path climbs up to a little col to the south, then passes around Llyn y Foel on its western bank. Daiar Ddu, the rocky east ridge which forms the southern arm of the cirque is then climbed pleasantly to the summit.

It is possible to climb **Moel Siabod** from Dolwyddelan in the Lledr Valley to the south, but this is not a very popular approach. Head north from the cross-roads in the village and take the public footpath through Pen-y-gelli farm. Above, a forest is entered and forestry tracks are followed over a ridge and down to cross the Afon Ystumiau. This stream is the outflow of Llyn y Foel, and after leaving its banks for a short while, the path regains the side of it and follows the gushing waters up to the lake in the cwm above.

This hill has its dangers. It has been reported that the lakeland poet Robert Southey (1774-1843) became stuck on these slopes over night,

Moel Shabot on the Llugwy by Joseph Barber

Moel Siabod, from the hills above Capel Curig from Illustrations of the Natural Scenery of the Snowdonian Mountains, *1829*

presumably before the coming of the forest, and in 1836, Haskett Smith wrote that a few years previously, possibly in 1830, a Mr Philip Homer also became benighted on **Siabod**'s slopes and died of exhaustion. The body was carried down to Capel Curig for burial.

Far to the south-west of **Moel Siabod**, the terrain rises from the moorland ridges of lesser hills to again clear the two thousand foot mark. These eight Hewitts of the main Moelwyns are centred in a vague horseshoe around Cwm Croesor. The village of Croesor lies a couple of miles up the valley from Garreg on the A4085, between the Aberglaslyn Pass and Penrhyndeudraeth. A car park in Croesor provides as good a place as any to begin explorations of the Moelwyns. Croesor itself was once a thriving mining community, though now, every other cottage seems to be owned by Englishmen and rented out as holiday accommodation.

Cnicht, spelt Cynicht on maps before 1924, 'the knight', reaches 2260'. It towers above the village and dominates the skyline, as indeed it does many views into the National Park from the coast around Porthmadog. From Croesor a track heads just west of north to gain the long south-west ridge of **Cnicht** low down, barely above the pastures of the valley. This path actually continues across the ridge and descends to Bwlchgwernog beside the Nanmor near the village of Nantmor at Aberglaslyn. The ridge up **Cnicht** is easy to follow though very steep. In fact it is this ridge, viewed head-on appearing more as a sharp gable, that gives **Cnicht** its popular 'tourist' name of The Matterhorn of Snowdonia. Frank Smythe, that prominent mountaineer of the early years of this century viewed the mountain from Garreg and pointed out that it bore 'a striking resemblance to the Dent Blanche'. While it fails by far to measure up to those Alpine giants in height, Cnicht is nevertheless a marvellous little mountain. The way is interesting throughout, with just a bit of easy scrambling near the top to add excitement to a day's outing. The summit is marked by a small cairn, which hardly seems necessary on such a well-proportioned Hewitt—the highest point could hardly be in doubt.

The ridge continues beyond the summit, dropping down to the north-east to a broad grassy col above Llyn yr Adar, which lies amid the wildlands to the north. The path here vanishes for a while, but a vague line of sheep tracks can be followed through the mat grass to gain an old fence post up on the wide summit plateau of **Ysgafell Wen**, the next Hewitt. In the heart of this elevated moorland rise a number of knolls and grassy bumps, two of which are listed as Hewitts. The higher of the two, by a mere ten feet, stands a little way east from the fence post at 2205' and is marked by a few stones on a rocky little protuberance. **Ysgafell Wen** translates as 'white ledge' and the second of the summits also makes use of the name, being simply **Ysgafell Wen North Top**. This stands at 2195', 400 yards northwards from the fence post. A peaty depression is reached if heading north, then a fence leads the way to the right of the next little knoll. The summit of the **North Top** is marked by a tiny cairn atop of this knoll. The ridge which continues to the north is that which eventually curves around to gain the long Moel Gîd ridge of **Moel Siabod**.

Ysgafell Wen can be climbed from the east by leaving the A470 just below the road pass at the head of the Lledr Valley. A track heads off around the minor top of Moel Dyrnogydd before contouring around to the headwaters of the Afon Lledr across rough heather and grass. A small knoll on the long north-east ridge of **Ysgafell Wen**, known as Moel Lledr can be climbed to gain the ridge itself, from where just over a mile of rugged terrain leads to the top of **Ysgafell Wen**.

To the south-east of **Ysgafell Wen** lie two tiny tarns amid much boggy ground. A vague path leads around the north side of these, Llyn Terfyn and Llyn Coch, then passes around the dome of the next Hewitt, **Moel Druman**. Leave the path before climbing up the easy gradient to the featureless top of this nice little viewpoint. **Moel Druman** means 'bare hill ridge' and stands at 2218'. Many beautiful tarns adorn the hills to the south, but by far the largest is Llyn Conglog immediately beneath **Moel Druman**'s south-eastern face.

Allt Fawr, 'big hill', at 2290' is a pleasant little Hewitt. Its short west ridge rises from across Llyn Conglog when looking east from **Moel Druman**. There are two other good ridges on **Allt Fawr**, sadly encompassing the most horrible sight in the whole of Wales, the slate tips of the Gloddfa Ganol Slate Mines. The north-east ridge falls from the summit to the top of the Bwlch y Gorddinan, or Crimea Pass as it is sometimes known, as an inn once stood there with that name. The ridge can either be gained direct, or a track can be taken on the Blaenau Ffestiniog side of the pass to an air shaft for the railway line which still carries passengers from the coast, down the Conwy Valley to Blaenau Ffestiniog. This shaft lies just uphill from Llyn Ffridd-y-bwlch, edging onto the waste screes from the mine. A steep pull up pathless slopes leads to Llyn Iwerddon, pleasantly away from the destruction of the mines below, from where the ridge lies just to the north. A path is then followed along the ridge to the summit of **Allt Fawr** with its rocky little rib and tiny cairn.

The south ridge falls towards the village of Tanygrisiau, terminating abruptly over the scattered crags of Craig Nyth y Gigfran. There are a number of rock climbs hereabouts, indeed two separate crags are mentioned on this nose of rock in the Climbers' Club Guide to the area. Craig y Clipiau lies at the entrance to Cwmorthin, the narrow, mine despoiled valley which lies to the south of the Hewitts mentioned above. Here there are a number of climbs in the harder grades, but the crag can hardly be called popular. Further along, above the Tanygrisiau bacon slicer factory lies the

Moel y Fridd, a pencil and grey wash sketch by John Baptist Malchiar in 1795

rambling Clogwyn Holland, another little visited place - hardly surprising really when you consider its position. A public footpath leads off down the ridge from the summit of **Allt Fawr**, but due to the quarries falling away on either side, I cannot recommend this as a good approach to these hills.

Across the ruined defile of Cwmorthin to the south a further three Hewitts are to be found, and to my mind these are by far the best mountains to be found in the Moelwyns, with the possible exception of **Moel Siabod**.

Llyn Cwmorthin dominates the bottom of the corrie, but above, steep slopes rise out of the detritus to gain the short north ridge of **Moel-yr-hydd**, 'bare hill of the stag', at 2126'. The summit itself is unassuming, being mainly grassy, but impressive cliffs fall away to the south while away across the mine-shattered col between Cwmorthin and Cwm Croesor rises the stark flanks of **Cnicht**, the start of our explorations on this, the main ridge of the Moelwyns. A tarmac road leaves Tanygrisiau and heads uphill for the Llyn Stwlan dam nestling in the crook formed by the final two summits of the main range, **Moelwyn Mawr** and **Moelwyn Bach**. A footpath leads up to the col between **Moel-yr-hydd** and **Moelwyn Mawr** from this access road, but is hard to follow at first. From the col, beside a rock outcrop, easy grass slopes climb the abrupt west side of **Moel-yr-hydd**.

The col mentioned above also provides a short approach for **Moelwyn Mawr**, 'big white bare hill' at 2526'. 500 feet of grass leads to the trig pillar on the flat summit. The southern side of **Moelwyn Mawr** is much more exciting. From the dam below Llyn Stwlan a path climbs up to Bwlch Stwlan, a narrow col with a public footpath leading down the other side to a minor road near Croesor village. From Bwlch Stwlan a delightful rocky ridge leads via easy, though exposed, scrambling over the minor top of Craigysgain to soon bring the flatter summit of **Moelwyn Mawr** underfoot.

It should be noted that a path traverses around the eastern façade of **Moelwyn Mawr** from Bwlch Stwlan to the col below **Moel-yr-hydd**. This can be used to provide a convenient means of traversing **Moelwyn Mawr** without having to retrace your steps across the summit. There are many old mine adits to be seen along this contouring path, but they are all fenced off to deter the curious.

From Bwlch Stwlan, the short north ridge of **Moelwyn Bach** leads easily to the summit of that mountain at 2329'. **Moelwyn Bach** means simply, 'small white bare hill'. The top is composed of a couple of compact grassy knolls, but the highest is obvious. The long west ridge can be descended to pick up the public footpath near the minor road at Croesor for those returning there. A small enclosed conifer plantation must be gained just before the road.

Dense forests mask the southern slopes of **Moelwyn Bach**, but a delightful track follows the course of the Ffestiniog Railway from a car park at Llyn Mair on the B4410 from Maentwrog to Garreg. This public footpath is well marked throughout, with signs to Tanygrisiau until the Tanygrisiau Reservoir is reached. Three hundred yards along the west bank of the reservoir, a faint path climbs uphill through rocky bluffs to gain the dam below Llyn Stwlan.

An eighteenth century print of a copper mine shaft in the Aberglaslyn Pass, with donkeys saddled with panniers for carrying ore

Blaenau Ffestiniog itself never fails to appal me, although that is perhaps a little unfair. It is certainly a dying town, although the Llechwedd Slate Caverns and the Gloddfa Ganol Slate Mines do attract tourists, as does the Ffestiniog Railway. Apart from the slate screes poised above the roofs of each house, the heavy rain, for which the area is noted, contributes towards an atmosphere of doom and gloom. An average rainfall for Blaenau Ffestiniog is around 100 inches per annum, making it by far the wettest town in Britain. Obviously the slate mines once provided much needed employment in the area, as well as housing materials, but it has recently been calculated that for all of the useful stone mined and quarried in the area, about twice that amount lies as wasted spoil on the hillsides around-about. As a lover of mountains and wild places, I find this appalling.

There are three more Hewitts in the Moelwyns, which if it weren't for completeness I would far sooner forget and exclude from this book alto-gether. **Manod Mawr** has two summits, both of which are Hewitts, but here the quarries have ravaged right up to the very tops of the hills. **Manod Mawr** itself is the highest point, 2169' above sea level. **Manod Mawr** translates as 'large snowdrift', but snow will be the last thing on the mind of anyone who climbs to the top. The way from the west climbs up into the heart of the Graig-ddu Quarry, and gains a dynamite blasted col, replete with access roads and warning signs. Fortunately the summit itself is a good way back from the ruins of its flanks. Faint tracks lead south from the col to the summit which is marked on the map as having a trig pillar. On my last visit during my Hewitt Traverse in 1998, it had been removed. A short wall surrounds the foundations of where the pillar once stood.

From the south the same col can be reached by leaving the A470 south of Bethania and taking a track up past Cae Ddu. This leads easily up to the southern shore of Llyn y Manod, with the wild slopes of Manod Bach, much lower than **Manod Mawr**, to the west. A green track rises gently along the western flank of **Manod Mawr** to gain the col, and so the summit.

Manod Mawr North Top's summit is ludicrously close to the lip of a quarried face to the south. It too can be gained from the col by following one of the quarry tracks, avoiding the heavy plant and loaded wagons that trundle past. The way is obvious and disgusting. The top is flat and rocky and is marked by a cairn at 2159'.

At last a scene of beauty beholds the walker who has just traversed the two Manods. Away to the north Llyn Bowydd and Llyn Newydd, though reservoirs, provide a foreground of delightfully lapping waters to the boggy moorland of **Moel Penamnen**'s southern acclivity. This, the 'bare hill of the top stones' marks the last of the high ground heading east from the Crimea Pass. The way from the Manods is rough, but navigationally easy. A fence

*A postcard of c.1913 showing Aberglaslyn Pass,
between the Moelwyns and Hebogs*

69

takes off from **Manod Mawr North Top** in the general direction of Y Ro Wen, the heavily forested ridge to the south, forming the eastern flank of Cwm Penamnen. This fence can be followed throughout until the top of Foel-fras, the minor little top to the east of **Moel Penamnen**. From there an easy grassy slope leads to the summit at 2044'.

An approach can be made to the south-west by following a public footpath alongside the Afon Barlwyd to the twin lakes of Llynau Barlwyd, then climbing the very steep western face of the hill, though the shortest way gains Llynau Barlwyd around the slopes of Moel Farlwyd from the top of the Crimea Pass.

Perhaps the better alternative is to start in the north at Pentre-bont, just south of and across the Afon Lledr from Dolwyddelan. The Roman Road, Sarn Helen heads south into the densely wooded valley of Cwm Penamnen from where a track leads up to the head of the corrie just to the east of Foel-fras. This way passes beneath the wonderful rock climbing ground of Carreg Alltrem, meaning 'steep-looking rock', high on the eastern side of the valley. Although the crag is small, it does provide some of the best middle grade outcrop climbs in the whole of Snowdonia. It was first discovered in December 1953 by Tony Moulam, then one of the leaders in pioneering new ascents in Wales.

My favourite way of climbing **Moel Penamnen**, probably because it avidly avoids all contact with the slate mines around Blaenau Ffestiniog, is also from Pentre-bont in the north. A track heads south-east, alongside the Afon Bwlch y Groes which borders the forest on the left. This track leads over the Bwlch y Groes on its way over to Penmachno in the east. From the top of the pass, the Bwlch y Groes, at an obvious little col, the broad northern flank of Y Ro Wen can be climbed to gain its north-east ridge. It is then a wonderful traverse along the ridge to the summit of that minor hill, before swinging around the head of Cwm Penmachno and across to Foel-fras, following the edge of the forest all the way.

The summit of **Moel Penamnen** is flat and grassy and is graced with a small cairn providing good views northwards to the higher mountains of Snowdon, the Glyders and the Carneddau beyond **Moel Siabod**.

THE MOUNTAINS OF EIFIONYDD

West of the busy A4085 from Beddgelert to Betws Garmon lies the Hebog Ridge, the hills of Nantlle and the isolated **Mynydd Mawr**. These, the Mountains of Eifionydd, provide the walker with perhaps some of the best ridge walking to be had anywhere in Wales. Although they are not as rough or craggy as many of the other ranges in the Snowdonia National Park, the grassy tops, softened by the conifers of the dark forests in the surrounding valleys of Nantlle, Colwyn and Pennant, provide the hillgoer with a very different, though pleasant alternative to the more familiar heights of **Snowdon** and the Glyders.

The main summits of Eifionydd are contained within two long ridges formed roughly as a letter 'T', with **Trum y Ddysgl** at the junction of the two. The Hebog ridge runs south to north with a noticeable drop to the col of Bwlch-y-ddwy-elor north of **Moel Lefn**, and has three principal summits, whereas the Nantlle ridge runs east to west and contains four Hewitts and three minor tops. **Mynydd Mawr** lies across the Nantlle valley and is distinctly separate from the other summits of the range. In all, eight of these hills are Hewitts, and all eight can be comfortably ascended in three days of fairly easy, and it must be said, excellent walking.

Dominated on the one side by Cerrig Llan, which according to Borrow is 'quite black and perpendicular', and on the other by the bulk of **Moel Hebog**, the village of Beddgelert will always be a popular place amongst hillgoers.

It is named, as most people know, after the faithful hound of Llywelyn ab Iorwerth. The story goes that Llywelyn left his son in his tent down in the valley one day in the mid-thirteenth century, under the watchful eye of Gelert, his dog, while he took his men on a campaign against the English. Returning that evening, Llywelyn was horrified to find the tent collapsed, and Gelert covered with blood, sitting alongside. Imagining that the blood was that of his own son, Llywelyn took up his spear, and in a rage of vengeance killed his dog. As his loyal hound lie dying on the ground, Llywelyn was startled by the sound of a child crying from beneath the tent. He pulled aside the torn canvas to find his son in his cradle, completely uninjured, and the dead body of a wolf near-by. As the awful truth dawned on

Llywelyn, he rushed to the side of Gelert, whom he now understood had saved the life of his son. His dog was barely alive, but did manage to lick his owner's hand before passing away. Llywelyn mourned the death of Gelert as he would a brother, and buried him with all honours in the valley, erecting a tomb over his body. A tomb remains to this day, near the river to the south of the village, which was actually constructed by a David Prichard, landlord of the Goat Hotel in the eighteenth century to try to boost the tourist trade. This is a bit of a shame really, as the heart-rending story of Gelert never fails to bring a tear to the eye of the many tourists who now flock to see the grave. Whilst the National Trust maintains the property and ensures that the legend lives on, it is now widely believed that the true derivation of the name Beddgelert is from a sixth century saint called Celert who is thought to have been buried nearby. Certainly 'Bedd' is derived from the Welsh for a grave.

Although one of Snowdonia's prettiest villages, most of its visitors come for the hillwalking. **Moel Hebog,** at 2569', is a magnificent mountain, and provides some of the most spectacular views of the surrounding mountains and coast of North Wales. It will always hold a special place in my affections. Although I made an ascent of **Snowdon** as a young lad, when, as far as I was concerned, **Snowdon** was the only mountain in Wales, **Moel Hebog** was the first mountain I climbed in Wales in the true spirit of a lover of mountains and wild places. I first caught sight of it, or at least first noticed it, towering above the trees as I drove my battered old Escort down Nant Gwynant. My partner, Rachel, and I thought how wonderful it would be to climb those grassy flanks and tread its summit, not because of it being a particularly high mountain, but simply because I knew instinctively that an ascent of **Moel Hebog** would be something special. Without much discussion about our plans, we set off early the next morning from Beddgelert. I remember it well. The day was what a Scottish friend of mine would call 'dreich'—in other words, it was one of those grey days of constant drizzle and low cloud, the kind that never really brings heavy rain, but takes a great delight in wetting you to the skin regardless. We followed the old, abandoned track of the Welsh Highland Railway for a short distance above the village after struggling to gain easy access to the hillside through a small housing estate. We did eventually find the path, and were soon clambering up into Cwm Bleiddiaid. The path wends its way over to the left of the cwm before making for the north-east ridge of the mountain. The beetling crags of Y Diffwys or 'the precipice' seemed to plunge down into the yawning gulf of the cwm to our right as we fought our way up the path which hand-rails the hanging valley below. The smattering of rock climbs which ascend this vegetated face

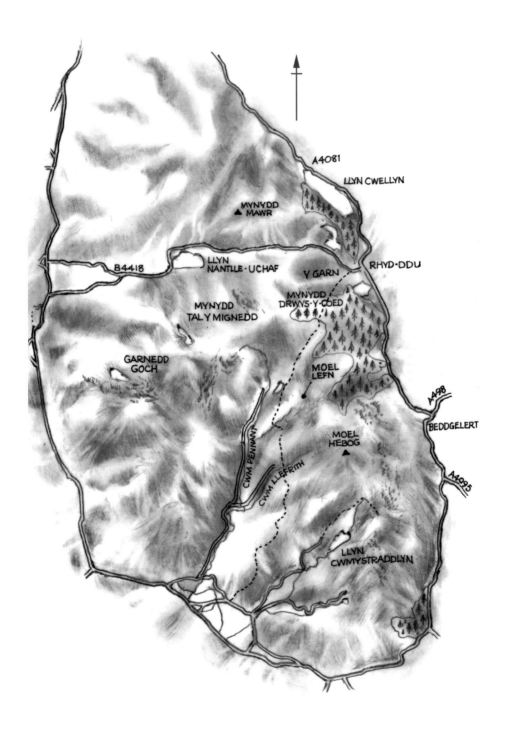

*Llyn Gwynant and **Moel Hebog** from an old postcard*

are not particularly popular, although at that time, looking for interesting lines on a sheer rock face was not really one of my main concerns. Higher up, beyond the sight of the cwm, the ridge becomes more apparent but also more rocky. Luckily for us the path was well marked with cairns and the scars of thousands of passing walkers. I say luckily, because at that time neither of us had the faintest idea of how to use the map and compass that we had tucked, rather hopefully, in the top pocket of a rucksack.

At last the summit was within our grasp. As if the darkest secrets of these ancient mountains were unravelling before our eyes, the clouds parted as we neared the stone wall and cairn which mark the highest point of the whole Hebog range. Behind us over Nant Colwyn, almost as if blocking our retreat, dark clouds were pelting the rows of conifers in the Beddgelert Forest with heavy showers of hail, while away to the south-west, the sun sparkled with apparent joy as it highlighted the flat-calm seas of Tremadog Bay with patchy flushes of golden amber reflections away over the St. Tudwal Islands beyond Criccieth.

The summit cliffs of **Moel Hebog** are particularly well known to lovers of ancient Welsh history. Although only providing the rock climber with one or two poor routes, they are more distinguished as being the site of one of the earliest recorded rock climbs. The current Climbers' Club Guidebook to the Tremadog and Cwm Silyn areas describes a climb known as Glyndwr's Ladder as: '250 feet - Easy - (first ascent c.1400). A solo test-piece of its time: the gully offers a few short pitches interspersed with noisy scree and good rock scenery.'

The story goes that as Owain Glyndwr was fleeing from his armed pursuers, he swam the Afon Glaslyn at Nantmor, which was tidal and much wider in those days, and climbed the mountainside beyond. He came across the summit cliffs of **Moel Hebog** and climbed Simnai Foel Hebog (or the chimney of Moel Hebog). The Climber's Club guide amusingly adds that 'A strong English party failed to follow!' He then made his way over to the cave on **Moel yr Ogof** where he hid for six months.

The ascent we took on that particular day is the most popular way of reaching the summit of this, the 'bare hill of the falcon', to give **Moel Hebog** its anglicised translation, although there are other ways of gaining the main ridge.

One way is to approach from the south via either Llyn Cwmystradllyn or over the minor top of Moel-ddu, although there are far too many walls to cross to make this approach really worth while. The reservoir in Cwmystradllyn was created in 1960 by raising a bank of earth to act as a dam. This transformed what I am told was a rather drab, reed-choked stretch of marsh, into a large expanse of water of great beauty, in an otherwise industry-scarred landscape.

Below the level of the reservoir in Cwmystradllyn lie the spectacular ruins of the old Ynyspandy slate mill, whilst higher up, above the lake, is the old slate quarry itself. Although other quarries seem to have succeeded in Wales, this particular enterprise proved to be a total failure. Within only a decade of the quarry opening up for business, the whole project was deemed unprofitable and was left abandoned. The cwm is a fairly quiet place these days, and other than being the site of some very ancient hut circles, does not offer much to the walker, except perhaps solitude.

The same, however, cannot be said for Cwm Pennant. The delights of this beautiful hidden valley are sadly becoming well known to the hoards of walkers who flock to Snowdonia every weekend. I say sadly, because of the detrimental effect that this has on the landscape in the way of erosion and litter. The approach from Cwm Pennant is usually made from Cwri-isaf via the grassy slopes of Cwm Llefrith as far as Bwlch Meillionen, and then ascending up the north-west ridge of **Moel Hebog**. This ridge provides the usual continuation onto **Moel yr Ogof** and **Moel Lefn** from the summit of **Hebog**.

Moel yr Ogof is reached by climbing directly north-west from Bwlch Meillionen, the pass of clover. The path leads upwards through a rocky cleft, but avoids a visit to Glyndwr's Cave. This lies further round to the right, but as a way for walkers cannot really be recommended.

Moel yr Ogof translates quite simply as, the bare hill of the cave, and really doesn't have much more to offer the explorer. The summit itself is quite interesting, being fairly rocky and having a number of outcrops containing fossils indicating that this whole area was once below the level of the sea.

Continuing north-west along the ridge, it is an easy ascent to the next summit, **Moel Lefn** or 'the smooth bare hill.' Walking over the grassy connecting ridge, the dark forests down in Nant Colwyn to the east are a constant reminder of man's intrusion into the wildest parts of Wales, and indeed all of our mountainous areas. A popular campsite is hidden away among the trees just north of Beddgelert, and provides the usual place to stay for many walkers in the area.

The summit of **Moel Lefn** is not a particularly interesting place in its own right, but does however, provide excellent views across the head of Cwm Pennant and Bwlch-y-ddwy-elor, or the 'pass of the two biers', to the Nantlle ridge. The ridge leads north, eventually to the pass which takes the old corpse road from Cwm Pennant to Rhyd Ddu, giving easy access to the ridge from either of those two valleys. This corpse road was used to take the dead of the Rhyd-Ddu area to the nearest consecrated ground, the church at Llanfihangel-y-pennant in Cwm Pennant.

Tucked away, under the western side of this ridge is a large cliff of perfect mountain dolerite. Although vegetation seems to abound, there are large areas of very steep rock, which give the rock climber some of the hardest courses in the district. This is Craig Cwm Trwsgl or 'crag of the rough hollow,' and is strictly a place for the hard men of climbing.

The usual descent from **Moel Lefn** back to Beddgelert is by taking the ridge north to the edge of a steep drop, where a faint path comes up from the right. This path goes downhill and soon bends to the left beneath a huge slab of rock with a prominent quartz stripe running through it. Beyond this is Bwlch Sais or 'the Englishman's Pass'. Further north-east, steep grass leads down to the chasm of Princess Quarry which should be passed on the left. Follow a wall down left to Bwlch Cwm-trwsgl at the edge of the forest, before gaining the forest track which contours the hillside above Llyn Llywelyn before reaching the road back to Beddgelert at the Forestry Commission campsite.

Walking north along the Hebog ridge, one cannot fail to notice the long switch-back of the Nantlle ridge section of the letter 'T', across the head of Cwm Pennant. This ridge is possibly one of the finest high level walks in the whole of Wales.

The usual starting point is the village of Rhyd Ddu on the busy A4085 road, $3^{3/4}$ miles north of Beddgelert. After a short walk across the flat valley bottom just to the north of Llyn y Gader, an incredibly steep path leaves the old corpse track heading for Cwm Pennant and takes to the south-east flank of Y Garn. Although only a minor top on the ridge, nothing more in fact than an extension of the northern ridge of **Mynydd Drws-y-coed**, Y Garn is part and parcel of the Nantlle ridge traverse.

Rock climbers may feel like making a real mountaineering day of it by gaining the summit via one of the excellent routes on the northern upper slopes of the mountain. Of the two better routes, the Eastern Arête is a very amiable Very Difficult (which by modern standards is actually quite easy) whilst Mallory's Ridge is a good deal harder at a Very Severe grade. The former was first ascended in 1905 by Walter Parry Hasket Smith, the father of British rock climbing, while the latter was climbed in 1911 by George Mallory who was to disappear on Everest in 1924 after being spotted just a few hundred yards from the summit. We shall never know if Mallory did actually make the summit, a remarkable 29 years before Hillary and Tensing, but many prominent mountaineers of today think it likely. Mallory is also famous for his off-hand answer to a question which is asked by many non-climbers even today. When asked why he risked life and limb in attempting to climb the world's highest mountains, his answer 'Because it is there' became well quoted, and is still a favourite quip in mountaineering circles. In British rock climbing history, Mallory's name will always be linked with the development of routes on the Welsh crags around the turn of the nineteenth century.

Following the ridge south across bouldery terrain, widely interspersed with the ever-present mat-grass (*Nardus stricta*), the easy pull up to the summit of **Mynydd Drws-y-coed**, taking in the occasional rock step *en route*, gives a clearer view of the rest of the ridge. This, the 'door to the wood mountain' is only the first main summit on what is a long walk, so using the sweeping drop into the cwm on the right as a good navigation aid, the next summit should soon be underfoot.

Trum y Ddysgl, 'ridge of the dish', at 2326' is a wonderfully lofty perch from which to view the Snowdon massif across Nant Colwyn to the east, whilst the scree littered ridges of Craig y Bera, scarring the southern flank of **Mynydd Mawr** across the Nantlle, dominate the scene to the north. As mentioned earlier, **Trum y Ddysgl** is the junction of the two ridges of Eifionydd. The ridge south from here drops steeply to Bwlch-y-ddwy-elor before abutting almost head-on with **Moel Lefn** on the Hebog ridge.

Again, using the huge drop into Cwmyffynnon to the right as a handrail, the next summit is soon reached just beyond a stone wall. This, the summit of **Mynydd Tal-y-mignedd** or 'mountain at the end of the bog' is memorable for its huge cairn, a stone tower built by local quarrymen to commemorate Queen Victoria's Diamond Jubilee.

A fence leads the way down the south ridge to gain the wide grassy col of Bwlch Dros-bern before the long trudge up through steeply inclined boulders and over-sized scree to the summit of **Craig Cwm Silyn**, and hence the

Llyn Nantlle Uchaf by William Pearson

summit of the Nantlle ridge. At 2408' this, the 'crag above the Silyn corrie' has a summit consisting of an ancient hollowed-out cairn, set in the middle of a boulder field.

The many ridges which fall northwards into the Nantlle valley can no doubt be ascended to gain the main ridge, but few walkers would relish a struggle with these hideous slopes of steep scree, and besides, many walkers have experienced access problems over the last few years, that is, away from the main paths and tracks in the Eifionydd hills.

North-west of the summit of **Craig Cwm Silyn**, high above the twin lakes of Cwm Silyn itself lies what is the most popular crag in the range—Craig yr Ogof, a crag distinguished by a prominent cave which gives it its name. The first climbing done here was in 1913 on what is now called Sunset Rib, although other much better climbs were to follow. Colin Kirkus and Menlove Edwards added their classic lines in the 1930s, although other much harder lines have been done since then, including Crucible and Jabberwocky now graded as Hard Very Severe and Extreme Severe (2) respectively.

Other crags ring the cirque rim of Cwm Silyn as well as Craig yr Ogof, although none are anywhere near as popular, and are also covered in vegetation.

Beyond **Craig Cwm Silyn** another minor top can be included in the walk, although if you are returning to Rhyd Ddu it is not really worth it.

Garnedd Goch forms the southern and western sides of Cwm Silyn, whilst Cwm Ciprwth falls down the southern flank of the mountain into Cwm Pennant. Another lake is cradled between Garnedd Goch and the next hill, Mynydd Graig Goch. There are one or two rock climbs on Craig Cwm Dulyn, but they are not really worth a visit unless botany rather than climbing is what you are after.

To return to Rhyd Ddu from **Craig Cwm Silyn**'s summit it is possible to descend diagonally south-eastwards to the head of Cwm Pennant near the derelict cottages of Blaen-pennant, then follow the corpse road up to the col of Bwlch-y-Ddwy-elor and over to Rhyd Ddu via the conifer-covered lower slopes of **Mynydd Drws-y-coed**. Personally, I prefer to retrace my steps along the entire ridge, missing out Y Garn at the end by descending steep slopes eastwards from the summit of **Mynydd Drws-y-coed**, but this is only because of my love of long ridge walks, rather than the way through the valley lacking any interest.

North of the Nantlle valley lies the last of the Eifionydd Mountains, **Mynydd Mawr** or 'big hill'. Rising from the shores of Llyn Cwellyn to the east, the Nantlle valley to the south, and gently from the waters of Caernarfon Bay seven miles to the west, this mountain is totally isolated from the rest of the range. The nearest connecting 'ridge', if it can be called that, is the drop down to Bwlchgylfin at 775' above sea level on the B4418 Rhyd Ddu to Nantlle road.

The usual place to start an ascent is Rhyd Ddu. The mountain is rarely, if ever, ascended from the west, whilst the steep slopes to the east falling into Llyn Cwellyn are generally avoided except by rock climbers. A track starting near the junction of the B4418 and the A4085 heads north through a forest before gaining a path on the left beneath a power line. Steep climbing gains the ridge above the forest which leads to the minor top of Foel Rudd. Easier slopes now head west above the crags of Craig y Bera. Although these cliffs seem to be composed of extremely poor, shattered rock, one or two good climbs do exist here, the best being Angel Pavement, a 600 foot-long Severe which is described in the Climbers' Club guide as 'An excellent route but only recommended to confident parties as protection is poor, the rock is often questionable and the pitches long.' For the less ambitious walker with a head for heights and some knowledge of rope-work, I would recommend the pleasant Sentries Ridge. Being more of a scramble than a rock climb it is an alternative way of gaining the main summit ridge.

From the ridge leading from the forest to the slopes above Craig y Bera the walker gets a good view of the picturesque lake of Llyn y Dywarchen. This is the famous 'lake of the floating island' and is also given particular

*The whole of the Eifionydd range from **Moel Eilio***

mention in *The Journey Through Wales* by Giraldus Cambrensis, published in 1188. Giraldus describes the island as being 'driven from one side to the other by the wind, shepherds beholding it with astonishment, their cattle while feeding carried to the distant parts of the lake.' The island was also visited by the famous astronomer Halley, of comet fame, who swam out to it in 1698 'to be satisfied that it floated.' If we are to believe this, and the many other pieces of documentation regarding the island, we can surmise that it remained intact for perhaps 600 years, although nothing can be seen of it today. An island still graces the lake but is shown to be fixed in position!

The summit of **Mynydd Mawr** is reached by gaining the southerly ridge which descends from the summit to the apex of the Craig y Bera cliffs, the going being fairly easy. The ascent of **Mynydd Mawr** is only likely to take around half a day from Rhyd Ddu, and provides an excellent view point of the surrounding mountains of Nantlle and Snowdon.

Here, above the base of the lake where it flows out into the Afon Gwyrfai lies the impressively steep, and often overhanging façade of Castell Cidwm. Rock climbers will be familiar with the name of this crag, if not familiar with the actual lines themselves, for Castell Cidwm is synonymous with difficulty when it comes to rock climbing. The crag had to wait until March 27th 1960 for its first ascent. This first climb, Dwm, is still one of the great classic test-pieces of British rock climbing, and perhaps no more need be said than that it took all of the talents of Joe Brown, the rock master of the 50s and 60s, to climb it and claim it as his own. Even then he didn't manage what climbers call a 'free ascent', climbing only on the natural holds on the face. The final roof succumbed only with the aid of three pegs, as the rock was running with water. This final pitch, the hardest of three, was led by Brown's mate, Harry Smith. Remembering his first visit to Castell Cidwm, Brown recalls that 'Our eyes went up and were transfixed by a fantastic wall

*Westwards to **Mynydd Tal-y-mignedd**, with **Craig Cwm Silyn** beyond*

overlooking the stream. It had breadth and verticality and was bristling with a fringe of overhangs ... The steepness of the face was awe-inspiring and we were at a bit of a loss where to look for a breach in the defences ... We got up 60 feet then none of us could climb higher ... The cliff had an unnerving character.' Brown and Smith climbed Dwm on their next visit. Although Dwm is graded as Hard Very Severe (not easy by anybody's standards) it is actually one of the easiest lines on the crag today.

Castell Cidwm is believed to be the site of a murder, going back to the times when the Romans occupied England and Wales. Legend has it that a warrior queen, Elen Lueddog, was following her youngest son to Caernarfon, when, from the slopes of the mountain to the west of Llyn Cwellyn, his older brother Cidwm, shot and killed him with an arrow.

Today, the name is believed to have derived from the Welsh word for 'wolf,' giving us 'the castle of the wolf.' Wolves were, of course, endemic to areas of England, Wales and Scotland, as they still are in other parts of Europe. Along with many other predators such as the bear and wild cat, they eventually became extinct. The last wolf in Wales is believed by William Condry, an authority on Welsh natural history, to have been killed in the tenth century, several centuries earlier than its compatriots in England and Scotland.

Another possible meaning of the word Cidwm is the ancient Welsh word for 'robber'. George Borrow in *Wild Wales* records a conversation with the Snowdon Ranger where he comments 'I shouldn't wonder ... if in old times it was the stronghold of some robber-chieftain; cidwm in the old Welsh is frequently applied to a ferocious man.' He then went on to say that if he ever came that way again, he would employ the Snowdon Ranger to guide him to there, though no 'castle' as such exists.

The view from the summit of **Mynydd Mawr** is extensive, taking in the flatlands of Cardigan Bay and the isle of Anglesey on the western horizon. The Nantlle ridge lies just across the valley to the south, whilst Snowdon, the Glyders, the Carneddau and even the Moelwyns can be seen to the east. The summit includes the remains of a Bronze Age cairn and a collection of wind shelters.

An alternative return can be made to Rhyd Ddu by heading north-east to the col above Craig Cwmbychan near spot-height 592 metres, by following a stream that leads steeply downhill to gain the Afon Goch just above Llyn Cwellyn. Aircraft remains can still be seen in this narrow valley, a sad reminder of the last war.

As can be seen, the hills of Eifionydd have much to offer the mountain lover. Two very good ridge walks and a single, solitary mountain can provide endless days of pleasure. The rock climber in search of quieter crags away from the hoards around Ogwen and 'The Pass' could do a lot worse than head west to these hidden cwms and peaceful ridges. The area is also steeped in history, and is a good place for the naturalist, offering as it does, typical plant species of a predominantly Ordovician rock base. Copper from the area has been mined at Nantlle probably from before the time of the Romans. The beaker-folk, who dwelt along the banks of the Rhine, are widely regarded as being responsible for the first use of metals in Britain— be it through invasion, immigration or a spreading of knowledge along trade routes—and heralded the start of the Bronze Age, perhaps 2,000 years prior to the invasion of the Romans. There is no evidence however, to prove that the copper used by these ancient races was from the Nantlle area of Wales.

Since the 1920s forestry has dominated the eastern side of the range. The conifers, rising as they do from Nant Colwyn and Nant y Betws, have provided much needed jobs in the area at the expense of the natural scenery. They do, however, provide a valuable habitat for many bird and mammal species including the goldcrest, polecat, pine-marten and red squirrel. One of the problems with widespread afforestation in the Beddgelert area is that it has effectively wiped out many rare and unusual plant species. This must be weighed up against the undeniable advantages of providing the community with jobs where the only alternative would be to rely on the locally dying trades of farming and quarrying, or else a move into the towns to find employment. The Forestry Commission does provide camp sites, picnic areas and car parks for visitors, and at Beddgelert, an orienteering course for the walker is an alternative to a day in the mountains.

Looking over the Suspension and Tubular Bridges on the Menai Strait towards Snowdonia c.1923

From near Aber on the north Wales coast looking into the mountains c.1920

On the sands at Penmaenmawr looking towards the most northerly of the Welsh Hewitts c.1920

Llanberis Pass

Llyn Crafnant c.1920

Dolbadarn Castle, Llanberis c.1907

Snowdon *from Llyn Llydaw,*
in a series of Views of North Wales c.*1908*

Nant Ffrancon c.*1909*

In Llyfnant Valley c.*1904*

Precipice Walk, Dolgellau

Cadair Idris *near Tal-y-llyn Pass* c.1930

Devil's Bridge, c.1950

Plynlimon Pass c.1930

Looking over Crickhowell towards the Black Mountains

THE RHINOGS

The six Hewitts of the Rhinogs, that wildest of mountain ranges, rise between the Afon Eden beside the A470, and the A496 coastal road. A mighty ridge of rough Cambrian Sandstone and ling and bell heather, mat-grass and bilberry, runs north to south from the Vale of Ffestiniog to Afon Mawddach near Dolgellau, and boasts five of these Hewitts along its crest. The outlying peak of **Y Garn** hides above the forests of Cwm Mynach and Coed y Brenin to the east of the main group.

Geologists call the area the Harlech Dome from the great beds of grit-stone and sandstone which are exposed throughout the range, and continue but fall well below the outcropping rocks of other mountain ranges in Snowdonia. The rocks of this Harlech Dome lies far beneath Snowdon itself, although these rocks are probably a hundred million years older than the Ordovician summits of the Snowdon region.

The Welsh simply call the range Y Rhinogau or Y Rhinogian, after the Welsh term for a door-post, 'rhiniog'. At the centre of the range is a mighty pass, crossing over from east to west and known as Bwlch Drws Ardudwy or 'The gap of the door to Ardudwy', leaving us to assume that the two summits at either side of the pass—**Rhinog Fawr** and **Rhinog Fach**—are the 'big and little door-posts', although the Nuttalls give the translation as being 'threshold'. All walkers who know the range simply refer to them as The Rhinogs. This pass is the pivotal point of the group, although the summits of **Diffwys** and **Y Llethr** to the south are both higher than the two 'main' Rhinogs.

This exploration of the group starts from the south. Three minor valleys drain southwards from **Diffwys** or 'The Precipice' at 2461'. Paths lead up the sides of the Afon Dwynant above Cutiau and the Afon Cwm-llechen above Bontddu and lead up over easy ground to the long west ridge of **Diffwys** via Craig y Grut and Braich respectively, but it's the third, and most easterly of these three valleys that gives the best walk onto the tops.

A minor road leaves the A496 near Pen-y-bryn and climbs steeply up, alongside the wooded banks of the Afon Cwm-mynach (the stream of the monk's valley). Cars can be taken up this road as far as a small car park deep in the conifer woods before Blaen-cwm-mynach. A notice board gives information about the local wildlife, forestry and also gold and manganese mining which once flourished in these hills.

A broad forestry track leads northwards, eventually opening out to give stupendous views across the cwm to the rocky west flank of **Y Garn**. A path heads off westwards into the trees atop a raised bed of cobbles, laid as a base for the tracks of the old manganese miners, and gives easy access onto the open fellside below the rocky outcrops of the east face of **Diffwys**. These manganese mines are no longer worked, although it is thought that much still remains to be mined in the future, should the need arise, as manganese is essential for the making of steel—though let's hope that never happens. This path winds in and out of the many knolls and spindly heather, but stops at the old levels just short of the grassy ridge top. From the levels a faint path gains the ridge at a col just north-east of the summit. A six foot high wall traverses the southern half of the ridge and gives an infallible guide in poor visibility. These magnificent structures, which in some parts of the range reach a height of eight feet, are said to have been built by French prisoners during the Napoleonic Wars.

Turning south, the trig pillar at the summit of Diffwys is soon reached overlooking the vegetated cliffs above the head of Cwm Llechan. Continuing along this wall brings you over a minor grassy bump, known simply as Diffwys West Top, to the long ridge of Craig y Grut, previously mentioned.

As you head northwards along the ridge the going underfoot becomes progressively rougher, turning from the grass and bilberry of the southern peaks, to the waist deep heather rooted in boulder scree, and outcrops and slabby pavements of grit of the northern half of the range. As you head north, you also become aware of the huge gulfs which fall away to the coast to the west. These cwms are among the most beautiful places in Wales, although they are sadly becoming more and more popular with day-trippers and large groups of teenagers. The most southerly of these is Cwm Ysgethin, holding three beautiful lakes. Llyn Irddyn, 'the priest's lake', lies below the broken western façade of Craig y Grut known as Llawlech; the dark waters of Llyn Bodlyn lie higher up the cwm, below the formidable vegetated fortress of Craig Bodlyn, the only major rock climbers crag of the area; and at the very head of the cwm, the tiny Llyn Dulyn graces a hollow just below the grassy col on the main ridge, before the climb northwards to **Y Llethr**. Paths lead up into the cwm from Tal-y-bont at the coast, and higher up, one diverts away from the valley bottom and climbs the ridge of Moelyblithcwm to the summit of **Y Llethr**, 'the slope', at 2480'. Still the terrain is predominantly grassy, though as you drop down to the enchanted

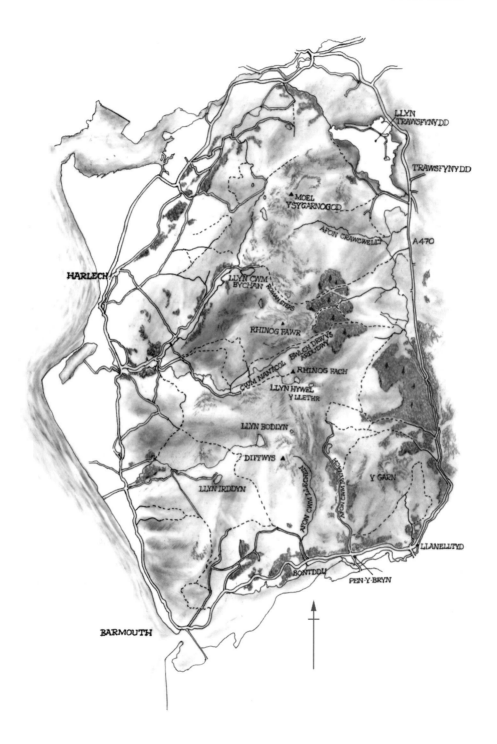

bowl of Llyn Hywel, the scene changes to one of heather and sweeping crags rimming the edge of the lake. A short distance eastwards from the col lies the quiet Llyn y Bi, or the magpies lake. This overlooks the vast, empty badlands of Cefn Cam, above the head of Cwm Camlan.

The climb up **Rhinog Fach** (2336') again follows the wall, heading first north, then around to the west to gain the summit cairn. This is the southern post at the door to Ardudwy. 1000 feet below to the north is the door itself, Bwlch Drws Ardudwy. Rough slopes lead down to this narrow col, but fortunately, a good path picks a way through the worst of the heather and boulders. To the east is the Afon Crawcwellt, a tributary of the Afon Eden, while to the west lies another of those wonderful coastal valleys, Cwm Nantcol. This is a delightful glen, wooded in its lower half, and gives a good way onto the tops from Llanbedr at the coast. The path up to Bwlch Drws Ardudwy is obvious, but faint paths can also be followed up to Llyn Hywel and its neighbour Llyn Perfeddau.

If there is a path of any kind up the south ridge of **Rhinog Fawr** (2362'), you will probably follow a different one each time you venture up the mountain from this side. A not too obvious rib of rock is hewn out of the peaty soil and runs northwards, well to the east of the summit. A vague sheep track seems to want to follow this, but makes a point of vanishing every so often. Once high on the eastern ridge of the mountain, more discernible tracks can be found that lead to the summit with its cairn and trig pillar.

A way can be found down the western side towards the head of Cwm Nantcol, giving the option of a good half day traversing over **Rhinog Fach** and **Fawr**, if you leave the car there and take the path up to Llyn Hywel. The main ridge however, goes on for a good deal further yet. A good path leads through peat and heather to the black waters of Llyn Du and heads either eastwards to the top of the Roman Steps leading down to Crawcwellt, or westwards to run beside a stone wall to gain the Roman Steps at Bwlch Tyddiad before they drop down into Cwm Bychan. These Roman Steps are certainly very old, but are probably not Roman. The pass was once an important trade route from Harlech to Bala and in medieval times was used as the main line of communications between Harlech Castle and London. On the Cwm Bychan side the hundreds of stone flags can still be seen and walked upon to this day.

Cwm Bychan is yet another lovely corner of the Rhinogs. Again, it is picturesquely wooded, and has at its head the tranquil lake of Llyn Cwm Bychan. A camp site at the lake is a useful starting point for exploration of the northern half of the range.

Between **Rhinog Fawr** and **Moel Ysgyfarnogod**, the most northerly Hewitt on the ridge, lies an upland of the toughest walking country south of the

The Mountains of Merionethshire from Criccieth, from Illustrations
of the Natural Scenery of the Snowdonian Mountains, *1829*

Scottish border. Deep, rocky fissures cross the range and beautiful hidden tarns
adorn the hills. This part of the range has been called 'The Celtic Badlands',
and even today, it is a confident walker who plans to continue along the ridge
towards **Moel Ysgyfarnogod**, the bare hill of the hare, at 2044'.

A way can be found to the 'lake of the maidens', Llyn Morwynion,
before the crossing of the rough bounds begins proper. Tough walking
through deep heather follows to Llyn Pryfed and the twin lakes of Twr Glas
over the compact rocky crown of Craig Wion, but at last the pavements of
grit fall away to a col where a path passes over from the head of Cwm
Bychan to Llyn Trawsfynydd.

A stile to the north, below the outcropping crags of Craig Ddrwg clears
a stone wall, and a path beyond passes between countless knolls and round
small lakes before the easy climb up to the summit of **Moel Ysgyfarnogod**.
This is the last of the Hewitts on the main ridge, although the crest continues
northwards over Foel Penolau and another Diffwys before dropping down
into Cwm Moch and the moorlands to the west of Llyn Trawsfynydd.

Few people with have the energy to complete the whole ridge traverse
from Bontddu or Barmouth in the south to Llyn Trawsfynydd in the north
in a single day. It is a long walk of 22 miles, over the wildest mountain
country in Wales. Better perhaps to take your time, and enjoy the deep cwms
of the western side, picking off just one or two summits each day. The area
abounds in wildlife, and if you are really lucky, you may see the feral goats,
said to be the biggest herd in Wales.

For an easy day out in the Rhinogs, the lonely, isolated summit of **Y
Garn**, 'the cairn', at 2064', sees few visitors and is worth a visit for its

stupendous views. The rugged grandeur of the main Rhinog ridge rises in a series of desolate switchbacks to the west, while across the yawning, wooded defile of the Afon Mawddach to the east, the forests of Coed y Brenin rise up the lower slopes of the Southern Arenigs in ridge after ridge of conifer festooned flanks to the top of **Rhobell Fawr**. To the south, beyond the point where the by now mighty Mawddach swings away westwards to the sea, lie the hidden cwms and crenellated ridges of **Cadair Idris**. Only to the immediate north does the terrain drop away to lesser heights, over the vastness of the Crawcwellt moors to the sad eyesore of Trawsfynydd Power Station.

For an ascent of **Y Garn**, a number of possibilities are open to the walker in search of the bliss of solitude, although stone walls can cause a problem on some of the approaches.

The southern side of the hill, overlooking the Mawddach estuary, is split into two short cwms, Cesailgwm and Cwm yr Wnin. The western edge of this flank is bordered by the semi-wooded ridge of Garn Fach, the eastern by Cefn Coch, with the ridge of Foel Ddu effectively falling in a prominent nose between these two cwms. A way-marked path 'The New Precipice Walk' contours the lower slopes of Foel Ddu and provides an excellent short stroll without actually gaining a summit. Information leaflets for this walk, and a number of others including 'The Old Precipice Walk' can be had from the Tourist Information Centre in Dolgellau.

Of the three ridges to the south of **Y Garn**'s top, only Cefn Coch is easy to follow, crossed as it is by a public footpath, leading over from the woods of Cwm yr Wnin to the beautiful Cwm Camlan. A faint path leads up the ridge beside a wall, which eventually must be climbed high up, just short of the summit. This ridge can also be gained from Cwm Camlan from a starting point at Ganllwyd, a preferable alternative. From Ganllwyd, a track follows the north bank of the Afon Gamlan above a series of waterfalls, then crosses the torrents via a footbridge and up into Cwm Las, eventually gaining the open hillside at the old, disused gold mines below the vegetated crags of Craig-y-cae. From the mines the ridge of Cefn Coch follows the skyline from left to right.

Cwm Mynach in the west gives a much wilder approach to the hill. A footpath heads out from Blaen-y-mynach on a long, sweeping arc to join up with the paths at the head of Cwm Camlan. Once clear of the forest, an amble uphill leads over the distinct north-west ridge to the summit, without the need to climb any stone walls.

They say that lower hills give far superior view-points for viewing loftier ones nearby. **Y Garn** is such a place, and every walker must feel the urge to gain its top sooner or later.

THE ARENIGS

This, a vast wilderness of isolated peaks, interspersed with empty tracts of heather moorland and forest, covers the huge area of country between the Rhinogs and the Aran - Berwyn ranges. The Afon Mawddach and its tributaries effectively cut off the range to the west, while its eastern border is formed by the deep 'U' shaped valley of the Afon Dyfrdwy and Llyn Tegid, the biggest natural lake in Wales. Only to the north do the Arenigs fall away gradually, though not by any means gently, through the barren wastes of the Migneint moorlands and on to the head of the Afon Conwy at its source.

The eight Hewitts in the group are concentrated around three distinct areas; north of Llyn Celyn and the A4212 from Bala to Trawsfynydd lies the **Arenig Fach** hills and associated Migneint moors; south of this road, but north of the infant Afon Mawddach as it flows westwards into the Coed y Brenin Forests lies the triple peaks of the **Arenig Fawr** group; whilst further south still, beyond the infant Mawddach lie the **Rhobell Fawr** hills.

This exploration starts in the north with the **Arenig Fach** Hewitts. Desolate moorlands of deep heather surround the two hills of the group to the west of the B4501 road from Frongoch to Denbigh, while to the east of this road, rough grass covers the isolated hill of **Foel Goch**.

Foel Goch, 'the red bare hill', can be ascended easily from Frongoch by any number of public footpaths which climb up into distinct little cwms and head for a gate at Foel Tyn-y-ddôl, just south of the minor top of Garnedd Fawr. A grassy path leads up to an electric fence that's been in place on my last three visits, running eastwards towards the summit. The fence turns north just a couple of hundred yards short of the top, but the path continues through heather to the summit cairn, trig pillar and boundary stone at 2005'.

Other paths lead up Ceseilgwm from Llangwm in the north and gain the ridge at a broad col just east of the top, but the most popular way of ascending this hill is from the south near Cefn-ddwysarn on the A494. A minor road heads up the valley northwards to the small hamlet of Pentre-tai-yn-y-cwm, then continues up Nant Cwm-da to the same col on the east ridge where the path from the north comes up. From here it is only a short distance up pathless grass to the summit, after climbing a fence via a stile.

A glance at the map will reveal countless possible variations to these walks, and it is easily possible to take in the minor summits of Moel Darren or Moel Emoel on this southern side, the long eastern ridge over Pen y Cerrig-serth with its wonderfully named Carnedd Benjamin and Orddu, or the equally enjoyable curving north-western ridge over Garnedd Fawr and Y Geseil. Although small by comparison with the other Arenigs, **Foel Goch** is ideal territory for an exploratory wander, and the views of the nearby peaks of the higher Arenigs, and the Hirnants and Berwyns across the River Dee really are superb.

West of **Foel Goch** rise the lonely peaks of **Carnedd y Filiast** and **Arenig Fach**. On my traverse of the Welsh Hewitts in 1998 I followed a path up Cwm Hesgyn from near Ciltalgarth below the dam of Llyn Celyn. This is a delightful moorland path, steadily climbing up the eastern flank of the minor top of Foel-boeth, then dropping down to the rushing waters of the Nant y Coed before an abrupt climb up to a col between the heathery ridge of Brottos and **Carnedd y Filiast**, 'cairn of the greyhound'. This really is a wonderful way onto the tops, with a good track underfoot and expansive views across Llyn Hesgyn and Cyfiau to **Foel Goch** and north-east to the Clwydian hills. The summit of **Carnedd y Filiast** stands at 2195' beside a corner of a fence marking the county boundary and is marked by a good wind shelter and a trig pillar. The same summit can be reached from the very head of Cwm Penanner from where a by-way climbs up the slopes of Foel Frech to the Bwlch Blaen-y-cwm. It is then a simple matter to follow the county boundary south-westwards to the summit.

Heading westwards across the Migneint, one of the boggiest tracts of high moorland in Wales, takes a real effort, although for the lover of wildlife there is the chance of seeing golden plovers as well as the more common snipe and lapwings. Your goal will be **Arenig Fach**, 'small high ground', at 2260'. The way follows a fence and as the terrain gets very tough in places, it is better to stay beside this and use it as a guide. A short descent to the head of Nant y Coed at Ffynnon y Waen, then an easy climb up to the minor summit of Carnedd Llechwedd-llyfn, is followed by a long stretch of bog to the headwaters of the Afon Gelyn. All the while the darkly vegetated crags of Creigiau Bleiddiaid dominate the view. Nestling at the base of these igneous cliffs is Llyn Arenig Fach, although you do not get a view of its dismal waters from this approach. There is a vague path of sorts heading through the heather, but everywhere the going is hard. At last an old line of fence posts heads off at right angles and climbs quickly up the northern side of **Arenig Fach**. There still isn't a path to follow, but here the vegetation has

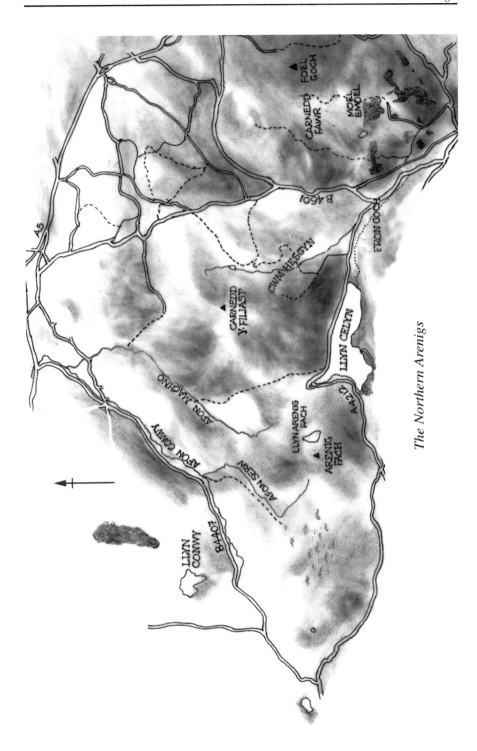

The Northern Arenigs

The Southern Arenigs

changed to bilberry and the walking is much easier, though steeper. The top levels out and it is a short stroll across close-cropped heather to the summit trig pillar and cairn known as Carnedd Bachgen.

If you do want a view of Llyn Arenig Fach, it is possible after crossing the Afon Gelyn to pick a way up beside the delightful stream of the Trinant—presumably meaning 'three waters'. A vague path heads off through the heather beside the left hand branch and makes for the broad ridge overlooking the lake. Again a bit of a path can be found climbing directly up the ridge, and so to the top.

To the north a public footpath finds a way through the boggy moorgrass beside the Afon Serw from near its confluence with the Afon Conwy, and gives a possible approach from the B4407, although the problems of crossing the Afon Serw from the path's end at Cefngarw, and finding a way up the west ridge of the hill from there, are likely to put all but the most ardent explorer off.

By far the quickest and easiest way to climb **Arenig Fach** is from the Cae-garnedd car park on the banks of Llyn Celyn, although the way up through the enclosures and onto the open fellside has to be carefully thought out. Once the ridge of Bryn Du is gained, a vague path ascends quickly through the rough terrain to the summit.

Llyn Celyn, the 'holly lake', is actually a reservoir, dammed in 1965 amongst much controversy to provide Liverpool with water. The village of Capel Celyn was abandoned and drowned and is today commemorated by a Memorial Chapel.

South of the lake, the highest peak of the range, **Arenig Fawr** (the big high ground) at 2802', rises amid igneous crags and grassy moorland and is widely considered to be one of the quietest big mountains of Wales. George Borrow wrote in 1854 that 'of all the hills which I saw in Wales, none made a greater impression on me', whereas an eighteenth century topographer said of the two Arenigs, 'Arennig mountain rises to the north of the lake of Bala and sheweth itself very boldly. It is beautifully shaped, having two summits [**Arenig Fach** and **Fawr**] of nearly equal height and falling in a ridge singularly broken to the west.' In 1771 the Honourable Daines Barrington conducted possibly the earliest rainfall experiments in the mountains of Britain on **Arenig Fawr**, stating that 'Rennig is commonly considered as the fifth mountain of North Wales in point of height.'

These two mountains share something other than name, for both have a huge glacier gouged depression on their eastern side, each holding a lake. Llyn Arenig Fawr is one of the most popular approaches to that mountain. A minor road leaves the A4212 and crosses the Afon Tryweryn at Pont Rhyd-y-fen, passing below the steep northern façade of **Arenig Fawr**. Leaving the car on this minor road near Pant-yr-hedydd, just west of Llyn Celyn, a good track heads around the slopes of Moel y Garth and up to the dam of the reservoir. Although none is marked on the map, a good path climbs up Carreg Lefain and onto the ridge top of Y Castell throwing broken spurs of rock down to the lakeside far below. The path crosses a stile, and shortly after another gives access to the upper mountain. Here the path vanishes from underfoot, but as the going is easy on grass and bubbly rock, the summit trig pillar of **Arenig Fawr** is soon reached.

Cars can also be left at Pont Rhyd-y-fen itself, and a way can be followed up the broken northern side of the mountain, aiming for Pen Tyrau, and then the easy north ridge to the top.

Another popular way of reaching the top of **Arenig Fawr** is to head off up the delightful banks of the Afon Llafar from the village of Parc at the western end of Llyn Tegid. A public footpath leads out of the woods near Blaen-y-cwm-uchaf onto the open fellside, and a good way can be found leading up over the minor top of Carreg y Diocyn and onto the ridge south of the main summit.

On this ridge, south of the main summit lies another minor top, known simply as Arenig Fawr South Top, and more confusingly, further south again rises another little eminence called Arenig Fawr South Ridge Top. These are all listed as separate summits by the Nuttalls, and although I would strongly contest their right to that title, I am the first to admit that this south ridge does provide a wonderfully airy way to the summit. Another minor road cuts right across the range from the western end of Llyn Tegid to Trawsfynydd and gives access to this south ridge. Just east of the point where the road crosses the wild Afon Lliw a footpath heads up into the boggy terrain of the col between the **Arenig Fawr** ridge and **Moel Llyfnant**. The south ridge near the many small tarns on Craig y Bychau can be gained by following the wall around to the east from near the top of this col. The way onwards to the summit is then straightforward, if not rather switchback.

Continuing over the col on the public footpath leads along the western flank of **Arenig Fawr** to Pont Rhyd-y-fen, and so gives a good means of return if the whole ridge is to be traversed.

West of **Arenig Fawr** stands the proud summit of **Moel Llyfnant**, 'smooth stream of the bare hill', at 2464' the second summit of the range. It is usually climbed from the col as described above, from where easy slopes of grass lead up to a fence just short of the top.

Another possible way is to continue from Pont Blaen-Lliw half a mile further upstream to the small farmstead of Beudy Uchaf. A way can then be followed up to the corner of a conifer plantation to the north-east, before climbing the mat-grass slopes eastwards to the summit.

A longer, and more round-about approach is to continue along the footpath past Beudy Uchaf to gain the crest of the **Gallt y Daren** ridge at Bwlch y Bi. Then, heading north to Moel y Slates, and eastwards along the boundary of the forest at Y Corsydd, the broad north-western slopes can be climbed, again easily over boggy mat-grass and cotton sedge.

The same approach can of course be used to climb **Gallt y Daren**, 'hill of the knoll', at 2031'. From Bwlch y Bi a fence heads due south for the top with its cluster of stones and remains of an iron mast and telegraph poles. Just above Bwlch y Bi there is a small cliff with a cave. Above this is a small cairn with a fading memorial plaque to 'Bonzo, the brave fox terrier who perished in this cave after eight days unsuccessful rescue attempt, which took place from April 23rd to May 1st, 1973', along with a list of those who attempted to dig him out.

Gallt y Daren can be quickly ascended from Pen y Feidiog, a mile and a half west of Blaen-Lliw. A fence leads up over the minor top of Foel Boeth, and on to the summit of **Gallt y Daren**. From the top, the Rhinogs stand out across the minor hill of Moel Oernant and the Crawcwellt moors, while to the south **Rhobell Fawr** and **Dduallt** tower above the surrounding forests. The scene to the north would be beautiful, but is dominated and spoiled by the Trawsfynydd Nuclear Power Station.

And so to the last two Hewitts of the Arenig range. South of the infant Mawddach, over the small, rocky knolls of Rhobell-y-big and Foel Gron, rises the lonely heights of **Rhobell Fawr**, 'the big saddle', at 2408'. In his classic book of the 1930s *On Foot in North Wales*, Patrick Monkhouse describes **Rhobell Fawr** as 'a noble mountain. It is not steep and shapely, but its slow curve has power and serenity'. Geologically **Rhobell Fawr** belongs to the same series of igneous rocks of the Ordovician period as Cadair Idris, the Arans and of course the other Arenigs, but its actual structure is much more complex than these surrounding peaks. There are large intrusions of limestone, much of which is of course deeply buried beneath the shroud of peat which covers most of the Arenigs.

Minor roads and forest tracks lead northwards from near Rhydymain on the A494 Dolgellau to Bala road, and lead easily up to a col in the forests to the east of the summit. A stone wall leads up this ridge, over rocky outcrops and through grassy marshes to another stone wall just east of the summit. A stile gives access to this lofty perch. A wilder approach can be made by heading south from the end of the minor road leading up into the headwaters of the Afon Mawddach, in Cwm yr Allt-lwyd. It is possible to make for the rocks of Foel Gron, and then across the bogs heading south up the long ridge to the top. Otherwise the col in the forest mentioned above can be gained by following a public bridleway southwards up the Nant yr Helyg.

The western flank is much rougher, and for the most part is guarded by the dense conifer plantations of the Coed y Brenin Forest. However, a track leads south out of the forest, bound for Llanfachreth over the Bwlch

Goriwared. A way can be followed up the obvious south-west ridge from this bwlch, and although the going is hard, this is an excellent way onto the summits for those wanting a quieter approach to what is a fairly peaceful mountain anyway.

East of **Rhobell Fawr**, across the dark forests, stands the rocky top of **Dduallt**, 'the black hillside', at 2172'. The main way of reaching its top is again along the forestry tracks from either Cwm yr Allt-lwyd in the north or Rhydymain on the A494 to the south. The O.S. map shows the forest as blocking all access from this, the west side, although just south of the highest part of the track, the trees have been cleared and give a way out onto the south ridge of **Dduallt**. From there it is an easy matter to follow the fence which borders the forest to the very top of the hill where a small stile gives access to the cairn.

The north ridge can also give a good ascent, although this invariably means fording the Afon Mawddach, while the face thrown down to the east is far too steep to afford a comfortable way to the delightful little cairn at the summit. It is among the broken rocks of this east face that the River Dee has one of its sources, along with the wild peat-bogs to the north of the summit. The same bog also has the source of the Afon Mawddach among its bed of mosses, rushes and heather.

To the south of **Dduallt**, where the rushing stream of the Afon Eiddon has carved a deep trench, the underlying limestone has been exposed at Craig y Benglog, which plays host to the rock rose, a true calcicole which is something of a rarity for Snowdonia.

As a whole the Arenigs are one of the most spacious mountain ranges in Wales, with the possible exception of the hills around the Elan Valley in mid-Wales. They give the walker a sense of freedom, and for some of the approaches, it helps if you set out with a pioneering spirit. Although some of the terrain is tough, this has an added appeal, and even the waist-deep heather of the Migneint holds a special charm, although this is by no means typical of the vegetation of the rest of the range. For the most part, this is traditional sheep-farming country, where, aside from the forests, you are more likely to be striding out on grassy ridges, than wallowing in the heather. Given the choice, I would go for a wander in these hills far sooner than many a more worthy mountain in Wales.

THE ARANS

This long ridge of high hills forms one of the most delightful elevated traverses in the whole of Wales. From the steep little dome of **Pen y Brynfforchog** in the south, to **Aran Benllyn** in the north, a crossing of the entire ridge, eleven miles in all from Ochr y Bwlch on the A470 Dolgellau to Dinas Mawddwy road on the southern fringe, to Llanuwchllyn at the southern extent of Bala Lake, the way throughout is wonderful. The range is parallel to the busy A494 which runs along its base to the west. To the east, the boundary is less well defined, as the moorlands of the Arans merge into those of the Hirnants, but are separated by a minor road from Dinas Mawddwy to Llanuwchllyn. This follows the course of the Afon Dyfi, then climbs steeply up to Bwlch y Groes before descending to the valley of the Afon Twrch in Cwm Cynllwyd. East of the main ridge of the Arans, which in itself accounts for six Hewitts along its length, two subsidiary ridges are thrown down into the quiet cwms on that side, one of which has one Hewitt, the other, more northerly ridge has three.

Pen y Brynfforchog, 'top of the forked hill' at 2247', is a nice little Hewitt to climb. It is usually combined with an ascent of **Glasgwm** to the north-east, but can also be climbed from the A470 from the south. A car park at the top of the pass gives a head start, being well over a thousand feet above sea level. A faint path runs along the east side of a fence which abuts onto the road at right angles. A stile gives access to this, and above, the way is very steep but soon eases as the short west ridge of a minor un-named summit (point 564 metres) is reached. It is possible to turn eastwards to climb this minor top *en route* for **Pen y Brynfforchog**, though a path cuts across its northern flank and makes for the col between the two if you wish to avoid any unnecessary ascent. Once at the col a path leads along the east, right side of the fence to a little dip between two little knolls at the top of **Pen y Brynfforchog**. This is presumably the reference to the 'forked hill' in the name. A small cairn sits atop the westernmost knoll.

A short way beyond the summit, heading north, a forest fills the little cwm of the Nant y Graig-wen. A path leads around this forest to the left and on to Bwlch y Fign before the easy climb up **Glasgwm** beside the fence, but another path climbs out of the forest almost at the corner and gives an alternative approach to climbing **Pen y Brynfforchog**. A public footpath climbs the slope of Cerist from Dolobran just to the west of Dinas Mawddwy, and gains a grassy col on Y Gribin, overlooking the impressive defile of Cwm Cywarch. On the southern side of the col a track heads off westwards into the trees. After 300 yards or so, a narrower path leaves the main track on the right and contours around to the open fellside on **Pen y Brynfforchog**'s north ridge. The col on Y Gribin, just short of the forest, can also be climbed direct from the minor road near Fawnog Fawr in the Cywarch Valley. The way is steep but is lessened by tight zigzags. This public footpath affords views of the main rock climbing crag of the Arans—Craig Cywarch. This rambles over the eastern façade of Glasgwm amid wild gullies and impressive walls and ribs. There is much here to tempt climbers of all grades but probably the most popular route in the whole of the range is Will-o'-the-Wisp, a classic Hard Very Difficult which winds a way up the South Buttress. Despite being a climb of such a relatively easy grade, it had to wait until 1972 to have its first ascent, by the redoubtable mid-Wales pioneer, John Sumner, a true sign of how far behind other areas mid-Wales is in rock climbing development.

Glasgwm, meaning 'blue valley', rises to 2559', and is a great little hill. Apart from the fact that Craig Cywarch nestles in its eastern flank, the very summit is of interest as it has a notable tarn, quite sizeable for such a high-point, just feet from the very top. As has already been pointed out, **Glasgwm** can easily be climbed from **Pen y Brynfforchog** by following the forest boundary to the north, then continuing alongside the fence from Bwlch y Fign to the summit. The fence is far from direct, but in poor visibility it is as well to keep it in sight. A stile has to be climbed beside the tarn (known as Llyn y Fign) just before the summit cairn is reached. The banks of Llyn y Fign provide an excellent high-level camp site for those with the means to make themselves comfortable at such a height. However, the site is very exposed and it would be as well to make sure you have a good tent before heading off for a night on the tops.

Glasgwm can of course be climbed from the col near the forest on Y Gribin to the south. The way starts off along a faint path, but this soon vanishes altogether on the broad incline of Bwlch y Gesail. Continuing over rough grass and stones, the fence soon comes into view however.

To the north a steep, rocky slope leads down to a broad boggy col with a public footpath crossing it from west to east. This path climbs through the pine forests above Rhydymain on the A494, and follows a tributary of the

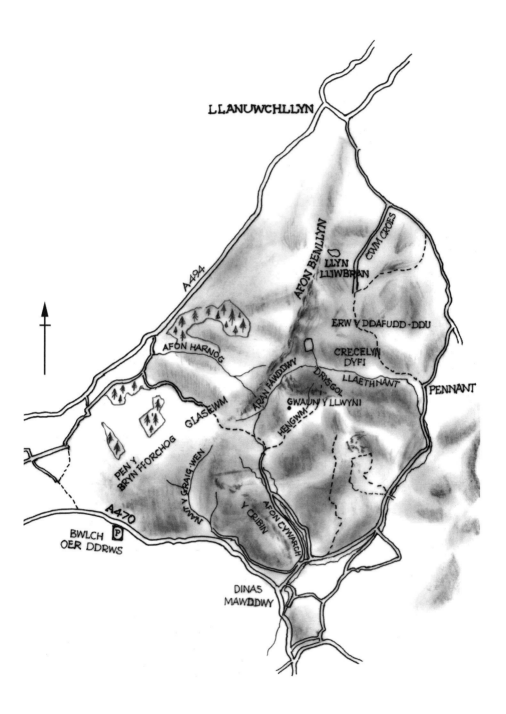

LLANUWCHLLYN

A494

AFON BENLLYN

CWM CROES

LLYN
LLIWBRAN

ERW Y DDAFUDD · DDU

AFON HARNOG

CRECELYN
DYFI

AFON FAWDDWY

DRISGOL

LLAETHNANT

PENNANT

GLASEWM

GWAUN Y LLWYNI

HENGWM

PEN Y
BRYN FFORCHOG

NANT Y GRAIG · WEN

Y CRIBIN

AFON CYWARCH

A470

BWLCH
OER DDRWS

P

DINAS
MAWDDWY

Afon Cwm-ochr before despatching the walker among the peaty hags of the col. The path continues as a well-worn route down into Cwm Cywarch to the east.

As the Arans once suffered greatly with access problems, the Snowdonia National Park Authority have taken pains to ensure that walkers on this section of the ridge do not stray from the permissive path which crosses the rugged land to the south-west of **Aran Fawddwy**. Planks and duck-boards form a basic pontoon across the worst of the bogs, and the paths are all well marked with signs, and even the occasional painted rock.

Crossing the duck-boards, the way slowly gains height and eventually reaches a track coming up from the forests of the Afon Harnog to the west. This track continues in a north-east direction to the summit of **Aran Fawddwy** and onwards along the higher summits of the range. But first, the delightful little Hewitt out on a limb to the south-east—**Gwaun y Llwyni**. This, the 'moorland of the bushes', is a nice little pointed summit when seen from the rocky col between it and the Drws Bach ridge of **Aran Fawddwy** to the north. It is an easy matter to deviate from the main track up **Aran Fawddwy** to gain the narrow perch which forms this summit at 2247'. High angled screes plunge down to the east into the upper arm of Cwm Cywarch, known as Hengwm, from the top of Gwaun y Llwyni, and the views across the cwm to the grassy ridges on the other side are good. The long whale-back of **Pen yr Allt Uchaf** is also a Hewitt.

Pen yr Allt Uchaf, at 2034' can hardly be said to live up to its rather glorious name. It translates quite grandly as 'top of the highest hillside'. It's a quiet little ridge, especially as most of the walkers heading for **Aran**

Dolgelly by John Sell Cotman, 1804-5

Fawddwy from Cwm Cywarch take a broad public footpath which climbs along **Pen yr Allt Uchaf**'s western flank, and avoids the summit altogether. Where this path gains the intervening ridge at a col marked as point 568 metres, a way can be forced through the peat hags and griffs to the south to bring a stile underfoot, and just beyond, the summit itself. This is unmarked.

To the immediate south of the summit lies another quiet corrie, Cwm Terwyn with its twin public footpaths climbing up onto the ridge along either bank of the little stream which drains the moors above. The way begins at Ty'n-y-maes in Cwm Cywarch, and either path can be followed up into the cwm, and so onto the ridge itself.

Heading north along this subsidiary ridge from the summit of **Pen yr Allt Uchaf**, the way first drops to the col, already mentioned above, then a wide path through grass climbs up and around in an arc over the summit of Drysgol to pick up a fence near the minor top of Drws Bach. At a prominent cairn there is a visitor's book in a tin box. The cairn itself commemorates the death of Mike Aspain, a member of the RAF St. Athan Mountain Rescue Team. Mike was killed by lightening whilst out on duty with the other members of the team. He was only eighteen when he died.

North from Drws Bach lies the highest point of the range, and indeed the highest mountain of Britain south of Snowdon itself—**Aran Fawddwy** at 2969'. This is what draws walkers to the range with its rocky ridges, plunging depths into crag-girt corries, and distant vistas of all the major mountains of North Wales. It is widely quoted that **Aran Fawddwy** is simply the Welsh equivalent of 'the mountain of (Dinas) Mawddwy'. Of course Mawddwy itself can be given an English equivalent, and in this particular case is very apt. W.P. Haskett Smith tells us that 'The word *Aran* means an "alp," or a "high place;" *mawdd* is said to mean "spreading," and the terminations *ach* or *wy* mean "water."' We are therefore left with 'the high place of the spreading water', perfectly descriptive of **Aran Fawddwy**. From Drws Bach the path crosses a stile then climbs up rocky slabs, knolls and boulders to gain the spectacular summit. Beneath your very feet to the east lie the tranquil waters of Creiglyn Dyfi, the source of the mighty River Dovey, or Afon Dyfi to be correct. Steep crags fall away to its rippling surface. This line of crags continue to the north, forming the eastern face of the rest of the ridge with just the occasional grassy rake to break the steepness. All of the rocks of the Arans are of the Ordovician series, or volcanic trap rock, as it is sometimes called. To the south, the younger beds of the Silurian series can be seen on the mountains and moorlands of mid-Wales. Even the Old Red Sandstone mountains of the Brecon Beacons can be seen from here on a clear day, over sixty miles to the south. The top of **Aran Fawddwy** is marked by a trig pillar atop a foundation of boulders and blocks.

The next summit, **Erw y Ddafad-ddu** is easily gained from Aran Fawddwy. More rocky ground leads down to a stile from where the path continues northwards to the small cairn which marks the top of this rather flat summit.

Erw y Ddafad-ddu means 'acre of the black sheep' and rises to 2861'. It has a broad though steep bank of grass leading down to the south-east, almost to the shores of Creiglyn Dyfi, and a line of eroded steps can be taken to climb to the summit from the Llyn, although no right of way passes by its waters. To the east of Creiglyn Dyfi lie a further three Hewitts, but the final high summit of the main ridge first demands our attentions.

Aran Benllyn, 'mountain at the head of the lake', towers above the southern end of Llyn Tegid, or Lake Bala, at 2904'. It is likely that it is this lake rather than the cirque lake of Llyn Lliwbran, which laps at its rocky east face, that gives it its name.

From **Erw y Ddafad-ddu** the path crosses a stile to the western side and traverses around rocky bluffs and boulders to gain a low stone wall at the summit of **Aran Benllyn**. The wall provides a good wind shelter. A ragged cairn marks the summit, and just beyond, along the north ridge, the tiny Llyn Pen Aran gives a sparkling foreground to views of Llyn Tegid in the trough of the Afon Dyfrydwy, better known as the River Dee, to the north-east. The ridge continues to the north, but decreases in height throughout. **Aran Benllyn** marks the northernmost Hewitt of the group.

The deep trench to the east is Cwm Croes, which splits higher up into two tributaries, Cwm Llwydd and Cwm Ddu, just below the craggy face of **Aran Benllyn**. The cirque lake of Llyn Lliwbran on the eastern side of the north ridge has much botanical interest. It was visited on April 17th 1682, by the youthful plant-hunter Edward Lhuyd. He thoroughly searched the area, including 'ye rivulets that run through ye rocks above Llyn Llymbran.' This unusual way of spelling the name is actually pretty much how you can still hear the locals pronounce it today. William Condry, in his book *The Snowdonia National Park* notes that this suggests a corruption of 'Llyn Bran', probably meaning 'lake of the crow', but also points out that 'Bran' is a name connected with very early Celtic folklore. He also records that some authorities have been known to insist on 'Llymbren'.

The way up **Aran Benllyn** from Llanuwchllyn near Llyn Tegid is easy to follow, first taking a track from the west side of the bridge over the Afon Twrch. It is a long haul over many false summits, but at least the way is direct and the views are good throughout.

From Creiglyn Dyfi it has already been pointed out that a further three Hewitts lie to the east. These have the steep-sided trench of the Llaethnant to the south, which affords a good way onto the main ridge from the east. The minor road from Dinas Mawddwy to the Bwlch y Groes, passes through the hamlet of Pennant and soon after, swings round in a wild turn to the right before climbing out of the valley. From the bend, a track heads off down to the river on the left below Nyth-yr-eryr, the 'eagle's nest'. Climbing from the valley bottom, the path soon rises again to the north of the stream to gain a cleft at Ceunant Briddell, the narrow col between **Foel Hafod-fynydd** and **Llechwedd Du**. You can either follow this path up onto Bwlch Sirddyn to gain access to these three Hewitts of the eastern Arans, or else ignore it and stick by the Llaethnant to gain Creiglyn Dyfi, and so the main Aran ridge via the grassy rake up **Erw y Ddafad-ddu**.

Assuming that you have descended from **Erw y Ddafad-ddu** to the northern shore of Creiglyn Dyfi, the next Hewitt on your round will be **Foel Hafod-fynydd**, 'bare hill of the mountain summer dwelling', at 2260'. This is a relatively minor hill which must be crossed *en route* to the peaty ridge out to the east. A fence is soon gained near a grassy col above the lake which is marked by a large boulder. The fence then leads quickly to the top which is marked by a small quartz cairn.

From Pennant down in the valley, the way is followed as described above to the spongy col of Bwlch Sirddyn, from where a fence leads up the steep northern acclivity of the hill. At the top turn right and follow the fence to the summit of **Foel Hafod-fynydd**. It should be noted that Bwlch Sirddyn can also be reached from the base of Cwm Croes via a track which contours along the western bank of the stream, then crosses over at the cwm head and climbs on a diagonal line southwards to the col.

North of Bwlch Sirddyn, more steep grassy slopes again follow a fence to our next Hewitt, **Esgeiriau Gwynion**, 'white ridges', at 2201'. The name probably refers to the long streaks of quartz which stud the hillsides to the west, and are particularly noticeable amid the lush grasses which flourish there. The fence from Bwlch Sirddyn should be followed throughout to gain the summit. This is graced with a few stones.

Across a mile of bleak tussock grass to the south, the elevation of **Llechwedd Du** is barely perceptible on the flat topped moorland. This, the 'black hillside' at 2014' is aptly named. Peat oozes from every griff of heather or grass, and eight-foot high mushrooms of eroded vegetation show dark sides of crumbling humus to the elements. These seem to float on a wash of black pools full of cotton grass. Thankfully, the fence can again be followed throughout, although this does not take a direct course. The summit is again marked by a small cairn of quartz atop a raised knob of grass and heather.

Llechwedd Du can also be climbed, if that is the right word to use to describe what is merely an exercise in bog-hoping, from the car park at the Bwlch y Groes. The way is arduous, but again makes use of the fence to aid navigation. Some of the peat wallows here are very deep, and it may be necessary to deviate substantially from the safety of the fence in order to avoid a thorough dunking. I would recommend avoiding this last approach, and indeed these final three Hewitts altogether, in anything but the driest of weather.

THE BERWYNS

The Berwyns seem to be gaining in popularity these days, and quite rightly so. This is splendid walking country, with airy ridges where it is possible to stride out along the high tops and not see a soul all day. Even the ubiquitous 'Berwyn Heather', renowned throughout the walking world as the worse possible terrain to have to cross, isn't anything to compare to that in the nearby Hirnants. Most of the higher ridges are actually grass-covered and the walking is easy. The entire range is outside the boundary of the Snowdonia National Park, which may account for its sense of spaciousness and solitude. The crowds used to simply pass it by, on the way into the Park.

The range is bounded to the north and west by the Bala fault line, which runs north-east to south-west and takes the winding River Dee, Llyn Tegid and further south, the Minffordd valley of Cadair Idris. Of the eight Hewitts in the group, five form the south wall of this geological fault, while the remaining three are mere summits on subsidiary ridges. The Tanat Valley forms the boundary to the south, while to the east, the moorland falls away to the English border near Oswestry and Chirk.

Across the Milltir Gerrig, the 'milestone pass', from the Hirnants, heathery slopes lead up onto the main ridge of the Berwyns. The first of the subsidiary ridges comes in from the south-east and has as its high point the little summit of **Post Gwyn**, 'the white pillar', at 2182'. A strange name, one might think, for a hill showing nothing about its top that could be called white, but the name does tie in nicely with W.P. Haskett Smith's definition of the meaning of 'Berwyn'. As mentioned earlier Haskett Smith is widely regarded as the father of British rock climbing, but one of his chief accomplishments was the writing of an incredibly detailed guidebook, supposedly to the climbing grounds of Britain, but which also contains a wealth of information on the gentler type of terrain in the mountains, such as that found in the Berwyns. In his *Climbing in the British Isles*, he records that the name Berwyn is said to signify 'White Tops', deriving from 'Bera-gwen'.

The **Post Gwyn** ridge is a true delight. **Post Gwyn** itself can be climbed from Milltir Gerrig, but is best tackled from either the Tanat Valley, or from the Afon Rhaeadr below the famous falls of the Pistyll Rhaeadr, 240' in height, and one of the real jewels of the Berwyns. In the deepest winters, this waterfall forms a cascade of ice, although this is becoming increasingly rare in these days of global warming. When it does freeze, two rivulets of ice are often broken up the centre by some residual liquid, forming two delightful, grade V winter climbs, grade V being the very hardest of winter climbing grades until very recently. It is these frozen streams that attract the few climbers who come to the area, for in summer conditions, the Berwyns are as devoid of good rock climbing as the lowlands of Holland. There are a number of other good ice-falls in the area, but again, they take weeks of hard frost to form into anything climbable.

Public footpaths lead up onto the **Post Gwyn** ridge from Pencraig and Llangynog in the Tanat Valley, sometimes written as Tanad Valley, and up around Craig y Mwn, 'crag of the ore', from Tan-y-pistyll. These gain the ridge around Y Clogydd, a mile and a half short of the summit, but easy walking over rough grass and occasional heather clumps soon have this underfoot.

Another possibility is to follow the path above Pistyll Rhaeadr into Cwm Disgynfa, and then pick a way up the eastern flanks.

Across the Afon Disgynfa to the north-east, the main Berwyn ridge can be seen sweeping round to the first of the Hewitts, **Moel Sych**, 'dry bare hill', at 2713'. Again, this can be climbed direct from the road at Milltir Gerrig, but there are other, better ways. From below Pistyll Rhaeadr, a public footpath climbs up beside the Nant y Llyn. This can be followed beneath towering ridges to Llyn Lluncaws, a tiny tarn, filling a glaciated hollow in the cirque, below the rough east face of **Moel Sych**. The two ridges which fall down from the summit, forming the walls of the cirque can be climbed over rough grass and heather. Either one being equally as good as the other. The left-hand ridge can also be gained from above Pistyll Rhaeadr, and to the east of Cwm-Rhiwiau, although this doesn't follow a right of way.

Heading north-east from **Moel Sych** alongside a fence, the first col marks the top of a long heathery ridge over Moel yr Ewig and Godor which separates the valley of the Afon Rhaeadr from that of the Afon Twrch. East again from Godor along this ridge, a public footpath crosses from one valley to the next and is a useful way of gaining height, although the intervening minor tops, before the main Hewitts are reached, may put walkers of modest ability off using this approach.

Just north-east again, the path beside the fence rises to the cairn of **Cadair Berwyn**, 'the chair of Berwyn', at 2723', perched atop the broken cliffs above the head of Cwm Maen Gwynedd. Much of the scenery in this

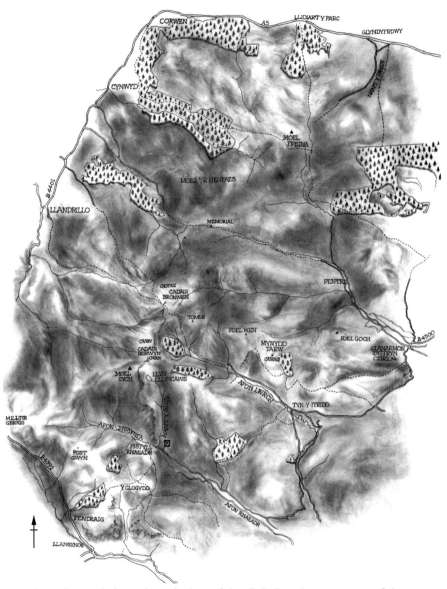

cwm has changed since the printing of the O.S. Landranger map of the area, as the forest which fills the head of this cwm is now cleared, and other conifers have been planted upon the Moel yr Ewig flank.

This summit is widely known as the 'New Top' of **Cadair Berwyn**, as that which is a couple of hundred yards to the north holds the O.S. trig pillar. It was widely believed that **Moel Sych** held the title of the highest peak in the range, until new surveys at first brought Cadair Berwyn (with the trig pillar) up to the same height, and then increased the height of the top in the middle of the two. This, it was believed until this new survey was undertaken, was only a minor bump on the ridge, but its new height is now given as 830 metres, a whole three metres higher than both **Moel Sych** and the old summit of Cadair Berwyn. Thus, the old Cadair Berwyn has become nothing more than an intermediate top on the way over to **Cadair Bronwen** in the north. This old summit is still regarded as a separate mountain by the Nuttalls, although the drop between the two summits can be little more than 20 metres.

And so you pass over the old summit with its trig pillar, then pick up a path through the short, wet grass above the vegetated crags of Craig Berwyn on the way down the ridge heading north.

From out of the Afon Twrch valley an ancient by-way climbs up the steep slopes to gain a col at what is marked on the map as a cairn. It is actually a standing stone which once marked a Roman route along this track, known as Ffordd Gam Elin, or 'Helen's Winding Road', Helen being the daughter of Octavius, wife of the Emperor Maximus. Sadly the standing stone no longer stands, but just lays recumbent, peacefully in the dewy mountain grass. From the col, Ffordd Gam Elin heads over the southern flank of **Cadair Bronwen**, sometimes called 'Fronwen', and leads down the Trawsnant ridge to Hendwr by the River Dee. This track makes a good way onto the ridge from either side.

One of the little known attractions of walking in this range is the likelihood of coming across one of natures floral wonders. This is the only known Welsh habitat of the cloudberry (*Rubus chamaemorus*), a low-growing, edible member of the bramble family. Locally it is known as mwyar Berwyn, or the Berwyn Berry. Another rare species found, or more often not found, thanks to its tiny size, is the little orchid known as the lesser twayblade. It only grows to a height of about two inches and displays tiny leaves and a minute spike of reddish flowers. The reason it is so hard to spot is that it thrives beneath the canopy of dense heather.

Staying on the main ridge for the time being, the dome of **Cadair Bronwen**, the chair of Bronwen, with its perfect plum-pudding-like cairn, rises next, to a height of 2575'. This, the legendary seat of Arthur, gives a fine termination to the main ridge, although two smaller Hewitts lay deep in the heather, either side of the ancient trackway of Ffordd Saeson, the 'Englishman's' or 'Saxon's' Road', to the north. However, first an exploration of the ridge out to the east.

108

East of the (not) standing stone at the head of Cwm Maen Gwynedd, a long heathery ridge passes over a number of summits, two of which qualify as Hewitts, and effectively forms the north wall of the cwm. From the col a fence leads over Tomle, a minor top, then turns left and down to a deep col before the climb up to the summit of **Foel Wen**, or 'the white bare hill' at 2267'. The actual top is unmarked amid a moorland of mat-grass.

Slightly further along the ridge, another gentle rise clears the second minor top before the more distinctive drop down to a boggy col. Rocky outcrops give something to aim for in the peaty morass, but a good path does help to find a fairly dry way through. A fence is climbed with the help of an old tree bough, then the easy climb up **Mynydd Tarw**, 'hill of the bulls', at 2234' follows. As you reach the top with its wind shelter, the views across the plains and distant moorlands of England spread out before you.

A small wood covers the slopes on the south-east flank and falls to Tyn-y-ffridd beside the Afon Twrch. From there a way can be found alongside the wood to this summit, or else a by-way leads around the southern flank to the col between **Foel We**n and **Mynydd Tarw**. The Nuttalls in their book describe an ascent up this ridge from the Afon Twrch, and around the skyline finishing on Godor across the valley to the south. This gives an excellent round of Cwm Maen Gwynedd, and takes in four Hewitts, including the minor diversion to bag Moel Sych, and involves much upping and downing over the minor little bumps that are the 'Nuttalls'.

And so, what of the two northern outposts of the Berwyn range. What do these heathery lumps have to offer the Hewitt bagger? I must admit that when I first came to these hills as part of my Welsh Hewitt Traverse, I really didn't expect to find the wonderful wildness of these empty moorlands above the forests of Cynwyd. Of the two, **Moel yr Henfaes**, meaning unknown, but possibly 'bare hill of the old field', at 2037', is the least delectable, being only a few hundred yards above a bulldozed track which climbs gently up from the River Dee at Hendwr. At the top of the pass, above which stands the summit, is a memorial to 'A Wayfarer 1877 - 1956 Lover of Wales'. This wide col has become known as 'The Wayfarer's Pass', and there is a visitor's book cached near the memorial.

A climb over a fence leads to a small cairn atop a rock beside another fence, amid a field of mosses and rushes. The name given for this hill in the tables of Welsh Hewitts by Alan Dawson, refers to the long ridge heading north-east from the summit, and the top actually seems to be nameless. The Nuttalls use the name Pen Bwlch Llandrillo Top, 'Top of the Llandrillo Pass', although that seems to be too much of an obscure mix of Welsh and

English for most people's liking. As this is a book about the Welsh Hewitts, I have kept to the name given by Alan Dawson.

The pass can also be reached from the east via the village of Llanarmon Dyffryn Ceiriog, and a parking spot at Pentre at the head of the valley.

The wild fastness of these, the northern Berwyns becomes more apparent as you leave the summit of **Moel yr Henfaes** and follow the fence over rough heather towards Cerrig Coediog, and ultimately **Moel Fferna**. In this lonely land there is nothing to tempt the eye but rolling hills of heather, although on my first visit, I enjoyed the cackling mating display of a pair of hen harriers idling through a murky sky above the boggy col below Cerrig Coediog.

At last the peaty path gives way to a main track coming up from Cynwyd in the west. This crosses the ridge on its way over to the England - Wales border and is the Ffordd Saeson, 'the Englishman's Pass'. The vague path along the ridge, crosses this ancient trackway and becomes much more distinct on its short climb up **Moel Fferna**, at 2067'. Like its southern neighbour, **Moel yr Henfaes**, the meaning of the name has long since vanished into the depths of ancient Celtic history.

A number of alternative routes climb **Moel Fferna** from the north, perhaps the best being that coming over from Glyndyfrdwy. A footpath along the eastern bank of the Nant y Pandy can be followed up to the edge of a forest. From here a path leads off westwards through the heather, and leads to the summit. A way from Llidart y Parc climbs up the wooded slopes beside the Nant Ffriddisel, whilst another climbs the broad north-west ridge of Bryn-llus from Corwen. This latter descends into the forests around Afon Trystion above Cynwyd, before gaining the Ffordd Saeson track.

This is deliberately only a brief outline of this wonderful hill country, and quite rightly so. Other more obscure ways can be found onto the tops, and indeed great walking days can be had even down in the valleys. The emphasis here is on exploration. The range lends itself admirably to generally 'having a nosy', and abounds in ancient cairns, stone circles and natural wonders. Even the problems of old that have contributed to a general misunderstanding about the type of terrain to be found in the Berwyns, that ancient bug-bear 'access', seems to be relaxing, and although many of the routes do not follow rights of way, the hill farmers of today seem more than happy to accommodate the sensible hillwalker. The actual main ridge route is private land throughout, although the landowner has given permission for the erection of stiles and way-markers along the entire ridge, a true sign of changing attitudes among the farming communities. So, by all means go and enjoy the beautiful Berwyns, but respect the land and those who choose to make a living from it.

THE HIRNANT HILLS

This range of predominantly moorland hills are usually considered a part of the Berwyns, but for the purposes of this book it seems logical to describe the two groups independently. The range as a whole take their name from the heavily forested valley of Cwm Hirnant, around which, with one exception, they are clustered. Cwm Hirnant rises southwards from the eastern end of Llyn Tegid and takes a minor road over a high pass to Llyn Efyrnwy (Lake Vyrnwy), which gives easy access to the hills nearby. There are three Hewitts on each side of the road as you drive up this pass.

To the west of the range is the deep defile of Cwm Cynllwyd and the boggy outposts of the Arans. Another minor road climbs over the moors to the Bwlch y Groes pass, again giving easy access to the single outpost of the group, **Moel y Cerrig Duon**. Just down the south side of Bwlch y Groes a junction takes one either eastwards to Llyn Efyrnwy, or southwards to Dinas Mawddwy. The eastern boundary of the range is the busy B4391 taking traffic from the Bala area to the Tanat Valley.

This exploration of these hills starts in the west, at the isolated dome of **Moel y Cerrig Duon**, 'bare hill of the black stones', at 2051'. From all angles it is a simple-looking hill. A car park at the top of Bwlch y Groes gives as a good a place as any to enjoy a short stroll over rough grass to the summit cairn, requiring nothing more than about 300' of ascent. Alternatively, down the Cwm Cynllwyd side of the pass, the soaring arêtes of Craig yr Ogof are bounded to the south by a stream which can be followed onto a wide, heathery col. Across the col a fence has a very faint path running alongside it, which leads southwards to the top.

Far across the moors to the north lies the second Hewitt of the Hirnants, **Foel y Geifr**, 'bare hill of the goats', at 2054'. While the rough moorland that lies in between can be crossed to link these two peaks, I can't really recommend it. This is the way I came during my Welsh Hewitt Traverse in 1998, and I found the whole crossing one of the most gruelling parts of the entire trip. However, if you do decide to plough on through it all, all I can say is that it is probably best to gain the ridge over point 605 metres.

The easiest and most popular way of reaching the summit trig pillar is direct from the minor road pass to the east. The way at first is rather boggy, but this is soon cleared and fairly gentle heather slopes lead up to the top.

Another good way, though again very hard going, is to take the minor road up Glyn Gower from the south side of Llyn Tegid. Before the road-end a public footpath heads off uphill, through the dense forest and up onto the ridge of Uwchafon. From here it is a long slog around the outside perimeter of the forest to the dome-like top of Moel Figenau, from where a fence leads over towards Mynydd Carnedd Hywel, the broad west ridge of **Foel y Geifr**.

Once the summit trig pillar has been reached, the attractive north ridge, over Trum y Gwrgedd to **Foel Goch** is a real delight. Dark conifer planta-tions shroud the hillside to the west, while to the east the miniature-like cars on the minor road can be seen struggling up to the top of the pass. A path leads off from the trig pillar of **Foel y Geifr** and runs through the heather alongside a fence to the top of **Foel Goch**, 'bare red hill', at 2011'.

The only alternative to gaining this short ridge is to start down in the depths of Cwm Hirnant at the point where a track heads off up Cwm yr Aethnen across the valley. Grass and bilberry lead up the northern nose of **Foel Goch** to reach its small collection of slaty stones which mark the summit.

Across the head of Cwm Hirnant, the peaty top of **Pen y Boncyn Trefeilw** rises 2119' above sea level amid an ocean of deep ling and bell heather (*Calluna* and *Erica*). Luckily, though few walkers would see such man-made desecration as fortunate, a bulldozed track leaves the top of the road pass at the head of the cwm and climbs the broad western slopes to within a few metres of the summit. This actually lies within a grassy field over a fence, and is marked by a boundary stone. The name itself is trans-lated as nothing more exciting than 'top of the hillock', but is ideal for a summit such as this.

It is also possible to gain the bulldozed track from the bottom of Cwm yr Aethnen down in the Hirnant valley via the track mentioned above.

Back on the bulldozed track, the way leads up and down over little heathery knolls and great sweeping ridges, with the Penllyn Forest covering the hillsides to the north. The next Hewitt is **Cyrniau Nod**, 'mark cairns', at 2188', and as such is the highest hill in the Hirnant range.

Eventually the track gains a slight elevation, then dips before cresting another. The summit of **Cyrniau Nod** lies in the boggy morass to the south, but if you stick with the track for a short distance further, a fence is reached,

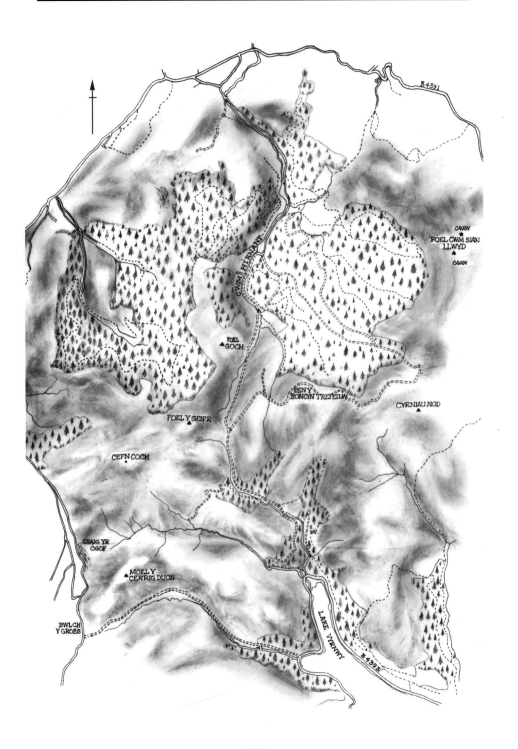

alongside of which is a vague path leading to the summit. This top marked the half-way point of my Welsh Hewitt Traverse in 1998, but found me at a low ebb, unable to enjoy the splendid views of the Berwyns across the moors to the east.

The bulldozed track heads off downhill, shortly after the point where the fence leads to the summit, and gives an alternative approach to **Cyrniau Nod** from Cwm Hirnant. A forest track goes up into the trees beside the Nant Ystrad-y-groes of Cwm Gwyn, and is easy to follow throughout. A good circular trip can be had by those who have parked down in Cwm Hirnant and began the day by climbing the north ridge of **Foel Goch**. This leaves the possibility of returning through the forests at sunset after climbing **Cyrniau Nod**, or if done in reverse, leaves the walker on the top of **Foel Goch** as the sun slips down over the long ridges of the Arans and Arenigs in the west. It is at times such as that that you witness the pleasures to be had from even relatively mundane walking territory such as this.

More pathless heather separates **Cyrniau Nod** from the last Hewitt of the range, **Foel Cwm-Sian Llwyd**, 'the bare hill of grey Jane's valley', at 2126'.

Perhaps the best way of climbing this hill is from a point just north of the top of the Milltir Gerrig, 'milestone pass', at a ruined cottage by the side of the road. A faint path crosses into the broad, shallow Cwm-Sian Llwyd, then peters out, but fortunately the going is fairly easy over compact heather and bilberry. A trig pillar marks the tops and gives superb views in all directions, while just north a few hundred metres stands an ancient cairn, made into a now derelict building.

From Aber Hirnan, mid-way up Cwm Hirnant a track heads up through the forest, and once on the open hillside turns into a fairly good path through the heather. It actually crosses **Foel Cwm-Sian Llwyd**'s southern flank on its way over to the Tanat Valley, but at its highest point, a small path leads off to the summit.

Obviously this same path can be gained from the Tanat Valley, via a delightful walk up Cwm Rhiwarth where cars that have careered off the B4391 high above, lay as burnt out wrecks on the hillside beyond Blaen-rhiwarth.

These Hirnant hills are by no means the most spectacular in Snowdonia, but perhaps for that very reason, they provide the walker with a real sense of solitude, a kind of 'away from it all' atmosphere. In this day and age that can be a very valuable commodity, and one worth pursuing.

CADAIR IDRIS

Cadair Idris, the Chair of Idris, forms one of the most popular mountain ranges south of the Snowdon massif, **Cadair Idris** also being the name given to the highest mountain of the group. Indeed, it is often quoted that Penygadair, the highest point on **Cadair Idris**, is the second most popular summit in Wales, **Snowdon** of course being the first.

On the whole the range is a fairly compact one, comprising just seven Hewitts, all of which lie within a three mile radius of **Cadair Idris** itself.

The A487 forms the south-eastern border of the range, along with that road's extension to the south-west—the B4405 through the old slate mining village of Abergynolwyn. To the north lies the sprawling township of Dolgellau on the Afon Wnion, while to the west the range falls over rough moorland and fertile livestock country to the A493, the Afon Mawddach and the coast at Fairbourne. Away to the south-west, the range drops well below 2000 feet and continues over countless low hills of farmland and uncultivated moorland to the sea at Tywyn, from where a deep sea-washed valley, that of the Dyffryn Dysynni, cuts back into the range.

There are a couple of claims for the 'Idris' part of the name. Tradition has passed it on by legend that there was a giant named Idris Gawr, but what seems more likely is that it took its name from Idris ap Gwyddno, a seventh century hero and Prince of Merioneth. It was he who led the Welsh against the Irish invaders in what came to be known as 'the Slaughter of the Severn and the Killing of Idris'. An Irish account of this battle backs up this story, mentioning 'the war of Idris, king of Britons, who fell therein.'

The Chair of Idris is generally taken as being the wild north-west facing cirque which holds Llyn y Gadair beneath the broken faces of rock that fall from the summit. **Cyfrwy** to the west and the ridge taken by the Foxes Path to the east form the 'arms' of the Chair. Some make mention of a rock near the summit of **Cadair Idris**, upon which if you spend the night, you awake either a poet or a madman. This is as it may be, but this legend has unfortunately been stolen from the rock known as Maen Du'r Arddu on **Snowdon**—the writings of Mrs Hemans, an English poetess, transferring the legend from **Snowdon** to **Cadair Idris**. Many others have written of

Cadair Idris, from Tennyson to Darwin, who wrote 'Old Cader is a grand fellow and shows himself off superbly with ever changing light. Do come and see him.' Darwin spent a lot of time holidaying in later life in Barmouth across the Mawddach. The Victorian parson and diarist Francis Kilvert climbed **Cadair Idris** on June 13th 1871 and declared it 'the stoniest, dreariest, most desolate mountain I was ever on.' His mood cheered somewhat upon descending and dropping below the clouds. 'Down, down and out of the cloud into sunshine, all the hills below and the valleys were bathed in glorious sunshine - a wonderful and dazzling sight. ... Above and hanging overhead the vast black precipices towered and loomed through the clouds, and fast as we went down the mist followed faster and presently all the lovely sunny landscape was shrouded in a white winding sheet of rain.'

Although only 2930' high and thereby 39' lower than **Aran Fawddwy** nearby to the north-east, it was once held that **Cadair Idris** was the highest mountain in the whole of Wales. In the eighteenth century William Camden claimed as much in his book *Britannia*, but went a step further by pronouncing **Cadair Idris** to be the highest mountain in the whole of Britain!

The mountain at the heart of this range is graced on all sides by the wildest of corries, crag-girt and tarn bejeweled, and as such, **Cadair Idris** holds a very special place in the hearts of many a well travelled hillwalker. There are a number of badly eroded paths to the summit, but one of the most popular must surely be the Minffordd Path. A car park and toilet block near the junction of the A487 and the B4405 is the place to start, and a well marked path heads off up into the Nature Reserve of Cwm Cau. Shortly before reaching the shores of Llyn Cau, another path begins the ascent of **Craig Cwm Amarch** along its narrow eastern ridge. Open gullies drop from the giddy heights into the cwm on the right, and the impressive crags around the Pencoed Pillar can be seen falling from near the summit of **Craig Cwm Amarch**, our first Hewitt. This, the 'rock of the Amarch cirque' rises in a pleasant little steeple to 2595', and forms the southern ridge of **Cadair Idris** itself.

The summit is unmarked by a cairn, but has a stile crossing a fence and a mad collection of boulders, sadly often crevice-crammed with sweet wrappers and banana peel. Craig Cau falls from beneath your feet, with its outstanding climbing on the famous Pencoed Pillar. This provides, among other routes, an excellent Very Difficult, first climbed in 1903 by Millican and H.G. Dalton. Millican Dalton is more often associated with the Lake District, though even there his first ascents are very few. Millican styled himself as probably the first ever 'Professor of Adventure'. Being some-

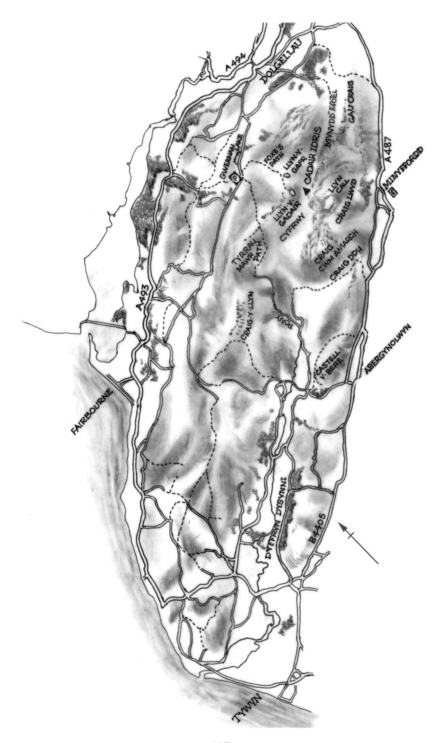

Cader Idris by John Glover

thing of a philosopher, he gave up his London office job to pursue life as a real pioneer, living in a hut in the Epping Forest during the winter months and offering 'Camping Holidays, Mountain Rapid Shooting, Rafting and Hair-Breadth Escapes' to adventurous tourists while living in a cave under Castle Crag in Borrowdale during the summer. Payment from his clients for these adventures was, more often than not, nothing more than cigarettes, his food being bought from money made from the sale of hand-made outdoor clothing and equipment. Most of his activities took place in the years between the wars and it is reported that Millican 'was vegetarian, teetotal and a pacifist'. He is known to have written to Churchill from his cave in 1942, asking him to stop the war. That his name is associated with a climb in this cwm guarantees that any would-be ascentionist today should prepare for a real adventure, even despite the lowly grade of the climb up the pillar.

Craig Cwm Amarch, often named as Mynydd Pencoed, can be climbed along another ridge which leaves the valley just a mile and a half south-west of Minffordd. A track passes to the north of Tal-y-Llyn (strangely named Tal-y-Llyn Lake on the O.S. map) and a public footpath climbs up into the lower reaches of Cwm Amarch from Pentre Farm. Once past the level of Graig Ddu on the left, the ridge above that crag can be gained and followed to the summit.

Llyn-y-Cau, Cader Idris by Richard Wilson, c.1765.
Craig Cwm Amarch *is the peak beyond the lake*

The way onwards to **Cadair Idris** from **Craig Cwm Amarch** is obvious and easy to follow. A path drops down to a col above Llyn Cau, from where a rocky slope leads up to the summit. It should be noted that the col mentioned can also be gained from the north shore of Llyn Cau, though of course, that approach misses out **Craig Cwm Amarch**.

A trig pillar at 2930' marks the highest point of **Cadair Idris**, with a little hut for shelter just a few yards to the north. The hut was built in the 1830s by Richard Pugh of Dolgellau, one of the early guides on **Cadair Idris**. It was said that this hut '... proved of great advantage to visitors who before were not unfrequently assailed by the teeming shower without an opportunity of shelter; and who had no spot for temporary refreshment while waiting for the dispersion of the misty clouds in order to enjoy the exquisite prospect. Here parties and individuals may have all convenient refreshments.' The summit is stony and wild, and it should be remembered that there are few easy ways down to either the south or the north, in fact the northern façade is even more crag girt than the south, and only the ridge taken by the Foxes Path can be relied upon to get you down safely in that direction, though even this path is very loose. In 1973 the Mid-Wales guidebook author, John Sumner and his partner R. Short were checking a climb on this north face, the Central Gully of Penygadair, when they came across

From Barmouth to Dolegelly we were highly gratified; the road wound along a ridge of rocks, that hang over the Avonvawr, an arm of the sea; which, at full tide, has the appearance of a large lake, surrounded with beautiful woods: The mountains on both sides, but particularly on the opposite shore, were strikingly grand; and above all, Cader Idris reared its head into the clouds, which, together with the sombre aspect of the evening, and the hollow murmurings of the sea gave an awful sublimity to the scene that cannot be described.

Dolegelly is a large and dirty town: we took up our quarters at the Golden Lion, a good hospitable inn and next morning, after breakfast, procured a guide to conduct us to the top of Cader Idris. We armed him with stores, and warlike preparations of all kinds (to wit): ham, fowl, bread, and cheese, and brandy, and began the ascent at nine in the morning, and continued to toil for three hours and a half before we reached the top. But, alas! expectation had again flattered us: for, though it was a most lovely day in the valleys, yet here we could not see fifty yards before us; the summit of the mountain is not of greater extent than the base of a common sized room; and, on one side, falls almost perpendicularly many hundred yards in depth. When I stood upon the edge of this precipice, and looked into the frightful abyss of clouds, it put me in mind of the chaos, or void space of darkness, so finely described in Milton, when the fallen archangel stood at the gates of hell ...

From A Pedestrian Tour through North Wales
in a Series of Letters by Joseph Hucks, 1795

the remains of a decomposed body, which it was subsequently discovered must have lain there for over six months. Perhaps this sufficiently highlights the dangers of wandering away from the main tracks on **Cadair Idris**. W.P. Hasket Smith in his *Climbing in the British Isles* mentions a Mr. Smith, a tailor from Newport, who in 1864 fell from the lip of the crags between **Cadair Idris** and **Cyfrwy**. His body was not found until the following year. It is worth remembering that if you have an accident while walking solo in the mountains, it could be a long time before someone finds you, even on popular **Cadair Idris**.

Across the head of the cwm to the west lies the rocky top of **Cyfrwy**, beyond which the ridge drops to a broad col then climbs gently to continue over a further two outlying Hewitts to the south-west before dropping to the seashore. But before these are described, I'll turn to the long eastern ridge out towards the Cross Foxes Hotel at the junction of the A487 and the A470.

A short way beyond the hut from the summit, a path swings off to the north and soon becomes scree covered and loose. This is the famous Foxes Path, once a popular way to the summit from the Gwernan Lake Hotel which lies down to the north along a minor road which is signposted as '**Cadair Idris**' from Dolgellau. A car park and picnic site are the start of this way up, which is well marked until up in the cwm holding Llyn y Gadair. Here, another path comes up from Llyn Gafr, an alternative way up from the Gwernan Lake Hotel. Above, the ridge is gained and horrible slopes lead to the top.

The Foxes Path to Cadair Idris from an old postcard

From the summit, where this path swings off into the depths of the cwm, the summit becomes plateau-like and a vague path leads around the lip of the vast crags which form the whole of the northern face of **Cadair Idris**. Within a mile, this leads to the summit of **Mynydd Moel** beyond a stile. A large cairn, hollowed out to form a windbreak marks the top of this, the 'bare mountain', at 2831'.

Mynydd Moel too has its share of crags, and halfway along this wonderful little walk between the summits, another, known as Twr Du, falls away also to the north.

*The long ridges of **Cadair Idris** as seen from **Y Garn** to the north*

At a much lower level to the east lies the last of the summits in that direction, **Gau Graig**, the 'hollow rock', at 2241'. A path leads around the rim of the cwm holding the little Llyn Arran, dropping to a boggy moorland before the little cairn at its summit is reached. This top gives good views of the Rhinogs, the Arenigs and the Arans, each separated from the other by the troughs taking the big rivers of the Afon Mawddach and the River Dee, with Llyn Tegid visible down the length of the latter.

Gau Graig can be climbed quickly from the top of the Tal-y-Llyn Pass to the east. A car park gives a good place to start, though this is not convenient unless you are content to retrace your steps at the end of the day.

To the north, a long rocky ridge falls from the summit of **Gau Graig**, and a path, not marked on the map, follows this down to an open little col near a prominent knoll, from which a public footpath leads down to the northwest, passing Bwlch-coch before picking up the minor road into Dolgellau. If ascending via this route, park in Dolgellau and take the road up past the hospital. There is little parking along this road, and none at all at its end.

To the west of **Cadair Idris**, huge columnar crags rise up from the shining levels of Llyn y Gadair. This awesome face is that of **Cyfrwy**, 'the saddle', at 2661'. From **Cadair Idris** a bouldery slope leads down to a col before a gentle rise over much loose rock to the summit, with the long sweep of the corrie rim on the right.

The best way to climb **Cyfrwy** for the mountaineer is via the long, though easy, rock climb known as the Cyfrwy Arête. This was first climbed solo by that redoubtable seeker of unclimbed faces, O.G. Jones in May, 1888. Even today, it is often done solo, though this can only be recommended for those with rock climbing experience. Initially the route avoids the broken rocks at its base, though the last time I climbed the line, with Andy MacNaughton, we managed to force a way through these piles of loose blocks to maximise our time on the rocks. The normal way heads off round to the left, then cuts back to the base of the ridge where a large 'CA' is carved into the hard Ordovician base. After this the way is enjoyable throughout, climbing a long ridge to the famous feature known as 'The Table'. This is a large, fairly flat block, about a third of the way up the Arête, and separated from the upper ridge by a steep-sided gap. The climb down into the gap is quite a struggle, then a traverse across to the left gains a spike before a remarkably steep pitch on good holds leads to an easing and then the top. The summit cairn is set back, around the head of a gully on the left.

To the west, broad, open slopes of boulders and grass fall down to a col via a vague path. The usual descent to the west, and only a variation on the path mentioned above, is to head around the rim of the corrie to the south, until a col is reached before the climb up to **Cadair Idris**. This col is marked by a big cairn. From there, a well marked track, the Pony Path descends in long zigzags to the north-west, then down into the valley of the Afon Dysynni to the south, but more on this approach shortly.

From the col one path continues alongside a fence straight ahead to the summit of the next Hewitt, **Tyrrau Mawr**, while another heads off to the north-east for the car park near the Gwernan Lake Hotel. This later is the best descent to the west from the peaks around the central part of the **Cadair Idris** massif, and is hard to miss.

The Pony Path starts down amid the sylvan beauty of the Dyffryn Dysynni to the south-west and crosses the range before leading down to the Gwernan Lake Hotel. This wonderful valley of the Dysynni is well-known to rock climbers for its excellent road-side crag, Craig yr Aderyn, or 'Bird Rock', which gives a wide variety of climbs of all grades. It gets its name from the fact that in the days before the sea retreated to its present position, Craig yr Aderyn was a sea cliff, and as such was a favourite nesting place for thousands of sea birds. Even today, though the crag is a good six miles from the sea, it is used by cormorants as a nesting ground, possible the only inland nesting site of this aquatic bird. This is also one of the few places in Britain that you can see the chough, a member of the crow family, but easily distinguishable from the other members of that carrion group by its bright red beak and feet.

Further up the Dysynni Valley we find the remains of Castell y Bere, a fortification of Llewelyn ap Gruffydd's time. He was the Prince of Wales until his death in 1292 when his brother, Dafydd took over. Their Grandfather, Llewelyn ap Iorwerth, Prince of North Wales had begun building the castle in 1221, but it wasn't to stay a stronghold of the family for very long. Edward I led over 3,000 men on a successful siege of the castle soon after Dafydd began his rule. A rebellion was started in an attempt to win back this, the last of the Welsh castles to fall to the English, but this failed, and soon after, Castell y Bere began its steady decline into the ruins we find today.

It is from near here, at the hamlet of Llanfihangel-y-pennant, that the Pony Path begins its ascent to the high tops, although it is likely that the origins of the track were simply a means of crossing the range from the Dysynni to Dolgellau. The way follows an obvious track throughout, bringing the walker to the col between **Cyfrwy** and **Tyrrau Mawr**.

Tyrrau Mawr, 'large towers', at 2169' is far from being an exciting hill to climb, and yet, as a continuation of the main ridge of **Cadair Idris**, running all the way from **Gau Graig** to **Craig-y-llyn** and beyond, it is simply superb. A grassy path leads up from the col to the ancient cairns of Carnedd Llwyd, the 'grey cairn' just before the ladder stile is reached near the highest point of **Tyrrau Mawr**. The summit itself is unmarked, but has some interest in the way of panoramic views across the Afon Mawddach to the Rhinogs. Below your feet to the north, plunging cliffs of broken rock sweep down to the minor road west of the Gwernan Lake Hotel.

From **Tyrrau Mawr**, a path follows the ridge to the south-west, and soon after a little col, rises again to the last Hewitt of the range, **Craig-y-llyn**, 'rock of the lake', at 2041'. Yet more broken crags continue the theme of falling away to the north that has been so popular throughout the whole range, and the small Llyn Cyri hides away beneath these to the west.

It is possible to climb **Craig-y-llyn** direct from the Dyffryn Dysynni via a hard-to-follow public footpath through Nant-Caw farm. There is a path marked on the map, but you cannot help but feel that you are trespassing when you try to follow it through padlocked gates and over low fences. Remarkably, a good track is soon reached which contours around the upper slopes of the hill, and a stile gives access to this over a high stone wall. The ridge of **Craig-y-llyn** lies above to the north and can be gained just about anywhere over rough grass and bilberry.

THE DOVEY HILLS

Although the three Hewitts of the Dovey Forest do not boast rugged peaks or rocky summits to entice the walker, these grassy, dome-like tops and Pennine-like ridges hold a certain charm all of their own. Being a compact group, bounded to the north and east by the A470 road from the Cross Foxes Hotel just east of Dolgellau through Dinas Mawddwy and on to Cemmaes, and to the west by the A487, rising across the tarmac to the heights of **Cadair Idris**, only approaches from the south offer anything like quiet ways to these summits.

The northern aspects of these hills show us pretty much what the rest of this range would have been like before the land was taken over and planted up by the Forestry Commission in the 1920s. These northern slopes fall away down incredibly steep grassy flanks to the Bwlch Oerddrws and the Afon Cerist tributary of the mighty Afon Dyfi, or River Dovey, and are for the most part still used for grazing for the hardy sheep of the district.

Being composed chiefly of slates and shales, the group closely resembles parts of the Skiddaw Forest in the Lake District, although nowhere near as high.

Many walkers start their ascent onto the ridge from the car park at the top of the pass known as Bwlch Oerddrws on the A470. A good path climbs up the rocky nose of Craig y Bwlch before joining a fence over Cribin Fach to the easy final slopes of **Cribin Fawr**, 'big serrated ridge', at 2162'. This is a nice, quick way onto the ridge, but leaves the problem of returning to the car if you plan to go on to climb **Waun-oer** and **Maesglase**, the former lying to the south-west, and the latter lying to the east, with **Cribin Fawr** sat firmly in the middle of the two. Using this approach you are faced with returning back over **Cribin Fawr** after bagging **Waun-oer**, and then again after climbing **Maesglase**. This is quite feasible, it is actually what I did during my traverse of all the Welsh Hewitts (see Part Two), but there are better ways to see these hills.

South of the ridge lies a vast area of forest, planted row upon row with conifers, totally blanketing the hills and valleys. This used to be a thriving slate mining centre, based around the village of Aberllefenni. Starting from the village, which can be reached from either Corris on the Minffordd to

Machynlleth road (the A487) or from Aberangell south of Dinas Mawddwy on the A470. From Aberllefenni, striking ridges festooned with pines and spruces climb up abruptly out of the valleys, but our way lies up Cwm Ratgoed, on the west bank of the Nant Ceiswyn. Beyond the cottage of Ffynnon-badarn, a way-marked path leads up a flight of steps to gain a forestry road. Further way-markers lead up through the forest to gain the ridge of Mynydd Ceiswyn at a fence. Following this to the right will lead easily up to the summit of **Waun-oer**, 'the cold moor', at 2198'. A trig pillar and solar panel mark the highest point.

A short descent leads to a narrow col then, still beside the fence, steep slopes lead up the west ridge of **Cribin Fawr**. The summit is just beyond a stile and provides walkers with an open debate of tussocky mat-grass, each little tussock looking higher than the next. The best I can suggest is that you leave your rucksack by the stile and run head-long around the small plateau for ten minutes like a crazed thing. Not only are you bound to pass over the actual top in doing this, but you will also provide any other walkers in the vicinity with a bit of light entertainment!

At the stile another fence heads off down the broad south-east ridge towards two grass and heather knolls. This is the way on towards **Maesglase** with faint paths on both sides of the fence. As you will need to be on the northern side, it is perhaps better to start off on that side anyway. Parts of this section of the walk are rather boggy underfoot, but shouldn't provide too much of a problem. A grassy col passes by before the first little knoll, then another before the minor summit of Craig Portas. Here the path swings around the head of the cwm to the north, with sweeping views down into the very depths of the valley head. Across the cwm rise the towering heights of the Arans. Soon the way crosses another stile near a broad heathery part of the western ridge of **Maesglase** known as Cae Afon. The fence heads dead north, but a peaty path can be seen cutting off the corner and making straight for the summit of the third Hewitt of the Dovey Forest, **Maesglase**, the 'blue meadow', at 2211'. A small cairn with a few bits of wood sticking up out of its centre marks the highest point, beside the fence. Beyond, the rough scree and broken rocks of Maen Du fall away shear to the valley.

From **Maesglase** the quickest return to the car at Aberllefenni is to retrace your steps back over Craig Portas to the second little knoll, then head south-westwards along the narrow ridge of Mynydd Dolgoed and down steeply to the head of Cwm Ratgoed.

Other approaches to these hills are possible, and being well off the beaten track are worth exploring in their own rights. The Mynydd Ceiswyn

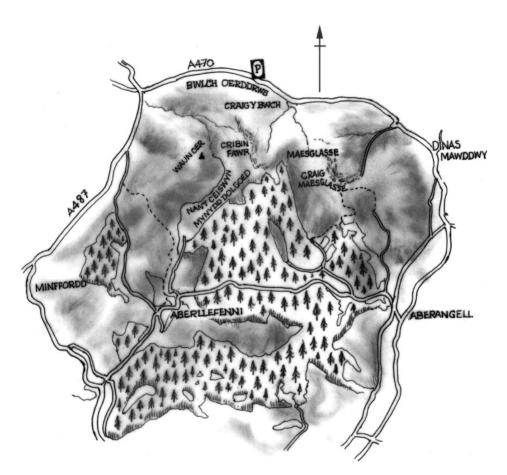

ridge of **Waun-oer** described above can also be gained from Waunllefenni, the head of a minor cwm leading westwards from Aberllefenni. This is an even quieter way onto the tops. Likewise an ascent to the col between Craig Portas and **Maesglase** can be made from the darkly wooded cwm of Nant Maes y Gamfa via the old quarries of Coed Mawr, although the last time I visited there was a lot of tree felling in operation, and it is likely that walkers will be discouraged whilst this continues.

The only other popular way of bagging the Dovey Hills is to climb up the Ffridd Gulcwm slopes of **Maesglase** to the Bwlch Siglen, direct through the woods above Dinas Mawddwy. This is the route taken by the Cambrian Way, a 265 mile, long distance footpath from Cardiff to Conwy. The last part of the ascent, after passing Bwlch Siglen is spectacular, hand-railing as it does around the edge of the cliffs of Craig Maesglase.

The Dovey Forest itself offers many good low-level walks, although it is beyond the scope of this book, concerned as it is chiefly with the Welsh Hewitts, to detail anything in particular. Better perhaps that you go and discover the area for yourself. One particular hill of note is little Mynydd Cwmcelli at 469'. It lies just south of the forest through-road from Aberllefenni to Aberangell, and for those ticking Marilyns (hills of any height with an all-round drop of at least 150 metres) as well as Hewitts, it is on your list!

For the lover of ornithology, these forests will already be known as one of the few likely spots where siskins breed in this country. Until the 1940s the siskin was not known to breed in Britain outside Scotland or Ireland. Breeding pairs now thrive in the Betws-y-Coed forests and occasional pairs have been recorded in the Coed-y-Brenin and also the Dovey Forests. There is also a likelihood that you might see crossbills hereabouts.

THE TARRENS

Contained within a rough triangle with the A487 as a boundary to the east, the estuary of the Afon Dyfi or River Dovey to the south and the B4405 to the north-west, the Tarrens are formed as a compact group of hills, chiefly of shales and mudstones, throwing up just two summits above the magical height of 2000'. There are a number of other, lesser tops within the area, but these are of little interest to the walker, indeed man's intrusion upon the range has meant that only dedicated Hewitt or Nuttall baggers frequent the range at all. In fact, if any hills in Wales can truly be said to have been exploited to the point of being almost re-landscaped by man, then the Tarrens fit that description nicely.

In the last century the village of Abergynolwyn to the west of the Tarrens was a thriving slate mining centre. Back in 1864 William Maconnell bought the by then already working Bryn-Eglwys quarry, or 'church hill quarry', south-east of the village and high up in the corrie between the two principal summits of these grassy hills. Maconnell mechanised the workings, built more houses in Abergynolwyn for his employees, and in 1866 constructed the Talyllyn railway to transport the quarried slate to the coast at Tywyn. This railway also served the local community as a means of transport, offering a regular passenger service. The quarry thrived for almost 100 years, before grinding to a halt in 1948. Almost immediately, the Forestry Commission bought the surrounding land, soon planting it up with regimental rows of young conifers which in time would be turned into chipboard, paper pulp and fencing materials. This land of the Tarrens is now only a small corner of what has become the Dyfi Forest, stretching as it does for many miles beyond Corris and the A487 to the east, eventually finding its boundary near Dinas Mawddwy and the A470.

Walkers in the Tarrens (it's best to avoid using the common phrase 'Tarren Hills' as the word 'Tarren' itself actually means 'hill' or 'knoll') are fairly few and far between, although the village of Abergynolwyn becomes busy in summer due to the Talyllyn Narrow Gauge Railway which continues to ply its trade, ferrying cargoes of tourists to and from Tywyn. Both of the two Tarrens that are Hewitts, **Tarren y Gesail**, or 'knoll of the hollow', at 2188' and **Tarrenhendre**, 'knoll of the winter dwelling', at 2080', can be ascended quite easily from Abergynolwyn by taking the track on the northern bank of the Nant Gwernol river. The railway terminates at Gwernol Station just a short way up the valley, and a new footbridge provides access to the station and the way onwards and upwards on the opposite, southern side of the river. A path continues to an old winding house before gaining the line of the disused railway beyond. Forest tracks slowly lead the walker uphill, running parallel to the stream of Nant Moelfre. The tracks continue zigzagging to eventually reach a break in the trees where the summit cliffs of **Tarrenhendre** can be seen above. An easy gully leads up to the right of the cliffs to gain the summit after following a fence for a short distance.

There is a connecting ridge to **Tarren y Gesail** to the north-east which heads first for the subsidiary top of Foel y Geifr, the 'bare hill of the goats'. Again, dark forested slopes need to be negotiated before the summit of this, the second Hewitt of the day is reached. Near the summit is an O.S. trig point—the summit, some 50 metres to the east, is one metre higher. The valley can be reached directly from here by aiming south-west for the site of the Bryn-Eglwys quarry and following the main track down.

The two Tarrens can also be ascended from the Machynlleth area in the south. Many different tracks leave the forest around Machynlleth, Pennal and Cwrt to gain the higher tops through the trees, but perhaps the best way is to take the minor road west of the hamlet of Cwrt and, after about a mile, take to the public byway on the right. Following this for about 1½ miles, another track branches off to the right and makes for the main ridge via the rough, moorland grasses on the minor tops of Trum Gelli, Tarren Cwm-ffernol and Mynydd Esgairweddan. The summit of **Tarrenhendre** lies just north of the ridge of this latter top. This way onto the ridge is wonderful for the views looking back down the Dovey Valley during the ascent, and the sudden panorama of the mountains of **Cadair Idris** as one gains the ridge.

An ancient pilgrims' path is said to cross the ridge at the col between the two Hewitts to connect the township of Machynlleth with Cadfan's Church at Tywyn. There is a strong possibility that pilgrims then travelled on by sea to the religious settlements on the holy island of Bardsey, as that is also known to have been founded by Cadfan in the sixth century. Cadfan's Church at Tywyn was well known even up until the Middle Ages.

For the most part the type of wildlife living in these forests is limited by the specialised habitat that is found there. In most areas the tree cover is so dense that the undergrowth has been shaded out, and only alongside the

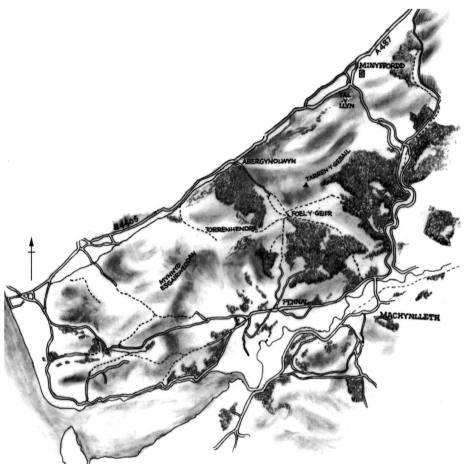

tracks or rides is found a more variable vegetative ground cover. The high-pitched notes of the coal tit and the goldcrest can often be heard along these corridors, though it takes a positive sighting by even the most experienced ornithologist to tell which bird is making the noise, the two songs being so alike. Siskins may also be found in the forests of the Tarrens, although it is not known if they have been recorded as a breeding species, and crossbills are a fairly common sight. In the older, darker corners of the forest there is always a good chance that the long-eared owl will have taken up residence, and if the overhead canopy is not too dense, dusk often see the woodcock, that shy, well camouflaged wader, 'roding' down a grassy ride. This is the term given to the strong, powerful and direct flight undertaken by this territorial bird.

Where the shelter belt is of mixed trees, or where a few broad-leaved, deciduous specimens have been left to encourage a more diverse ecology,

131

squirrels will often be present, though many see these as more of a natural nuisance than a species to be encouraged. Squirrels are notorious for stealing the eggs of birds, and make no bones about whether the species providing then with a meal is a rarity or not.

Above the tree line, the bird life is less diverse still, though on my last visit to Tarren y Gesail I spied a short-eared owl quartering the ground to the south of the summit. This is the only diurnal owl in Britain, and so is easy to identify, even at a distance.

And so, even if the Tarrens offer little to the serious hillwalker, it call be seen that the dank forests around their slopes do provide something of interest to the lover of natural history, even if only of those species which favour this type of environment. Personally, I enjoy a wander through these forests almost as much as a day on the open heights of the nearby Cadair Idris group, and certainly prefer the comfort of their shelter on wild days to being continuously swept off my feet on those higher, wind-blasted tops.

A magnet for the tourist in the Dyfi Forest is the Centre for Alternative Technology on the A487 just north of Machynlleth. The centre aims to promote a deeper understanding of the environment and a more thorough knowledge of what can be done to improve the way we live by relying more on natural resources such as solar, wind and wave power. But that is not all that this centre is about. Even down to studying the most effective ways to make your own garden compost, or building your own energy efficient house, the staff at the centre seem to have an answer for every question relating to the issues which threaten our planet.

PLYNLIMON

In his book *Coming Down The Wye*, Robert Gibbings begins with the simple words, 'Plynlimon is the kind of mountain I like. It is neither too high nor too steep, and there are few precipices. In fact, you can't break your neck without an effort. It is a friendly hill.' When I first read that, I couldn't help but agree with him, Plynlimon is a friendly hill, and as a range has been softened and mellowed even further by the vast cloaks of conifers which cover its shoulders. But do not be misled, in times of bad weather, the five hills of Plynlimon (the Welsh spelling for these hills is Pumlumon, pronounced 'Pimlimmon', which means 'five summits') can be as harsh as any other untamed mountain group in Britain.

Of course, not all of these 'five summits' are Hewitts (indeed it is not clear which five summits the name refers to), but as they are a compact group, it is not unreasonable to bag a number of lesser heights on a round of the four main tops.

The range is bounded to the south by the A44 from Rhayader to Aberystwyth, to the west by the Afon Rheidol and Nant-y-moch Reservoir, to the east by the dense forestry plantations of the Hafren Forest above the small community of Staylittle, and to the north, by mile after mile of open moorland and more forestry, before falling in deep secretive cwms to the Dyffryn Dyfi (Dovey Valley) at Machynlleth. Immediately to the north of the main ridge, the Afon Hengwm effectively separates the range from this wild landscape of conifers and heather.

The old county of Cardiganshire claimed Plynlimon as its highest mountain, but as such, the range as a whole is more like a stray bit of Snowdonia, for geologically, it has formed as a plug of typical North Wales Ordovician rock amid a blanket of Silurian slates and shales which cover much of the rest of mid-Wales. Lead mining was one of the chief providers of employment in the area, before the coming of the forests.

It is also an important range as far as its streams are concerned. Gibbings wrote 'from the sheltered slope on which I sat I could watch the silver line of the Wye winding towards the old lead mine above Pant Mawr. A mile to the west the Severn started on its course. Behind me the Rheidol had its source in the flanks of the same great hill.' And although he may have got a few of his facts muddled, the source of the Severn rising to the east of the Wye, not the west, and nearer to two miles than one, Gibbings is right—great the range certainly is.

The Afon Rheidol is believed to have derived its name from the Welsh word rhedeg, meaning to run, and if so would make the Rheidol, 'the fast stream'. This is of course entirely appropriate for a river that rushes to the sea only 16 miles from its source, whereas the Severn, rising only two miles north-east of the Rheidol, ambles for over 200 miles before joining the sea. The River Wye meanders its course through the most beautiful parts of mid and South Wales before finally joining the Severn at Chepstow. That these two rivers run very different courses through Wales and England from a source only two miles apart on the same mountain mass, and finish up flowing out to sea together, really is remarkable. George Borrow visited the sources of these great rivers on his tour of 'Wild Wales', and 'took possession' of them, as he himself put it, by taking a drink. Rather him than me!

And so, what of the four Hewitts of the Plynlimon range? A single, isolated hill known as **Y Garn**, 'the cairn', at 2244', marks the western extremes of the higher hills, and rises up gently from the shores of the Nant-y-moch Reservoir. Nant-y-moch is Welsh for 'stream of the pigs', perhaps indicating that this was once a habitat of wild boar. The stream rises at the col between **Y Garn** and **Plynlimon** and forms a broad cwm to the north of the former. It is likely that this is the only Hewitt of the range that is frequently climbed as a single hill in a short day out. Apart from a direct assault from the reservoir beside Nant-y-moch, it can also be climbed from Dyffryn Castell, an old inn on the A44, or from near Hirnant on the minor road alongside the Afon Rheidol, to the west of the Dyll Faen Forest.

The other three, **Plynlimon**, **Plynlimon East Top** (or Pen Pumlumon Llygad-bychan as the Nuttalls have named it), and **Pen Pumlumon Arwystli** are closer together to the north-east, and as such are more often than not climbed in the same trip. All four can of course, be linked easily together, and this is how they are usually done.

A lay-by at the top of the road pass at Eisteddfa Gurig on the A44 provides a good starting point. In *Climbing in the British Isles*, Haskett Smith records that 'an amusing notice used to be seen at Steddfa Gurig [then an inn] ... "The notorious hill Plinlimon is on the premises"'. From here a track leads uphill westwards to the north of the little knoll of Foel Wyddon. Ahead is the Dyll Faen Forest and a path follows the edge of this around to the north. After a while a good track swings away towards the top of

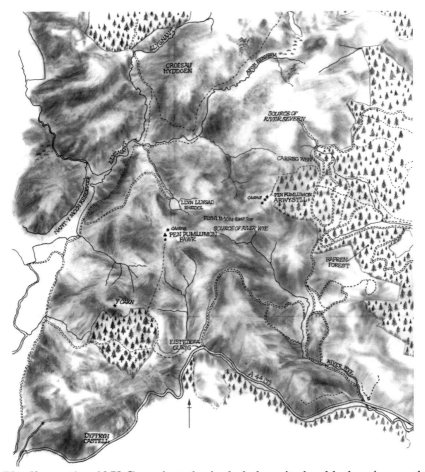

Plynlimon, but if **Y Garn** is to be included, as it should, then ignore this and continue over grass to cross a fence at a corner. Staying beside the forest all the way, a fence leads to the top of this, the first Hewitt of the range, with its ancient cairn and wide views of the Nant-y-moch Reservoir below. On these grassy flanks, Owain Glyndwr raised his standard after defeating the English in a bloodthirsty battle in the reign of King Henry IV. Returning to the fence at the corner, it is possible to either continue beside this along the ridge, above the wastes of Cwm Nant-y-moch, or to head off slightly to the right to pick up the good track seen earlier. This latter passes twin tarns just above the half way point, and easy grass slopes lead on, to the top of **Plynlimon** at 2467'. On good days the view from these higher tops is extensive, stretching way over to Snowdonia in the north, and southwards, beyond the empty land of the Cwmdeuddwr Hills, to the Brecon Beacons and Black Mountains of South Wales.

What once the Druids told, how great those floods should bee
That here (most mightie hill) derive themselves from thee.
The Bards with furie rapt, the British youth among,
Unto the charming harpe thy future honor song
In brave and loftie straines; that in excesse of joy,
The bedlam and the girle, the grandsire and the boy,
With shouts and yearning, cries, the troubled ayre did load
(As when with crowned cuppes unto the Elian God
Those priests his orgyes held; or when the old world saw
Full Phoebes face eclipst, and thinking, her to daw
Whom they supposed falne in some inchanted swound,
Of beaten tinkling brasse still ply'd her with the sound)
That all the Cambrian hills, which high'st their heads doe beare
With most obsequious showes of lowe subjected feare,
Should to thy greatness stoupe: and all the brooks that be,
Doe homage to those floods that issued out of thee:
To princelie Severne first; next, to her sister Wye,
Which to her elders court her course doth still apply,
But Rydoll, young'st, and least, and for the others pride
Not finding fitting roomth upon the rising side,
Alone unto the west directlie takes her way.
So all the neighbouring hills Plynillimon obey.

From 'Poly-Olbion' by Michael Drayton, 1622

The summit is crossed by the fence from **Y Garn** which sticks closely to the ridge, and is decorated with a number of wind shelters, two ancient cairns and a trig pillar.

From **Plynlimon**'s main summit, a track heads off towards the top of the broken cliffs above Llyn Llygad Rheidol. A path leads down to a col to the east, then continues beside the fence to a cairn at the top of **Plynlimon East Top**, at 2385'.

All around, the terrain is predominantly mat-grass and bilberry, though much of the land on these flat-topped mountains is boggy.

The last Hewitt on the round is **Pen Pumlumon Arwystli** at 2431', which lies along the watershed to the east, beyond the source of the River Wye. This is just over a hundred feet down the slope to the south and can be visited by those wishing to 'take possession of' the Wye. The way over to **Pen Pumlumon Arwystli** is again fairly easy going, although the terrain around these summits can be confusing in mist. On my Welsh Hewitt Traverse, I had a job on navigating precisely to each summit, as although the terrain looks well defined on the map, in actual fact it is pretty featureless in poor visibility. The summit of **Pen Pumlumon Arwystli** is marked by two large, bronze age cairns, each one hollowed out in the search for archaeological remains. Of the many ancient cairns in this area, it is believed that the only two that haven't suffered this fate are those on Carn Biga to the north-east. Those nearby at Carn Fawr and Carnfachbugeilyn, 'the little cairn above the shepherd's lake', have been excavated.

Just beyond **Pen Pumlumon Arwystli**'s summit, a forest covers the whole of the huge tract of land to the east. This is the Hafren Forest, Afon Hafren being the Welsh word for the River Severn, and was planted up in the 1930s by the Forestry Commission to provide wood for paper pulp, fence posts and chipboard. You can follow the edge of the forest for a short distance before picking up a track down through the trees southwards to the Nant-lago lead mines, and then over the ridge of Cripiau Eisteddfa-fach and back to the car. However, you may wish to follow the fence around to the north which crosses great moss-bogs to the source of the River Severn. The whole area is just one oozing marsh of peat and cotton-grass, and it can be a real problem deciding exactly which sodden spot is the true source of the mighty river.

Deep in the Hafren Forest is a picnic spot beside the River Severn, with a toilet block and forest walks in the area. A path can be followed from here, up beside the stream to the open hillside at the edge of the forest, just to the north-east of **Pen Pumlumon Arwystli**'s summit at Carreg Wen, 'white rock', and gives a useful short approach to the three main hills of the range.

The Afon Hengwm to the north of the range has a good path along its banks, and if used from a car parked at Nant-y-moch, can give access from the north up any one of the four ridges which fall from the main ridge to this fast-flowing stream. Further approaches from the northern side are impractical unless you are set for a very long day. A camp site at Rhiwgam above the Afon Dulas, south-east of Machynlleth, can ease this problem, but still gives a long trudge through deep heather just to reach the Afon Hengwm, which must then be forded prior to an ascent. Similarly, the car park at the Glaslyn Nature Reserve at the head of the Afon Dulas brings the walker from the north slightly closer to these hills via Bugeilyn and the head of the Afon Hengwm.

All in all, this is a marvellous range for those who love to explore, and indeed one of its chief attractions is the many smaller hills which abound in the area. I have always found the Plynlimon range to be very quiet, but these smaller hills, such as Drosgol or Disgwylfa, both of which are listed as Welsh Marilyns (hills of any height with an all round drop of at least 150 metres), above the Nant-y-moch Reservoir are incredibly peaceful. As is the intention with much of this book, the main aim is to encourage walkers to discover these places for themselves, and so no further details of routes across this grassy wilderness are thought appropriate. Go and find them for yourselves, and the reward will be that much greater.

THE CWMDEUDDWR HILLS

Quite simply, there is nothing in Wales to compare to the wildness and sense of utter solitude that surrounds these vast empty moorlands. The atmosphere is unique, and though not really rugged in any way, these lonely Hewitts, three in all, encompass all that is beautiful and spacious of our desolate lesser heights. This is wilderness, but not in the sense of being untamed by man, for dense forests cloak many hillsides, and valleys have been dammed to form large open stretches of reservoir water, but it is wilderness nevertheless. It is no coincidence that when the red kite was widely believed to be extinct in Britain at the turn of the century, the last few pairs where discovered clinging to a tenuous existence in the lonely cwms of the upper Afon Tywi. Likewise the pine marten. It is not known if this species of mammal has been totally wiped out in Britain, but many believe that there may still be some small family groups, surviving in the ample forestry cover of these moorlands of mid-Wales, far away from the eyes of the general public.

It is hard to define boundaries to such a huge area of wild land, as endless empty tracts continue from horizon to horizon, but generally, the three Hewitts of the area should be taken as two very separate ranges. Nestling in the forests to the south of the A44 and Plynlimon, a solitary hill just manages to clear the tops of the trees. South of here, the moorland ridges of Cwmystwyth form a border. This hill is **Pen y Garn**. It has its feet in the Afon Mynach, which tumbles down the impressive falls at the well-known tourist spot, Devil's Bridge, three miles to the west.

Pen y Garn, 'top of the cairn', at just 2001' has few hillwalking devotees. Its summit has been taken over by students of botany and meteorology, and it is likely that if you meet anyone else at its top, they will be students of one persuasion or another. This is a shame as there are one or two good ways of attaining that mediocre height.

The B4574 runs south-westwards from Devil's Bridge to Cwmystwyth and at about the halfway point between the two, reaches a low col, deep in the conifers of the Forestry Commission property. The Arch, built in 1810 by Thomas Johnes of Hafod Uchdryd to commemorate the fiftieth year of King

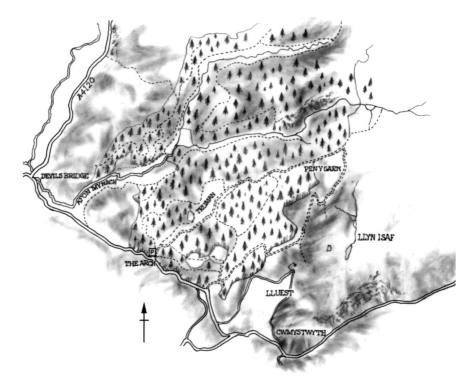

George III's reign, spans this old turnpike road, and passing beneath it, a car park can be found in the trees on the left. The turnpike once took stage coaches from London to Aberystwyth, in the days of more romantic travel.

A forestry track leaves the car park and climbs steadily uphill, around the eastern flank of Truman. Over the last couple of years the trees around Rhos Peiran to the right have been cleared, and the land has now been replanted with young spruce and pine. Once this part of the forest has been gained the summit of **Pen y Garn** can be seen, barely rising above the trees to the east. Higher still a viewing platform gives wonderful vistas of the afforested slopes of the low hills immediately to the north, across the Nant Rhuddnant, a tributary of the Afon Mynach. A bench to the right of the track gives a good enough spot to enjoy this peaceful corner of the country.

Just a short way beyond the bench, the track leaves the forest, and soon a gateway on the right gives access to the top of **Pen y Garn**. A number of stiles have to be climbed as small enclosures have been made with fencing to mark out areas of study on the hillside, then the summit trig pillar and cairn is reached. To the north, the views take in the semi-rugged ridges of Plynlimon, while to the south, miles and miles of emptiness, a bleak though intensely beautiful desolation, formed by a vast plateau-land of tussock grass and barren peat bog, fills everything to the furthest horizon.

Over a fence from the summit a track leads south onto the Banc Myheryn ridge, and soon takes the walker down to the village of Cwmystwyth. A lot of the hillsides around here have been mined for lead from as far back as the seventeenth century, but now little remains of what was a prosperous industry. By 1885, British lead was far too expensive to mine when compared to that available on foreign markets, and business throughout the country collapsed.

A few hundred yards above the point where this track becomes a tarmac road, just above the cottages of Lluest, the track swings back into the forest and leads back to The Arch.

It is possible to follow a public by-way along the true left bank of the Afon Mynach, and this gives a good approach to the forest from where a track leads uphill to join the one described above near the ridge of Truman. The problem here seems to be that there is a good landrover track along the banks of the stream that bends into every little contour of the hillside. The by-way marked on the map doesn't always follow this track exactly, preferring to go more or less dead straight. Although this track follows much rough ground, the landowner has erected signs warning walkers that they must stay on the right of way. This does seem ludicrous when you see the good track, often within ten or twenty yards to the right, but in cases such as this, it is better to adhere to the landowner's warning. Once the trees have been gained, you are pretty much free to wander where you like.

South again from Cwmystwyth, empty hills of tussock grass eventually fall away to the false beauty of the Claerwen Reservoir, and the much flooded Elan Valley. Beyond the Elan Valley, heading even further south, more tussock grass ridges rise up, forming two hills of just over two thousand feet, before dropping to the peaceful tranquillity of the River Irfon and the A483. These two hills, **Gorllwyn** and **Drygarn Fawr** have as their natural boundaries, the River Wye to the east and the upper streams of the infant Afon Tywi to the west.

I believe that this wonderful corner of Wales deserves a whole book of exploration to itself, the deep valleys, forests, tarn speckled moorlands and minor hills are all worthy of the walker's attention, but as this book is chiefly concerned with the Welsh Hewitts and the discovery of their immediate environs, it must be left to the individual to discover those areas away from the main hills. Besides, I would not claim to know the area well enough to write authoritatively on these windswept, unfrequented moorlands, away from the two hills above 2000'.

An engraving of Devil's Bridge

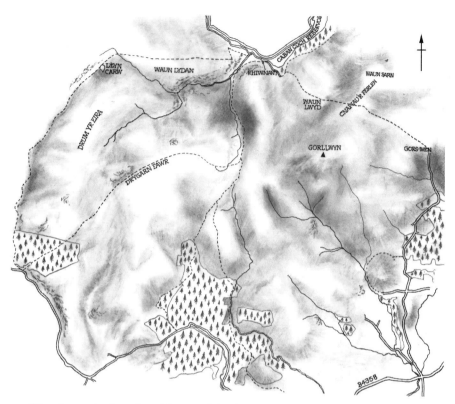

Thanks to the local residents of the last century, we today have the right to wander at will anywhere within the water catchment area of the Elan Valley. In 1892 the population of these secluded valleys fought for the right of unrestricted access upon the building of the first reservoirs in the region. An act was passed in parliament giving the freedom of these lovely hills to anyone with the wish to enjoy 'air, exercise and recreation'. This of course, applies only to unenclosed land, of which there is no shortage in these hills. In 1984 the National Trust made the announcement that they had purchased 16,500 acres of land in the Abergwesyn Common, to the south of the Elan Estate. The purchase was made with grants from the Countryside Commission and the National Heritage Memorial Fund. This, alongside the neighbouring estate of the Elan Valley, ensures that this freedom to roam now covers a huge acreage of wonderful upland walking country.

To get an indication of what was lost to the reservoirs in the Elan Valley we must again turn to that great little book *Climbing in the British Isles* by W.P. Haskett Smith. Under the paragraph for Cwm Elan, he wrote that it 'is a very pretty spot, and the gorge of Cefn Coch is exceedingly striking.

Mackintosh says that the height is not less than 800 ft. and the cliffs are in many parts mural and quite perpendicular. He declared that, while the cliffs on the left-hand side of the river are very fine, he had seen nothing to surpass those on the right. This from a hill traveller of his experience is remarkably high praise ... The Birmingham reservoir is to submerge several miles of this cwm and the two houses in which Shelley stayed.' This just makes me pine for the Elan Valley of old, although there can be no denying that it is still a very pretty spot today.

The region was favoured by Bronze Age man as the hundreds of cairns, standing stones, stone and cairn alignments and tumuli which dot the hillsides prove. These sites of antiquity are far too numerous to name here, but one of particular note is that of Carn Gafallt, a small hill to the immediate south-east of Elan Village. Four Bronze Age gold torcs have been found on this hill and are now on display in the National Museum of Wales.

Drygarn Fawr at 2103', is the highest of these two Hewitts, and is perhaps the most popular, if such a term can be used for the ultimate in quiet hillwalking country. The name is said to come from the Welsh for 'three big cairns', although the exact position of the third is a mystery.

Most Hewitt-baggers make their ascent from the north, usually from the western end of the Caban-coch Reservoir, and take in **Gorllwyn** while they are at it. The Caban-coch Reservoir, like the other four in the valley, provides Birmingham with water, feeding that city by a 73 mile-long pipeline. Gravity alone forces the water through this, and a drop of 170 feet is needed for the water to make the journey.

A public bridleway climbs up alongside the slowly gurgling waters of the Nant Paradwys. The way splits at the col of Bwlch y Ddau Faen, but as is often the case in these parts, the track to the right, traversing just below the summit of **Drygarn Fawr** to its south, is not evident on the ground. For many of these public paths marked on the map in mid-Wales, it is usually a case of using your own judgement and just wandering at will. Once above the bogs of Bryn Rhudd, a bit of a path can be picked up, leading directly to the first of the two cairns on **Drygarn Fawr**'s summit ridge. These huge structures were built by Bronze Age man between 2000 and 1500 BC, but have been rebuilt a number of times since. This first cairn is noticeably lower than the one further west which marks the actual top. Twenty yards west again, an O.S. trig pillar stands amid bilberry and hardy grasses.

A number of other ways to the top are open to the walker. It is possible to climb westwards from the hamlet of Rhiwnant on the Caban-coch

Reservoir, onto the rough ridge of Waun Lydan. A broad ridge sweeps round the headwaters of the stream known as Rhiwnant, passing lonely Llyn Carw, Cerrig Llwyd y Rhestr and the tussock grass ridge of Drum yr Eira before the short climb to the trig pillar from the north-west.

The map shows public bridleways climbing up from the River Irfon to the south-west, and although I find this approach delightful, again the paths underfoot do not always bare close resemblance to those marked on the map. I would recommend following the ridge to the east of the Afon Gwesyn, passing the trig pillar on Pen Carreg-dan *en route*.

On my Welsh Hewitt traverse of 1998 I climbed **Drygarn Fawr** from the east, via **Gorllwyn**, and descended into the forests around the upper Afon Tywi to the west. An ascent from the west is a possibility, but a long forested ridge, almost 2000' high, running north-south between the Tywi and Irfon streams must be crossed before you even set foot on the lower slopes of **Drygarn Fawr**. There is a wonderful bothy deep within the forests to the west, but as is the policy of the Mountain Bothy Association who maintain these open buildings for the use of all who enjoy the countryside, the exact location of this bothy must remain unpublished. If the MBA were to start publishing these details, bothies throughout the country would be over-run with litter-louts and maintaining the properties would become impossible. For those who have not come across bothies in the countryside before, I will explain. Many disused buildings in the wilder places of the country are no longer used by the landowners for their original purpose, be it as a shooting lodge, forester's hut, coastal shieling or whatever. Under consultation with the landowner, the MBA take over the maintenance of the building, with the proviso that it will be kept clean and tidy and litter-free. The MBA do this voluntarily, and rely on membership subscriptions to undertake this work. The bothies are open and free for all to use, and often have sleeping benches and a fire place. The location of these bothies is either passed on by word of mouth, or as should be the case, is discovered by the walker during a thorough exploration of an area. Although most of the bothies in Britain are in the Highlands and uninhabited coastal regions of Scotland, there are also quite a number in Northern England and Wales. I have given the address of the MBA in Appendix 5 for those who may be interested in becoming a member of the association.

Running east from Rhiwnant, a public bridleway skirts the edge of the reservoir before climbing up the grassy slopes of Waun Lwyd to the broad, peaty col of Cnapiau'r Ferlen. It was here in 1998 that I first saw a red kite wheeling in majestic arcs above the tiny cotton-grass tarn to the west. A series of boundary stones lead south-west over low-growing bilberry to the cairns and trig pillar at the summit of **Gorllwyn**, 'above the grove', at 2011'.

Cnapiau'r Ferlen can also by gained from the south by following the minor road along the valley of the Afon Chwerfri from just east of Llanafan-fawr on the B4358. A bridleway leaves the road near its end at Gors-wen, and though hard to follow, basically runs along the south side of the stream until high up in the cwm. Cross the stream and gain brackeny slopes which lead steeply up to the col.

From the summit of **Gorllwyn**, a vague path leads off down the western ridge and is again marked by boundary stones. This soon has the boggy depression of the Bwlch y Ddau Faen underfoot at the head of Nant Paradwys, and the ascent of **Drygarn Fawr** can be started as described above.

Since my first visit here in 1998, I have returned for a number of weekend visits, each time taking in different aspects of the hills and moorlands of the area. Although I have become very familiar with the three Hewitts described here, the most wonderful thing about the district is that there is still much for me to discover. These Cwmdeuddwr Hills offer a lifetime of exploration for those with the will to struggle through the desolate bogs and dense forests. For those who do, the rewards are great indeed.

RADNOR FOREST

The high hills of Radnorshire, forgetting for the time being the term 'forest', rise as a great dome of Silurian rock in the form of shales and flagstones, forming for the most part a characteristic upland scene of gently undulating moorland of grass and heather, totally isolated from the other hill ranges of Central Wales. They are bounded at a distance to the north and east by the River Lugg, once the Llugwy, to the west by the river Aran, a tributary of the Ithon, and to the south by the Summergill Brook, a tributary, via the Hindwell Brook, of the Lugg. These heights are chiefly of interest to the walker, offering no extensive rock outcrops to entice the climber.

The three principal summits of the range, each one above 2000' and all Hewitts, are clustered in a compact group to the north of New Radnor on the A44, and for the most part are usually ascended from that ancient town—its name belies its age—now a very quiet village, its rights to township lapsing long ago. A minor road runs north from New Radnor alongside Mutton Dingle, from where a public bridleway takes the walker around the western slopes of Knowle Hill to a small col at the edge of the forest.

The large castle mound that still dominates New Radnor, has a notably see-saw history. Probably begun in 1070 the castle had a relatively quiet initial century, until captured by the Welsh under Rhys ap Gruffyd in 1182. Its troubles then began. The Marchers appear to have retaken it in 1095, only to lose it to the Welsh once more the following year. It was re-occupied, probably by King John, in 1208, lost to rebel Marches in 1215 and recaptured by John in 1216. Rebuilt by loyal Marchers, it was lost to the Welsh under Llywelyn ab Iorweth in 1231. Retaken and rebuilt by royal forces, it was again lost to the Welsh, this time under Llywelyn ap Gruffydd in 1264, but regained the following year. It also saw service during the wars with Owain Glyndwr in the early 1400s, and stories persist of a massacre of its garrison after the fateful nearby Battle of Pilleth where many Marcher gentry were killed or captured.

Although originally the name 'forest' in this area, like on so many of the large Highland estates of Scotland, referred to an ancient hunting ground, in this particular case much of the high land in these hills has been planted up with regimental rows of conifers, mainly spruces, larch and pine, by the Forestry Commission and so is once again 'forest', now in the modern sense of the word.

An old mill pond, now a muddy hollow and overgrown with willows, marks the point where the footpath begins its climb uphill through the trees, soon gaining a wide forestry access track. A little above this, where this track emerges from the forest, a large metal barn stands in the corner of an enclosure, and the track continues as a grassy track, turning left at a fork. This leads over a heathery col with a fence to the east. A stile here gives easy access to a path leading over another stile to the summit of **Bache Hill** or Small Hill, at 2001 feet high, only just making it into the ranks of Welsh Hewitts. An O.S. trig pillar stands atop an ancient tumulus and marks the highest point.

Away to the north-west lies **Black Mixen**, named after the Old English term for a dunghill, the next Hewitt on the round. Back at the col the track heads down to a corner of the forests which adorn the northern flanks of the range. In the forest a track heads uphill, and after half a mile, another track leads out onto the open moor at a gate. A short easy track leads towards a radio mast, and the actual summit lies in the boggy heather to the left. Again this is marked by a trig pillar.

The last of the three Hewitts of Radnor is the great hulking dome of **Great Rhos** or Great Moor, the highest hill of the group. Across Harley Dingle to the west it rises almost imperceptibly above the surrounding moorland as a long whale-back, but to reach its top, you must first head north-west to a low, muddy pool, the Shepherd's Well, source of the Harley Dingle itself.

The deep valley of the dingle is used as a rifle range by the M.o.D., hence the long detour round, although in actual fact taking in the Shepherd's Well on this walk involves nothing more than following the natural lie of the land. To go direct down the dingle and up the other side would provide much harder walking, regardless of the fact that you might get shot whilst doing so!

A path leads over to the Shepherd's Well from **Black Mixen**, and again you gain the edge of the forest. A faint path can be seen alongside the boundary, and you should follow this round to the left. A long straight section, heading westwards is soon reached, and within a quarter of a mile along here, a public bridleway climbs up out of the forest and makes for the broad north ridge of **Great Rhos**. There are paths and tracks heading out towards the top, but these can often be confusing in poor visibility so a simple compass bearing can be followed to gain the trig pillar of **Great Rhos**.

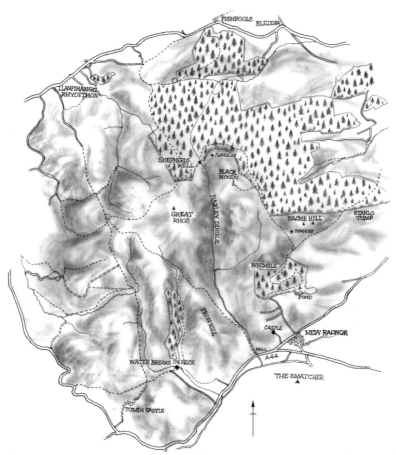

The normal descent from **Great Rhos** for those starting at New Radnor, heads off south towards the col before the long ridge of Fron Hill. A public bridleway leads down to the south-east into Harley Dingle, then contours round the southern slopes of Whimble back to New Radnor.

Another popular way of ascending **Great Rhos**, if popular is not too grand a term for these seldom visited hills, is to leave the A44 at a point about a mile west of the Old Town Wall of New Radnor, and follow a good track to the tumultuous falls of Water-break-its-neck. A rather enthusiastic nineteenth century guide used to write of this waterfall, 'a small stream drops seventy feet into a rugged and gloomy dell amidst the wildest alpine scenery.' A bit fanciful, I admit, especially since the falls are all too often dry in summer these days, but nevertheless, they are still worthy of your attention. A path above the falls climbs up over the ridge of Esgairnantau through newly planted conifers and on to the open hillside above the dry bed

A view towards Radnor Forest with Old Radnor Church in the centre.
The Whimble is the prominently shaped hill on the right.
From an engraving of c.1840

of Davy Morgan's Dingle. Much of this area suffered from the great moorland fires of 1976, and long bulldozed tracks can still be seen on the ground
which were made during the battle to put it out. Just above this point the
path becomes faint and bends around to the east to eventually pick up the
one along the south ridge above Harley Dingle.

The range can also be accessed from the north at Fishpools or Bleddfa,
although this involves much more woodland walking then routes from the
south. Forestry tracks lead up Cwm y Gerwyn towards the Shepherd's Well,
and there is also an old by-way from Llanfihangel Rhydithon in the north
that leads over the western flanks of **Great Rhos** to Tomen Castle near
Llanfihangel-Nant-Melan in the south which can be followed by the diligent
today. This by-way can be reached at the half way point from the west at
Llanevan via a bridleway alongside the Mithil Brook and gives partial views
of a narrow gorge at its top. This was the spot I used for a camp site after
traversing the Radnor Forest from a morning start at Hay-on-Wye, although
the area does not lend itself well to this practise. Cascob and Kinnerton
villages, both east of the range, give good access points for **Bache Hill** and
Black Mixen, the former via the long ridge of Stanlo Tump, the latter up the
heavily forested Cwm Mawr.

MYNYDD DU

There are two ranges of hills in the Brecon Beacons National Park of South Wales going under the name of the Black Mountains. This has caused much confusion among visitors, as the two groups are separated by the mountainous and moorland country of the Fforest Fawr hills and the Brecon Beacons. It has become the practise on maps and in guidebooks to refer to the eastern range, outlined later in this book, as The Black Mountains, and to give the Welsh translation to the western range. This section covers that range—the Mynydd Du.

The Hewitts of the Mynydd Du have as their boundaries the A4069 from Brynamman to Llandovery in the west and north-west, the lowland hills of the Mynydd Myddfai around the Usk Reservoir to the north, the A4067 separating it from the hills of Fforest Fawr to the east, and the busy conurbations of the Swansea area to the south.

It is a wild upland area of great beauty, and has two distinct geological regions. The rushing Afon Twrch rises beneath the highest mountains of the range, and flows out to the south-west, but three miles from its source is joined by a smaller tributary, the Twrch Fechan, which rises on the boggy col between Waun Lefrith and **Garreg Las**. West of the Twrch Fechan the underlying and outcropping rocks are predominantly Carboniferous Limestone, occasionally with caps of millstone grit, while to the east where the ground rises higher, the rocks are of the Old Red Sandstone.

Consideration is first given to the lonely limestone hills of the western half of the range. The limestone screes fall from the summit of **Garreg Lwyd** westwards to the pass at the top of the A4069, giving a very short approach to that lovely little Hewitt. West again from the road, lesser hills continue for miles towards Llandeilo and the lower reaches of the Afon Tywi. The road itself was built by a Turnpike Trust, set up in 1790, and rises to height of 1618'.

I will always have a soft spot for lowly little **Garreg Lwyd**, for it was the first hill that I climbed on my Welsh Hewitt Traverse in 1998; a squally day of mixed hail showers and sunshine. On that occasion I started from the top of the pass where a small car park often sees dozens of tourists admiring the local residents—the Welsh Mountain Ponies, of which there are hundreds in these hills. George Borrow passed by here on his tour of 'Wild Wales' on November 10th 1854, a fact that is well recorded in books about the area. He was travelling from Llandovery to Swansea and passed through the tiny village of Capel Gwynfe before crossing the pass. He tells us that the name signifies 'the chapel of the place of bliss', although interviews with a local revealed that no such chapel existed. Borrow continued up the track, passing the toll-bar at Cowslip Gate and on up to the summit of the pass. Seeing little in the dense hill fog, he recorded on his descent that 'I could just see that there was a frightful precipice on my left, so I kept to the right, hugging the side of the hill.'

From the top of this pass a short ascent over scree and bilberry soon brings the summit of **Garreg Lwyd**, 'grey rock' at 2021' underfoot. A huge ancient cairn marks the top beside a trig pillar.

Out to the east stands a grassy dome known as Foel Fraith which just fails to make it into the ranks of Hewitts by a mere 8 metres. Beyond this hill, a bridleway crosses a boggy pass from the Afon Twrch in the south to Cwm Sawdde Fechan in the north. Either of these two paths can be followed to Blaenllynfell, a small cotton-grass filled pool. A line over shake holed ground leads to the open top of Foel Fraith, then down to the col between that hill and **Garreg Lwyd**, above which easy slopes lead to the summit. Both of these give a round-about approach to that western most of the Mynydd Du Hewitts, but take the walker into some pretty wild country.

Blaenllynfell drains south down the Nant y Llyn to join the Afon Twrch, across the valley from the rocky flank of Tyle Garw. Rising northwards from the apex between these two streams is a long ridge of a hill, running south - north and giving a good walk over limestone pavements. This is **Garreg Las**. The way to the summit from Blaenllynfell is at first very rocky, with a short limestone scar to pass on its southern side. This scar is detached from the main hillside by a block-filled gorge and is quite a remarkable site. Once above the scar the way is pathless but obvious, as the steep ground to the west can be kept in sight all the way up to the twin ancient cairns of Carnau'r Gareg-las, huge mounds of stones, hollowed out in the middle, probably by seekers of Bronze Age antiquities. The northern-most cairn marks the top of **Garreg Las**, 'blue stone', at 2083'.

Garreg Las can be reached on foot from the north by heading south along the lane from the centre of the tiny village of Llanddeusant. Above Gellygron the way passes through woodland and become a public bridleway. This climbs up the broad north ridge but doesn't make for the summit. Instead it passes to the east of the hill, eventually splitting into a

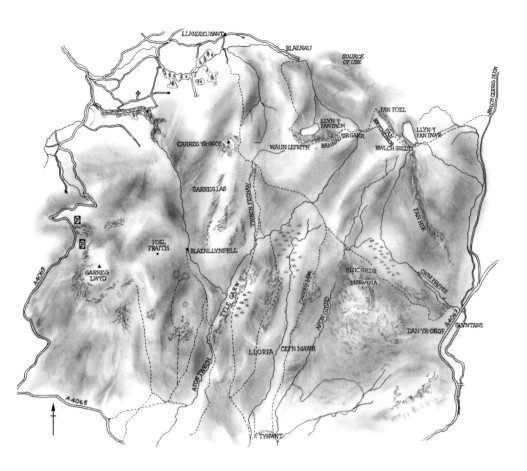

number of tracks, three heading south towards Cwmgiedd and another leading south-east to Glyntawe on the A4067. Instead of continuing along these tracks, branch off to the right and make for the bouldery top of Carreg yr Ogof with a trig pillar at its top. This little hill marks the northern end of the high ground along the ridge of **Garreg Las**, and only a shallow col separates it from the top of that higher hill.

The clustered villages and towns around Ystradgynlais on the A4067 to the south of the Mynydd Du provide a number of possible starting points for **Garreg Las**, all of which converge before passing just to the east of the summit as mentioned above. Two bridleways leave the minor road end above the Nant Gwys at Tyhwnt. For the most part they are hard to follow, but can be if a diligent approach is taken. One crosses the stream immediately and follows a good ridge to eventually run parallel to the Afon Twrch above the craggy slopes of Tyle Garw, while the other finds a way up the broad ridge of Llorfa to an un-named summit with a trig pillar amid a wild sea of limestone slabs and boulders. Both of these tracks descend to cross the Afon Twrch, then climb up beside the Twrch Fechan where the going becomes more obvious.

From the village of Cwmgiedd a track follows the wooded eastern bank of the River Giedd, crossing over via a bridge at a picnic site. Above the bridge the way leaves the wood and climbs up the ridge of Cefn Mawr to pass over the rocky crown of Carreg Lem. Just beyond this minor top of grass, another track comes in from Glyntawe to the south east. The way now leads over the infant Afon Twrch to pass Esgair Du, 'the black ridge' on its south side, and so on to the rocky eastern flank of Carreg yr Ogof, the northern outlier of **Garreg Las**. All of these approaches from the south are lengthy, but take the walker into quiet areas of outstanding beauty. In its upper reaches the Afon Twrch and its tributaries encompass much wild land; open, barren and craggy, a must for the seeker of solitude.

The three Hewitts of the eastern half of the Mynydd Du are more mountainous than the western, and are composed of the Old Red Sandstones. From the camp site at the Dan yr Ogof Caves in Glyntawe a path zigzags steeply through wooded hillsides to gain a fairly straight path above Cwm Haffes. Broken scars and slabs of limestone form the rocky hills and knolls of Disgwylfa to the south. Haskett Smith compares this name to that of the word 'dysgwyl', meaning to watch or expect, making it a parallel of Cumbrian hill names such as Watch Hill or Lookingstead.

The bridleway leads across the open bogs and gurgling stream of the upper Afon Giedd before joining the path described above and crossing the Afon Twrch. The Afon Giedd is marked on the map as beginning its life high up beneath Bwlch Giedd, a windswept col between two of the highest mountains in the range, **Fan Hir** and **Fan Brycheiniog**. It flows for two and a half miles in a south-westerly direction, then disappears beneath the ground at Sinc y Giedd, seemingly rising again within half a mile and flowing in the same direction. However, what the map cannot tell us is that it turns towards the east during its short spell underground, and is actually the stream that issues forth from the Dan yr Ogof Caves. This subterranean passage has managed to fool the cartographers at the Ordnance Survey, but if you take a look at the map, you will see how easy it is to make that mistake. So, the Bwlch Giedd and upper part of the Afon Giedd would appear to be wrongly named. The Afon Giedd actually has its source on the broad rocky flanks of Disgwylfa and Carreg Lem.

The Dan yr Ogof Caves are partly open as show caves to the general public, and have walkways and flood lighting to ease the passage of the many tourists who come to witness what is usually only on offer to the speleologist. Beyond the show caves are an endless series of tortuous passages, avens, boulder chokes and open caverns, displaying stalactites and stalagmites, though these areas are only reachable by the experienced caver.

From the point were the path crosses the Afon Twrch, a steep hillside can be climbed directly to the north. This is a flank of **Bannau Sir Gaer**, better known as Carmarthenshire Fan, and leads up Brest Twrch to the rim of the crumbling north facing cliffs on the main summit ridge. To the west the minor top of Waun Lefrith forms the continuation of the ridge in that direction, and gives a possible means of ascent from **Garreg Las**. Beneath ones feet the dark waters of Llyn y Fan Fach nestle at the foot of the huge drop into the corrie bottom. To the north, surrounded by deep conifer plantations lies the Usk Reservoir, which gives water to Swansea. **Bannau Sir Gaer**'s highest point is marked by an ancient cairn and is often named as Picws Du, 'black peak.' It stands at 2457' above sea level.

From Llanddeusant a minor road runs eastwards to Blaenau by the Afon Sawdde. From there a track runs up the broad north ridge of Waun Lefrith, gaining the summit of that minor top around the edge of the steep drop into the cwm rimming the Llyn y Fan Fach. The path continues around the rim to the summit of the Hewitt, **Bannau Sir Gaer**.

The next summit along the ridge of the Mynydd Du, and the highest of all, is **Fan Brycheiniog**, 'Breconshire Beacon,' at 2631'. Beneath the precipitous eastern face of this mountain lie the cheerless waters of Llyn y Fan Fawr, and the source of the Afon Tawe. For those approaching from **Bannau Sir Gaer**, it is an easy matter to descend to the col between the two, and climb the steep western flank to the summit wind shelter and trig pillar.

Other approaches do exist, but are not so easy. One possibility is to park in a car park by a minor road that cuts through the forests to the south of the Usk Reservoir and heads for Talsarn. The Carmarthenshire and Powys County Boundary can be followed southwards, along the infant River Usk to its source, from where a steep ascent up the northern ridge of Fan Foel, a minor top of **Fan Brycheiniog**, can be climbed. A cairn marks the top of Fan Foel, and a path leads along the edge of the vegetated cliffs to the summit of the Hewitt.

The other possibility is to take a minor road from almost opposite the Tafarn-y-Garreg in Glyntawe. This minor road heads north along the true left bank of the upper Afon Tawe, and from the highest point of the road, a pass called Bwlch Cerrig Duon, a path leads westwards to the outlet of Llyn y Fan Fawr. The path climbs very steeply up to Bwlch Giedd just south of the summit of **Fan Brycheiniog**.

The escarpment that forms the eastern face of **Fan Brycheiniog** continues south-east to pass below the summit of the final Hewitt of the range, **Fan Hir**, 'long beacon' at 2497'. From **Fan Brycheiniog** it can be climbed easily by heading south to Bwlch Giedd. **Fan Hir**'s top, a small scattering of red sandstone rocks, lies just a few hundred yards beyond that col.

From the path above Cwm Haffes, which leads uphill from the Dan yr Ogof Caves down in Glyntawe, it is possible to cross the River Haffes above the first steepening and gain the long southern ridge of **Fan Hir**. This gives an enjoyable walk to the summit, along the very top of the sweeping flank of the mountain's eastern flank.

Geologically, this eastern flank is quite remarkable. Towards the end of the last ice age, there would still have been a considerable build up of ice and snow on this eastern wall of the Mynydd Du, though the angular summit blocks of the Old Red Sandstone would have been thawing out in the rising sun, at the top of the ice slope. When the ice holding the blocks to the parent mountain finally melted, these blocks slid down the slope in their hundreds, and formed a long, low ridge or mound down at the base of the snow slope. This is known as snow-scree, and today is covered by wind blown soil and much vegetation. The gully in between the two has now formed the bed for a little stream.

I always thoroughly enjoy a visit to the Mynydd Du, but that is probably due to the fact that the area partly reminds me of my beloved Yorkshire Dales. Regardless of that, the range is beautiful whilst also being dramatic, the scenery is forever changing, and there is more likelihood of having a quiet day here than in the other ranges of South Wales. In all, the Mynydd Du is a wonderfully unspoilt region, in an otherwise over-crowded National Park.

FFOREST FAWR

As is the case with the Radnor Forest in mid-Wales and many of the large estates of Scotland such as the Ben Alder Forest and the Abernethy Forest, the term 'forest' here actually applies to the old name for a hunting estate, rather than a huge acreage of trees. In the Middle Ages, the Great Forest of Brecknock was a royal hunting-ground. Until its enclosure in 1819 it was used by the surrounding villagers as a common on which they could graze their livestock of cattle and sheep. Now, huge areas of its 40,000 acres are turned over to forestry, particularly in the south, but in the Middle Ages all of the high land was open, grassy moorland, only the valleys being densely wooded.

In all there are six Hewitts in the group, two of which rise to the west of a minor road which dissects the range from Ystradfellte on the Afon Mellte to the south, and Heol Senni on the Afon Senni to the north. The Fforest Fawr hills are sandwiched in between the Mynydd Du to the West and the Brecon Beacons to the east, although the range as a whole has strictly defined man-made boundaries. To the south lies the A465, while to the north is the A4215. The A470 to the east separates the group from the Brecon Beacons, and the A4067 in the west from the Mynydd Du.

Fan Nedd and **Fan Gyhirych** are the two Hewitts in the west of the range, and as a pair are fairly unexciting. **Fan Nedd**, 'Neath beacon' at 2175' can be climbed from Blaen-nedd-Isaf on the Afon Nedd to the south by following rough moorland slopes up onto its south ridge. The summit is a wild ridge of heather, bilberry and mat grass and has a trig pillar at its southern end. Its northern end is marked by a prominent cairn. The quickest and usual way of reaching its top is to leave the car on the minor road which slices the range in two from north to south, at the standing stone of Maen Llia. This Bronze Age monolith stand about eight feet high and was almost definitely used as a marker for travellers crossing the range, although originally it could possibly have been a memorial stone to someone called Llia. It is also no surprise to find that Sarn Helen, that great road of the Roman times, crossed the range here. It is widely believed that the particular Helen in question was a British wife of a

Roman emperor who persuaded her husband to build this road right through Wales. However, William Condry, author of many well-regarded works on history and natural history, and Wales in particular, claims that Sarn Helen should more correctly be called Sarn Elen. In his *The Snowdonia National Park* (remember that Sarn Helen runs the full length of Wales, north to south), he writes that *'sarn* means a road, especially a paved road, and *elen* is a changed form of *y leng*, meaning of the legion.' So, perhaps the name Sarn Helen is simply the modern form of what was built as 'The Road of The Legion'.

From Maen Llia a permissive path climbs quickly up the boggy slopes of the north-east ridge to gain the cairn at the northern end of the summit block of **Fan Nedd**.

West of **Fan Nedd**, across the inhospitable headwaters of the Afon Nedd stands the lonely Hewitt of **Fan Gyhirych** at 2379'. The meaning of Gyhirych is unknown. A broad, bulldozed track crosses the hill along its eastern and southern side, passing within a few hundred metres of the summit, and provides the only practical way of climbing this undistinguished Hewitt.

To the south-west of the summit lies a small enclosed forest of pines, spruces and larch, from which the bulldozed track emerges at a gate. This track can be gained from Glyntawe by following an old railway line, now disused, northwards from the abandoned looking hamlet of Penwyllt. Industrial detritus from the nearby quarries detract from the pleasure of walking hereabouts, but this is soon left behind as you stride out along the cinder tracks. After a mile a path heads off from the railway line, climbing easily uphill to enter the forest at a gate. Steeper climbing through the trees brings you out onto the wild moorlands of **Fan Gyhirych**'s south ridge. The bulldozed track is followed until it swings away to the east, just short of the actual summit dome. The top is marked by a trig pillar, and is reached by following an indistinct path through short heather and grasses. A small cairn sits atop the steep northern face of the hill.

Alternatively, the summit can be gained quickly, though very steeply, from a lay-by on the A4067, across the road from a prominent tower.

The bulldozed track which narrowly misses crossing the actual summit swings around in a series of short arcs and bends to eventually settle on a general northern heading, after bordering the enclosed forests below Bwlch y Duwynt. It looses height over the western flank of the ridge of Y Gelli, and joins the minor road which heads off eastwards from the A4067 above Cray Reservoir, signposted to Heol Senni.

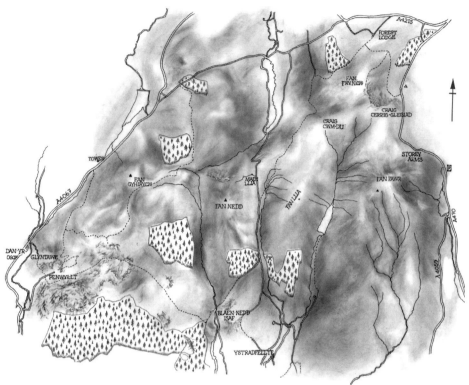

From the south a network of bulldozed tracks and public footpaths criss-cross the Ogof Ffynnon Ddu Nature Reserve, and provide a lengthy approach from the Nedd Fechan and the road head at Blaen-nedd-Isaf.

There is a connecting path between **Fan Gyhirych** and **Fan Nedd**, initially following the main track, then heading off down to a boggy col to the north-west of **Fan Nedd**. The way is hard to follow, is only a permissive path, not actually a public footpath, and is closed to walkers during the lambing season, from 15th April until 10th May each year.

To the east of the minor road which splits the range into two parts, grassy slopes lead up from the summit of the road pass near Maen Llia to gain the long ridge of **Fan Llia**, 'Llia's Beacon'. A fairly good path follows this south-west to north-east trending ridge, and can be followed from a picnic area in the woods, two miles beyond the village of Ystradfellte. Crossing a stile to gain the grassy fellside, long easy slopes lead up the ridge of Cefn Perfedd, making for the prominent sandstone cairn just short of the summit itself. There is a real feeling of spaciousness to be found on this wonderful short walk, and infrequently seen views of the other hills of Fforest Fawr rise gently all around. The summit itself is marked by a small collection of stones atop a flat rock and is at 2073'.

On my Welsh Hewitt Traverse of 1998 I climbed **Fan Llia** from the north-west, the top of the road pass near the standing stone of Maen Llia. The way is pathless and rough, crossing as it does, the headwaters of the Afon Llia. This route in reverse does however, provide a continuation for those heading for **Fan Nedd** to the west.

Continuing north-east along the ridge from the summit, still named on the O.S. map as Cefn Perfedd, the way is easy and very grassy, reminiscent of the Pennine moors of England. This is the way onwards to the two most northerly summits of the Fforest Fawr hills. First the path dips to the head of the broken crags of Craig Cwm-du, boggy but easy to cross. Then a good path climbs up eastwards to gain the flat plateau-land of **Craig Cerrig-gleisiad**, 'blue stone rock', at 2064'. Long before reaching the summit the path vanishes from underfoot and is replaced by peaty pools of slime and rivulets of slow-moving moorland water. The highest point is marked by a small cairn, just short of a fence which borders the crags of the **Craig Cerrig-gleisiad** Nature Reserve. A path skirts the edge of these cliffs and provides the usual way of climbing this hill, along with **Fan Frynych** just to the north.

From a lay-by on the busy A470, on the northern side of the road pass in Glyn Tarell, two miles beyond the Storey Arms Centre, a path starts off beside a small stream which issues from the craggy cwm above. Once above the intake wall, the path splits, one way heading left for the short but steep eastern ridge of **Craig Cerrig-gleisiad**. The other turns right and follows the top side of the intake wall, eventually rising above it to gain a small col beside a stand of larch trees up on the north-east ridge of **Fan Frynych**. Other paths climb up into the heart of the wild cwm, but these are recommended only for

Maen Llia

those intent on spending time exploring the Nature Reserve. This is a desolate cwm backed with impressively vegetated crags, famous as being one of the richest sources of alpine plants in Britain. The cwm floor is chiefly a heathery scattering of boggy hollows, with a raised outer curve of morainic mounds. These hollows are the remnants of former cirque lakes which would once have bejeweled this beautifully wild place.

As I have already mentioned, there is another, second summit on the lip of this hollow. **Fan Frynych**, 'the ox hill beacon', stands at 2064', precisely the same height as **Craig Cerrig-gleisiad** less than a mile to its south.

The path in between **Craig Cerrig-gleisiad** and **Fan Frynych** is obvious and easy to follow, though can be boggy at the broad col at the half way point. Also at the col, a stile must be climbed over a fence.

To link the two summits of the Nature Reserve together in one short walk, the east ridge of **Craig Cerrig-gleisiad** should be climbed from the car park north of the Storey Arms Centre, as described above. The path can then be followed to **Fan Frynych**, and the continuation of this heads downhill on a steadily narrowing ridge to a small triangle of larch trees. Just beyond this, at a small col, the path heads back southwards, beneath the crags, and joins up with the other described above, which follows the upper side of the intake wall.

The small col on the north-east ridge can also be gained from the two tiny ponds in the wood at Forest Lodge near the A4215. A public footpath passes to the south of these two ponds, then, at a cross roads of tracks, climbs steeply uphill to the col.

There are also paths leading up to the top of **Fan Frynych** from the west, starting uphill from a public bridleway which contours around the whole western edge of these hills from the headwaters of the Afon Llia to Forest Lodge near the A4215. One of these tracks follows the course of the Nant Cwm-du, below the broken crags of Craig Cwm-du mentioned earlier. The other climbs the ridge to the north of this steep sided valley. The two join just half a mile short of the summit with its trig pillar.

To the south of the Nature Reserve lies the highest summit of the range. **Fan Fawr**, the 'large beacon', stands in solitude at 2408', with the Ystradfellte Reservoir to the west and the Taf Fawr Valley to the east. Its only connection to the rest of the range is a broad, peaty col above Craig y Fro to the north. Beyond this col the terrain rises gently up the open slopes of **Craig Cerrig-gleisiad**'s southern ridge.

The quickest way of gaining the small cairn which marks **Fan Fawr**'s summit is from the top of the road pass to the east. The A470 climbs above the many reservoirs of the lower Taf Valley, and offers a good car park at its highest point, across the road from the Storey Arms Outdoor Centre. A well-worn path climbs the bleak slopes of Bryn Du, becoming boggy before tackling the final summit cone.

The only other popular way of climbing this hill is from the south-west. Just north of the village of Ystradfellte a bridge spans the confluence of the Afon Llia and Afon Dringarth. Across the bridge the road climbs steeply for a short way before a track leaves it on the left. This continues all the way to the dam of the Ystradfellte Reservoir, and it is possible to climb **Fan Fawr** via these wild western slopes. When approaching from this direction, a trig pillar is reached, strangely lower than the summit, and a good half a mile short of it.

On my traverse of all the Welsh Hewitts in 1998 I descended from a rock outcrop below the summit of **Fan Fawr**, south-eastwards towards the Beacons Reservoir. I have since climbed the hill from here, and though the way is pathless, the wide trough of the Nant Pennig is a wild and open landscape. Also the broad ridge of Cefn yr Henriw provides an alternative descent to the starting point at the dam of the reservoir.

I would never claim that these hills of the Fforest Fawr are anything other than boggy, unfrequented lumps, sandwiched as they are between the much better ranges of the Mynydd Du and the Brecon Beacons, but I like them, and do enjoy wandering over their quiet heights and through their windswept cwms. Personally, I would sooner go for a solitary stroll in these hills than be bombarded by the hundreds of walkers who pour over the eroded ridges of the more popular hills nearby.

BRECON BEACONS

Striking ridges of glowing sandstone and open moorland of heather and grass, growing amid acidic peaty soils. This is the Brecon Beacons. Although the National Park is named after this range, the group of hills that make up this section of the book form the central part of the Park, and are distinctly separate from the Black Mountains to the east and the hills of Fforest Fawr and the Mynydd Du to the west. In the north, beneath the vegetated escarpments which invariably form the northern faces of all the high land in the range, the River Usk, or Afon Wysg to give its unfamiliar Welsh spelling, forms a natural border. Westwards, the busy A470 winds its way up the valley of the Afon Taf Fawr, while to the east the village of Llangynidr on the Monmouthshire and Brecon Canal marks the extremities of the range in that direction. In the south, the A465 and Merthyr Tydfil form the southern border.

There are four Hewitts in the main Brecon Beacons, all linked quite easily by a well eroded path which follows the rim of the north facing craggy flanks. Joined to the main group by a tenuous col above the Taf Fechan Forest lies the solitary hill of **Cefn yr Ystrad**, far to the south of the other Hewitts.

Geologically the mountains and moorlands of South Wales are vastly different from those of the north. Devonian rocks are represented in the Brecon Beacons by the Old Red Sandstones which cover much of the range, and are composed of layers of brownstones, consisting of interbedded red marls, brown sandstones and conglomerates with the harder beds protruding as short crumbling cliffs and shelves. It is largely this layering that has formed the plateau-like 'table-top' summits of the range.

Only to the south of the Brecon Beacons does the rock formation differ. Here we find Carboniferous Limestone displaying regular features of karst country such as shake holes and exposed pavements, giving scenery similar to that found in the limestone dales of Derbyshire and Yorkshire.

Of the Hewitts in the Brecon Beacons, the four of the main ridge are all composed of outcropping Old Red Sandstone, which is very evident to all who walk these ridges, while **Cefn yr Ystrad** to the south is predominantly

Carboniferous Limestone. This too is much in evidence, although for a very different reason. Huge limestone quarries disfigure the whole of the northern side of the hill, right up to the last rise before the very summit.

Walkers wishing to make the ascent of **Cefn yr Ystrad** will invariably make a start from the west. The village of Pontsticill, at the southern end of the reservoir of the same name, is as good a place as any to begin the short climb.

A minor road leads downhill from the village, crossing the Afon Taf Fechan below the dam of the reservoir. Almost opposite to the entrance to the water works, a public footpath leads up a grassy slope, enclosed by fences, to pass beneath a low railway bridge taken by the Brecon Mountain Narrow Gauge Railway. The way climbs diagonally up alongside a hawthorn hedge, eventually passing through a gate and out onto the grassy flank of the hill above the intake wall. Welsh Mountain Ponies often roam with the flocks of sheep here, but usually aren't much of a menace. The path isn't very obvious at first, but eventually, another track which contours higher up is reached, and leads around the western flanks of the hill, into the open valley of Cwar yr Ystrad. Short outcrops of limestone dot the hillside, and it is an easy matter to pick a way between these to gain the mat grass of the summit ridge above. The summit area is composed of a number of grassy knolls, and two ancient cairns stand by the highest point, which is marked with a trig pillar. The views out to the Black Mountains across the valley of the Usk are superb. The trig pillar stands at 2024', the highest point of this hill. Its name translates as nothing more remarkable than 'ridge of the dale'.

Cwar yr Ystrad can also be gained from a point about halfway along the eastern bank of Pontsticill Reservoir, by climbing up through a conifer wood along a public bridleway and contouring around into the valley above its steepest part. Of course, there is no road access to the eastern side of the reservoir, but a good, way-marked path runs between the shore and the narrow gauge line of the railway. This path can be gained from a minor road which runs atop the dam at the southern end, or else from a car park at the northern end of the reservoir, crossing it via a bridge to Dolygaer scout camp and outdoor pursuits centre.

Another option is to follow a path up into Cwm Callan from behind the outdoor pursuits centre at Dolygaer, and upon leaving the forest, continue for a short way until a vague col is reached at Bryniau Gleision. From here it is a simple matter to head south into the quarry wastes just below the summit.

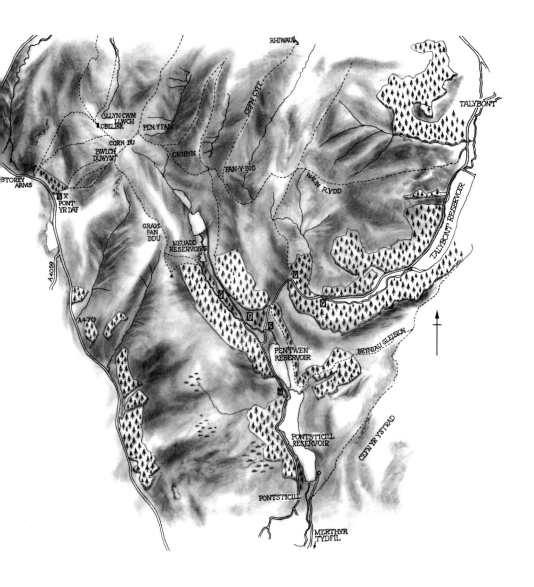

The familiar shape of the Brecon Beacons, as seen in an old postcard

Following the system of reservoirs upstream into the cwm of Taf Fechan, the scenery becomes more rewarding, with wooded slopes and open stretches of water, for here are the Pentwyn Reservoir just above the Pontsticill, and the twin Neuadd Reservoirs higher up, surrounded by a domination of moorland ridges and high summits.

From the Neuadd Reservoirs a good path climbs westwards onto the ridge of Twyn Mwyalchod, gaining it at a trig pillar. The way northwards is superb, leading as it does along the edge of the huge vegetated drops into the upper cwm to the right, and reminding one of the gritstone edges and peaty moorland of the Kinder Plateau in the Peak District. The way lies along Graig Fan Ddu, Craig Gwaun Taf, and eventually, down to the col at Bwlch Duwynt. This is an important col in the range as it is also the point that a good path climbs up from Pont ar Daf on the A470 in the Taf valley to the west. Immediately to the north-east rises the flat-topped hill of Corn Du, traditionally regarded as a separate summit of the Brecon Beacons, but as it only rises a few metres above the col between it and **Pen y Fan**, it does not qualify as a Hewitt. Corn Du is often approached from the west at the Storey Arms Centre at the top of the pass on the A470. From there, one path climbs pretty much directly, aiming just slightly to the left of Corn Du's summit, but dropping into a cwm along the way, whereas the public foot-path heads north-east for the little hill known as Y Gyrn, before skimming

Seen from a less familiar angle, from above Pontsticill

the edge of the cwm round in an arc to an obelisk. This commemorates the death of Tommy Jones in 1900. This five year old local lad became separated from his father as they made their way over to visit relatives from Brecon Station, and his body was not found for a month.

There have been other deaths in these mountains, and Haskett Smith mentions a picnicker who died somewhere hereabouts. He quotes a report in the *Times Index*, stating that the unfortunate man fell 12,000 feet to his death, pointing out that these figures are 'somewhat startling'. I should say!

The obelisk overlooks the hidden tarn of Llyn Cwm Llwch from where an ascent can also be made. A car park at the road end up Nant Cwm Llwch gives the starting point, and the way passes amid wonderful craggy scenery before gaining the obelisk. Above this point the way lies up a short, narrowing grassy ridge to the top of Corn Du. The path from Storey Arms, via the obelisk is by far the shortest way of reaching the main ridge, taking about an hour.

Only a short distance to the east of Corn Du rises the red mass of eroded rock that is the summit of **Pen y Fan**, 'top of the beacon', at 2907', the highest of all the mountains of South Wales and indeed, the highest point in the British Isles south of Cadair Idris. From Corn Du the way leads down a short ridge to a col, then up an obvious path to the cairn at the summit. The same point can be reached from Bwlch Duwynt along a path which contours the sides of Corn Du's southern flank. From the summit of **Pen y Fan** the views stretch out as far as the Malverns, the Bristol Channel and Plynlimon, although for views as extensive as this you must wait for a really clear day.

It is only as you look along the lengthy escarpment of the northern edge of this Old Red Sandstone series, from the summit of **Pen y Fan**, that the uniformity of the southward sloping aspect of all of the mountains of the National Park becomes apparent. It is obvious from here that the many summits which dot the edge of this northern scarp are merely the angular tip of a huge tilted bed of Sandstone, and as this bed recedes in altitude to the south, that is where the Carboniferous Limestone has bedded down on top, forming the karst scenery and lowland hills of the south. Beyond that lies the South Wales coal fields. This same geological structure forms all the high hills of the Mynydd Du far to the west, the nearer Fforest Fawr hills, and to a less obvious extent, the Black Mountains to the north-east. Only in Scotland does the Old Red Sandstone series rise to a greater height than it does here in the Brecon Beacons. This ancient landscape amply illustrates the massive effect of glaciation, as the huge cirques which fall to the north from the main ridge effectively show, and the area is also remarkable as being the most southerly habitat of a number of plants which really belong to the Arctic zones. Nowhere further south than this will you find wild species of purple saxifrage, mossy saxifrage, roseroot or northern bedstraw.

Following the scarp eastwards, the next Hewitt of the chain, **Cribyn**, stands as a proud peak above the surrounding cwms, throwing down a long ridge to the north, called Bryn Teg, meaning 'fair hill', into the lower part of the Afon Cynrig near Brecon. The way to **Cribyn** from **Pen y Fan** is obvious, following the edge of Craig Cwm Sere down to a col, then with a short, steep ascent up to the summit. **Cribyn**, 'the summit', at 2608' gives another good view point from which to gaze not only at the other heights of the range, but also of the openness of the Usk Valley, and the distant smudges of the Cwmdeuddwr Hills and **Plynlimon**. It is said that even **Cadair Idris** can be seen to the north on a really good day, and that Exmoor stands as a vague smudge beyond the Bristol Channel to the south, although that is something I cannot vouch for.

The north ridge of **Cribyn**, Bryn Teg mentioned above, can be climbed to the summit quite easily from the road head in Cwmcynwyn, and gives a good, fairly quiet way onto the tops. From the top of **Cribyn**, a path goes off down the south-east ridge of Craig Cwm Cynwyn to a grassy col, Bwlch ar y Fan. This is crossed by a busy bridleway, reputedly dating back to Roman times, but if not that far, it is certainly an old pack-horse road.

If you are planning on having a short day out, and need to return to the Neuadd Reservoirs, this track can be followed southwards, around the flanks of Tor Glas, taking you back to the car in a mile and a half.

Bwlch ar y Fan can also be reached along the track from the north. It starts at the same point as the path up Bryn Teg on **Cribyn**, but follows a line more along the flanks of Cwm Cynwyn rather than climbing straight up the ridge.

East again from the col, a short but very abrupt climb up eroded grass leads to the summit of **Fan y Big**, 'beak beacon', at 2359'. The Nuttalls record that a trig pillar marks the highest point, which indeed it used to, but on my last visit, during the summer of 1998, there was no sign of it. A small cairn marks the highest part, and slightly to the south, a good wind break offers shelter on really wild days.

Like the other Hewitts of the range, **Fan y Big** throws down a long grassy ridge to the north, Cefn Cyff which can be gained at a minor road end, near the farmstead of Rhiwiau, south of and uphill from the Afon Cynrig. It is perhaps these dark, north-facing cwms that separate the many ridges of the range that provide the solitude required by some visitors to the area. Cwm Oergwm has a good system of footpaths along its bottom, taking the walker through delightful mixed woodland from the road end at Rhiwiau as a quiet alternative to a day on the tops.

The eastern side of Cwm Oergwm is formed by yet another long ridge, throwing down a subsidiary ridge from the peat moors around Craig Cwareli, the mid-way point on the escarpment between **Fan y Big** and the next Hewitt eastwards, **Waun Rydd**. A minor depression takes a stream up into the shallow Cwm Cwareli before this eastern ridge of the main valley heads out north along Gist Wen towards Llanfrynach. A public footpath follows the ridge of Gist Wen, and gives a good approach to the Hewitts at this eastern end of the Brecon Beacons. Once on the main ridge, near Bwlch y Ddwyallt, 'the two hills col', this path continues over the pass, and down towards the head stream of the Talybont Reservoir. This path follows the steep, narrow ridge of Craig y Fan Ddu from a car park at the road pass from Pontsticill Reservoir to Talybont Reservoir in the south, and is a delight to walk throughout, with deep semi-wooded valleys dropping away on either side. After the Second World War, much of the land in this part of the National Park was leased to the Forestry Commission who began planting trees in the early 1950s.

Waun Rydd itself is an unassuming mound, covered in mat grass and very reminiscent of the wild, high moors of the Yorkshire Dales. **Waun Rydd**'s name translates roughly as meaning 'free moorland,' and its tiny summit cairn stands at 2523'. A good path crosses the ridge of Waun Rydd heading eastwards towards Talybont Reservoir, but just fails to actually cross the summit, passing it to the south.

The east ridge of **Waun Rydd** is a wonderful walk, and is one of my personal favourites for gaining the eastern end of the Brecon Beacons. It starts at a car park near the dam of the Talybont Reservoir. The work on this was completed in 1938, and the streams which form its catchment area provides Newport with water. A good path, well sign-posted, heads west, steeply uphill at first, but levelling off near Twyn Du, 'the black knoll'. Ahead, up the ridge of **Waun Rydd**, a magnificent cairn can be seen, spearing the sky as you approach. This is Carn Pica, a ten foot high construction which provides a wonderful viewpoint across the River Usk to the Black Mountains in the north-east, and down the valley towards Crickhowell and Abergavenny.

Above Carn Pica the small summit plateau of **Waun Rydd** is soon underfoot, and the continuation westwards to the other Hewitts can be started. The only problem with starting your ascent from Talybont Reservoir is that it is awkward to return at the end of the day, without retracing your steps along the ridge, although with such wonderful walking as is to be found in the region, this option could hardly be seen as posing a problem— you simply get twice the value from your day in the hills!

170

THE BLACK MOUNTAINS

This, the second range known as the Black Mountains in the Brecon Beacons National Park lie well to the north-east of the main chain of Old Red Sandstone Hills. The wide rift of the Usk Valley separates the group from the Brecon Beacons themselves, while to the east, the border with England forms a useful man-made boundary. The large town of Abergavenny lies to the south, while the northern border is formed by the valley of the River Wye. The old castle town of Hay-on-Wye forms the northern apex of the National Park in that direction.

Hay-on-Wye takes its name from the Norman French word 'haier' meaning 'to enclose'. So The Hay, as it used to be called, means quite simply 'the enclosed settlement'. The Hague in Holland is derived from the same verb. Today Hay is famous for being the book capital of Britain, with seemingly every other shop being devoted to selling the written word.

The Offa's Dyke Long Distance Footpath takes to the streets of Hay after descending from the high ridge of the hill known as **Black Mountain**, and for walkers intent on leaving Hay for the hills, the Offa's Dyke Path is a useful way-marked route to follow. Offa was King of Mercia, that huge Anglian kingdom which in the 6th century stretched from Wessex to Northumbria and had Wales as its western boundary. During its latter decades Mercia was an earldom under Canute and remained as such for his successors until the Norman Conquest of the eleventh century. Offa was king from 757 until his death in 796. It was he who caused to have built a series of earthworks running from near the mouth of the River Wye to the mouth of the River Dee as a boundary between Mercia and Wales. Today, Mercia is often used as a convenient group name for the counties of Shropshire, Herefordshire and Worcestershire. As an Official Long Distance Path, Offa's Dyke provides a not-too-difficult walk of 177 miles from near the Severn Bridge at Sedbury Cliffs in the south to Prestatyn on the north coast. The only really hard walking on the entire route is the short section in the Black Mountains, and crossing the ridge of the Clwydian Hills near the end.

From Hay the Offa's Dyke Path climbs up a ridge of farmland and woods, crossing an expanse of common land above Cadwgan Farm before joining a minor road which cuts across the range from Hay to the Vale of Ewyas and the tiny village of Capel-y-ffin. At a stone circle just a short way along the road a path climbs up the steep northern face of Hay Bluff, a wonderful little hill, but not high enough above the col between it and **Black Mountain** to be classified as a Hewitt. A trig pillar marks the top of Hay Bluff and gives an expansive vista across the whole of the middle valley of the Wye. To the north lies the forested smudge of the Radnor Forest, while to the left of those rounded hills, the vast emptiness of the Cwmdeuddwr hills roll away to the mountains of Snowdonia.

A good path, still the Offa's Dyke route, heads south along the border of England and Wales. The way is peaty but not too rough, and in places, paving slabs of sandstone have been laid to ease the passage of the thousands of walkers who come this way every year. Usually the top of **Black Mountain**, which lies just over a mile south of Hay Bluff, is unmarked, but on my last ascent during my Welsh Hewitt Traverse of 1998, the highest point had a pile of pallets stacked at its top, probably used us duck-boards before the laying of the stone flags.

Black Mountain rises as a long whale-back to an undistinguished top at 2306'. The actual summit is often hard to define among the heathery mounds. There is another, lower summit along the ridge to the south-east, listed in the Nuttalls book, but not a Hewitt. This is known simply as Black Mountain South Top. A public footpath leaves the Vale of Ewyas just down from Capel-y-ffin at The Vision Farm, and climbs to the north-east to gain the ridge just below this lower summit. It is then an easy matter to follow the well-trodden Offa's Dyke Path to the summit of **Black Mountain** itself.

The other convenient start for an approach to **Black Mountain** is from the top of the minor road between Hay and Capel-y-ffin. This is known as the Gospel Pass. The whole of the Vale of Ewyas is deeply connected with early Christianity in Wales, though the name of the pass, which in Welsh is Bwlch yr Efengyl, probably dates back to the recruiting tour made by Archbishop Baldwin and Giraldus Cambrensis, Archdeacon of Brecon, for the Crusades in around 1118. There is a car park at the top of the pass from where a good track heads off for the top of Hay Bluff and so on to **Black Mountain**.

Black Mountain is the only Hewitt that is listed in both the Welsh and English lists, its summit being right on the very border, and as such can also be climbed from the Olchon Valley on the English side. Numerous tracks and public footpaths gain the ridge, but those emerging onto the flat heathery moorland near the summit leave the valley from Upper Blaen at the road head. This upper part of the Olchon Valley has another upland wall to the east, that

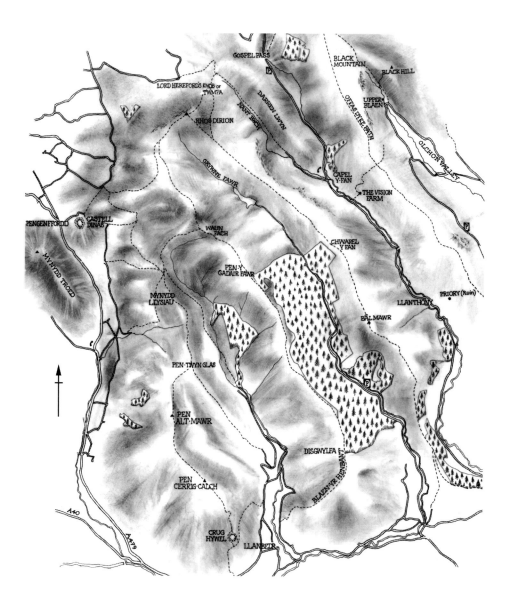

We now began to ascend its steeps; but before we had risen too high, we turned round to take a retrospect of all the rich scenes together, which had left behind. It was a noble view; distance melting into distance; till the whole was closed by a semi-circle of azure mountains, scarce distinguishable from the azure sky, which absorbed them.

Still ascending, the spiral road round the shaggy side of the mountain, we arrived at what is called its gate. Here all ideas of cultivation ceased. That was not deplorable: but with it our turn-pike-road ceased also; which was finished, on this side, no farther than the mountain-gate. We had gotten a guide however to conduct us over the pathless desert. But it being too steep and rugged to ascend on wheels, we were obliged to lighten our carriage and ascend on foot.

In the midst of our labour, our guide called out, that he saw a storm driving towards us, along the tops of the mountains: a circumstance indeed, which in these hilly countries cannot often be avoided. We asked him, How far it was off? He answered, Ten minutes. In less time, sky, mountains and vallies were all wrapt in one cloud of obscurity.

Our recompense consisted in following with our eye the rear of the storm; observing, through its broken skirts, a thousand beautiful effects, and half-formed images, which were continually opening, lost, and varying; till the sun breaking out, the whole resplendent landscape appeared again, with double radiance, under the leaden gloom of the retiring tempest.

A day spent on the Black Mountains from
Observations on the River Wye, and several parts of South
Wales etc., relative chiefly to Picturesque Beauty; made in the
Summer of the Year 1770, by William Gilpin

of Black Hill, which though only a ridge of **Black Mountain**, can be climbed as a pleasant prelude to a day on the main ridge. A picnic site lies at a tiny col between Black Hill and the knoll of Little Black Hill, from where a good track climbs this subsidiary ridge and then bends around to join the main tops between **Black Mountain** and Hay Bluff.

Bronllys Castle and the northern and western slopes of the
Black Mountains, from a drawing of 1805

To the west of the Gospel Pass the first of the summits which form part of the main Black Mountains massif rises in a curved ridge to the summit of Lord Hereford's Knob, or **Twmpa**. From the pass the way is easy and cannot be confused. The summit is marked by a cairn at 2264'. **Twmpa**, the usual name given to the hill, means simply 'mound'.

A short ridge cuts down into the head of the Vale of Ewyas from the summit, and forms a minor valley to the west. This is taken by the Nant Bwch, while the ridge itself is named as Darren Lwyd, a nice way to gain the summit from Capel-y-ffin. A public bridleway contours the nose of this ridge low down, and can be gained from the two valleys that fall to either side of the ridge. The track along the ridge climbs direct up the nose of the ridge while another climbs in steep zigzags from a point just up from the Capel-y-ffin Youth Hostel in the main valley of the Afon Honddu. Once on the ridge the going is very easy over grass with a gentle slope to the top of **Twmpa**.

To the south-west a high col separates **Twmpa** from Rhos Dirion, a minor top. From Blaen-bwch at the road head of the Nant Bwch valley, a public bridleway heads straight for this col, and by turning right a short ascent over grass leads to **Twmpa**.

As you climb these boggy little hills of the eastern Black Mountains, it will become increasingly clear that the whole range is composed chiefly of long ridges trending from a northern scarp in a general south-east direction. Each of these ridges are carved by deep valleys whose streams flow from a source on the southern bank of this main scarp. It will also be clear that as the terrain swings southwards in a gentle arc to the west, displacing this northern scarp to become more north-west facing, the hills rise to a greater altitude with **Waun Fach** forming both the highest and the pivotal point of the entire range.

From Rhos Dirion, **Waun Fach** lies to the south, across the deep defile of the Grwyne Fawr valley, but before this wild trench is crossed, another Hewitt rises to 2228' on the long south-east ridge of Rhos Dirion. This Hewitt is **Chwarel Y Fan**, 'quarry beacon'. The map marks a small conifer plantation at the very summit of this little hill, but in actual fact this has recently been harvested, and the only trees are much lower down the declivity, filling the lower part of the Grwyne Fawr valley.

The old Benedictine Monastery at Capel-y-ffin has a good public bridleway rising behind it which climbs steadily beneath craggy slopes to a col near a cairn to the north-west of **Chwarel y Fan**. A path then follows the ridge to this little summit with its good cairn.

From Rhos Dirion a track runs the entire length of the ridge, passing the col above Capel-y-ffin, and so on to the summit, and beyond. The continuation climbs to a trig pillar at Bâl-Mawr, then descends into the forests near Cadwgan where a car park and picnic site give a good access point onto this ridge. The way follows a good path along the ridge throughout.

Across the Grwyne Fawr valley, another, much higher ridge forms the western wall of this long corrie. From Rhos Dirion a path heads south-west, then picks up a line along the main ridge to the south, bringing the boggy summit plateau of **Waun Fach** underfoot. This translates as the 'little moor' which is quite surprising considering that **Waun Fach** is the highest mountain in the whole of the Black Mountains range, rising to 2661'.

The main ridge-top track continues from the summit towards the next Hewitt, **Pen y Gadair Fawr**, while another track descends to the west to a narrow col before a further three Hewitts are to be gained to the south. These tracks provide really the only good ways of reaching the summit of **Waun Fach**, although I have forced a pathless way up from the dam of the Grwyne Fawr Reservoir. This follows a narrow cleft then emerges among deep heather and tussock grass. It is far better to follow the main ridges.

From **Waun Fach** a boggy path leads to the south-east to the little dome of **Pen y Gadair Fawr** at 2625'. This, the 'head of the great chair', can be climbed along forest tracks from the depths of the Mynydd Du Forest in the Grwyne Fawr valley, or for a long ridge walk, from Llanbedr just to the north of Crickhowell. A public bridleway climbs around Blaen-yr-henbant, and narrowly misses the trig pillar on Crug Mawr before gaining the edge of the forest at Disgwylfa. It is then an easy, though lengthy, matter to follow the ridge alongside the trees, over Pen Gwyllt Meirch and Pen Twyn Mawr to the summit of **Pen y Gadair Fawr**. In all, this is an excellent way of climbing to the higher Black Mountain tops.

The path down to the col at 617 metres, to the west of **Waun Fach**, is again very boggy, but soon a narrowing ridge, marked on the map as Pen Trumau, brings it underfoot. A number of public bridleways climb up to the col from the west, leaving the valley around the knoll holding Castell Dinas near Pengenffordd on the A479 between Crickhowell and Talgarth. Castell Dinas is now in ruins but was the site of an Iron Age fort which the Normans thought so well placed as to build there own castle on the same spot. The bridleways are easy to follow, as indeed many are in the range, being much used for pony trekking by the many centres in the area. Another track climbs to the col from the south-east, following the banks of the Grwyne Fechan from Cwm Farm, upstream from Llanbedr.

The narrow ridge of **Mynydd Llysiau** has at its northern end, over-looking the col, a little cairn near the spot height at its summit. This is the 'herb mountain' though in fact the flora doesn't seem to be that much different from that of the other hills in the range, predominantly grass but with occasional clumps of heather and bilberry. The summit is at 2175'.

The way southwards lies along a delightful grassy ridge, rising slightly to the Nuttall of Pen Twyn Glas. Here a track heads off along the wonderful little ridge of Tal Trwynau to Neuadd-fawr at the edge of Cwm Banw. This gives a good approach to the hills at the centre of the range.

The main path climbs above a col to the rocky summit of **Pen Allt-mawr**, 'big hill end' at 2362'. There is a trig pillar on top of the millstone-grit summit blocks.

The path continues southwards, splitting over Pen Gloch-y-pibwr. One track heads off for the ancient cairns at the south-western lip of the heathery summit plateau, then drops to the A479 near Tretower, though this way is unmarked on the map, and so is probably over private land.

The main track swings around a peaty depression, then climbs to the wonderful summit dome of **Pen Cerrig-calch**. This, the 'limestone head', is an aptly descriptive name for the only hill of the range to be capped with carboniferous limestone. This cap is self evident in small white blocks which adorn the plateau near the ancient cairn and trig pillar.

Beyond the summit, which is 2300' high, the way continues to the south-east before zigzagging down to the brackeny col behind Table Mountain. It is sad that this, the fort of Hywell has been anglicised even by the local people who are now entirely English-speaking. Indeed the town of Crickhowell which lies at its base is still named 'Crug Hywel', Howell's mount, in Welsh, and it is a shame that the hill has lost its identity. It is said that Hywell Dda, or Hywell the Good, was the grandson of the great Welsh king Rhodri, back in the ninth century, and that his fort on the flat-topped hill was the first settlement in the immediate area.

A public footpath descends through fields of livestock and passes the farm of The Wern before entering the market town of Crickhowell, and the end of our exploration of these wild mountain ridges.

PART TWO

TRAVELOGUE OF A WELSH HEWITTEER

Travelogue of a Welsh Hewitteer

This second part of this book follows the ups and downs of accepting a challenge to walk all the Welsh Hewitts in one fell swoop. I hadn't given the slightest thought to bagging every Welsh Hewitt in one go until about six months before setting off, a fact that startled many of the people I was to meet during the walk. The whole idea seemed pretty preposterous to just about everyone but me. Likewise, when the walk was completed, a number of people wanted to know how I could prove that I had in fact climbed them all. They were missing the point. I hadn't planned to climb them so that anyone else would know I had done so, I was climbing the Welsh Hewitts to satisfy my own quite selfish love of the mountains.

Although I thought it quite possible that no one had actually walked all of the Welsh Hewitts in one go before, I was quite prepared to continue with my plans even if they had. Shortly before setting off I received a letter from the Nuttalls wishing me well and pointing out that Anne Bowker had actually done all of the summits on their list in one backpacking trip a couple of years before. Others may have also completed the round in one, more will have climbed them all over an extended period. The first person recorded as doing so was Edward Moss who completed the list on 22nd July 1951. Moss had written previously about the mountains of Wales in the Rucksack Club Journal for 1940 in an article entitled 'The Two-Thousands of Wales'. It is not known how many have completed them since Moss's achievement.

Once it was agreed that this book would include my walk across all of the Welsh Hewitts, I spent a couple of hours pouring over maps, drawing a black ring around each summit so that I could see the whole country laid down before me with each Hewitt high-lighted. This made plotting a rough route quite simple, a bit like a huge 1:50,000 scale dot-to-dot, spread over eight sheets of Ordnance Survey Landranger map. I could then get down to the more intricate details of which paths I would use, where I would camp, what distance I would cover each day and when I would have a rest day for shopping and washing clothes.

As far as organising equipment, I had been lucky on that score. Obviously I had quite a lot of necessary gear being a Mountain Walking Instructor, and keen rock and winter climber. However, I hoped that the commercial sector would be pleased to help me out with anything that needed replacing from my existing store. I spent hours scanning the shelves of the outdoor shops both in my immediate locality and in the further flung reaches of Scotland and the Lake District, deciding such things as what would be the most comfortable rucksack without compromising on durability and size, or the best sleeping bag to cope with the wide range of altitudes I planned to camp at, from the valley floors to the very summits. These and a hundred other things I had to take into consideration. Put simply, I wanted the best I could lay my hands on for use in the Welsh hills. Obviously I could have looked for the most expensive item in each case, but that would have invariably meant that say, the tent in question would have been designed for use during a howling blizzard at camp five on Everest and might have been just a touch over the top for two months in Wales, not to mention three or four times as heavy as the one ideal for my purposes. When I had finally produced my shopping list of things I simply couldn't do without, I kept a tight hold of my wallet (well, I am a Yorkshireman after all), and sent a query letter to the manufacturer in question. The response was amazing to say the least. Within weeks Global Mobility had produced a camp stove, Weatherstop (my local retailer) donated the best possible sleeping bag from their range and the Brasher Boot Company decided that I was to become their Expedition Award Winner for April 1998—an honour that ensured the safe delivery of a pair of Hillmaster Classic boots, and a pair of trekking poles thrown in for good measure. A quick photo-session at Weatherstop where I was presented with these goodies gave a bit more welcome publicity both in the local press and in 'TGO' magazine. Before long I also had a Hilltrek tent from the new range by Robert Saunders, an Archipelago rucksack from Adrian Moore of Aiguille Alpine Equipment, a huge selection of soups and pasta sauces from Knorr and a large box-full of Ovaltine Power from Novartis Nutrition Ltd. Half way through the walk a pair of Porelle Dry waterproof socks from Porvair arrived via the express mailing of Rachel, my partner.

Of course, not everyone was so helpful, I chased around endlessly trying to persuade someone to give me a set of waterproof clothing, but to no avail. I therefore had to make do with an extremely tatty Gore-Tex jacket and trousers in which I had been knocking around the hills for years.

By this time I had pretty much finalised my plans for my walk. All that remained was to wait until the first weekend in June when I could shoulder my rucksack and stride out across the lonely limestone pavements of the western Mynydd Ddu.

CHAPTER I
Tentative First Steps

Saturday 6th June ~ The Start

A burning sun rising behind glowing ridges of Old Red Sandstone; waking early to avoid the blistering heat of midday, taking a siesta in the welcoming shade of an ancient oak tree with a good book during the really scorching hours and resuming my walk later in the afternoon, finishing for the day by an idyllic gurgling stream alive with wagtails and dippers bobbing along on water-worn boulders; occasional camps on almost breathless summit ridges, just the slightest breeze keeping the midges at bay as I gaze longingly north-wards towards my ultimate goal, squat little **Tal y Fan**, well beyond sight over the farthest horizon, with a solitary curlew melodically bubbling away across the heather moor with its familiar call of, 'cur-lee'. Of course, it never crossed my mind that the first couple of days in the Brecon Beacons National Park could, in reality, differ greatly from these lazy, pre-trip dreams.

That they did came as something as a shock, although I managed to convince myself that the torrential rain that started almost the moment we drove over the English / Welsh border wouldn't last for very long. Instead it was the start of possibly one of the worst summers on record. The rain itself wasn't a problem, but the fact that the windscreen wiper on the driver's side wasn't working, was. And this was only the second major problem of the day. The first had been a blow-out at 70 mph—the car was borrowed for the trip and the spare tyre in the boot was flat. Rachel and I approached a nearby farm to ask if we could use the phone. The elderly couple were only too pleased to assume the role of our knights in shining armour and willingly allowed us entry to their front room. A two-way conversation with a very nice man from the AA on the phone and the farmer's wife shouting her address through from the scullery combined to give an atmosphere of utter pandemonium, but we were soon waiting by the road for help to arrive. The AA sent out a local man from a garage who pumped up our flat spare and advised us to buy a new tyre to replace the burst one. An hour later, and £30 short, we were once more on our way.

All went well until somewhere around Abergavenny when the heavens opened and the windscreen wiper did its little party trick. Luckily, Rachel had an older version of the Metro we were driving and knew that all we needed was a spanner to tighten up a nut that had come loose. Making do with a combination of Rachel giving me directions of the 'left-a-bit', 'sharp-right', 'don't knock the policeman off his bike' variety and me leaning out of the window to operate the wiper manually whilst driving, we made reasonably good progress in search of a garage that would sell spanners. I say 'reasonably' good progress because we had managed to miss a vital turning, not realising our mistake until eight miles later. Eight miles isn't usually worth worrying about, but at our wiperless speed of somewhere around 10 miles an hour it added considerably to our journey time and our already frayed tempers.

At last we managed to rebuild the offending machine, just as the rain stopped and a weak sun made an effort to shine through the pile of wet towels that were the South Wales clouds.

The camp site in Glyntawe is owned by the same farmer who owns the Dan yr Ogof caves, a Shire Horse Centre and various other tourist-type crowd-pullers, so we were a bit surprised to find that apart from ourselves there were only two other tents on the site. After a meal in the pub we turned in for our first night in my new Saunders tent. Although they had agreed to let me choose any tent from their range back in early April, I had only taken delivery of one of their Hilltrek models just days before leaving for Wales, and so had had no time to even pitch the thing, never mind actually test it. As the heavens re-opened for my tent-testing benefit we tried to get to sleep as the monsoon rains pounded the canvas (or whatever they make them out of these days) just feet above our heads.

Sunday 7th June ~ A Lazy Beginning

I awoke at 8.00ish to find the tent being pelted with yet more rain. I listened for a while as it drummed heavily above our heads before burying my head in my sleeping bag and going back to sleep—I knew that I only had a short walk ahead of me, whilst Rachel's drive home shouldn't take her much more than about 6 hours.

It was 1p.m. before we emerged from our bags, late-breakfasted and packed up what we each needed for the day. I left the tent pitched at Dan yr Ogof and got Rachel to drop me off at the summit of the A4069 above Brynamman before she began the drive home.

Knowing that it would be almost a month before we'd see each other again, we'd spent the morning constantly stalling and putting off the inevitable. We'd never been apart for this length of time in all our years together and I think we both knew that it would be a real wrench when I stepped out of the car and made for the grass-covered limestone screes of **Garreg Lwyd**, my first Hewitt of the trip.

However, within minutes of leaving Rachel at the tiny car park at the top of the pass which takes the A4069 across this, the western slopes of the Mynydd Ddu, I became entranced by the wonders of these glorious hills, and immersed myself fully in the mountain environment, an environment which I knew well, but not one with which I had ever cohabited for such a length of time. I could only wait to see how the relationship would develop.

The difference in height between the road pass and the summit of **Garreg Lwyd** is only a little over 400 feet, with easy grassy slopes leading me past typical limestone shakeholes and up over scree to the plateau-like top at 616 metres. The ancient summit cairn is huge, and is made out of thousands of irregular rocks hewn by the wind, each crevice giving a toe-hold for dark green mosses and lichens. The centre of the cairn is hollowed out and gives a welcome wind shelter for the walker.

Dark clouds were piling up far out to the west and a strong breeze threatened to blow them my way as I headed, again down easy slopes, this time covered in mat-grass and ground-hugging bilberry, towards the wide col between **Garreg Lwyd** and the minor top of Foel Fraith. At the col grow wind-scarred junipers, each laying low and spreading spiky branches over the stony ground.

Foel Fraith was soon behind me as I plodded past the peaty pool of Blaenllynfell before taking to the long south ridge of **Garreg Las**. Flat pavements of limestone, reminiscent of my beloved dales of Yorkshire, led up the ridge towards the summit. A number of small crags, some of which are separated from the parent mountain by wide crevasses, fall away to the west. Rowans grow out of these crevasses, thankful for the shelter the outside wall of limestone provides against the elements. Twin cairns, again of giant proportions, marked the top of **Garreg Las**, and I took shelter from the wind in the hollow of one of them, both to check the map and to have a bite to eat. Cold winds brought a quick shower of hail as I sat hunched up in the shelter eating, and soon had me on my feet heading down to the next col.

A public bridleway connects the Sawdde valley away to the north to the Tawe valley to the south-east and crosses the ridge near the col before the pathless climb up to Waun Lefrith on the main ridge of the Mynydd Ddu.

As I neared the col, I came across what I at first took to be a dead sheep. It lay motionless on its back, and it wasn't until I drew closer that I noticed its lamb crouching beside it. As I approached, the ewe began flailing its legs about in a desperate effort to turn over, but just couldn't manage it. Ignoring its panic-stricken eyes, dark with fear, I quickly put my hands under its damp back, grabbed a fist full of warm fleece, and with a great heave, righted it. The ewe sprang away, lamb in tow, and was quickly out of sight.

Confident that this display of kindness towards a helpless animal could only guarantee brilliant weather for at least the rest of my trip, I found a stream to follow uphill to gain the main ridge of the Mynydd Ddu. Sure enough, within minutes the hail stopped and the sun made an effort to do better in the future.

From the col-of-the-capsized-sheep the geology had changed quite noticeably. The outcropping rock of the Garregs is a delightful whitey-grey carboniferous limestone, but as I climbed higher onto the main ridge, this gave way to beds of the Old Red Sandstone, common on the higher mountains of the Brecon Beacons National Park.

At Waun Lefrith breathtaking almost-vertical slopes of grass, interspersed with broken crags and scree plunge down to the lake of Llyn y Fan Fach to the north. I scanned the rippling waters for signs of a woman. The mother to the legendary Physicians of Myddfai is said to have come from out of this lake, and after being beaten three times by her husband, returned there only to be seen once more, by her three sons, upon whom she bestowed the knowledge to make them great men of medicine. All I could make out was a man in a bright red jacket having a sandwich beside a small building.

A good path led me around the rim of the cwm and up to the third Hewitt of the day, **Bannau Sir Gaer**, or **Carmarthen Fan** as it is commonly known. Black rain clouds swept the valleys to the south as I dropped down to the col away to the east and began the long climb up to the summit of **Fan Brycheiniog**, my highest of the day.

An Ordnance Survey Triangulation Pillar marks the summit along with another good wind shelter. I rested for a while and took in the stepped ridges of the mountains in the Fforest Fawr, Brecon Beacons and Black Mountain ranges stretching away to the east. Heading south-east across the top of the sweeping slopes of the mountain, the next, and last summit of the day, **Fan Hir** came easily.

Although no path was shown on the map, I could make out a bit of one descending the ridge of **Fan Hir** directly towards Glyntawe. I took to this and quickly lost height, eventually gaining a public footpath alongside the Afon Tawe before joining the main road back to the camp site.

Cocooned in my tent with a plate full of pasta and a good book, I felt reasonably pleased with myself. In only five hours I had completed the hills of the Mynydd Ddu, five in total, and although I had a longer day tomorrow, I felt confident that I would do as well then. But for now, I had only to relax until about half past nine when I had told Rachel that I'd ring her to see that she had arrived home safely. Apparently, the exhaust fell off the car near Merthyr Tydfil, and being a Sunday, the AA man that came to her rescue had a hard job in trying to find a garage that was open and willing to fix it. She had only got home minutes before, after an exhausting eight hour drive!

Monday 8th June ~ A Foul Day

I had been looking forward to rubbing noses with the hills of the Fforest Fawr, an ancient hunting forest, as it was one area of South Wales, along with much of the Black Mountains further east, that I had never visited. However, the sound of heavy rain failed to inspire me and instead I lingered over Graham Greene's *The Honorary Consul* and a cup of peppermint tea. It became increasingly obvious that I was in for a bit of a soaking, and I eventually prised myself from my warm sleeping bag.

Once I'd broken camp I headed off for the old railway track which contours the opposite slopes of the Tawe valley. Passing through small limestone quarries before gaining the track, I came across a field of friendly ponies who escorted me at very close quarters.

Welsh Mountain Ponies in the Brecon Beacons

From the cinder tracks of the old railway, another bulldozed track led up through dripping conifers and on to the south ridge of **Fan Gyhirych**. Again, as I gained height the geology changed from the limestone of the valleys to the Old Red Sandstone of the mountains. The bulldozed track continued to within a short distance of the summit before it veered off to the east. I reached the almost pathless summit in a howling gale, which drove stinging rain and hail into my face as I fought to gain the small cairn which marks the top. I found it very hard to stand, let alone walk in a straight line, and was only too grateful that for the greater part of the day, the wind would be on my back.

I returned to the bulldozed track and found a permissive path, the gate to which was guarded by a herd of cattle, which took me down boggy slopes to an even boggier col before the climb up to **Fan Nedd**. I followed a stone wall for a while, but it soon began contouring rather than climbing, so I abandoned its undoubted aid to navigation and took to bilberry covered slopes. Within a couple of hundred feet of rough climbing, I came across a path which I had been walking almost parallel to, and soon had the summit ridge underfoot. At the northern end of the ridge stands a proud cairn, beside which I left my rucksack while I headed off to bag the summit. Although I often worried about somebody finding my rucksack and deciding that they would like to take it home, leaving it against a prominent feature such as a cairn while I went off to bag a summit was something I was to do fairly regularly over the coming weeks. It seemed pointless carrying it all the way to a peak, only to have to return with it perhaps half an hour later, if I could just leave it and save myself the extra strain.

With the wind playing games on the top, I didn't linger long. I just touched the tiny cairn with the toe of my boot and turned tail to flee. Picking the rucksack up at the cairn I soon descended to the minor road near the ancient standing stone, Maen Llia.

Plodding up towards the north-east ridge of **Fan Llia**, the rain still wasn't showing any signs of giving me a break, and as I seemed to be strug-gling I knew I would have my work cut out to reach the ridge across the valley to bag **Fan Fawr** if I planned to stay the night at the Llwyn-y-celyn Youth Hostel. I hadn't booked a bed there, but I really didn't fancy trying to pitch a tent with the wind gusting from all quarters. There were two choices, neither of which I was comfortable with. If I went out on the ridge to bag **Fan Fawr**, I would have to find a site for the tent somewhere on the col before the rise up to **Craig Cerrig-gleisiad**, whereas if I left **Fan Fawr** to get to the Youth Hostel that night, I'd have to make a separate trip to bag

Fan Fawr tomorrow, putting me a day behind schedule. I reasoned that as my plan had been to climb all of the hills in the Fforest Fawr today anyway, and that was clearly out of the question in the present conditions, I was behind schedule already and so might as well make the effort to get to the warmth and comfort of the Youth Hostel.

I left the undistinguished summit of **Fan Llia** and took the grassy ridge over Cefn Perfedd. An endless path through the grass led eventually to the col above Craig Cwm-du where for the first and last time that day the cloud cleared revealing the slopes of **Craig Cerrig-gleisiad** and the far-off col below **Fan Fawr**. I knew then that I had made the right decision. Even before I made it as far as the col the clouds had merged together again to form a grey blanket around me.

Long slopes led up to the boggy plateau before the summit of **Craig Cerrig-gleisiad**, and just beyond, a fence bars the walker from straying over onto the cliffs of the nature reserve. Following this fence northwards, I soon picked up a good track heading down to a muddy col before a style led over to easy slopes towards the summit of **Fan Frynych**.

After nine hours of hard going, for much of the time over featureless ground and in consistently heavy rain, I sloshed down north-eastwards to gain a public footpath heading back south into the cwm below the cliffs of the nature reserve. Feeling much the worse for wear, I gained the road and plodded along in a daze to the Youth Hostel.

The warden appeared from a back room as I entered looking totally bedraggled, and kindly told me that the hostel was full. I just couldn't believe it! I had battled against possibly the worst weather of the whole year, never mind the season; it was an incredibly wicked night in the middle of nowhere and this huge building, which, like all Youth Hostels, was originally intended to offer shelter to weary walkers, climbers and cyclists—in short anybody who had arrived under their own steam—was full to the rafters with tourists and motorists. Making me even more upset was the fact that I'd given up the chance of bagging **Fan Fawr** for the sake of a good night's sleep in a Youth Hostel and the possibility of drying out some clothes. And that was only the start of my problems. I had lost a day from my schedule and still didn't have a clue were I would be sleeping that night.

Hoping for suggestions from the warden I eagerly awaited his return from his little room at the back of the hostel. Return he eventually did with an "Oh. Still here." Upon further questioning, he waved an arm in a general northerly direction and muttered something about there being a campsite at a place whose name I didn't quite catch. I asked how far, and with a grin he muttered, "Well actually, I'm not sure if it's there anymore, but if it is, it can't be much more than about six miles."

This was way beyond what I could take without desiring to slap the little fellow about the face, so I stuffed my hands into my rainwater-collecting pockets to keep them out of harm's way and fell outside into the weather.

There appeared to be only one thing for it, I would have to find a site in the corrie of the Cwm Cerrig-gleisiad Nature Reserve—strictly against their by-laws, but by that time I was pretty desperate.

The wind up in the cwm had lost all direction, howling round the cliffs, first clockwise then counter-clockwise and finally, for a bit of variety, in a vertical descent from the rim of the beetling cliffs.

After an age, I had the tent pitched of a fashion, and throwing my rucksack inside, followed it as another squall of wind-driven hail tore at the flimsy nylon flysheet. The whole thing bellowed in and out like the inside of a huge green lung and it was immediately obvious that unless I wanted to lose it, I would have to get outside and batten down the hatches more securely for what was building up to being a really wild night. After getting in and out for the nth time, I gave up and dived inside to make a meal. Emptying my rucksack I could have wept when the soggy mess of pasta shells, soup packets and once-dried milk powder flopped onto the floor of the tent in a mangled stew of rainwater. My food bag had taken a real soaking but at least the contents should still be just about edible. I got the stove going and dumped some gruel into a pan. My next priority was to get out of my wet clothes and into my sleeping bag. I peeled off my tatty Gore-Tex outers, sponge-like fleeces and drenched underwear, and unrolling my sleeping bag discovered that it too was soaking. With a fibre-filled bag this wouldn't have been too much of a problem as they still provide warmth even when wet. However, I had plumped for the much lighter, warmer (when dry) and more expensive duck-down version, which is next to useless when damp and may as well be thrown in the nearest bin when really wet. As I had by now begun to shiver uncontrollably, I hardly dared inspect my spare clothing. Luckily everything in that sack was totally dry, so I put on every stitch and gobbled down some food. The meths burner on the stove had run dry so I refilled it and set about getting a real fug going in the confines of the tent. Cooking in tents is usually discouraged, and for very good reason. Tent nylon, though extremely light-weight, waterproof and durable is also highly flammable, but there are times, such as in my present predicament when to attempt cooking outside would be verging on idiocy. For a start, the wind would have instantly whipped the stove and pans away across the dark, lonely expanses of the cwm.

Pertex, the outer material on my sleeping bag is also highly flammable, but as the stove was my only source of heat, I carefully dried it out above the flames.

During all this palaver the wind was having a pretty good attempt at flattening my tent, but to be totally fair to Saunders, the manufacturers, I don't think I'm over-exaggerating when I say that brick houses would probably have been blown flat that night in that tempestuous corrie.

As I didn't know what surprises the night would bring—I might easily have to abandon everything at any moment—I packed most of my gear, left my torch handy and made an effort to try to cram as many high calorie foods into my mouth as I could possibly eat before finally lying down to sleep at 1.30a.m. What with worrying about the wildly flapping tent, and the fact that my plans were in tatters, sleep didn't come easily.

Tuesday 9th June ~ More Hard Grind

At 5.30 I could stand it no longer. The tent had survived the night, but the shear weight of the rain combined with the still heavy winds were battering the flysheet down onto the inner tent and collapse seemed imminent. Time to abandon ship, but at least the dim, grey light of morning had arrived.

It was obvious that I must find a camp site where I could dry everything out. The question was, did I head down Glyn Tarell with the hope of finding the camp site recommended by the Youth Hostel warden—if it still existed, or did I head over the pass at the head of the cwm and make my way down the valley of the Afon Taf on the other side where a site was marked on the map at the village of Llwyn-Onn.

Although Llwyn-Onn was a good deal further, it would leave my options open for continuing with the outlying peak of **Cefn yr Ystrad**, even if the main Brecon Beacons ridge would be slightly harder of access. But what to do about **Fan Fawr**? The obvious answer would be to bag it on the way over to the Taff valley as it lies only one mile south-west of the summit of the pass at the Storey Arms Outdoor Centre. However, the wind was still howling madly from the south-west, and in my sleepy state of retreat, I didn't want to even think about going up high today, let alone into the very teeth of the storm.

I made some porridge for breakfast, washed it down with a couple of mugs of tea and stepped out into the utter chaos of Cwm Cerrig-gleisiad at the unearthly hour of 6.30. Despite the wind and rain gusting merrily into my face, the way up to the Storey Arms Centre went remarkably quickly, following as it does the well marked path of the Taff Trail.

From a car park at the summit of the pass a path begins the 1000 feet ascent to **Fan Fawr**'s summit. In a mad minute of enthusiasm I decided to go for it, but first took shelter in the phone box beside the road to nibble on some chocolate.

Back in the wind I struggled uphill, counting steps to keep a good momentum going, rather than as a way of measuring distance. The angle isn't too steep and the wet grass underfoot was kind to my sore feet.

Allowing myself a short rest after every 400 steps, I found that I began to gain height relatively easily, and actually began to enjoy battling against the elements. True, the rain was still pelting down and having no problem finding its way up the sleeves of my jacket, but there is some satisfaction to be gained from testing oneself against the elements and coming out on top.

Just above a marshy depression between two knolls, a rocky outcrop gave an ideal place to leave my rucksack, allowing me the freedom to race on to the summit without its extra weight. Although the remaining height to gain the summit ridge was soon behind me, the wind found new strength (I nearly said it gained its second wind!) and made a mockery of my efforts to remain upright. This was one of those rare occasions when I wished I'd kept my rucksack on—the extra weight would have acted as ballast. Visibility was not much above zero yards, so I paced out the distance to the top.

Finding a few sandstone cobbles piled as a small cairn, I turned my back to the wind and thankfully raced on down to my sack.

Heading south-east towards the Beacons Reservoir, now emerging from the cloud below me, I soon picked up the Taff Trail again and followed the signs through the dripping pine forests above the Afon Taf Fawr. My spirits were up, having snatched a summit in the foulest summer weather I've known for a long time. I paused in the drizzle to admire the magenta flowers of the rhododendrons in the forest, and just above the Cantref Reservoir, a sandy fox made a dash for cover into a dense thicket of scrub.

At last, only the minor road alongside the west bank of the Llwyn-on Reservoir remained before the plod across the dam to the insignificant village, and the camp site at Grawen farm.

Not finding anyone home, I found my own spot beneath a clump of ash trees and got the tent up as the sun came out to have a bash at drying it for me. Lambs in a nearby field found me most interesting and made a point of chasing up to the fence each time I passed, while grey squirrels made it obvious that they considered my food bag easy pickings, even though I left it in the inner tent with the door zipped up.

Although the odd squally shower made a hash of my efforts to dry out the tent completely, I discovered a tumble dryer in the toilet block and wasted no time in throwing everything in.

The owners of the site were typically pleasant Welsh farmers. They'd lived at Grawen for over 30 years as tenants of the various Water Boards who had owned the land. Although their main source of income had been livestock, they were finding that the camp site had grown into a pretty lucrative enterprise. Plans had been forwarded to the National Park Authority for increasing their number of electrical hook-ups for caravans, but had so far been rejected. Both the farmer and his wife showed a great deal of interest in my walk, particularly as they have a vested interest in providing their visitors with information on what to do in their local area. They could appreciate that a guidebook about the Welsh mountains would be of particular interest to these visitors.

After my chat with them, I recovered the last of my clothes from the dryer and headed off to my tent for a meal. As the stove purred away, the occasional patch of blue sky flitted between whitening clouds and cast dappled shade onto the roof of my tent through the pale green leaves of the ash tree canopy above—it looked like my luck was changing.

Wednesday 10th June ~ Regrouping

Although I woke to a bright and cheerful morning, my first priority was to pop down the road to Cefn Coed to buy a rucksack liner, for I knew I was partly to blame for the soggy mess in my rucksack. Even the most expensive modern rucksacks are seldom waterproof, but for some reason I'd convinced myself that my new Aiguille Alpine Equipment one would be. I usually use a tough plastic sack to line my rucksack and keep its contents dry, but strangely, hadn't bothered for this trip. This was something that I had to remedy if I wanted to avoid dying of hypothermia the next time the heavens decided to open. On any walk into the mountains, keeping spare clothes dry is absolutely essential, especially on an overnight trip. I had learned this lesson long ago, but luckily had only had to suffer a sleepless night for my neglect and lunacy.

So, despite the perfect weather, today was spent trying to find a shop which sold large plastic bags. I also needed some more methylated spirits for the stove, as trying to dry my sleeping bag out in Cwm Cerrig-gleisiad had used up about half of my reserves.

As a keen rock climber, I tend to be always on the look-out for any climbable piece of rock wherever I go, and so as not to have a completely wasted day, I had a good look at the limestone crags of Darren Fach above the busy A470 to Merthyr Tydfil. Blank-looking walls and one or two broken arêtes looked worthy of attention, but would have to wait until I could return with all the paraphernalia of my climbing rack. Yellow rock roses adorned the vast screes below the crag as well as one or two clumps of purple vetch.

Just beyond Darren Fach a minor road took me into the centre of Cefn Coed with its scattering of shops. A fish and chip lunch bucked me up, as did the next shop along, a hardware-cum-grocery store. I found a couple of black bin-liners to use as a rucksack liner, but couldn't see any meths on the untidy shelves among bottles of white spirit, bleach and weed killer, so I found the assistant.

"Excuse me," I began, "I don't suppose you sell methylated spirits?"

"That'll be the purple one, is it?" she asked in an accent typical of South Wales.

"Yes. That's right."

"No. Sorry we only have white spirit and the other white one ... er ..."

Obviously needing some assistance herself, I offered, "You mean turps."

"Er, no. We don't sell that one either I'm afraid," and then as the name came to her, "It'll be turpentine that we sell. Do you want some of that?"

Trying to suppress my grin, I declined and paid for the two bin-liners. If the weather took another turn for the worst, these two simple bags could prove to be the most valuable items of equipment I had bought for the entire trip.

Back at the site I spent the remainder of the afternoon alternately basking in the sun and diving for cover from the infrequent showers. Although on the whole the weather had made a vast improvement during the course of the day, away to the north a long dark smudge hid the upper-most slopes and ridges of the Brecon Beacons and Fforest Fawr hills.

I could hardly wait to see what the morning would bring when I would step back into the fray and resume my journey along the spine of the Cambrian Mountains.

Thursday 11th June ~ Cefn yr Ystrad and to the base of the Beacons

I'd heard from the farmer that the weathermen had forecast a vast improvement for the coming weekend. Boosted by this news and keen to get on, I'd actually woken at 4a.m. to find a regular storm blasting the hills of South Wales, and finding it hard to get back to sleep, I'd read for a while. Waking again at 9.30 with my torch on and my book still open on my chest, I began making a brew of Horlicks as more rain blew down the valley.

By way of perfect timing I read the last few paragraphs of *The Honorary Consul* as the last pitiful drops of rain fell from a speedily clearing sky. Equally quickly, I washed the breakfast pots and struck camp. I took the road northwards for a couple of hundred yards before gaining a bridle track which wound its way uphill, first through conifer plantations and then onto open moorland around the southern flank of Garn Ddu.

I knew I would only be bagging one Hewitt today, **Cefn yr Ystrad** away to the east, so I deliberately took my time on the easy contouring slopes that lead towards the village of Pontsticill above the reservoir of the same name.

Around the boggy depression of the Nant Cwm-moel I made acquaintance with some more Welsh Mountain Ponies, which I managed to frighten the life out of. Unfortunately, I got the impression that sooner or later, these semi-wild horses were going to frighten the life out of me!

A track became a minor road and led out onto the public road near the junction to Vaynor Church. Here I turned left and plodded tarmac to Pontsticill village.

Weather-wise things were really improving. For the most part the sky was a rare world of blue, with just the odd fluffy cumulus to add a bit of variety to the scene. It actually looked like I might be in for a completely dry day, although the wind still blew hard from the west, with an ability to carry storm clouds my way without much trouble.

Snack-wise I was starving, and having only half a packet of Love-Hearts (don't ask!) and a chocolate biscuit handy in the pocket of my rucksack I began to think about buying a sandwich in one of the shops or pubs in the village. There didn't seem to be any of the former, and although I tried both the Butcher's Arms and the Red Cow in the latter category, they both were completely deserted. I'd have to starve until I could be bothered to delve deep down into my rucksack.

Once down in the valley I crossed the road and ducked under a bridge taking the Brecon Mountain Railway. On the climb up from the other side, I stopped to take my top off. The incredible had happened—for the first time in five days of walking I was hot enough not to need a fleece pullover.

The bridleway marked on my map was not easy to follow through the wonderful karst-paved pastures of this typical limestone hill, but with a bit of guess-work and a bit of a fumble around, I soon made the summit of **Cefn yr Ystrad**.

Food time. I took some grotty looking water from a pool near the summit and dropped in a couple of sterilising tablets, then wandered over to one of

*Layers of Old Red Sandstone form **Pen y Fan**, along with most of the other high mountains of South Wales*

the two big cairns which mark the top, along with a trig pillar. The views to the north towards the Brecon Beacons had been superb all day, but as I'd neared the top, the whale-back ridges of the Black Mountains had filled the north-eastern horizon. Away to the south the heavily industrialised valleys of South Wales dominated the scene.

I had a brew up and a bit of a snack, then began the descent through the vast quarries which have all but obliterated the northern and western sides of the hill. On the way down I picked up the unmistakable smell of some- thing very dead and rotting. I followed my nose for well over 700 yards to find a maggoty dead horse at the base of a small limestone outcrop. A boggy bridleway led on down to the railway alongside Pontsticill Reservoir, through a semi-harvested conifer plantation.

The four Hewitts of the Brecon Beacons actually began to look quite easy as I headed north towards Pentwyn Reservoir, the next in the chain up the valley. I was almost tempted to have a bash that night, but the problem with that idea was that I'd planned to camp at Crickhowell, nine miles to the east, after bagging those four, and that, on top of what I'd already walked would be perhaps asking a bit too much. For that night, my plan had been to find a wild site somewhere around the Neuadd Reservoirs further up the Taf Fechan, and so have easy access to **Pen y Fan** the following morning. However, as I'd not been there before, I wasn't sure if there would be anywhere suitable for a camp in the area, and if it was far enough away from any habitations so as not to cause a problem. I remained undecided as I walked on.

I gained the end of a minor road at Dolygaer Outdoor Centre and Scout Camp, which led over the dam of the Pentwyn Reservoir and along the west side. Where another road heads off eastwards over a pass towards Talybont Reservoir, I caught a glimpse of a large Duke of Edinburgh Award Expedition camping down in the trees by the river. This put my mind at rest as far as wild camping in the area went, and I even considered going down to join them. However, it was very likely that they were just a group of kids doing a Gold Award, in which case they would be camping alone without a leader, which would mean that they would either have been extremely noisy throughout the entire night, or else absolutely terrified of this strange bloke pitching his tent next door. I changed my mind and pushed on.

It became obvious that doing the Brecon Beacons that night would be out of the question unless I fancied it in the dark, so I looked for a camp site, eventually settling on a large flat area surrounded by rhododendrons below the dam of the Lower Neuadd Reservoir.

The camp site really was ideal. I was literally at the very foot of tomorrow's climb up **Pen y Fan** via the long moorland ridge of Graig Fan Ddu, so I couldn't be better placed. The stream ran just yards from my tent door, gurgling over pebbles and gulping in the small stoppers made by bigger boulders.

I put a pan of pasta on the stove and contented myself with the sight of a dipper flitting in quick wing-beats from one water-washed boulder to another. Just as in my pre-trip dreams, a grey wagtail joined him for a while atop a curvaceous sandstone block.

Later that night a minibus pulled in at the car park above my camp and a hoard of teenagers fell out. For a moment I thought they were going to camp next to me, but luckily they just passed behind me on the dam and took to the slopes of Graig Fan Ddu as the sun filtered over the dusky ridge in an orange smudge, silhouetting each young walker against the evening sky.

Friday 12th June ~ The rest of the Brecon Beacons

Another good day, starting with an adult dipper trying to teach a juvenile the rudiments of successful fishing, right outside my door.

Full of enthusiasm, I rose at 7.30, and after a quick breakfast and an even quicker paddle in the rushing stream, was sweating up the slopes of Graig Fan Ddu an hour later, under a perfectly cloudless sky.

I followed the rim of the heavily vegetated sandstone cliffs around in an arc to the north-west, over Graig Fan Ddu and Gwaun Taf to the obvious col at Bwlch Duwynt. From the col I considered taking in the summit of Corn Du, but it not being a Hewitt as it is not a separate peak, I decided that the day's walk would be long enough without this addition. A path contoured around this minor summit for a short way before gaining a small col before the easy climb up to the lofty summit of **Pen y Fan**. On this last section, walkers seemed to emerge from every direction, a good few of us making this, the highest summit of the Brecon Beacons National Park, at the same time.

The red screes down Craig Cwm Sere were partly paved in an effort to lessen erosion caused by the thousands who come this way every year, and I was soon passed by the less heavily encumbered walkers.

At the summit of **Cribyn** a huge party of teenagers didn't inspire me to linger so I nipped down Craig Cwm Cynwyn to the next col. As I arrived there, a squad of young army recruits were being put through their paces, at least half of them on the verge of collapse. I'd seen them running up the wide path in Cwm Cynwyn to the north. Absolute madness in the blazing heat.

Heading up **Fan y Big** a group of fell ponies posed for a photo before I plodded on uphill in the searing heat of the late morning. At the top I became convinced that the actual summit was a grassy knoll to the south, rather than that marked on the map. It certainly looked higher from where I was sitting, but as I was heading that way anyway, it would be no problem to bag it on the way past. The over-head sun picked out the dark peat griffs on **Waun Rydd**, my next summit, across Cwm Oergwm.

Half an hour later, as I looked back along Craig Cwmoergwm, the south ridge of **Fan y Big**, it was obvious that the little grassy knoll along the ridge that I had made a point of bagging in case it was the highest part of the mountain, was in fact well below the summit marked on the map. Oh well!

The path contoured around in a big arc to the east before crossing the grassy **Waun Rydd** just south of the summit. The path itself actually passes a big cairn which most walkers probably take as being the top, although this is actually seven metres lower than the true summit.

Beginning to feel the heat, I bombed down the long east ridge towards Talybont Reservoir. Initially the path was very steep over rough grass, but soon levelled out to become a gentle gradient all the way down to the shore.

Retailers the world over seem to delight in discussing with absolute strangers the state of business and the success of their own little enterprise. The owner of the ice-cream van by the reservoir's dam was no exception. Trade was terrible, he told me, partly because of the rain (which was a fair

Fan y Big *across the head of Cwm Cynwyn*

199

*Looking back to the higher Beacons from **Fan y Big***

comment) and partly because of the extreme cold (I'd been boiling all day). Apparently, he'd had to scrape ice off his windows that very morning. I heard this last detail with total disbelief as I'd been snug as a bug in a rug in my little tent below the Neuadd Reservoirs. However, a conversation with Rachel on the phone later on, revealed that there had been warnings of a ground frost—it must have affected north-facing ground as my cwm had had its foot to the south.

Over the dam a total confusion of paths led up through a wood to gain the minor road which skirts the west side of Tor y Foel—a prominent hill of just below 2000 feet. A signpost for a bridleway crossing the road was rather misleading, pointing to a dangerous scramble over a high barbed-wire fence. I wandered 30 feet to the right and took a good path by a hawthorn hedge.

Skirting the wooded hillsides above the almost parallel River Usk and Monmouthshire and Brecon Canal, I managed to disturb a middle aged couple who were, shall we say, making the most of each other's company! Despite the fact that I was clattering along the path, Brasher Trekking Poles clicking at every step and whistling a merry tune for good measure, it took a good loud cough before the semi-naked pair became aware that I wanted to go through the gate that they were leaning against. With a 'we weren't really doing anything' air, the man nearly fell over himself and his pants in an effort to open the gate for me, while the woman ashamedly hid her face in case she knew me. I passed through the gate, thanking the man for his courtesy and remarking on what a nice day it was for it.

Crossing over the canal via an old iron bridge, I began toeing the towpath in a Crickhowell-bound direction. My feet were beginning to feel a tad sore and my shoulders were grumbling under the strain of continually carrying a heavy rucksack.

A series of locks at Llangynidr added a delightful tone to the canal path, and picnickers and dog walkers were everywhere. A real 'away from the mountains' atmosphere prevailed, and an old couple stopped to ask me if I was backpacking along the length of the canal. The actual truth astonished them.

At last, at 6.30 I took a track from the towpath down into the hamlet of Dardy and followed the B4558 into the quaint market town of Crickhowell. The camp site immediately got my vote of confidence by having excellent showers and a laundry. After throwing a pair of worn out socks into the nearest dustbin, I headed into the town for a burger and chips. It had been a long day; 20 miles with over 1000 metres of ascent, but again I felt as if the fight was back on, and I could afford another rest day as I wasn't due at the Youth Hostel at Capel-y-ffin until Monday night.

Crickhowell Castle, set in a park in the town

Saturday 13th June ~ A Day in Crickhowell

Rising late, I spent a pleasant day wandering through the streets of Crickhowell, buying fresh groceries for the next two days, stocking up on socks, meths for the stove, and books from a charity shop to keep me from going mad, as well as writing to people back home.

Once again the weather had managed a complete about-face,

bringing heavy showers throughout the day. At 11a.m. the cloud base hung low and rain fell in hard-stinging sheets, but by 11.30 the top of Crug Hywel, or the fort of Hywell, after whom the town is named, could be seen rising high above the town on the slopes of **Pen Cerrig-calch**. Hywell Dda, or Hywell the Good, was the grandson of the great Welsh king Rhodri, back in the ninth century. Although maps today show two names for the summit of this flat-topped hill, Crug Hywel and Table Mountain, it is unfortunate that many local people now refer to the hill by it's meaningless anglicised name. It would surely be a great loss to ancient Welsh history if this hill fort lost its identity and became known simply as Table Mountain.

Sunday 14th June ~ The Western Black Mountains

I was soon plodding up a farm track towrads Crug Hywell, scattering redstarts from the hedgerows as I went. My rucksack felt its usual unwieldy self and I couldn't see myself getting much further unless I could make the load more comfortable. I sat in a buttercup meadow beyond the farm build-ings of The Wern, and completely emptied the sack. A couple of walkers passed me by as I began carefully re-packing all of my gear. Each morning I'd packed it within the confines of my tent, and had just thrown things in. This time I made sure that there wasn't anything sharp or hard digging me in the back and also that the load was evenly distributed. I shouldered the pack and instantly knew that I had got things right for once—I had relearnt another lesson.

I took the path around the east side of Crug Hywel rather than the steeper one directly over the nose in front. Stopping high on the ridge of Trwyn Ysgwrfa for a drink, a fox darted across the brackeny col behind me. Although the whole hillside was providing rough grazing for sheep and young lambs, the fox dashed between them and strangely, they didn't bat an eyelid. I know that foxes rarely kill lambs, much preferring the easy meat of carrion, but I would have at least expected the sheep to make a run for it.

At last the going became easier as I topped out on the broad shelf of the summit of **Pen Cerrig-calch**. Away to the south-east rose the cone of Sugar Loaf above Abergavenny, but nearer at hand my eye was drawn by the striking quartzite-like rocks which adorn the summit in a blaze of white. I continued straight over the top, with its trig pillar and ancient cairns, making for the path above Cwm Banw to the east.

Just before the rise to **Pen Allt-mawr**, a lazy shower began to fall, so I wearily donned waterproofs despite the heat of what had already been a claggy morning. A large group of young schoolgirls adorned the summit of **Pen Allt-mawr** in various stages of collapse so I beat a hasty retreat down the long ridge leading on, over Pen Twyn Glas to **Mynydd Llysiau**.

Although the rain was mildly sporadic, like a complete idiot I decided to grab a bite to eat just as the heavens opened in earnest. Of course my new method of packing the rucksack meant that my food bag was somewhere near the bottom, requiring virtually everything else to be taken out first and making damned sure that everything got at least a bit of a soaking. Cheered up by this lunacy of mine, I had a good excuse for putting my rediscovered rucksack-packing skills to the ultimate test—a speed packing exercise in the pelting rain.

The rain came and went, and then came again as I made good progress up the rocky nose of Pen Trumau and across the boggy col beyond. I'd always considered Kinder Scout in the Peak District to be boggy until I came upon the slopes leading up the final summit ridge of **Waun Fach**. At least Kinder Scout is usually only boggy on the horizontal bits. The water on **Waun Fach**, however, seems to be totally unaware that it is supposed to be drawn down by gravity, eventually to the sea, on anything even remotely resembling a gradient. The west ridge of **Waun Fach** was a 45° quagmire of stinking swamp, oozing peat and putrefied sphagnum, gurgling in a boot gobbling frenzy with every step I took. Maybe I'd just caught it on a bad day. As for the flat top of the mountain, well—perhaps I need say no more!

On the way over to bag **Pen y Gadair Fawr** to the south-east, it began to rain properly. No more of this weak drizzly dreich. Huge bullets of water hurtled down from out of the dismal clouds all around as I doggedly followed a compass bearing to pick up an unseen path. I left my sack at the col just before the final rise, and wasted no time in running up to bag the top. I was back in minutes, and quickly descending the convex slopes towards the Grwyne Fawr Reservoir.

I now faced a bit of a problem. It was only 12.45p.m., and as my pace for the day had been cracking, I was only about half an hour from the bothy where I had planned to stay the night. No self respecting mountaineer-cum-hillwalker would be seen dead calling it a day at such an early time, and I could hardly have claimed to be tired. Just over the ridge across the valley was the Youth Hostel at Capel-y-ffin, but I wasn't due there for another day, and I didn't fancy trekking extra miles today just to be told that the hostel was full for the night. I decided to contemplate my options on the descent to the reservoir.

Once there, I plumped for crossing the ridge. Only 120 metres above the reservoir, my sixth Hewitt of the day could be seen tempting me onwards. I had planned to climb this, **Chwarel y Fan**, along with **Twmpa** tomorrow, but if I could bring my booking at the Youth Hostel forward one day from Monday night, I could then bag **Twmpa** and **Black Mountain** tomorrow on the way to Hay-on-Wye.

The way up **Chwarel y Fan** was easy as I soon found a path through the thick grasses and hard rushes of its western flank, and in no time at all I had reached the summit, fringed just below the ridge with the stumps of recently harvested conifers.

I arrived at the Youth Hostel to find that, yes, they had plenty of room. I settled in for the night with my fellow hostellers—a couple of cyclists; an old fellow whom I had passed the time of day with earlier on, on the way up **Waun Fach**; a quiet pair of Flemish girls; and a young man on a pony trekking holiday.

The hostel is pleasant, very basic but homely, and the evening passed comfortably amid much discussion of horses. The Youth Hostel has quite a number of ponies and runs its own pony trekking courses with the aid of Howard, a burly but friendly type who evidently uses Capel-y-ffin as his second home.

Monday 15th June ~ To Hay-on-Wye

Jack Evans, the Youth Hostel warden, greeted me with a request to fill the coal buckets before I headed off. This is an old tradition with Youth Hostels in Britain, though one that is now dying out. Youth Hostels were originally used by young people who had arrived under their own steam, be it on foot or by bike, and provided cheap lodgings for the night in return for the hosteller helping out with one or two chores to help keep costs down. These days it is only the smaller, out of the way hostels which insist on this, as quite often the bigger hostels are filled with foreign tourists or motorists trying to get away from it all. Although I am more than happy to share a hostel with these tourists, it is a shame that the genuine hillgoer has a real problem finding low-cost lodgings in the hills. Over the past couple of years, the Youth Hostel Association has actually taken this a step further and has closed down quite a number of smaller hostels in mountainous areas, putting the money so raised towards building new, state-of-the-art hostels in our cities. In short, the Youth Hostel Association has turned its back on the hillgoer, and has sold its soul to tourism.

For this reason I was more than happy to help with the task alloted me. After breakfast, I set too with a will and soon had half a dozen coal buckets lined up beside the old stove in the entrance hall of the hostel.

*Storm clouds brewing up over the Vale of Ettwys
from the south ridge of **Twmpa***

By about 9a.m. I was on my way, making for a track which zigzags steeply up, onto the long ridge of Darren Lwyd. A kestrel hovered overhead, while across the wooded trough of the Vale of Ewyas, a cuckoo welcomed the morning of another drizzly day.

The summit of **Twmpa** was nothing particularly special, just a small cairn with a big view. The whole of the Wye Valley lay at my feet in a dismal swirl of low cloud.

At the Gospel Pass where the minor road up the Vale of Ewyas crosses the ridge and drops down towards Hay-on-Wye, motorists sat picnicking in their cars, rain streaming down their windows. I picked my way through the steady stream of slow-moving traffic and found a grassy path to the top of Hay Bluff. After a quick bite to eat at the trig pillar, moated by a dark, peaty pool, I picked up the track along the ridge to the south.

This is part of Offa's Dyke Path, and as I went, a number of weary walkers plodded by in the other direction. Straddling the English / Welsh border with a leg in each, I followed stone flags to a pile of pallets, evidently used as duck-boards prior to the laying of these slabs, which seemed to mark the highest point of **Black Mountain**. I continued on to bag the next couple of humps just to make sure I'd reached the top and came across a red grouse with its chick, desperately trying to chase it away from me. The chick, however, was unaware it should be afraid of me. Showing a great deal of interest in this strange fellow walking around with a huge hunch-back, it waddled ever closer. Its mother by this time had literally gone berserk, and in a wild, flapping cackle, flew off across the heather, leaving its youngster to fend for itself. Not wanting it to be abandoned, I turned and quickly retraced my steps to the trig pillar on Hay Bluff.

I dropped down to the road coming down from the Gospel Pass and followed the Offa's Dyke Path into Hay, as the weather made an effort to improve on its recent bad behaviour. Picking tiny wild strawberries as I went, I note I'd bagged 24 Welsh Hewitts so far. I now had to face the loneliness of the wild, empty spaces of mid-Wales before entering the more familiar ground of Snowdonia. I had 113 Hewitts to go. At least I felt I'd made a start.

Taking the Clyro road out of Hay, I crossed the broad River Wye and found a delightful camp site just up the hill. I was looking forward to a relaxing day in Hay, browsing through the book shops and satisfying my appetite in the various cafés and pubs. That night I slept the sleep of the just, knowing that for once I could get away with not setting the alarm.

CHAPTER II
Discovering mid-Wales

Tuesday 16th June ~ Relaxing in Hay

For once the day was notable only as being wonderfully clear, a day of brilliant sunshine. I spent the day in Hay as planned, browsing through the astonishing variety of book shops, initially being delighted at the chance to explore such an Aladdin's Cave of winding passages replete with second-hand and antiquarian bookshops. Some specialise in one particular subject such as photography, natural history or children's books, while the majority are more than happy to stock just about anything. Some appear to flog nothing more than junk at an inflated price—the kind of ancient paperback novel that you can pick up at any charity shop for 10p is marked for sale at £3.50. True, there are also some wonderful bargains to be found and I was pleased to find an immaculate hardback copy of Fraser Darling's *Island Years* for the remarkable price of £2.50.

Later on, I retired to the tent for a spaghetti bolognese, a bottle of Murphy's Stout and a few chapters from *Kramer Vs Kramer*, one of the books I had acquired in Crickhowell. It is hardly the type of book I'd usually read, but as during each day my mind was fully engrossed with walking and navigating around Wales, I'd given up trying to get enthusiastic about a mountaineering book or exploration travelogue after a hard day in the hills. I found that a novel with a simple plot, or even none at all, suited me fine. Still, *Kramer Vs Kramer* was positively less than wonderful, being far too predictable. About half way through, I fell asleep.

Wednesday 17th June ~ To Radnor Forest

Back to the old routine. Heavy rain heralded my return to the challenge. I packed up the camp and headed off as the deluge continued. I followed a succession of minor roads and parts of Offa's Dyke Path to the tiny village of Newchurch, then on, along the 'B' road to Gladestry. There I took cover from the rain in the pub, in no particular hurry to leave the warmth of the quiet little lounge-bar and to cross the hills to New Radnor.

It was still pouring when I finally stepped outside and followed a dead-end road which became a track, then dropped to cross the swollen Gilwern Dingle via a footbridge just before reaching the dripping eves of the small collection of houses and tiny chapel that is the hamlet of Yardo. Outflanking the semi-wooded knoll of The Smatcher on its east side, I finally arrived at the quaint village of New Radnor at about four o'clock.

The Ordnance Survey map shows a caravan site beside the A44, on the edge of the village. The map couldn't have been more correct. It was a caravan site—of the 'no tents' variety. A sign in the gateway told would-be visitors that they should first report to the owner at 'Westfield' before entering the site. With the intention of persuading the nice owner that he really did want to let me camp on his field for the night, I set about looking for 'Westfield'. I found a village shop (closed), a couple of pubs (both closed) and a tourist information centre (not sure whether it was open or closed. The door was open, but it looked rather like there had been a burglary—papers and leaflets were scattered everywhere and rubbish was piled in every corner. But the computer was in its place on a desk and switched on. I called out for some tourist information, but no one was home).

Back on the tearfully rain-swept streets of this strange ghost-town, I resumed my search for 'Westfield'. At last I came across it on the far side of town, but yet again the place was totally deserted. I doubt if the owner would have objected to me pitching on his caravan site without his permission, in fact he probably wouldn't have even found out, but instead I decided to head up into the shaley hills of Radnor Forest. I figured that whatever I climbed that night would be saved off tomorrow's journey.

I took the bridleway up behind Knowle Hill as the rain subsided at last. The Ordnance Survey map has a definite pond or small lake marked as being on the col north of Knowle Hill, and I initially thought of pitching my tent there for the night. However, at the col, although there was a definite marshy depression, I couldn't actually find any water as the whole area was overgrown with a dense thicket of willows. I crossed over the col and headed uphill through dripping branches of pine and spruce. By the time I had reached Whinyard Rocks I still hadn't found a water source and as the evening was still young, I began to form a plan to bag the three Hewitts of the Radnor Forest before nightfall. If the going was harder than predicted, there was always the possibility of finding water at the Shepherd's Well at the very head of the deep grassy trench of the Harley Dingle to my west. My

The hills of Radnor Forest viewed from the Smatcher

route was going that way anyway to avoid crossing the M.o.D. Danger Area between **Black Mixen** and **Great Rhos**.

It was about 6.30, but at least the clouds had lifted allowing sufficient visibility to aid quick navigation and speedy walking. I took to the good track which headed north-east towards **Bache Hill**, my first Hewitt of the day. The bridleway actually rises above the farm track to quickly turn north-westwards, up and over a heathery col to the west of the summit. At the col I dumped my rucksack, and taking a path to the right of a fence, climbed over a couple of stiles to reach the trig pillar atop this undistinguished hill.

Back at the pack I bombed down the heaths to gain a forest track at another broad, grassy col. Within 700 yards, another track headed out of the forest and going over a locked gate, I continued through the mist to the eerie peace of the summit of **Black Mixen**, dominated as it is by a radio mast and small collection of attendant buildings.

The next section looked like being boggy, so I had a quick snack, donned my new gaiters and took a faint path through the peaty moorland towards Shepherd's Well. As expected it isn't a well as such, and in fact provided no water whatsoever.

However, it was only 8p.m. with about two hours of daylight remaining so I followed the vague path which leads around the forest perimeter to a point where a bridleway emerges from Cwm Gerwyn in the depths of the pines, larches, spruces and occasional broad-leaved tree. This heads south-west over the north ridge of **Great Rhos** just 400 yards from the summit. As I'd yet again risen into the all-enveloping clouds, I took a bearing, measured the distance on the map and paced it out to find the trig pillar at the top. I found it easily, and began plotting the next short leg of my journey. I'd bagged all three of the Radnor Forest Hewitts and now had as my main priority the problem of getting down, out of the clouds, to a water source as quickly as possible before darkness closed in. I would have been quite prepared to continue navigating after dark, indeed one of the most essential skills I had had to master when training to become a Mountain Walking Instructor was safe, accurate navigation in all weathers, and in all conditions, regardless of terrain, both day and night, so I wasn't unduly worried. However, the ground about was pretty boggy, and in that pea-soup mist seemed virtually featureless, so night navigation wouldn't have been much fun. I took the necessary bearings and wasted no time in losing height. I managed to pick up a disjointed series of tracks which where going roughly in the right direction, and following these, soon found myself descending the ridge of Esgairnantau through newly planted conifer plantations. A brand new forestry track led me down to a dingle, perhaps half a mile above the famous waterfall of Water-break-its-neck, from where I turned right and following it upstream found a nice grassy site for the tent amid a million baaing sheep. At 9.45, I slipped into my sleeping bag and began brewing drinks and some rice for a meal, as the hounds of Llanevan farm began baying at me from down the valley to the west. All-in-all I had had quite a day. Over 22 miles, and 1220 metres of ascent, I had managed to cram two days walking into one, and boy did I know it!

Thursday 18th June ~ Low Spirits

Unfortunately, the dogs from the farm seem to have decided to devote the entire night to barking at me. I'd camped well out of sight of them, I wouldn't have dreamt of camping close to the farm without permission, and I would have thought that I was out of their hearing range when I'd first pitched the tent in the gathering dusk of the night before, being a good mile further up the valley from the farm.

Half expecting to be woken up in the sma' wee hours, by an angry farmer and his shotgun, I'd not had the best night's sleep, and by 5.15a.m. decided that I'd be better off struggling on to Newbridge-on-Wye, and spending the afternoon dozing there. Peering out of my tent, I couldn't see a thing for thick mist, although being light I knew that the sun had risen behind the grey curtains long before.

After packing up, I took the bridle path down through wildly scattering sheep flocks to the farm at Llanevan, and passing through gates with rusty hinges as quietly as possible, made it to the road leaving in my wake a huge heard of stampeding cows and young bullocks, wreaking havoc across the grassy pastures.

Dropping below the cloud at 200 metres, further wearying rain began as I took the lane towards the forest edge on Llandegley Rhos. Heavily hooded and hands deep in Gore-Texed pockets, I plodded onwards, head hung in dismay. Although I had had one or two good days, I was starting to despair of the seemingly continuous rain. Those pre-trip dreams of halcyon days in the sun had long since been forgotten, and had been replaced instead by the thought that I had stopped enjoying myself, and as such, couldn't really see much point in going on. But my immediate priority was sleep, and as the nearest likely place on my route where I could begin the long journey home via countless buses and trains was almost certainly going to be Builth Wells, south of Newbridge, I thought that I may as well head to Newbridge for a rest, and to see if the weather and my mood would improve any on the morrow.

And so the morning passed in an embittered spree of self pity, over the Gilwern Hills and down into the valley of the River Wye. Almost with my chin on my chest, I plodded tarmac through the village of Crossway and past the camp site at Disserth. Contributing to my mood of dismay, countless trials bikes regularly thundered past, each taking part in the ill-fated Welsh Two Day Trials. Belching carbon monoxide into the already heavy atmosphere and adding to the pollution with a stirring whring as they passed, each bike managed to drench me even more, if that was at all possible, with oily spray from their wheels.

I eventually arrived in Newbridge as the sun seemed to be making an attempt at forcing a way through the dark clouds of morning. As I had expected, it was half-day closing in Newbridge, but I still had over an hour to buy a good supply of luxuries to cheer me up during the afternoon. By 11.30 I had my tent pitched beside the murky waters of a very swollen River Ithon.

Lying in my bag, listening to the drizzle falling through the canopy of ash leaves overhead, I calculated that out of 13 days in Wales, I had only had three really good days of sun, and one of those had been a rest day in Hay. With such happy thoughts I dozed away the afternoon.

Forcing myself out of my sleeping bag at 6p.m. I walked back into the village from my camp at Pont ar Ithon with the intention of sharing my misery over the phone with Rachel, and giving her advanced warning that I would be home in a day or two. Before I could break the bad news, she seemed to sense my mood and made a quick point of giving me the weather forecast for the next couple of days. Incredibly, Friday had been pencilled in for a mini-heat-wave and the summer weather was supposed to remain into the middle of the following week. Within seconds, and without telling Rachel anything of my decision to pack it in early, my mind was racing over what route I would take to bag the three scattered peaks around the wild shores of the Elan valley reservoirs. With the bit firmly between my teeth, I made plans for a great day tomorrow, crossing **Gorllwyn** and **Drygarn Fawr**. As I put down the phone, my immediate thought was, 'Snowdonia, here I come!'

Friday 19th June ~ Bog hopping south of the Elan Valley

As I needed to visit the shop and post office in Newbridge before heading off into the wilds of the Cwmdeuddwr Hills, I set the alarm for 8a.m., with the intention of knocking on the post office door at nine. Unfortunately, I slept in, and what with one thing and another, including a short, heavy downpour, spending a good quarter of an hour by the river bank admiring the dazzling array of blue damselflies and bottle green demoiselles, I didn't leave the site until nearly 11.

Already the clouds had departed and left in their place a perfect blue sky. After mailing some notes and a map home to Rachel, I took the B4358 towards Beulah.

Quite apart from the weather making a distinct improvement, the very seasons seemed to have changed almost overnight. Beside the road the rhododendrons had begun to lose their gay, magenta flowers, although this was probably due to the rain as much as anything else, and the lower trumpets on each foxglove spike had fallen, to be replaced by plump seed pods. It takes a good few months of course for this process to repeat itself all the way up to the top of the spike, by which time these lower pods are bursting with vitality, and only a light pressure applied to the brown cases will pop them open, revealing hundreds of tiny black seeds, ready to take part in the next biennial propagation cycle of their species.

As I strode happily along the road in the sweltering heat of midday, more demoiselles leafed their way through the gentle breeze, and a dozen or more bullfinches chased among the roadside vegetation.

My way lay up Cwmchwefru, but on my map I had spied a pub in Llanafan Fawr, the next village along, and so continued along the road with the hope of having a coffee. The sign outside read 'The World Famous Red Lion Inn - Voted the best pub in Llanafan Fawr for the 547th year running', so I had a good idea what I was in for before I even entered—for it is, of course, the only pub in Llanafan Fawr. More important to me was another sign which read 'Free coffee with every meal, plus 10% off main courses at Lunch Time.' Now that was what I needed. Inside, I ordered a steak and kidney pie and a coffee and sat in the bar chatting to the landlord and his staff. The conversation soon turned to my walk, and in a show of true hospitality, the landlord was quick to donate a hand-full of Mars bars to help me on my way, with the suggestion that I name this book *Welsh Walks from the Great Red Lion Inn*, or similar words to that effect.

I returned to the minor road up Cwmchwefru, the road becoming a track and crossing the little Afon Chwerfri via a footbridge beside a ford, to join another minor road. As I walked I pondered on the hospitality shown at the pub. There was no doubting that they were good, genuine people. However, I was often to meet people who would either totally ignore me, or even be openly hostile until I mentioned that I was writing a book, when suddenly, pseudo-niceties would be easy to detect in their manner and conversation.

Crossing the Afon Chwerfri

Along the pleasantly shaded route, scores of female redstarts flitted around beneath the old oaks in a cacophony of ticking which is their usual alarm-call. Behind the cottage of Gors-wen, far up the valley, I finally left the minor road and took to a confusion of paths and tracks which is marked on the map as a single bridleway. In the end I gave up trying to follow the right of way and found easier going beside the stream. Still the sun beat down, so higher up in the cwm, below the grassy slopes of Bryn Moel, I took off my boots, peeled off my socks and plunged my feet into the swirling waters of the rushing stream. Even the water seemed lukewarm, so I had a good old paddle and a wash to the obvious interest of a couple of gnarly old sheep.

At last I managed to prise myself away from the oasis, and climbed the bracken-covered slopes to the broad peaty col of Cnapiau'r Ferlen. As I crested the ridge top, a forked-tailed raptor with distinct white under-markings sailed gracefully overhead. Even though I'd never seen one before I knew instantly that I was looking at a magnificent red kite, resplendent in its natural setting, the heartland of Wales. Its elegant beauty and balletic grace held me captivated in the brief seconds it took to clear my field of vision in a long swoop over the ridge behind me.

I felt really privileged to see such a wonderful, though very rare, bird of prey—only around fifty pairs breed in Britain each year, and these are endemic only to mid-Wales. But on occasion, large numbers flock over from the continent during the summer months, resulting in what seems like a population explosion. I would imagine that 1998 was such a year for I soon discovered in the next couple of days that I could rarely look into the sky without catching sight of at least one red kite, and sometimes would see half a dozen or more, wheeling above the old oak forests and barren hillsides of the area. At the turn of this century, red kites had all but been totally wiped out in Britain. Before then they were common throughout the country, even scavenging food in the streets of the major cities. Thanks to relentless persecution by man, by 1900 there were only three pairs surviving in the British Isles—in the remote upper Tywi valley of mid-Wales. Members of the British Ornithologists Club set about protecting the birds and tried to introduce additional red kites from the continent. As red kites are a very shy bird when on the nest, the only way of bringing these continental birds into the country was as fresh eggs, introduced into a buzzard's nest with the hope that the buzzard would hatch and raise the kite as one of its own. Although many hatched successfully, the main problem was that Spanish red kites, from which the eggs were taken, are migratory birds and out of 31 that were hatched and reared by buzzards in 1928, all of the young dispersed with the coming of the late autumn, and did not return the following year. However, over the years, changing laws regarding wildlife protection, and changing attitudes towards the use of illegal poisons in agriculture have helped to provide the kites of Britain with a more acceptable land in which to make their home. With luck, red kites will spread into other areas of the country.

Along the ridge an easy path led through grass and bilberry, via a delightful un-named tarn to the summit of **Gorllwyn**. 200 yards in front of me the kite breathed out of the valley on the still air and hovered ahead. As I walked on, the distance between us stayed the same. It seemed to be using me as a kind of beater, allowing me to flush out any small mammals or birds that lay in my path. Having little luck on that score, it eventually lost interest as I neared the trig pillar at the summit, and dropped with the grace and agility of a swift into the valley below.

As time was pressing I passed straight over the summit and on towards the grassy depression around the broad col of Bwlch y Ddau Faen. The terrain became increasingly difficult to walk over, being composed mainly of dense tussocks of mat-grass and hard rushes around the really boggy bits. This is real ankle snapping territory, and I made sure that I took even more care than usual. If I'd have had an accident, the chances of anyone else finding me within the next couple of weeks would have been pretty slim.

Just before the initial climb up **Drygarn Fawr**, along the broad slopes of Bryn Rhudd, I came across a slow-moving stream, struggling through the rushes down towards the distant Caban-coch Reservoir. Thankful for the trekking poles provided by the Brasher Boot Company, I now used one as a probe, much as I would with an ice-axe to cross rotten snow-bridges at the end of a winter season. At one point I poked about in a horrible peaty morass and unfortunately, put more weight than intended on the pole. It went in much deeper than expected, closely followed by myself performing a kind of half somersault, along with my rucksack as ballast. In an effort to avoid a dunking in the slime, I over-compensated with a twist of my leg to try to gain a tiny tussocky island. I watched with horror as my left boot just managed to gain a purchase on the edge of the island, and then slid off into the drink. In a real panic I belly-flopped onto the island with my legs dangling down into the slime on one side and my head being pressed face first, down into the mud on the other, and being held there by the weight of my rucksack, which in my inverted position had slid up my back and now rested its whole weight on the back of my neck. Regaining a modicum of composure I extricated myself from the mud, threw my sack back across to the dry bank from which I had just left, and jumped across after it. I was soaked to the skin with a dark brown slime of the kind only usually found at the very bottom of a newly filled silage pit, and the smell was even worse than that! The most frightening thing about the whole episode was the fact that although I had gone in almost up to my arm pits, neither foot had actually touched the bottom. The most annoying thing about the whole incident was that just 10 yards further downstream, I managed to cross easily without so much as getting any more mud on the soles of my boots. And that was just an innocent looking bog—no more than perhaps seven yards wide.

Although the sun still beat down from a cloudless sky, a stiff breeze had been building up ever since I had gained the ridge, and was whipping the heat away from my wet body. The only sensible thing to do was to strip naked and wring out my clothes, then put them back on again. It would have been pointless to get dry clothes from out of my rucksack, as I didn't know whether I would have any more similar incidents before reaching the bothy that night, and it would also be nice to have clean, dry clothes to change into once there. I was soon standing on a small patch of bilberry, desperately trying to drain as much liquid (I still hesitate to call the stuff water) from my clothes as possible. I half expected a couple of dozen geriatric ramblers to emerge from over the ridge at any minute, even though I hadn't seen a soul since leaving the road head. Thankfully, I managed to get myself dressed again without flashing at any excitable grannies.

At last, after taking one or two more minor plunges, I reached the first of the giant cairns which crown the top of **Drygarn Fawr**. An easy path led along westwards to the higher of the two and then on to the trig pillar. I crammed a lump of cheese and a Mars bar, courtesy of the 'World Famous Red Lion Inn,' into my mouth and sped off down the broad west ridge.

More torturous tussock grass led over a minor ridge and down to the clear waters of the Nant y Rhestr where I paused for a drink, and then on over a shoulder of Esgair yr Adar and into the forests of the Tywi valley. With the

Resting by the huge summit cairn on **Drygarn Fawr**

dusk I followed forest tracks until a desperate swim across the swollen waters of the Afon Tywi led me to the bothy, my haven for the night.

As the bothy came into sight, it was immediately obvious that someone else was in residence. Smoke belched from the chimney and children's voices, gay with the freedom of the hills, carried over the sound of the rushing water.

A red-headed woman, lithe from country living, was pitching a large family tent outside in the overgrown garden, and kids scampered every-where. I received a cheery welcome from all, apart from two cyclists who had taken over the one room in the bothy with a fire-place—The Snug. This young couple chatted fairly pleasantly, but not so much as to invite either me or the families outside to come into their room and share their space. I made my bed in the only other room, which for that night seemed to be more of a bike shed.

On my window sill a young meadow pipit had been abandoned for the moment by its mother, and seemed unable to fly. I had a chat to the three women outside over their fire, and we decided that it would either fly away of its own accord, or else would have gone in the morning, having been taken by something during the night.

The children were delightful, speaking for the most part in English, as their parents are English living in mid-Wales, but occasionally reverting to the Welsh that they learn in school.

Having covered a hard 19 miles to bag just two Hewitts, I turned in by 11, and was fast asleep within seconds.

Saturday 20th June ~ To Devil's Bridge

I became vaguely aware of the two cyclists leaving very early, wheeling their bikes out of my room at some ungodly hour, but didn't actually wake up properly. At 8.30 a shock of red hair came around the door and kindly offered a mug of tea.

We sat around in The Snug making small talk and breakfast as drizzle poured down the murky panes in the windows. The tea continued to flow as we swapped notes on our respective jobs, the problems of finding work in mid-Wales for an English Ex-Pat, as they jokingly referred to themselves, the bothies of Wales, the plight of the pine marten and on, via talk of the Cairngorms, to the reindeer sanctuary near Aviemore, and its owner Tilly Smith, whom we both knew. What a small world we live in!

As I pushed my way up through the dripping branches of the pines behind the bothy, I met a couple of the young lads who had stayed there last night. They'd been out exploring on their bikes and regaled me with tales of their latest adventure—seeing who could ride furthest into the ford down the road. Having crossed it yesterday I knew that it was at least four feet deep, and couldn't help showing my astonishment.

My original plan had been to head north across the vast expanse of tussock grass to climb **Pen y Garn** before turning eastwards to find a bothy hidden in the forest above Cwmystwyth. However, I really didn't fancy more knee-jarring, pathless terrain in view of the weather, and so had chickened out and gone for the longer but easier option of taking the road up to Devil's Bridge, and bagging **Pen y Garn** from there.

I gained a wide forest track and followed it on towards Strata Florida as the drizzle turned to familiar rain. Forestry trucks rumbled past, and I

Strata Florida Abbey

stopped to pass the time of day with an ageing cyclist.

Beyond the deserted village of Strata Florida I popped in to another Red Lion pub at Pontrhydfendigaid, but this time was disappointed. The place was far from welcoming and I settled down in a cold corner for a greasy platter of sausage, egg and chips.

Absolutely drenched, I plodded more dismal tarmac towards Devil's Bridge. The sun did put in an appearance round about Ysbyty Ystwyth, but was soon replaced by yet more rain.

At Devil's Bridge I booked into the Woodland's Camp Site for two nights, intending to bag **Pen y Garn** on a short circular foray from the tent. The site was a big place full of tourists, cyclists and walkers, and in my renewed low state, did me just fine.

Later, the rain cleared, so I cooked a meal outside on a picnic bench, watching the kites, now too numerous to get too excited about, wheeling in the sky above the site. Occasionally, one would fold a wing and go into a well-controlled spiral, pulling it back just before hurtling into the hillside.

Sunday 21st June ~ A Rest Day

Deciding to take a rest day to do a spot of laundry, I spent the morning lazing around the site, watching the kites, and toddling off down to the café at the site reception for a cup of coffee. I soon realised that it would make sense to spend the day wisely, if not profitably, by doing the tourist thing and shelling out £2.20 to have a look at the famous Mynach Falls below the Devil's Bridge. The price seemed a bit steep, especially once I'd realised that it didn't include the view of the three bridges themselves. For that I'd have to fork out another £1 across the road.

Just as I clicked through the turnstile, the rain began, so hood-up, I trotted from one 'viewing platform' to another. Occasional views of the heavily wooded slopes of the upper Afon Rheidol could be glimpsed through the humid shade of dank oaks. In the space of about an hour I took in all the sights and sounds of the glorious waterfalls pounding a time-worn passage through the underlying rocks. My only complaint was that for the most part, the over-abundance of trees made photographing the falls very difficult, if not impossible, although of course, I'd be among the first to make a stink if anyone suggested chopping a few down.

For me the most impressive notion is the fact that the trough of the Afon Rheidol way below to the west is actually not the original course of the main stream. That along the old valley floor flowed in a north / south direction, eventually joining the River Teifi near Strata Florida. Being a much stronger river than the minor Mynach which joined it from the east, it gouged out an incredibly deep trench, causing the Mynach to fall a much greater height to the valley floor, hence the impressive falls that we see today. Now of course, at the confluence of the Afon Mynach and the Afon Rheidol, just below Devil's Bridge, the course of the river has changed yet again, and instead of flowing south, has taken the line of least resistance and rushes out to the sea to the west.

219

After another cup of coffee in the café, I paid my dues and had a look at the Mynach from the other side of the road. The attraction here is the three bridges, built one above the other.

It is said that a lonely old lady called Marged once lived by the Mynach with her dog, Smala and her cow, Malen. One day Malen somehow strayed across the river. Because of the steep gorge, Marged didn't know how to get it back. The Devil appeared, disguised as a monk and by way of a deal, said that in return for the first living thing that would cross it, he would build a bridge to span the gorge. He of course, expected Marged to cross the bridge to fetch the cow herself. After she had agreed to his terms, Marged threw a crust of bread across the new bridge, and her dog, Smala scampered after it. The Devil became the proud owner of a flee-bitten mutt, and the old lady got her cow back.

The lower bridge has actually been dated as being built in medieval times, the middle bridge in the eighteenth century and the higher bridge, now used to take the busy traffic along the A4120, was built in the nine-teenth century.

Monday 22nd June ~ Pen y Garn

Leaving my tent and all the heavy gear at the camp site, I packed just the necessities for a short walk to bag **Pen y Garn** to the east.

Although I'm not a great fan of road walking, I enjoyed the easy ascent to the top of the pass at The Arch along the B4574. The sun had cleared the rain clouds that had swamped the hills that morning, and there was a wonderful freshness to the air.

The Arch itself is just that, a rustic-looking stone archway across the old turnpike road. It was built in 1810 by Thomas Johnes as a commemoration of George III's Golden Jubilee. Johnes was largely responsible for the planting of over four million trees in the area between 1796 and 1813, as a way of replenishing the mine-devastated natural beauty of this part of the country.

From The Arch a forest trail leads steeply uphill, high above the infant Afon Mynach. Newly planted spruce on the slopes of Rhos Peirian gave an emerald foreground of early summer

Thomas Johnes' arch above the Afon Mynach

*Meteorological paraphernalia on the top of **Pen y Garn***

foliage to the grassy slopes of **Pen y Garn** beyond. Older trees closed in as I climbed up to a clearing above Banc yr Adarn giving stunning views across the wooded flanks above the Nant Rhuddnant, to the hazy smudge of the four Hewitts of Plynlimon away to the north. I had a break on a well placed bench and took in the details of the range, knowing that I would be scaling those heights next morning.

Just around the next bend, a muddy pull-in gave a not-so-convenient car park for a couple of young lasses who looked as if they were preparing for a long day on the hill. This seemed a bit strange as they were parked within four hundred yards of the summit of the only notable hill for miles around.

I untied the sizzle holding a gate and pondered on the use of a number of squat cages, pegged to the ground on the easy slopes to the summit. Over a stile a host of meteorological equipment was liberally scattered about a small enclosure, across which another stile led to a path past a couple of solar panels to a large dry-stone-walled shelter and the trig pillar.

A vast emptiness that is the Cwmdeuddwr hills filled the horizon to the south, highlighting the difficulties of the terrain that I would have had to cross had I not opted for the easier route around to Devil's Bridge by road. To the north, Plynlimon still barred views of Snowdonia.

As I retraced my steps I stopped to have a look at the low cages below the meteoroloigcal station. It appeared they were being used to measure the differing growth rates of moorland plants and grasses when isolated from the ever hungry Welsh Mountain Sheep and other non-domesticated herbivores. Suddenly it was obvious that the two girls I had seen were either studying the local flora, or were meteorologists. I resolved to ask them about the project as I held the gate open for them, but it became apparent that neither of them were too chuffed at witnessing me plodding my size ten boots around 'their' botanical specimens. They passed through the gate with a new cage to erect tucked under their arms, with stony glances and a barely audible 'thank you'. Perhaps their university owns or has exclusive rights to the summit area of **Pen y Garn**, or perhaps they just think it should have.

I took the same forest trail back down until I reached a broad col in the trees, where another track headed around the back of a little knoll marked on the map as Truman. A good path led down to, and along the banks of the gurgling waters of the Afon Mynach.

Back at the site, I made a quick foray to the camp shop to buy in some supplies for the next couple of days and paid another night's camp fees. By way of evening entertainment, I called in at the Three Bridges Bar to watch England being easily thrashed by the Romanians in the World Cup.

Tuesday 23rd June ~ Plynlimon

Woken early by the girl from the camp reception trying to do me out of an extra night's fees, I had a leisurely breakfast in the sun and was away by just before 10a.m.

I followed the A4120 for a couple of miles up the Rheidol valley, then branched off right to find the footpath up onto the **Plynlimon** ridge near Dyffryn Castell. I considered popping in for a quick drink and a bite to eat, but for once managed to keep a check on my hunger.

The path led via a series of new stiles up onto the open fell-side. On the whole the weather was quite good, although one or two brief showers poured in from the west, and upon reaching the crest of the ridge, I could see, or rather couldn't, that the main ridge of the Plynlimon range was shrouded in hill fog. Again, the path on the ground didn't bear close resemblance to that on the map, but it was easy to follow and seemed to be heading in the right direction, so it did me for the time being.

Around the edge of the Dyll Faen forest the going was more obvious on a good path through bilberry and cotton-grass bog, while across the small valley to the north, the summit knolls of **Y Garn** intermittently peeked out of the clouds and revealed a blue sky behind.

Where the main track headed north for the summit of **Plynlimon Fawr**, a less obvious path over grass led west towards **Y Garn**. At a junction of fences, I dumped my rucksack and headed off into the clouds, a couple of minor ups and downs leading to the cairn which gives the summit its name. The dammed valley at my feet to the north-west contained the Nant-y-moch Reservoir, now glimmering in the late morning sun, leaving me wishing I'd not left my camera in the rucksack.

Plynlimon itself wasn't having such a good time of it. Dark, rain-heavy cumulo-nimbus had been scudding in from the coast all morning, and by now had obliterated the three highest peaks of the range. I retrieved my sack from beside the fence and headed up grassy slopes into the thick of it.

I gained the cairn-marked path and instantly lost all visibility. The clouds rolled over me but still hadn't produced any rain. Nevertheless I donned my jacket and trousers and waited for the onslaught to start.

Crossing a fence via a stile, a good summit shelter just south of the trig pillar kept me out of the wind and gathering rain while I fumbled around in my sack for a hat, gloves and a chocolate bar.

Paths seemed to lead off in all directions, so I ignored them all and followed a bearing down to a col and up to the east top of **Plynlimon,** counting steps all the way. A cairn near an obvious boundary stone marked the highest point. Further short legs with the compass led over to the boundary which led over wet, grassy ground to the summit cairns of **Pen Pumlumon Arwystli**. Such a bleakness I would usually have fled from, though I did consider dropping down into Cwm Gwerin to the north-west, more to lose height as quickly as possible than it being the best route to take. However, I decided to brave the elements for a while longer, and continued beside the boundary as far as the two tarns near the source of the River Severn.

Grassy slopes at the head of Cwm Hengwm led me down out of the cloud, but brought the first of the day's heavy rain. At least I had finished with the high mountains for the day. Across the cwm I could pick out the dingle that I would follow to the east of the minor top of Foel Uchaf, to gain the heathery expanse of moorland known as Llechwedd Crin. My only problem was crossing the Afon Hengwm which of course was in spate.

A couple of bold leaps soon had that obstruction cleared and, once across, a sheep track led up into the boggy bottom of the small hanging valley. Huge boulders of quartz dotted the top of Foel Uchaf to my left as I climbed, and away to my right a kestrel hovered gamely on the wind.

At 5p.m. I squelched into the basic but pleasant camp site at Rhiwgam where I was given a pitch out of the wind, along with a flock of sheep. I was their only customer.

Wednesday 24th June ~ Through Machynlleth

I left Rhiwgam in a nice heavy shower by way of a change, and in a bit of a depression took a sequence of minor roads down the Afon Dulas to Machynlleth, eating wild strawberries along the way.

Market day in Machynlleth brought a late morning sun, so I made an effort to be cheerful and did a spot of food shopping. Having long since finished reading *Kramer Vs Kramer*, *The Loneliness of the Long Distance Runner,* and *The Widower's Son*, another offering from Alan Sillitoe, although one which I had failed to really enjoy, I set about looking for a new book. In an instant my eyes focused on Steven Fry's *The Liar*, a caption on the cover promised to make me laugh out loud, so I immediately bought it—and devoured it over the next few days.

The sun by now was truly out, so under the enormous weight of my newly replenished food sack, I crossed the Afon Dyfi, chatting there for a while with a fly-fisherman who just happened to be from my own area of Yorkshire, then took the minor road along the east bank of the Afon Dulas towards Corris.

Just beyond the Centre for Alternative Technology, the camp site at Llwyngwern looked promising, so I pitched the tent beside an enormous felled tree, and draped its decaying boughs with all my wet gear.

CHAPTER III
Into Snowdonia

Thursday 25th June ~ A Gentle Day

I did a spot of washing before taking a stroll down to Nora's village shop-cum-post office-cum-pub in Ceinws, the next village towards Corris. Although I didn't really have a great deal planned for the day, reading, eating and drying out my clean clothes were about the order of it, this suited me fine. I fully exploited the opportunity to pig-out on luxury items of food that I wouldn't normally want to carry about on my back, so it was a huge spaghetti bolognese for tea, followed by tinned fruit with cream, a packet of biscuits and gallons of peppermint tea.

Later on, a camper-van arrived and duly managed to get stuck up to the axles in deep mud in the middle of the camping field. A young bloke in the next tent and I went over to offer our assistance, but the owner of the camper-van just glowered and muttered something uncharitable about withdrawing his membership of the Caravan and Camping Club. Not really seeing how this would help him get out of the rut, the pair of us trotted back to our respective tents to watch the entertainment. Unfortunately, it was short lived, as great buckets-full of gravel were brought into play, and throwing these under his wheels, gave our happy camper enough purchase to spin his way out, throwing caution, and gravel, to the wind.

By way of consolation the fellow next door popped over with his wife to offer a lift 'into town', an offer which I felt compelled to turn down—but it was a nice thought anyway.

Friday 26th June ~ The Tarrens

Friday dawned mucky and grey. The rain was back with a vengeance, so I packed up, and had a quick publicity chat with a young lad across the field who was particularly interested in my tent. Then I made my escape down the road to Pantperthog.

A forestry track led steeply uphill on the right, along the north bank of the Nant y Darren, its waters unseen in the dense hill-fog below, but clearly heard rushing down to join the larger Afon Dulas. Although the rain continued to pour, the trees provided a shield from the high winds, and it became incredibly warm as I toiled up the track.

Higher up, in the eastern corrie of **Tarren y Gesail**, the trees diminished, and the steep flanks of my first Hewitt of the day could be seen falling shear from the summit ridge. The hillside hereabouts was actually nowhere near as forested as my map suggested, although it did look as though all that may change in time—much of it was already cordoned off with fences. Quarries are marked on the map as being totally surrounded by the forests, but those I passed on the east ridge looked as though they had always been well above the tree-line.

Triumphant that the rain had at last called a halt for the time being, I decided to have a bit of a poke around in some of the old adits and spoil heaps of the quarries. Moss and duck-weed-covered pools of stagnant water barred the entrance to many of the adits. One in particular looked easy of access, so I tip-toed across uneven stepping stones of slate towards its yawning void of an opening. Nothing much to see really. Just a long, low archway leading into a tunnel, its entrance barred by a pool of stinking slime. Pirouetting on my stepping stone to effect my exit, my boot slipped on the wet slate, catapulting me backwards into the cess-pit behind. For once seeing the funny side of my downfall, I immediately burst out laughing, and in a bit of a childish giggling fit, extricated myself from the grime.

Abandoning thoughts of further exploration, I again wrung out the soaked parts of my clothing—the damage thankfully being minimal—and made my way over to the foot of the east ridge of **Tarren y Gesail**.

I dumped the sack beside a stile leading into a wood, and slogged it up the hill. A vague bit of a track led alongside the sweeping drop into the cwm on my right, and soon led to a fence along the broad summit ridge. I turned left and followed this to the trig pillar and small wind-break which marked the top. Although the rain had kept off, the cloud was still low, so without pause, I turned and retraced my steps back to the sack.

Clouds kept lifting and falling like huge waves, and the odd window would open up for a short time in the denseness below, revealing the forested slopes above the Dyffryn Dyfi, mounted in a murky frame.

Picking up a track along the flanks of Foel y Geifr, I contoured around a knoll and found the path leading up the east ridge of **Tarrenhendre**. Rain again began to beat down, and the simple act of walking became a real

226

trudge. I counted steps, just as a way of keeping the momentum going, and soon the boggy summit was underfoot. A scattering of fences complete with stiles gave access to the two cairns which marked the top. Again no view other than the bleakness of a marshy summit plateau.

Before heading up onto the summit I had taken a compass bearing from the map, planning to head off down the north-west ridge, but once at the summit I came across an obvious path, marked by regular stakes, running down the much shorter north ridge. From the edge of the forest a bit of a quagmire beneath the trees led down and emerged onto a good forest track. I followed this, first contouring and then dropping steeply down the slopes of Hendre.

Across the Afon Gwernol, a good path led alongside the quick-flowing waters, through a Woodland Trust property, and on to the old mining village of Abergynolwyn.

After a pint in the Railway Inn, I dragged my weary bones over to the camp site at Llanllwyda, beside the Afon Dysynni. The sun had again peeled back the clouds, and away down the valley lit up the eastern facade of Craig yr Aderyn—The Bird Rock. This huge pillar of stone blocks the middle reaches of the Dysynni valley, and is reputed to be an old sea cliff. For centuries its many faces have been inhabited by colonies of cormorants which give the rock its name.

I pitched camp and settled down for a meal. The sun became obscured by 9p.m., and soon after, the rains began. It continued for much of the night, waking me frequently. At 3a.m. I lay awake listening to it hitting the roof of my fragile home. As I lay there, I realised that not a single drop could be heard—each one fell en masse with thousands of others, giving a sound like one long, continuous, dull roll.

Saturday 27th June ~ Cadair Idris

I awoke at 7.30 to find weak rays of sunlight flooding the tent. I made a leisurely breakfast to give it a bit more time to improve itself and come up with something decent for a change.

At last I was to set foot on the mountains of the Cadair Idris range, and I couldn't help feeling a tad excited about my prospects for the day. Although I was pleased with my progress so far, these mountains of Snowdonia are among the best in Britain. Cadair Idris, though very popular, must surely rate as one of the true jewels of southern Snowdonia with its many hidden cwms bearing a myriad of tarns and pools, each flanked with soaring precipices, curving arêtes and steep walls. Most people make their ascent to the lofty summit of **Pen y Gadair** from either Minffordd, via the path above Craig Cau, or from the west via one or other of either the Foxes or Pony Paths.

My way to the high tops led along the lengthy ridge of **Craig-y-llyn** and **Tyrrau Mawr**, before crossing the col at the Pony Path and climbing steep zig-zagging slopes to the summit of **Cyfrwy**. From there I hoped to head out to the top of **Craig Cwm Amarch** before bagging **Pen y Gadair**, the summit of Cadair Idris itself, and then on eastwards to **Mynydd Moel** and **Gau Graig**. This way I could bag all seven of the Cadair Idris Hewitts in one day. As I packed up my tent and headed for the hills, I only hoped the weather would keep dry.

I left the site at 9, full of hope and enthusiasm for the day. Hardly had I crossed the meadows in the valley bottom via an ill-defined path and picked up the public footpath above Nant Caw than the heavens opened in a real cloud-burst. A quick fumble in the sack for waterproofs saw the rain stop almost immediately, so I left them in there and puffed uphill in a vague direction towards a track that I could see far above on the upper slopes of Craig Maes-y-llan. After perhaps half an hour of possible trespassing, I came upon the track and followed it over the col between **Craig-y-llyn** and Mynydd Pennant to the south. Easy grass and bilberry slopes led over to the ridge overlooking Llyn Cyri to the north-west, and away to my right a small jumble of slate and quartz stones marked the top of **Craig-y-llyn**. By now the weather had improved a great deal. Out towards the coast, the surf pounded the slim peninsular which takes passengers on the narrow-gauge railway out into the estuary from Fairbourne, and dashing white horses could be clearly seen thrashing the beach at Barmouth over the Mawddach. Over to the south, yesterday's drowned Tarrens where basking in the sun. Only the higher tops of Cadair remained clothed in grey smudges of cloud. Away to the north the rocky ridges of the Rhinogs retained a flirting cover of cloud-wisps as I stood on **Craig-y-llyn**, my 37th Hewitt. Only 100 to go, I told myself as I pushed on down to the boggy col before **Tyrrau Mawr**. Almost without thinking I crossed its summit in patchy cloud and began my countdown— 99 to go!

Crowds of weekend walkers joined me as I plodded on up the zig-zags above the point where the Pony Path joined mine. A broad path, well marked with cairns led exactly to the col between **Pen y Gadair** and **Cyfrwy**, from where my unknown companions left me in the mist to make straight for the higher top. I trotted my lonely way around the rim of the cwm to the summit of **Cyfrwy**, one arm of 'The Chair of Idris' after whom the range is named, with the dark waters of Llyn-y-Gadair invisible below on my right. Retracing my steps to the col, I took a bearing for another col at the head of the Llyn Cau National Nature Reserve, and followed the compass over bouldery slopes to pick up the Minffordd Path just above the col. My next summit, **Craig Cwm Amarch** lay above in the mist, so I followed the Minffordd Path to its summit. At a small windbreak, nestling behind a big boulder in the crook of a wall, I stopped for a bite to eat, then took off my waterproof trousers for what seemed like the first time in weeks. Although the clouds were still pretty dense, it didn't feel like rain.

Turning about-face I joined the happy throng of weekend summit baggers, and retraced my steps to the col above the Nature Reserve. From there a good path led up to the trig pillar of Cadair Idris's summit, **Pen y Gadair**. I took shelter in the summit refuge along with a National Park Warden, then followed a bearing down and across a plateau to cross a wall at **Mynydd Moel**'s summit. Still the clouds were playing games, one minute completely enveloping me, the next flirtingly revealing a shapely flank of hillside across the Bwlch Llyn Bach. These flanks were the rocky lower slopes of the Dovey Hills, my aim beyond the Rhinogs and southern Arenigs. From **Mynydd Moel**, **Gau Graig**, my next Hewitt, looked ridiculously tiny away on the east ridge. I dropped down boggy slopes into the sunshine, and bog-trotted over to this, my final top of the day.

The huge 'U' shaped valley containing Llyn Tegid, or Bala Lake, led towards the English border to the north-east via the River Dee, whilst the Arans, Dovey Hills, Rhobells and Rhinogs blocked further views in all directions. Only the dark, satanic buildings of the Trawsfynydd Nuclear Power Station provided relief from the overwhelming scene of natural beauty up the Afon Eden to the north. How they ever got permission to build such a monstrosity within a National Park, I shall never know.

Although there wasn't a path marked on my map down the north ridge of **Gau Graig**, an obvious one on the ground led to the minor road-head at Bwlch-coch. From here I was soon wandering the streets of Dolgellau, having pitched up for the weekend at Tan y Fron. I'd planned to meet Rachel in Dolgellau the following weekend, and so reckoned that I could easily bag all of the Rhinogs, including **Y Garn**, and the southern Arenigs of **Rhobell Fawr** and **Dduallt**, before she arrived, even if I took the next day off for shopping, washing and loafing around in general.

Sunday 28th June ~ In Dolgellau

It certainly started off as a 'sun day' as I lounged around reading magazines and brewing up. My altimeter was reading an all-time-low, so the atmospheric pressure must have been high, indicating more stable weather conditions to come.

At the Tourist Information Centre in the market place, I came across a new edition of Thomas Pennant's *A Tour in Wales* which I snapped up. It was an abridged version of the classic book, but still, it kept me out of trouble for a while. I posted home a huge parcel of used maps, books and camera film which instantly made my load lighter, and me happier—I couldn't wait to get to grips with the Rhinogs on the morrow.

By early afternoon the rain came on in a drizzle, but as the pressure was still high, I kept high hopes for the next couple of days.

Monday 29th June ~ On The Rhinogs

Five days in which to bag the rough bounds of the Rhinog range. I'd never set foot on the main Rhinogs before, but had long since respected the tortuous ridge of summits, stretching south to north from **Diffwys** to **Moel Ysgyfarnogod**, in a line almost parallel to the sea. I would go so far as to say that I even held them in some kind of awe, although in reality, I had no idea just what to expect from these notoriously rocky mountains.

I left Dolgellau with a warm following breeze and dry clouds topping the high summits across the Afon Mawddach. A toll-bridge (charging 20p for foot passengers) led across the narrow channel at Penmaenpool and I was soon gaining height on the north bank of the estuary. A road led up Cwm Mynach through heavy deciduous woodland, eventually giving way to more regular plantations of conifers. Crossbills are said to haunt the area, but I saw nothing of ornithological interest as I took the left-hand track before Blaen-cwm-mynach. Strangely enough, crossbills are one of the few species of bird that I have yet to see in Britain. I say strangely because I regularly come across their northern cousin, the Scottish crossbill—now recognised as an individual and endemic species, whilst walking in the ancient Caledonian Pine Forests of Glen Feshie and Rothiemurchus in the Cairngorms. These Scottish crossbills are very rare indeed, and supposedly harder to spot.

High above Llyn-cwm-mynach, I came across an old miners' tramway which led up towards the main Rhinog ridge. Huge boulders and warty tors of volcanic rock scatter the hillside and are interspersed with dense heather, so I was glad to have this good paved path underfoot, winding an easy way

***Rhinog Fach** and **Fawr** above Llyn Hywel*

onto the tops. I contoured round into the upper reaches of Cwm Llechan and gained the ridge via grass-covered slopes, sending sheep stampeding off into the heather. The cloud had descended and now cloaked the summits, but as a good stone wall led along the ridge, I wasn't worried about naviga-tion. Half a mile to the south-west was my first Hewitt of the day, **Diffwys**. I left my sack and followed the wall easily up to bag its summit. The trig pillar made a welcome make-shift tri-pod for the camera and a photo shoot, before I bombed back to pick up the sack at the col.

Contouring around to the col above Llyn Dulyn, the clouds parted for a while and gave profile views of the main crag of the Rhinogs from a rock climbers point of view—Craig Bodlyn. This fine, tall crag clings to the northern flank of the minor, west top of **Diffwys** and gives excellent friction climbing in the middle grades. I vowed to return in better weather with my rack of climbing gear and a trustworthy companion.

The wall led on northwards, up the grassy ramparts of **Y Llethr** where a small, inconspicuous cairn marked the highest point, then on, down steep craggy slopes to the rocky shores of Llyn Hywel. Finding a spot out of the wind above the col, I brewed up as ever-expanding views opened up of the crag-girt flanks of **Rhinog Fach**, the upper part of Cwm Nantcol and the sad eye-sore of Trawsfynydd to the north.

After a bite to eat I again followed the wall to the dark, cloud capped summit of **Rhinog Fach**. The way was rocky but the cairn was soon gained.

At the top I made the classic mistake of not checking my map or compass. Mist still swirled around and the view was minimal, but seeing a bit of a path heading off straight ahead, I just presumed that it would lead down to Bwlch Drws Ardudwy, and so set off into the gloom. Within 50 feet the path vanished, and I was left scratching my head wondering whether to continue. I got out my compass and checked the bearing. Surely it couldn't be right, I thought. I had been walking something like 100° off course, so I retraced my steps back to the cairn at the summit and did it properly. The new bearing seemed to be heading back almost the way I had come, and so left me wondering if my compass was faulty. I sat at the cairn and considered my predicament. Should I follow my instinct or the compass? I have often relied on my instinct when making mountaineering decisions and judgements in the past and have usually been right, but I had to admit that the compass is usually infallible. Thankfully I came to my senses. I rechecked the compass, got the same result as before, and followed it with a will. A good path soon emerged underfoot and zig-zagged down heather slopes to the trench-like col at Bwlch Drws Ardudwy. The compass had been right! It just goes to show how disorientating mist can be on unfamiliar terrain.

I had planned to camp at the col for the night, but as it was only around 5.30 I decided to head off up **Rhinog Fawr** and to worry about where to camp later on. Connecting ill-defined sheep tracks together, I happily clambered over little rocky bluffs up the broad east ridge of the mountain, before turning due west to find the trig pillar in the murky gloom of a cloudy summit.

A rough bouldery descent led down to Llyn Du where, for the umpteenth time that day, I dropped below the cloud level. I navigated across a couple of re-entrants to the top of Bwlch Tyddiad and the remarkable path of the Roman Steps. These led down directly to the camp site at the head of Cwm Bychan.

A large Duke of Edinburgh Award group were the only other campers, so after pitching up, I joined their two teachers for a bottle of beer and a chin-wag. They were kind enough to offer a share of their evening meal, but I explained that I might as well eat my own, to save having to carry it the next day.

They were particularly interested in my trek, and indeed my way of life as a writer-cum-mountain walking instructor. The older of the two was a touch concerned that young instructors such as myself couldn't possibly have enough mountain experience to supervise children in the hills, until I pointed out that, even though I was only 27 at the time, I had been leading groups on mountain walking trips since the age of 12, as an adventurous Patrol Leader with my local Scout Troup. I also wondered whether those in their early 20s could possibly have enough experience of life to teach, and be responsible for children in a class room. He took my point and diplomatically changed the subject.

Personally, I was quite surprised that these two, neither of whom had any formal mountaineering qualifications, though without doubt possessing masses of outdoor experience, were allowed by their Local Education Authority to bring a large group of teenagers to one of the wildest and most remote mountain ranges south of the Scottish border, and to pretty much let them loose on their own. Throughout the country there was supposed to have been, during the last couple of years, a big shake-up of all those running adventurous outdoor courses for the under eighteens. New regulations had been drawn up by the government following the Lyme Bay canoeing tragedy a couple of years before, supposedly making it almost impossible for unqualified people to instruct teenagers in adventurous pursuits. My personal feelings are that there are simply too many groups of teenagers in the mountains of Britain anyway, many of them unwilling participants. As a teenager I often went off into the hills alone or with a small group of friends, and I believe that it does a world of good to let young adults discover their full potential in our wild and mountainous places, to take charge of themselves, and be responsible for their own actions. However, I feel this should only be an option for those with the will to discover the mountains on their own initiative. Once that initiative has been undermined, and the responsibility has been lifted from the individual and given to an adult leader, that leader must do everything in his or her power to ensure the safety and well-being of the party, including undertaking relevant formal qualifications and assessments. They owe it to the people in their care to be fully proficient at their job. There are some aspects of mountain-craft that it is impossible to learn without the specialised skills of an instructor, and it is a fact that no matter how much experience a candidate has before entering into the Mountain Leader Training Board's schemes, they always learn something new.

Tuesday 30th June ~ Moel Ysgyfarnogod

I awoke late with the happy thought that only 450 metres of ascent and eight miles of walking separated me from my next planned camp at Trawsfynydd, via **Moel Ysgyfarnogod**, the last Hewitt on the main Rhinog ridge.

The teachers were just turning their mini-bus through the gate as I emerged, though there was a chance that we would meet up again later that day, as they too were heading for Trawsfynydd. Their pupils had left for the easy walk over the pass earlier that morning.

My way up to and around the little knoll called The Clip on the southern ridge of **Moel Ysgyfarnogod** was straight forward. A good path climbed easily up to a stile over a wall at the col below Craig Ddrwg, from where the main path to Trawsfynydd led down hill to Wern-fach and the minor road on the south shore of the lake. My track headed up the left-hand hill-side from here. Another stile gave access to the rough slopes of **Moel Ysgyfarnogod**, continuing as a faint path to the first of two tiny tarns on the ridge. Great beds of volcanic rock are laid down as vast horizontal slabs along this section of the ridge, and frequently ended atop little crags. Although it was dry, the cloud was still low enough to reduce visibility to about ten feet, so I had the job of picking a careful way across this hectic terrain. Deep cotton-grass bogs made navigation all the more difficult, requiring regular boxing, a technique used to clear obstructions and each awkward bit of ground whilst navigating, whilst also pacing to keep a check on your distance covered (See Appendix 2). Each boxed section made the likelihood of a minor navigational error occurring all the more likely, but as it turned out, the steep slopes leading to the summit were soon underfoot, proving that no error had occurred. Searing wind hurled loose bits of moss and grass about the summit, so I quickly touched the trig pillar, took another bearing, and bombed off down the eastern flank to pick up a good grassy track above Cwm Crawcwellt.

As I gained the minor road lower down the cwm, four totally washed out girls from the group at my previous night's camp crawled out of a bog, well off the course they should have been on. They wearily followed me down the road to Llyn Trawsfynydd. They were using the site on the western side of this large lake, whereas I intended to use the one in the village.

I crossed the lake via the long footbridge at its eastern end and had a nosy around Trawsfynydd. Countless crumbling terraced houses in a damp air of decay were all I could find at the spot marked on my map as the camp site, so I asked the advice of a young woman who was just going into her house.

"It's next door," she told me.

I looked along the row of terraced houses and wondered which of these semi-ruins would be likely to have a camp site in their back garden. The same woman must have seen me looking gormless through one of her grimy windows, for she came out to put me straight again.

"That one there," she nodded to her immediate neighbour's dwelling, as though it were obvious, "they won't be in yet, but you could wait." With this she slammed the door without even waiting for a thank you for her helpful advice.

I really couldn't imagine a more unlikely place for a camp site, and didn't know how long I would have to wait for the owners to appear. 'Oh well,' I thought, 'I might as well forget it and make my way towards **Rhobell Fawr**. I'll just see what turns up!'

As I walked along the minor road towards the Afon Gain, I began forming a new plan in my head. Although I'd plotted a very careful route from the comfort of my home before setting out, I'd realised that I might want to change a few minor details once en route. It now seemed pretty obvious that the best course of action would be to continue down the Afon Gain, on down the Afon Mawddach at their junction below the Pistyll Gain and up into the Coed y Brenin Forests to a little known bothy for the night. It was still quite a way off, but the weather seemed to be improving, and the night was young, so why not? As a bonus it would give an ideal starting point from which to bag the solitary peak of **Y Garn** to the west in the morning. I could then bag **Rhobell Fawr** and **Dduallt** from a camp site to the south near Dolgellau. This immediately seemed like the perfect plan.

The secretive bothy, a huge farmhouse, was well hidden amid the trees. It had three big rooms downstairs, each with a fireplace, and three more rooms upstairs. After many nights cocooned in my tent, the place seemed like a luxury palace, and what's more, I had it all to myself. I gathered arms

The bothy in the Coed y Brenin Forest, a real home from home!

*The distant view of **Rhobell Fawr** from the Coed y Brenin Forest*

full of fire wood, decanted water from the old tank above the buildings and settled down to a night by the fire with the bothy book and a plate full of curry with rice.

Outside the evening had improved. The clouds had peeled off the summit of **Rhobell Fawr**, whose top had been capped by menacing nimbus all day,

The sad remains of the gold mines beside the Nant Las framing
Rhobell Fawr

236

as had the summits of the Aran and Dovey Hills to the south, although of course, I had to wander down onto the main forest track to see this, as the bothy was totally surrounded by thick conifer trees.

Various farming families had lived at, and worked the land around the bothy for centuries, relying on gold-mining and of course, forestry as well as livestock as a means of income. The last family is recorded as leaving in 1965. With the landowner's permission, the Mountain Bothy Association had taken over the maintenance of the buildings in the early 1980s, converting the main farmhouse into the wonderful bothy of today.

Turning in for the night, I listened for a while as the roof slates creaked under their own weight, the floor boards heaved quietly into place for the night and a little owl screeched right outside my open window. I was at peace with the world.

Wednesday 1st July ~ Y Garn

I awoke to a cheery morning of bright sunshine filtering through the tops of trees outside my bedroom window. What a great day for **Y Garn**. After a leisurely breakfast I packed my sack, swept the floor, burnt some rubbish and collected some fresh wood to replace that which I had burnt the night before.

*Vegetation on Craig-y-Cae keeps all but the keenest climber away from **Y Garn***

*Distant views of the sea beyond the Afon Mawddach estuary from **Y Garn***

I crossed the Afon Mawddach and took the minor road beside the Afon Gamlan at Dolmelynllyn. Within minutes a footbridge led over the chattering waters into the shade of an ancient oak wood. A supposedly secretive jay cawed loudly revealing his position to all and sundry in a clump

The head of Cwm Mynach and the Crawcwellt moors separate
***Y Garn** from the main Rhinog ridge*

of larch as I climbed up towards a stile and bridge over the Nant Las, and into the cwm below the beetling crags of Craig-y-cae. Ruins of the old gold-mining industry remained among the brackeny slopes of this, the eastern side of **Y Garn**.

I gained a wall at the boundary of the National Trust property and followed it north-westwards, high above the cliffs. The long ridges of Cadair Idris stood out as a deep purple smudge on the southern horizon, while away to the west rose the long switch-back of the main Rhinogs. Although strictly speaking I was still in the Rhinog range, the deep wooded trench of Cwm Mynach separated me from the higher western summits.

It became obvious the further I walked that to reach the summit of **Y Garn** I would have to climb the stone wall, a practise that I usually avoid at all costs. Once on the other side, easy grass slopes led up to the little rocky top complete with its ancient cairn, after which the hill is named. All the summits of Snowdonia could be seen, from the Dovey Hills to **Snowdon** itself.

Feeling an uncomfortable twinge in my stomach, I began the descent down the south-east ridge into the forest above Cwm Wnin, and on to Llanelltyd. An easy path alongside the Dolgellau golf course led back to the smart market town itself, and after a quick shopping spree in the supermarket, I followed the busy A494 trunk road to the Dolgamedd camp site at Bont Newydd, ready for an ascent of **Rhobell Fawr** and **Dduallt** the next day.

After a meagre ration of pasta, I spent the best part of the evening and a good portion of the night commuting backwards and forwards to the toilet block. For the most part I managed this in a semi-dignified stroll, but on the odd occasion, this evolved into an all-out sprint that would have put Linford Christie to shame. All I could point the finger of blame at was the water from the feeder-tank at the bothy. A big sign had advised that if water was flowing from the over-flow, then it was safe to drink—with all the rain this was not in doubt, so I had presumed it to be safe. By now I had begun to have serious doubts!

Thursday 2nd July ~ Stomach Problems

What a day. My planned ascent of the Rhobells just didn't happen. I awoke at 11 feeling awful. I lay in bed sympathising with myself, wishing that there had been someone else there to do this for me. I made a trip to the phone box to ring folks at home, and also my pal Andy in Scotland to arrange when he would be coming down to do part of the walk with me. I also made a hell of a lot more trips to the toilet block, thanks to the ever worsening symptoms of 'Dolgelly Belly'. Towards the end of the day I even considered moving my sleeping bag in there to save on a lot of unnecessary mileage.

At least I knew that Rachel was due the next day, so all I wanted was to make sure that I had done the Rhobell Hewitts before she arrived so that I could have the whole weekend off, giving me time to recuperate and bag some real sympathy. I hoped to then be fully fit to tackle the Dovey Hills and Arans, starting first thing on Monday morning.

Friday 3rd July ~ The Rhobells

It took a long time for me to fall to sleep that night, finally starting to doze fitfully by about 2a.m. I'd set the alarm for 8, and just about managed to struggle out of my pit by 9.30. As yesterday, it was another bright and cheerful day with just the faintest sign of a breeze keeping the midges at bay and the temperature bearable.

Although I'd still been paying regular visits to the loo throughout the night, I'd began to feel a tad stronger, and so decided to go bag **Rhobell Fawr** and **Dduallt** before Rachel arrived, taking a loo roll for company.

Heading east along the main road, a turn-off on the left led uphill along a series of minor roads, each one gated, to where a track headed off towards the Ffrith yr Castell Forest to the south of my first objective of the day, **Rhobell Fawr**.

The weather remained impeccable; cloudless skies and just breezy enough to make walking the hills enjoyable, but not so chilly as to require a fleece top. Buzzards wheeled clumsily in wide-circumference circles above grassy hillsides full of meadow pipits and wheatears, bouncing along on the moorland wind. Only my stomach troubles could spoil the day, but mercifully, seemed to be controllable for the moment, although my legs felt much weaker than usual.

I contoured around the southern flank of the mountain, and soon after the path leads along the edge of another pine forest, I plunged off up the open slopes. Just above the track, a 100' high crag adorned the hillside. At the left hand edge of the clean rock, an off-width, two-pitch chimney looked like giving a good old-fashioned thrutch or struggle, whilst round to the right, the other side of a huge flake which also formed the wide chimney, a thin, finger width crack looked a bit more desperate, but still good fun. I'd no idea if there were any recorded routes on the crag, but immediately vowed to return later in the year. Upon returning home I did a bit of checking up, and was pleased to find that this whole crag is almost definitely virgin.

Above the crag, and over to the right, a stone wall led easily uphill, and after scaling a wall via a stile, the summit cairn and trig pillar could be seen on the horizon away to the south. Another wall needed climbing just before the short climb up to the little knoll of a summit. Haze blurred the distant views, but the nearer Hewitts of the Arenigs, Arans and Manods stood sepia-like above the lush valleys.

Retracing my steps back to the forest track, I hot-footed it northwards in search of a fire-break to lead me onto the upper slopes of my next Hewitt, **Dduallt**. At last, at the final rise to a broad col hidden in the depths of the forest, a wide break led off right into the thick of the trees. After a couple of hundred yards, I came to a junction, and following my instinct took the one heading right. This led first southwards, then round in a big arc to the east then north, north-west, and west for a while before swinging back east to eventually settle on a general northerly bearing. This was all good fun, but my guts had begun to play up, the trees were acting as a block to the cooling breeze and a couple of dozen flies had began to hover around my face. In all honesty, I felt pretty miserable. Although I knew that I couldn't really be much more than about half a mile from my summit, I seriously considered turning back. Only the thought of having to come all this way again after the weekend made me grit my teeth and press on. At last I decided to get the compass out and to try making some sort of sense out of the map, which typically didn't show any fire-breaks in the forest I was almost definitely lost in. By using the compass to measure the aspect of slope, that is, the rough direction straight down the albeit very slight gradient, I could deduce which area of the forest I was in. My altimeter told me roughly which contour line I was walking on, and the bearing I was following meant that if I ever came out of the trees, I should be pretty much in line with the main ridge of the Arenigs, with the summit of **Arenig Fawr** at the furthest point. Within a hundred yards the unmistakable outline of Arenigs Fawr's ridge came into view dead-ahead—I had then only to work out how to reach the top of **Dduallt**. I decided that if I walked in a northerly direction for long enough along this fire-break, I must come to a fence at the edge of the forest, the fence then heading pretty much directly for the summit. Sure enough I was spot on again, and was soon drying out my sweat-soaked top on a sun-scorched rock at **Dduallt**'s rocky summit.

There was no way I'd choose to retrace my steps through that damnable forest again, so I headed south along the edge of the plantation, across boggy grass-land and heather slopes to eventually pick up the forest track back to the network of minor roads, and so back to the site.

In retrospect it hadn't been a bad day. I'd bagged my 50th and 51st Hewitts of the trip, had managed to stay dry for the entire day, and didn't even need to use that loo roll!

The author on the first day of the Hewitt walk

Clouds clearing in the Mynydd Du from Waun Lefrith

Bannau Sir Gaer *in the Mynydd Du*

The hills of tomorrow—looking east from ***Fan Hir***

Broken sandstones of the Mynydd Du

Sepia tones of sunset as a final view of the Brecon Beacons National Park

*Craig Aderyn—the crag of the birds—in the **Cadair Idris** range*

*Another storm clearing over **Cadair Idris** from the south*

***Craig-y-llyn** from Llanllwyda*

*The soggy looking Tarrens from the slopes of **Craig-y-llyn***

The boundless tracts of the Rhinogs beyond Dolgellau

Arenig Fach *framed in the col between **Moel Llyfnant** and **Arenig Fawr** from the boggy summit of **Dduallt***

Mynydd Mawr *from the Snowdon range across Nant Colwyn*

*The first of a winter's powder snow on **Mynydd Mawr**, 'the elephant mountain', from the Snowdon Ranger Path above Llyn Cwellyn*

*Lifting clouds above Allt Maenderyn on the way up **Snowdon***

Y Lliwedd, *queen of Welsh Mountains*

Yr Aran across Cwm Llan from Bwlch y Saethau,
with the Hebog ridge beyond

Ruby slabs of immaculate rock above Pen-y-Pass below **Crib Goch**

Sunset over the Pass of Llanberis

*The eastern Carneddau from **Moel Siabod**'s lower slopes*

Across the Afon Llugwy to Pen yr Helgi Du and Pen Llithrig y Wrach

Pen yr Ole Wen *across the shining levels of Llyn Idwal*

Yr Elen *in her winter cloak*

CHAPTER IV
Wildness to the East

Monday 6th July ~ The Dovey Hills

Having spent two wonderful days of doing nothing much, other than hanging around Dolgellau with Rachel, I felt ready to move on and tackle the Dovey Hills. My chronic 'Dolgelly Belly' had just about done with making my life a misery, so I packed up and made to leave Dolgamedd.

A heavy mist blanketed the hills as I walked along the minor road to Cae-ceirch, then trotted uphill to Bwlch Oerddrws on the A470 to Dinas Mawddwy. A car park at the top of the pass had a couple of vehicles parked, so there was a chance that for once I might actually meet someone on the hill. A good path led up Cribin Fach as the sun beat through the final wisps of early morning mist, persistently clinging to the slopes of each shady corrie and the dank tree-covered hillsides of the pine forests to the south. An elderly chap, unmistakably an old army type, stopped to pass the time of day. He was quick getting round to telling me that he was a 'mountain guide', but tried to change the subject once I mentioned that I am also in that line of work, albeit with a much less impressive qualification. It was soon obvious that he'd never even heard of the Mountain Leader Training Board or the Association of British Mountain Guides, but with a wink, pointed out that as he now lived in the area, he didn't think that formal qualifications were at all necessary—after all, he'd been doing 'this sort of thing' with his army boys for over 30 years. As his clients are all above the age of 21, he's probably right, but I couldn't help wondering what his insurance premium would be without these 'unnecessary' qualifications. Turning to a more amiable subject, I quizzed him on the coming weather forecast, and whilst pleased to hear that the next day was set to be a scorcher, less so the news that it would gradually worsen towards the weekend. After a few more pleasantries, we wished each other luck with our respective enterprises and I headed off into the heat-haze.

Maesglase in the Dovey Hills

Just before the summit of **Cribin Fawr** I spied a cluster of ruined quarry buildings on the east flank overlooking Penantigi Uchaf, and as I knew I'd be heading back that way later in the day, decided to stash my rucksack there.

I took out my waterproof jacket, map, compass, a bit of food and some precautionary toilet roll, and wandered over to the undistinguished grassy top of **Cribin Fawr**. I made my way easily down the south-west ridge towards the tiny col before **Waun-oer**. Dewy grass made the way down precarious, but the climb up out of the other side was nice and simple, and I soon had the next Hewitt underfoot. The summit of **Waun-oer** was just across a fence beside a solar panel.

The whole of the south side of this range is heavily forested, and as I made my way back to the col, I could see a track, unmarked on my map, wending a way across the southern slopes of **Cribin Fawr** towards Craig Portas, a subsidiary top on the way over to **Maesglase**. If I took this, I figured, it would save crossing **Cribin Fawr** three times in the day, as I would have had to do to bag these three summits from the north. A mossy gully led down from the col to a small scarp of shaley scree above the track, and within minutes I was again heading uphill towards the grassy tops of Craig Portas.

Along the ridge a couple of walkers struggled up from out of the forests of Nant Maes y gamfa, and turned eastwards towards **Maesglase**. By now I was really moving, feeling fit and healthy again, and without my rucksack to slow me down, I soon passed the couple at a stile before the heathery final slopes of the hill.

Just short of the top, I heard a shout, and looking around saw a young couple in the heather waving to me. I walked over to discover they were a Dutch couple walking the Cambrian Way. They were highly delighted to meet me as they had not seen any other walkers during their entire trip. We sat for over an hour, chatting about walking, climbing and travelling world wide, and I made myself useful by explaining some of the finer details of our Ordnance Survey maps. They were confused as to what the broad purple stripes indicated around the forests, and why did they obscure the contour details beneath? These are new features on Ordnance Survey maps, and as mine didn't have them marked, I wasn't particularly helpful on that score.

Eventually I wandered over to bag the summit, before rejoining them for the walk across to **Cribin Fawr**. Wishing them luck, I returned to find that my sack was thankfully still in place, and made my way down to the A470, the now empty car park marking the last of the Dovey Hills for this trip.

This had been a range I hadn't previously visited, and I had thoroughly enjoyed their grassy tops and narrow connecting ridges. In many respects they reminded me of the slaty domes of the Skiddaw Forest in the Lake District or the Howgills of the Pennines—steep sided with huge corries of crumbling shales and slates, but without any of the bare-rock so typical of the more frequented peaks of the area to hinder the walker.

I had planned to camp for the night somewhere about the pass, but as it was still quite early, I thought it best to continue up onto the southern extremes of the Arans and find a site there.

*Looking over Cwm Cywarch to **Pen yr Allt Uchaf** from a high camp on Y Gribin*

I took my time up the very steep slopes of **Pen y Brynfforchog** above Bwlch Oerddrws, and, passing around the knoll at 564 metres, soon came to the tiny summit ridge with its small pile of slates.

It was unlikely that I could climb **Glasgwm** before dark, so instead I wandered down into the forest around Bwlch y Fign.

A boggy path led through the pines and eventually out onto the wide access track on Y Gribin. A grassy col at just below 2000' gave an ideal camp site for the night, overlooking Cwm Cywarch with its wall of grassy Arans towering overhead, beyond the upper pastures of the valley. **Aran Fawddwy** dominated the view but, nearer at hand, vegetated crags fell almost shear from the plateau of **Glasgwm**'s summit.

The evening stayed dry and clear, but a stiff wind picked up and rattled the tent throughout the night, bringing back memories of my high camp in Cwm Cerrig-gleisiad in the hills of Fforest Fawr.

Tuesday 7th July ~ The Arans

I slept well through the windy night, perched on my little col, and awoke to yet another sunny day. Two such days on the trot felt like being spoiled, and to make my delight greater, I knew that I had an easy start to the day having climbed up to about 2000' the night before. Rubbing my hands with glee at my good luck at choosing a perfect night to camp high, I set off at 9.30, up the easy slopes of **Glasgwm**. Occasional wispy clouds blew across the ridge in front of me as I walked, limiting my vision, but as the exquisite little tarn of Llyn y Fign came into view, the sun peeled back the cloud curtain and revealed the summit cairn just beyond.

*The view southwards, over **Gwaun y Llwyni** and **Glasgwm** to the Dovey Hills from the cairn atop **Drws Bach** in the Arans*

The source of the Afon Dyfi, Creigllyn Dyfi beneath the east face of Aran Fawddwy

A steep path led down beside a fence to a broad, boggy col. The National Park Authorities had placed duck-boards and planks over the worst bits, so the walking was still very easy. The planks led over a small rise to a point just short of the col before Drws Bach. On a subsidiary ridge, heading back to the south lies **Gwaun y Llwyni**, a superbly situated Hewitt. Vast grey screes tumble down into the upper reaches of Cwm Cywarch from its very summit, and it really is a magnificent view point. I left my sack at the col and enjoyed the gentle path leading to the neat little top.

Back at the col I shouldered the sack and set off up the steep, pathless slopes of Drws Bach. This ridge of **Aran Fawddwy** leads down to a wide col via the minor top of Drysgol, and further out on the ridge, the summit of **Pen yr Allt Uchaf** basked in the rising sun. To reach its top requires a lot of walking of the out-and-back variety, about four miles in all. I stopped on the highest point of Drws Bach for a second breakfast of TUC biscuits and a drink of spring water to suss out the route. It would obviously be sensible to leave the sack here at the top of Drws Bach, but this worried me somewhat as there were already a lot of people climbing up towards Drysgol from Cwm Cywarch. In the end, however, I decided to leave it, as I reasoned that most, if not all of the people up on the hills that day would be walkers, and would probably have enough gear of their own to carry without stealing mine.

Before I left for **Pen yr Allt Uchaf** I noticed a silver box tucked into a cubby hole under the cairn beside which I sat. This contained a visitors book. The very last entry was by Bill Owen of the Wirral, making his 50th ascent of **Aran Fawddwy**! Pretty impressive stuff. He'd passed by that way only one hour before me. I added a few details of my own walk to the pages of recorded ascents and trotted off over Drysgol.

All went well as I flew along the ridge, making good going without my sack once again. Down at the col I passed a large Duke of Edinburgh Award group, making slow progress up towards **Aran Fawddwy**. Boggy ground led up **Pen yr Allt Uchaf**, and over a stile, a slight rise marked the summit, along with a couple of decaying bits of wood.

Bombing back to get my sack I was surprised to be greeted by a solitary walker coming towards me, "Now then Graham. Only 70 to go eh!" He introduced himself as Myrddyn Phillips, a keen peak bagger who has done numerous rounds of the Welsh and English Nuttalls. He'd read of my trip in the visitors book back on Drws Bach and was obviously impressed by my attempt on the Welsh Hewitts. After sharing a drink with me, he asked if he could take my photo, after which we went our separate ways. We were to meet up again about a month later, again by chance, on the very last day of my walk.

Back at my sack I caught up with the Duke of Edinburgh group, and after a bite to eat passed them again on the claggy slog up **Aran Fawddwy**.

The rocky slopes of the last hundred metres gave an opportunity to get to grips with a bit of easy scrambling, making me wish, just for a second, that I had spent the summer rock climbing. How could I think such a thing? I was having a whale of a time. I spent a couple of minutes on the summit gabbing to a young bloke who was just making his first forays into the Welsh hills, having just completed a round of the Wainwrights in the Lake District. He wanted my opinion of the **Crib Goch** Traverse, as he had done all the other 3000'ers of Wales, but didn't have the nerve to do **Crib Goch**. I encouraged him by comparing it to the harder parts of Sharp Edge on Blencathra, but he said he hadn't dared to do that either. When the hoard of teenagers arrived with their D. of E. leaders, I said goodbye and beat a hasty retreat northwards to **Aran Benllyn**, by-passing **Erw y Ddafad-ddu** as I would be bagging that on the way down to Creiglyn Dyfi later.

Incredibly, the weather was still holding, only a sharp breeze remained to blow the tops clear of midges and keep the temperature down. Without it, it would have been approaching 'sauna' level.

I rested behind a long, low wall on **Aran Benllyn**'s summit. The youngsters passed me yet again, and one of them treated me to a very posh "Good afternoon". I think they'd enjoyed our little race across the summits.

Now back along the ridge to bag **Erw y Ddafad-ddu** before gaining steep grassy slopes leading down to Creiglyn Dyfi, the impressively crag-girt source of the mighty Afon Dyfi. I had originally planned to camp there for the night, but as I had been going so well, and the day was still young, I couldn't see the point in pitching up there and then. I might as well keep going while the going's good, I thought.

First things first though. By that time I had begun to feel a tad queasy and dehydrated, so I popped off down to the shore of the lake to fill my water bottle, then brewed up some peppermint tea, then a Knorr soup, closely followed by a mug of Ovaltine Power, while I buried my head in Bill Bryson's hilarious *Notes from a Small Island*.

A pour over the maps convinced me that I could press on and bag three more Hewitts that evening, before finding a camp somewhere around the Bwlch y Groes road pass. I had a quick paddle, changed my worn out socks in an effort to try making my feet feel less like tenderised steak, then took to the easy western flank of **Foel Hafod-fynydd**. The few quartz rocks marking the summit are only 100 metres above the lake, so that Hewitt was soon behind me. Next, along a fence over pathless grass to the dried-up bog of Bwlch Sirddyn, then incredibly steeply up the south side of **Esgeiriau Gwynion**. The only thing harder than climbing the hill was trying to pronounce its name! The wind had built up to a real gale-force, taking all the heat out of the sun's rays and leaving me wondering about my lodgings for the night as I plodded over more dry bog towards my final summit, **Llechwedd Du**. I considered pitching up on the leeward side of one of the great mushrooms of peat that pepper the summit plateau, but thought that if it rained at all during the night, I'd wake in the morning in a sea of newly hydrated bog and cotton grass—no thanks! With this in mind I plodded ever more wearily on.

At last, after what seemed like a lifetime of bog-hopping, I reached the pass at Bwlch y Groes without seeing anything that looked even remotely inviting as a place to spend the night. Four options confronted me: Firstly, Carry on over **Moel y Cerrig Duon**, the first of the Hirnant Hewitts, and only 80 metres higher than the pass—but how would I know whether the terrain on the other side would be any more welcoming than that I had already crossed? Secondly, start looking for a friendly farmer down in Cwm Cynllwyd, who might just be persuaded to let me camp on his land for the night. Thirdly, look for an equally friendly farmer in Cwm Pennant to the south, or fourthly, look for one down in Cwm Eunant above Llyn Efyrnwy. I eventually chose Cwm Cynllwyd.

Golden arêtes of slabby, vegetated rock fell down to the very side of the road at Craig yr Ogof and looked inviting, but at the time I'd no idea if they'd been climbed before. After finishing the walk I returned to Criag yr Ogof with my climbing partner, Andy MacNaughton. On a blustery November day we managed to force a way up through two of these arêtes, thereby beating the local activists to these first ascents. The farms at the

Golden slabby arêtes of Craig yr Ogof
above the busy farm of Tan-y-bwlch

head of the cwm were a real hive of activity, mowing the pastures and bringing in the bales as I approached Tan-y-bwlch. Three collies rushed at me from under a Land Rover and liberally went berserk as I knocked on the farmhouse door. Within minutes the farmer's wife had taken me in hand and pointed out a delightful flower meadow across the infant Afon Twrch. She filled my water bottle, and generously refused any offer of payment for her hospitality. I don't suppose Welsh hill farmers are given much to reading books on walking the Welsh mountains, but if by chance the good folk at Tan-y-bwlch happen on this one, I'll take this opportunity to thank them for allowing this knackered walker to collapse in one of their fields.

It had been a big day. I'd bagged nine Hewitts over sixteen miles, and had ascended over 1400 metres with a very heavy load. By the time I had cooked up a meal, it was just past 10p.m., and I fell to sleep without even getting into my sleeping bag. Outside my flimsy walls, the tractors passed by, threshing and reaping, but I didn't hear a sound.

Wednesday 8th July ~ The Hirnants

Back to the fray with the first of the Hirnants, another totally new range to me. I would also pass the half-way point on my walk.

A bit of rain had brought the cloud base down overnight, but it mercifully seemed to be rising again, and patches of blue shone through the murk.

I wombled around the farm looking for someone to thank, but the distant drone of tractors meant that they had all been busy at work for some time. Even the dogs didn't seem to be at home to wish me a fond farewell, so I regained the road, and took to the fellside just south of Craig yr Ogof.

I crossed a col to the east and stumbled through pathless heather to gain a fence along the National Park boundary. Here I left the sack and struggled uphill to the top of **Moel y Cerrig Duon**. Great belching clouds of smoke filled the otherwise clean air over Llyn Efyrnwy to the east, as the annual cycle of heather burning got underway. This is largely essential on grouse moorland, as the birds feed on the fresh shoots of the bell and ling heather which flourish following the burning off of the old stems.

Across a vast expanse of this moorland stood my next objective for the day, the **Foel y Geifr—Foel Goch** ridge. The distance between me and them looked immense, but beyond the ranges, across the minor road at the head of Cwm Hirnant, three more Hewitts would have to be bagged before I could bed down that night. It was going to be a long day.

Looking across the heathery head of Cwm Hirnant to the distant Berwyns

My map assured me that the distance to **Foel y Geifr** was only about two and a quarter miles as the wind blows, but I was not travelling as the wind blows. The map showed a bold, dashed line, alternated with dots, and merging on one side with a half smudged yellow band, heading more or less directly for the summit of **Foel y Geifr**, falling short by an easy kilometre. Obviously something pretty substantial would be in evidence on the ground to show this county boundary-cum-edge of the National Park, I thought. Surely something more useful to the hill wanderer than the decrepit wire fence which made a bee-line for some intolerably boggy ground in the space between. How wrong could I be?

I returned for the sack and with a spring in my step that I can now only put down to the fact that I really had convinced myself that there would be an incredibly good path to follow, I headed off through bog and fen, moor and marsh for what seemed like hours of hard toil and sweat. Slowly the awful truth began to dawn. There wasn't a path at all.

251

*A rest stop on the **Foel y Geifr** - **Foel Goch** ridge*

Walking through thigh deep heather is about as toilsome a terrain to cover as I can think of, with the possible exception of quick drying cement. To clear the leg-grasping vegetation with each step, you have to lift your leg cruelly high, somewhere round about the point where your knee comes within a cat's whisker of your chin seems to be about the norm, making you look like a bit-part player in a Ministry of Funny Walks sketch. But the cruel thing was that the damned trig pillar standing proudly aloof atop **Foel y Geifr** didn't seem to have got any closer despite my efforts.

Glancing feverishly at the map for a better route, it began to dawn on me that if there was going to be a path of any sort, it was bound to be on the ridge top to my left. I mean, who would wallow around in all the muck to the east, when the option of striding along a trouble free crest presented itself within half a mile to the west? Only an absolute idiot, I can tell you.

I turned sharply left and made for the ridge just beyond point 605 metres. Whilst no obvious path appeared and there was still masses of heather everywhere, at least I had gained a bit of height.

But then my progress improved, and I soon came upon a fence marking an obvious line along the ridge from Foel Figenau towards **Foel y Geifr**. The occasional mountain ash saplings pushed timid leading shoots up through the dense ground cover as I neared the top of the hill.

Another fence cut across at right angles, and most remarkable of all, was crossed by a stile. This was quite plainly, extravagantly ridiculous. I mean, who in their right mind would want to climb **Foel y Geifr** from the west when a car can be driven to a height of 500 metres and within half a mile of the top over in the east? It would take a real lunatic for sure. With this in mind I ambled over to the trig pillar and stumbled across an actual path heading off for **Foel Goch**. Within minutes I had reached the smallest possible cairn at its top, retraced my steps as dark clouds scudded quickly by on their way to the Berwyns, and dropped down eastwards to the road leading over to Llyn Efyrnwy from Bala.

A bulldozed track led up to within yards of **Pen y Boncyn Trefeilw**'s summit, then down, keeping just above the edge of Penllyn Forest before I again had to leave the track to bag **Cyrniau Nod**. A faint path led beside a fence to a big cairn with a stake in its heart. I stood there silently for a while pondering on what I had achieved so far, with my 69th Hewitt of the trip. 68 to go—at last I was over half way.

This feeling of elation didn't last long however, as soon after regaining the track, I had to abandon it again for more strength-sapping heather. More dark clouds filled every horizon and threatened to engulf me as I gazed with despair upon the rough terrain that lay between me and **Foel Cwm-Sian Llwyd**. Half of Wales seemed to separate me from its ancient cairn. Gritting my teeth, I focused on my immediate goal and waded into the heather.

Half an age passed as I floundered in the morass, and then, way in the distance, I spied a post stuck up out of the heather. At that stage in my exhaustion I had no problem in convincing myself that it must mark the start of a path. With something much closer to focus my attention on, and give me something seemingly more feasibly achievable in the near future, I gained my second wind and virtually sprang across the rough intervening ground. I collapsed by the post, face down in the heather, and just lay there for perhaps a minute, breathing heavily. Despite the heavy weight of my pack, I managed to right myself and checked to see if the path was heading in anything like my direction. The truth came as a bit of a shock. There wasn't a path. The post was just that, a wooden post, plain and simple, and didn't seem to mark anything at all. To make matters worse, the long black cloud that had been following me for some time, had caught up and fallen around me like a blanket on a bird cage, leaving me alone with just a heavy rucksack and a useless fence post for company. For the first and last time on the entire trip, I felt completely alone.

I fumbled with the straps of my sack and dumped it in the heather, then flopped down next to it. Taking my good old friend the compass from the top pocket I leaned against the post and began checking the bearing to the top of the hill. Snuggled up in the deep heather out of the wind, fatigue began creeping up on me, and I actually began to feel a tad sleepy. I closed my eyes for a few seconds and was at once at peace with the world. To think, I was huddled up in the heather in the middle of a vast empty wasteland of moor and bog, with not a soul in sight and the nearest house miles away. Solitude at last. What a great place for forty winks. Just a shame it was a bit on the chilly side ... 'My God, what the hell am I doing?' I awoke with a start, not really sure how long I had actually been asleep. I was chilled to the bone, but this only helped to snap me out of my semi-conscious state all the quicker. I realise now that I was probably very close to becoming hypothermic. I was tired, undernourished, the sweat that I had generated struggling through the heather had become cold and clammy on my skin, and I had had an over-whelming desire to just lay there and go to sleep.

Coming to my senses I pulled on a hat and gloves, my spare fleece pullover and wind-proof top, wolfed down some chocolate, cheese and biscuits then quickly checked the bearing and ploughed on to the top. It just goes to show how easily you can be caught out by the weather, even in summer, and also just how stupid I can be at times. I was really quite annoyed with myself for failing to spot the obvious, sooner than I did.

Just short of the summit I crossed the path from Bala to the Tanat Valley, from which another ran to the trig pillar at the summit. I had begun to warm up by that time, but still forced myself to eat a large slab of fruit cake that I had been saving for just such a time.

An indistinct path led off to the south-east, and as the wind was increasing all the more and I was becoming a bit short on food, I decided to postpone my attempt on the Berwyns the following day, and instead make for the camp site at Llangynog beside the Tanat where I felt sure I'd be able to have a good meal and restock on some supplies. With this in mind I made good time, cheering my spirits with a hearty rendition of a medley of songs from the later years of the Beatles. I'm not sure if there was anybody else in the area that day, but at that point I couldn't have cared less. 'Maxwell's Silver Hammer' followed 'Hey Jude' which followed 'Revolution'. I even had a bash at McCartney's 'Mull of Kintyre', all sang with a loud, sheep-scattering passion, and by 'eck was I on form!

Henstent Caravan and Camping Park in Llangynog seemed about the best site I have ever had the pleasure to pitch my tent on. After a browse in the site's library (yes, library!) I paid a visit to the pub for a Tanat Valley

Mixed Grill—well, it had been a hard day. 21 rough hill-miles over six Hewitts. The peaceful, pastoral atmosphere of the valley won me over, and I booked in to the site for another night. I felt I'd earned a rest day.

Thursday 9th July ~ Resting

A day of very high winds but long sunny periods. Perfect for lazing on a bench (how civilised) by the gurgling waters of the Afon Eirth reading *Notes from a Small Island*. Fish surfaced occasionally and blue tits, great tits, chaffinches and siskins fed off aphids in the now flowerless Prunus trees throughout the site.

Friday 10th July ~ The Berwyns

The time had come for me to rub noses with the Berwyns. I really wasn't sure what to expect from the range as I had never walked among these hills before. I took the path towards Pistyll Rhaeadr with mixed feelings—on the one hand, if the walking turned out to be like that of the Arans, then I was in for a great day striding over the tops, but on the other, if these were predominantly heather hills, like the neighbouring Hirnants, then I was in for another long hard slog.

The path led up the east side of Craig Rhiwarth before gaining the long east ridge of **Post Gwyn**, at a pass known as Y Clogydd. Imagine my delight upon cresting the ridge and finding gentle grassy slopes leading along the top to the summit. There was even a vague path beside a fence to follow for a while, but that hardly mattered, for the sun was shining, the birds were all of a happy flutter and I could really stride out.

Post Gwyn was soon behind me, but I could see that the connecting ridge route round to **Moel Sych** was going to be tough. More heather barred the way. This heather seemed to only extend from the west as far as Cwm yr Eithin, a broad subsidiary ridge running down towards Afon Disgynfa, so instead of following the main ridge round, I descended the short heather slopes to cross the Afon, then struck a course up Cerrig Duon to the east. The going underfoot was much easier than it would have been across the heathery tops, with just short growing mat grasses and clumps of bottle green hard rushes to contend with.

As I gained the main ridge the wind fairly howled across the desolate empty spaces from the west and literally propelled me up the good path to the top of **Moel Sych**. Struggling down into the teeth of the tempest came a couple of old blokes, scattering a pair of snipe as they went. I immediately recognised them as the leaders of the D. of E. group I had raced along the Arans just days before. We stopped to exchange pleasantries which gave me a good opportunity to thoroughly examine the younger one's exposed skin. It's true that the sun was shining brightly, but I do think the poor chap had been a bit over-indulgent with the old sun block—his face, neck, ears, arms and hands were plastered with about half an inch of the milk-coloured, putty-like stuff. With a 'seeya' from me, a spirited 'tally-ho!' from the older chap and a 'cheerio' from his plastered accomplice I was again on my way.

A 'permissive path' led over a stile to the actual summit, whilst a small sign tacked to the stile informed me that the next Hewitt was indeed **Cadair Berwyn**. The lonely, and I must say, pretty foul looking waters of Llyn Lluncaws lay in the hollowed cwm to the east where I had originally planned to camp overnight. I was glad that circumstances had forced me to do otherwise.

Cadair Berwyn's top consists of two summits, perhaps 300 metres apart with a dip of about 50 feet between the two. The rocky first top houses a big cairn-cum-windbreak, while the second plays host to a trig pillar. This is confusing as it is actually the southern top which is the higher, by a staggering three metres!

The next col saw the start of some serious back-tracking so I dumped the sack next to the fallen 'standing' stone and took the path eastwards over the

Craig Berwyn from Tomle.
There is almost cleared forest below the cliffs

minor top of Tomle. This two mile long ridge has four distinct tops to it, two of which are sufficiently elevated above their neighbours to be Hewitts. Beyond Tomle stands the summit of **Foel Wen**. On the same small plateau is another minor top before the slightly rocky col and rise to **Mynydd Tarw** and the end of the ridge. A substantial cairn marked the top and the point for me to turn around and head back to the rucksack.

At the sack I had a bite to eat and a bit of a relax, well content with my lot. After maybe 10 or 15 minutes I rose and startled a huge buzzard, not more than 10 feet away, into flight. Ochre feet, gleaming eyes and talons flashed in a blur of mottled feathers as it soared away with the building wind to its rump. How on earth I had managed to approach without its knowing I just couldn't understand. I hadn't even known it was there until it made off, but for it not to see me coming, or to hear me shuffling around in my food bag for a quarter of an hour was quite remarkable.

With the departure of this impromptu entertainment, I packed up and contoured round to Bwlch Maen Gwynedd, before climbing easy slopes to **Cadair Bronwen**'s windswept top.

The north-west ridge led down over Trawsnant as I tarnished the wild gusts of the wind with more Beatles ballads and one or two Dylan and Donovan numbers. Surely I can't be the only solo long-distance walker to entertain themselves this way? Although my voice leaves a lot to be desired, I just love a good rousing song. I remember reading in Mike Stroud's *Shadows on the Wasteland*, the account of his and Ranulph Fiennes unsupported trek across the Antarctic wastes, that he regularly passed the time by making up songs about his chickens back home, usually (or should that be unusually?) to the tune of 'The Milky Bar Kid'! So perhaps my efforts weren't quite so bad after all.

Down at Hendwr camp site by the mighty River Dee, I whiled away the hours of a blustery evening with the final chapters of *Notes from a Small Island* and mug after mug of Ovaltine Power.

Saturday 11th July ~ The remaining Berwyns

I called in at the camp shop for a couple of bits and pieces for the walk that day, leaving most of my gear in the tent. I was planning to return to Hendwr that night after bagging the last two of the Berwyn Hewitts, **Moel Fferna** and **Moel yr Henfae**s above Cynwyd just down the road.

A young lad was getting served by Dorothy, the elderly camp warden at the counter, and a sweet old lady was idly leafing through pamphlets for the Centre of Alternative Technology, Trawsfynydd Power Station, Electric

Mountain and the Ffestiniog Steam Railway by the window. I picked up what drinks and chocolate bars I wanted, and just as the lad took his change the old lady finished looking at the leaflets and turned to face the counter across the shop. Being a true gent, I politely waved her in front of me with a charming, "Sorry, do you want to go first?"

This dear, frail old thing immediately turned into a witch and looked at me as if I were an irremovable stain on her best Axminster. "No. I've got all the time in the world," she barked with a mouth full of marbles, and in a tone that implied that she was incredibly busy, but had been forced to rush out to buy something unbelievably essential.

"Oh. OK. Thanks," was my shocked answer, and I paid for my goods and went outside to put them in my sack.

"Oh, Dorothy," I heard her cry in apparent despair, "I never realised that you had to contend with that sort of person, you poor dear."

I just couldn't believe it. What could I have possibly done during my few hours at the site, most of which I had spent cocooned in my sleeping bag, I might add, to upset the old dear to such an extent? And what did she mean by 'that sort'? Did she have a real fear of hillwalkers or what? She obviously was under the impression that 'poor Dorothy' was fully entitled to danger money for simply being in the same country as me. Now, as a Northerner, I know that I don't speak as if I'm auditioning for a bit-part in a Jane Austin period drama, but does my Yorkshire twang really instil so much fear in the elderly classes? I really don't know. However, I must add that 'poor Dorothy' made no comment whatsoever, and in fact changed the subject immediately, thus restoring my general attitude of goodwill towards little old ladies. During my short stay at Hendwr, I always found Dorothy to be cheerful, helpful and at times quite comical, even if she does have a demented old lady as a friend.

I took the main road to Cynwyd where I stopped to buy a sandwich, then strolled along the minor road along the north bank of the Afon Trystion, scattering bullfinches as I went. The road soon turned into a forest track and slowly gained height. Beyond the limits of the forest it continued around the south side of **Moel Fferna** and at a gate on a col, a path led northwards up to its easily bagged summit cairn. The trig pillar shown on the map no longer marks the top, and it is not obvious where exactly it once stood.

At that point I'd covered at least half of the day's walk in a little under two hours, and as the day was dry, though overcast, and I only had one more Hewitt to bag, I delved into my sack for a book to read. I had come across *To Catch a Spy*, a collection of spy stories introduced by Eric Ambler, and although I'm not really a fan of spy stories it was the best I could come up with in anticipation of finishing *Notes from a Small Island*. I'd decided that an anthology boasting works by the likes of Somerset Maugham, Compton Mackenzie, John Buchan and Graham Greene had to be better than the only other alternative in the camp shop, a seedy looking novel from the seventies called, rather excitingly, *Avalanche*. I mean, an avalanche travels at an incredible speed, and I really couldn't imagine getting gripped over a novel whose only possible action would be over in a little over thirty seconds. On the whole, I think I'd chosen wisely.

I sat at **Moel Fferna**'s windswept top until a light drizzle descended, and so packed up and headed south over Cerrig Coediog. I'd donned my water-proofs by this time, but a wild chattering overhead made me swipe off my hood in surprise. A large, pure white raptor quartered the hillside above, as I watched spellbound. Only its wing-tips added relief to its colour, these being a jet black. The whole thing was about the size of a buzzard, but much lither looking, and very bull-headed. I'm not a keen naturalist, but I enjoy seeing anything wild in its natural habitat and like to be able to put a name to what I have found, be it a polecat, salamander, stonechat or alpine ladies mantel. That was the exciting thing about this bird—I didn't have a clue what it was. I eventually settled on a montague's harrier, though I didn't have the foggiest idea what a montague's harrier looks like, nor for that matter a hen harrier or marsh harrier. But at least my mind seemed to be settling on a member of the harrier clan.

As I watched, another joined it, although at first it wasn't immediately obvious that these two were of the same species. This second bird was slightly larger, but was a mottled brown all over with the exception of its rump which again was a prominent white colour. She chattered like her partner, and I watched them winding together on the breeze, parting and skimming away across the heathery flank of the hill, before wheeling round and returning to each other with more excited chatter. Very occasionally the bigger, predominantly brown bird let out a loud piercing shriek, like that of a buzzard. I had the same sense of awe that I felt when I first saw a red kite on the summit ridge of **Gorllwyn** weeks before. I knew that I was very, very lucky to be there, and so privileged to be able to witness this wild, courting couple of the air.

I happily pondered on this as I quietly made off across the heather, stopping just occasionally to glance back at one of the wonders of our natural world, knowing that I would like to stay there all day, but also knowing that my presence undoubtedly disturbed them. Upon returning home, I did a good deal of research and found that I had actually seen hen harriers, quite rare throughout Britain, but the one harrier that you are likely to see in the wild.

The path beside the fence passed the top end of three small conifer plantations just before reaching the grassy top of **Moel yr Henfaes**. A small cairn atop a rocky bed marked the actual summit.

South again, a bulldozed track beside a memorial to a 'lover of Wales', cuts across the range from south-east to north-west, and led north-westwards back to the valley of the Dee, and the tent at Hendwr.

CHAPTER V
Heading for Familiar Territory

Sunday 12th July ~ To Bala

A wild day of dripping leaves, puddles on roads and continuous drizzle. Basically, I had no Hewitts to climb until I reached the Northern Arenigs beyond Bala, so was quite content to plod down the road through Llandrillo.

During the walk the wind continued to build into a frenzy, leaving me happy not to be going high that day. On Llyn Tegid, or Lake Bala as it is more often called, it was all a frothy upheaval, although I spied a couple of brightly coloured sails of one or two hardy windsurfers dancing among the choppy foam.

I arrived early at the Penybont Camp Site, too early for the reception to be open, and so pitched up behind a screen of trees and ambled back into the town centre to do a spot of shopping and to generally be a tourist.

Later, when I returned to the site, I presented myself at the camp reception, and foolishly handed over a £20 note to cover the two nights I was to spend in Bala. The odd-job man-cum-receptionist-cum-con-man gave me change to the tune of £3.10. After a bit of haggling we estab-

The Arans, grey beneath storm clouds over Llyn Tegid

lished that he thought £8.45 per night was quite reasonable for a single bloke with a tiny tent, no car and no pets. We also established that I wasn't happy about it. The long and short of it was that I pointed out that it was in fact cheaper to stay at the Youth Hostel up the road, while he in turn pointed out that I would be the only one staying there as it had closed down a short while before. He showed me the small print in a pamphlet, stating that £8.45 is the going rate for his site, and I showed him that that very same pamphlet also states that that price is for two people, with a car and a dog. Additional cars cost £2 as do additional people and pets, and so by my reckoning he should have deducted £2 for me not being with a second person, £2 for not having a car and £2 for not having a dog with me—leaving a much more realistic total of £2.45, pretty much what other camp sites I'd stayed at were charging at the time. The whole thing ended with me demanding my money back, and him showing me, in that annoying, cocky way he had, the even smaller print on the pamphlet stating that refunds could not be given. Knowing when I am beat is one of my main traits, so I stormed off to my tent to have a good old sulk.

Monday 13th July ~ Book Hunting

Incredibly, the warden, the same bloke I'd had words with the day before, had the nerve to come over first thing to ask me to leave as he said I'd only paid for one night. Keeping my cool, I at first refused, just long enough for him to get ridiculously high and mighty with me, before producing my receipt to prove him wrong. This clearly pissed him off, and he skulked away with his tail between his legs, the score firmly fixed at 1:1.

I spent what turned out to be a very wet and windy day exploring the drab streets of Bala, trying to find a second-hand book shop.

Tuesday 14th July ~ Foel Goch

Although it rained heavily during the night, the day began sunny and luke-warm, so I hung around Penybont, just long enough to let the tent dry thoroughly, and to let the warden think I'd decided to stay another night.

My goal for the day was lowly **Foel Goch**, a small but isolated Hewitt a few miles north of Bala. I packed up and headed out of the town on the A4212 road to Ffestiniog. Within 2 miles I came across a good, down-to-earth camp site on the farm at Tynddol Isa. The simple plan for the day was to pitch up here, and leaving all the gear behind, bag **Foel Goch** from its west side.

I knocked on the door, and timidly enquired how much it would set me back to pitch the tent for a night. The old hill farmer's saddle-bag face took on a thoughtful, ponderous look, and muttered, almost as if he half expected me to walk off in disgust, "Would £1 be all right? It's what I usually charge backpackers." I pitched up a happy man. Basically the site had everything that Penybont had, with the exception of hot water on tap.

From Tynddol Isa I crossed the main road and climbed up through broad-leaved woodlands and attractive farmyards to gain the grassy footpath along the ridge from Maes Bras. I walked on into the gathering hill fog of a real dreich to pick up the county boundary just east of Garnedd Fawr. The boundary itself is marked by an electric fence which stopped just short of the summit, and on the south side, a vague path gave easy access to the trig pillar, boundary stone and cairn which mark the top of this unremarkable little hill.

For a slight variation on descent, I took the track through Llaithgwm amid barking collies and sturdy looking cows. Down on the B road, the farmstead of Tair-felin was a hive of activity. A dappled-grey collie was rounding up the sheep and having a particularly hard time of it. One old ewe would insist on chasing after the poor mutt and head-butting it at every possible opportunity.

At Frongoch the heavens opened with a certain menacing vengeance, so I took cover in the post office and persuaded the post-master to warm up a steak and kidney pie for me in his microwave.

I was soon ensconced in my warm bag back at the tent, stove a-blazing and boots steaming away under the flysheet, thankful for the good, honest country folk in the Welsh Hills, and the fact that the forecast for the morrow was a cracker.

Wednesday 15th July ~ More Arenigs

At last a day of good weather, although the drumming rain on the flysheet when I awoke didn't immediately inspire me with confidence for crossing the dreaded wastes of the Northern Arenigs and the Migneint.

After breakfast I glumly packed my bags within the shelter of the tent. At 10.15 I felt I could not put off the inevitable any longer. Even as I unzipped the door, the last few heavy drops fell as a speedily clearing sky revealed itself directly overhead. Squelching through the long wet grass of the flowery paddock that had been my home for the night on the way over to the toilet block, the clouds cleared further and a watery glare of sun filtered through the pile of grey towels that covered the surrounding hillsides.

*The bliss of solitude. Looking north to the Snowdon, Glyder and Carneddau ranges from **Carnedd y Filiast***

I took the main road up through Frongoch and continued until just beyond the canoeing centre at Ciltalgarth. My first stop for the day was to be the summit of **Carnedd y Filiast**. A good farm track led up above Cwm Hesgyn and on to gain the heathery moors of Foel Boeth. My track headed north to cross the murky, swollen waters of the Nant y Coed, its bank resplendent with healthy looking mountain ash and bilberry. The path continued more steeply to the summit of the Hewitt, marked by a cairn and trig pillar. Away to the north stood row after row of mountains, each still to be climbed, and far away to the right of these, a tiny ridge, notched between compact heathery knolls, stood my ultimate goal—**Tal y Fan**. A strong,

***Arenig Fach**'s summit trig pillar*

Outside the tiny bothy below **Arenig Fawr**

steady wind blasted the summit, and even the occasional clouds which dared to hang around the summits of **Snowdon** and the Carneddau were soon blown off.

Due west a fence led out across the wildness of the Migneint, eventually curving round to pass over the heathery north ridge of **Arenig Fach**, my next summit. Again, being back on heather, progress was difficult, but with the rapidly improving weather I still made good progress and was soon standing atop this, my second and last Hewitt for the day.

I needed to drop down to the road to the south before heading over to the bothy which nestles below the beetling, vegetated crags of **Arenig Fawr** for the night. A judicious use of numerous gates and stiles led easily down to this.

At the bothy I was delighted to find a good fire place and a large bag of coal so I went in search of dead heather stems for kindling and a water supply. As the Trangia hissed away with a pan of Knorr soup over it, I put a match to the kindling and immediately wished I hadn't. Great billows of dense smoke filled the tiny room and in spite of the fact that I opened the door, making having a fire in the first place totally pointless, it stayed full of smoke for the next two hours. At last, at 8.30 the smoke cleared and revealed a few hot embers on the grate. I closed the door and bedded down for the night.

Thursday 16th July ~ The Remaining Arenigs

Another great day looked like being on the cards. Above Llyn Arenig Fawr, to the east of the actual summit of **Arenig Fawr** itself, I struggled uphill in a mini-heatwave, slogging around the rocky flanks of Y Castell. Higher up, early morning mists still hung around the main mountain mass and gave welcome relief from the heat. Steep grass slopes and delightful scrambling on bubbly volcanic rock led up to the summit of **Arenig Fawr**'s main top. Across the deep defile to the west, the steep sided bulk of **Moel Llyfnant** stood proud and isolated from all else, leaving me wishing I didn't have to lose so much height before tackling its abrupt slopes.

Sheep scattered as I climbed up from the boggy col separating the two mountains, but I was soon perched among the breezy summit rocks of my second Hewitt of the day. Only **Gallt y Daren** remained, but again called for a long descent before I could tackle the rough slopes leading to its top.

Or did it? The O.S. map shows a fairly obvious ridge route connecting the two tops, and although it is undoubtedly much further to follow this round, I suspected it would actually work out easier than losing yet more height. I plumped for this and despite some fairly tough bog-hopping, it wasn't too bad. And the weather remained good. Perfectly cloudless skies matched my mood of happiness, and with purposeful strides, I soon swallowed up the intervening miles.

From the summit of **Gallt y Daren**, I could see a broad farm track, away over the hard rush moors of Moel yr Wden, leading towards the A4212. Although the track wasn't marked on the map, and would inevitably be private, I thought 'what the 'eck' and went for it. At least it was heading in my direction. Sure enough I was soon plodding tarmac westwards from Pont Dolydd Prysor, and under the shade of an amply foliated ash tree above Glanllafar Farm, I peeled off my sweaty boots, and had a snooze in the warmth of the afternoon breeze.

I hadn't really got a clue where I would be pitching up that night, but didn't really care. Something would turn up, so long as I made it to the Ffestiniog area. That would then leave me in an ideal position to bag the principal tops of the Moelwyns before meeting Rachel in Blaenau Ffestiniog on Saturday morning.

I made an effort to follow the not-so-obvious Roman Road of Sarn Helen, passing the Practice Works and Amphitheatre, but managed to make a bit of a hash of it. The problem was that it was just one of those stroll-along-with-your-hands-in-your-pockets days, and whistling a happy tune, I did just that. Not a care in the world. However, it soon became obvious that the particular path I'd chosen for this amble wasn't going to play fair. It would insist on leading me towards Trawsfynydd, a place where I had no intentions of spending good walking time knocking on grimy terraced house doors on the off chance that they might just happen to have a camp site tucked away somewhere in their back garden. No sir, I'd been there before!

After a bit of head scratching, and ponderously studying the map, I was soon on the right path once more, and bound for Ffestiniog. This particular path led to the main road near Gellilydan were a caravan site is marked on the map. Unfortunately, it was another in the New Radnor 'No Tents' variety. Luckily the warden was good enough to point me across the road to the Bryn Arms pub and a fellow called Archie. Archie was only too pleased to bung me in a small, enclosed copse of trees with a couple of over-friendly ponies for the night, at no charge whatsoever. How lucky can a camper be? So, for the price of less than a fiver, I got a hearty meal in his pub, a bed for the night and the chance of being stampeded to death in the small hours by the ponies. Quite good value for money really.

Friday 17th July ~ Starting on the Moelwyns

I stayed in bed until a heavy shower eased, finally unzipping to a bright world of blue skies, fluffy cumulus and dour horses' breath.

Down the road beyond Maentwrog a public footpath, raised on an embankment of earth, ran along the north bank of the Afon Dwyryd, then up through flowerless rhododendrons to the small station of Dduallt on the Ffestiniog Steam Railway. Yet again the day was a real boiler. Hardly a

Narrow guage trains ply their trade on the Ffestiniog Steam Railway, with **Manod Mawr** *behind*

breath of wind stirred the tree tops and empty blue skies filled the horizon beyond the Manods to the east. What's more, I thought it really looked set to stay that way. How wrong could I have possibly been?

The path follows the tracks of the railway, with only minor diversions all the way to Tanygrisiau Reservoir, from where I followed a less distinct trail through rocky knolls to the higher reservoir of Llyn Stwlan. Here the cloud was down with a great, grey, sulky vengeance. The Welsh Gods of weather clearly had other ideas for anyone wishing to bag a few easy summits that day. Heavy rain came, then grew heavier as I climbed up to the col between **Moelwyn Bach** and **Mawr**. Nearing this high level pass became a real struggle against the elements as the wind threatened to tear me from the hillside and thrust me headlong back down the steep slopes I had just climbed. Being barely able to stand upright, let alone walk any further uphill, the only sensible option seemed to be to pack it in for the day, and lose height as quickly as possible. It wasn't an easy decision to make for it would create a problem.

I had spent a good deal of time at Bala re-planning these last few weeks of my trip, and had decided to make good use of the extensive network of Youth Hostels which abound in Snowdonia. This would mean that when Rachel arrived for the weekend, she could take home the tent, which although it had served me well, was a heavy burden to lug around the mountains of Wales when the option of spending virtually every night in a Hostel was a possibility. For the remaining fortnight I would only need to camp out on two occasions, and was quite prepared to use a Gore-Tex Bivouac Bag for those nights. Again I had been particularly lucky on that score. Mountain Range, a North Pennines manufacturer of outdoor gear, had been good enough to let me have an excellent bivvy bag and a few other bits and pieces at trade prices. This bag was only about a third of the weight of my tent, which as far as tents go is considered to be quite light-weight anyway.

To avoid arriving at a fully booked Hostel, as I had at Llwyn y Celyn in the Brecon Beacons, I had pre-booked all of my Hostel nights for the remainder of the walk. To change my plans now because of a playful wind would cause much rearranging of plans.

With this in mind I battened down the hatches as it were, gritted my teeth and fought my way up into the gathering storm. Only 400 feet above the col, a cairn marked the top of the highest point of **Moelwyn Bach**, so turning my back to the wind, breathing easier with my face to leeward, I pelted it back down to the col.

Deciding that my task would be easier without my pack, I dumped it behind a boulder and tackled the easy scrambling of **Moelwyn Mawr**. Immediately the terrain became more interesting. Dark pinnacles with huge white bosses of quartz embedded in their bases loomed out of the gloom, and the scrambling kept my brain ticking over. Numerous false tops were passed by in the mists and I made mental notes of obvious landmarks to aid my descent—a tight squeeze through a notch, a large band of quartz, a rocky, granite like knoll—I would tick these off in my mind on the way down.

At last the top became more dome-like and grassy and the trig pillar rose out of the gloom. I followed my nose back to the pack at the col, glad to have these two summits behind me and only a much smaller **Moel-yr-hydd** to tackle next.

Overlooking the reservoir (not that you could see it that day) on the east face of **Moelwyn Mawr**, a good old miners' track contours at the exact height of the col and deposited me below the easy, grassy slopes of my final Hewitt for the day.

Again I dumped the sack, and passing through an electric fence via a gate, I gained the path on the other side and soon had **Moel-yr-hydd** behind me. Back at the sack the wind and rain continued with malice, but I didn't care, I was heading down to the flesh-pots of Blaenau Ffestiniog having done my share of fighting the elements for the day.

Menacing grey houses, industrial detritus, gutters overflowing with rubbish and more dark skies welcomed me to Blaenau. I shuffled through the dank grimness of a long-dead mining town hoping for a camp site, knowing my search was futile but not knowing what else to hope for. The staff at the Tourist Information Centre advised me to get on a bus or train and look elsewhere, and even though I pointed out that I'm not supposed to use any form of transport during this walk, it was obvious that they simply couldn't help me. I headed back outside and walked the streets lined with redundant shops and empty cafés. If I'd known that in just over a week I would break my self-imposed rule of not using public transport, I'd have been on the first train to the Lledr Valley, for there lies a homely Youth Hostel. Instead, I decided to call on the good hospitality of a local friendly farmer, and went off in search of a likely lad.

Way out beyond Bethania a sign for a guest-house with acres of fields around it offered hope, so I crunched up the long drive and knocked at the door. The owner of this 16th century farmhouse was in the strange position of not actually owning any land to farm, and was quick to point me in the direction of the landowner's house across a meadow.

Only a pack of collies intent on rounding me up made life difficult, but within minutes I was once again cocooned in my own little home, stove boiling up a pasta concoction behind the tiny farmhouse beneath the steep slopes of **Manod Mawr**.

Saturday 18th July ~ More Moelwyns

I'd actually arranged to meet Rachel in the centre of Blaenau Ffestiniog at midday, but wanted to get the three summits of the Manods out of the way first so that I could bomb over the remaining Moelwyns on Monday to Beddgelert.

An obvious path soon had me by the shores of Llyn Manod, and an old miners' track climbed steadily to gain the monstrous desecration that is the short summit ridge of **Manod Mawr**. The main top lies some way back from the spoil heaps of the open cast quarries along the ridge, and within half an hour of leaving the lake, I was striding along the bouldery top to the summit. Only the base of the trig pillar remained at the top, which is a pity as the Gorphwysfa Mountain Club, of Pen-y-Pass fame, are essentially responsible for its upkeep.

Gorphwysfa is the old name for the hotel which stands atop the Pass of Llanberis to the east of the Snowdon massif. In the early part of this century it was one of the main centres for Welsh mountaineering, from which exploration of the surrounding mountains and crags took place, along with the equally well known Pen-y-Gwryd Hotel just below the pass down the road. It was the regular venue for the famous climbing parties of the 1920s and '30s hosted by the late Geoffrey Winthrop Young, then one of the most prominent figures in world mountaineering. Later, it became the Pen-y-Pass Hotel, and even in its modem form as the Pen-y-Pass Youth Hostel, is still a popular spot for those intent on scaling the heights around. Thomas Pennant tells of an ascent to the pass which was 'either over loose stones or solid staircase and was exceedingly steep.' His party refreshed themselves at 'a spot called Gorphwysfa (The Resting Place)', although he does not record what sort of building, if any, graced the top of the pass. The Gorphwysfa Mountain Club presumably continues the tradition from Winthrop Young's legendary parties, in gathering climbers and hillwalkers together for expeditions near and far, including the lofty top of **Manod Mawr**.

Winthrop Young himself was born of good stock, being the son of Sir George Young who made the first ascent of the Jungfrau in the European Alps in 1865. Geoffrey lost a leg in the Great War but continued to climb with an artificial one that he invented. As early as 1907 he tried to amalgamate the leading climbing clubs of the time, but was unsuccessful. However, in 1943 he tried again, with the result that the British Mountaineering Council was formed in 1944. This is still thriving and fights for access, safety tests for equipment and represents British climbing on the world scene. Geoffrey Winthrop Young married Eleanor, daughter of Cecil Slingsby, the leading British mountaineer of the final few decades of the last century. Young was President of the Alpine Club, but also did much in the way of exploring the crags, hills and moorlands of North Wales. He died in 1958, but it would seem that the Gorphwysfa Mountain Club make a point of keeping his traditions alive, from a base at Pen y Pass Youth Hostel.

A few years ago the Ordnance Survey announced plans to remove all trig pillars from the British countryside, as they no longer use them for carto-graphic purposes, relying on satellite images instead. There was a huge outcry from the hillwalking fraternity, who rely on the pillars as invaluable aids to navigation. The Ordnance Survey were eventually persuaded to hand over the maintenance of all their pillars to selected members of the public, who in turn must endeavour to maintain them. I was therefore very surprised to find, or rather not to find, the pillar on **Manod Mawr**. Perhaps it had been removed by members of the Gorphwysfa Club for renovation with a view to reinstalling it at a later date. Who knows?

Manod Mawr's North Top lies almost at the very rim of the quarry workings and even as I walked, the sound of heavy plant machinery carried on the breeze from over the ridge to the east. I easily reached the summit cairn, then, glad to see the last of the gutted hillsides and mountains of slaty spoil, I turned back northwards and picked a path over rough heather towards **Moel Penamnen**.

It was obvious that I wouldn't make my rendezvous with Rachel in Blaenau at noon, but knew that if I didn't bag **Moel Penamnen** before heading down, I'd only have to waste half a day bagging it on Monday. I fairly belted along beside the fence which joins these tops in a long irreg-ular arc, then cut off the last big corner around Foel-fras to pick up a succes-sion of vague paths heading from the top and my final summit of the day.

Although the weather was on the whole staying fine, the wind had again built up to a crescendo, whirling around from all directions as I quickly lost height down Penamnen's western flank. I passed the twin lakes of Llynau Barlwyd on the right, then over boggy meadows to the top of the Crimea Pass and the main road back into Blaenau Ffestiniog.

I arrived at our meeting point an hour late and in a real fluster, only to find that Rachel hadn't yet arrived. She turned up a further three-quarters of an hour later, and for the remainder of the weekend I could forget all about the high summits of Wales.

Monday 20th July ~ The Last Moelwyns

A wet plod back along the road to the top of the Crimea Pass saw my joyful return to the hills. The plan for the day was to bag the remaining Moelwyns of **Allt Fawr**, **Moel Druman**, the two tops of **Ysgafell Wen** and finally **Cnicht** before finding my way to the Forestry Commission camp site on the edge of Beddgelert, but as the water streamed down the hillsides around me, I immediately began having serious doubts.

Soggy grass and bog led up easily to the tiny dammed lake of Llyn Iwerddon at the base of the north-east ridge of **Allt Fawr**, but beyond, the complexities of navigating in the dense hill-fog engrossed me pretty much for the rest of the day. **Allt Fawr**'s summit stones stood atop a compact rocky rib and gave a good, positive reference point from which to begin pacing along the bearings taken from the map.

Moel Druman and the main top of **Ysgafell Wen** posed little problems other than having to work out which side of an electric fence to walk on, whilst a wooden stake marked the junction of the path heading for the northern peak of the latter, across a short section of bog and peat hags.

Returning to the stake after bagging **Ysgafell Wen's North Top**, I again followed the compass along the intervening ground to the north-east ridge of **Cnicht**. The path vanished from underfoot occasionally and caused a few minor headaches, but soon a good path steadily began climbing the ridge and narrowed, leaving no excuse for navigational error.

The rain had stopped by this time, but the thick pea-soup still clung tenaciously to the wildness of the grassy Moelwyns. Yawning voids could be sensed falling away on both sides, and the odd bit of scrambling underfoot added real interest and mild excitement as I neared **Cnicht**'s summit.

Beyond, I continued along the obvious ridge, though dropping much more steeply than I had climbed, eventually descending below the cloud-base at about 100 metres above sea level. A minor road to Nantmor led on to the torrent of dark, frothy waters, squeezing through the rocky defile of the Aberglaslyn Pass. Although it seemed as if it had rained pretty much for weeks, with only the odd hour or two in-between showers to catch my breath, I was hardly prepared for the rushing, tormented surge of run-off from the surrounding watershed, gushing along beside me. A popular track along the course of the old Welsh Highland Railway managed to just about keep me out of the water, and after passing through the railway-blasted tunnels in the Pass, the village of Beddgelert was a very welcome sight.

CHAPTER VI
Mountains of My Youth

Tuesday 21st July ~ The Hebog Ridge

Having only eight miles to cover along the Hebog ridge to my bed for the night at the Snowdon Ranger Youth Hostel in the Cwellyn valley, and not being able to book in there until they opened their doors at 5p.m., I wandered down into the village for a late coffee and pizza after spending the morning doing a spot of laundry and general idling.

It was well gone 1p.m. by the time I finally headed off into Cwm Cloch and, setting a nice slow but steady rhythm, I soon gained the ridge leading to the top of **Moel Hebog**, and stuck my head in the clouds at about 700 metres. The wind howled across the open boulder slopes and made standing difficult and walking harder. Other walkers were being blown down from the summit slopes like hell-bent kites, but at last I lurched up to the trig pillar beside the poor shelter of the stone wall. The rain had started in earnest just below the top, so I took advantage of this mild excuse for a windbreak and struggled into my waterproofs.

The wall acted as an infallible guide down to the col before **Moel yr Ogof** where a sorry-looking group of walkers huddled together in the tempest. I waved over to them and followed the path up into the dark, scree-choked chimney which leads out onto the upper hillside. The walls of this cleft were bottle-green with moss and slime but looked like providing a climb or two in better conditions. A vague path above continued into the mist to the small cairn at the top.

After a quick snack I headed off into the wind and rain. It took a minute or two for me to realise that either the wind had changed direction, or I was again off course. Earlier it had been on my back blowing from the south-east, and though the ridge was fairly straight between the three Hewitts which grace its top, it was now trying to bowl me over from dead ahead. Feeling a bit useless, I ambled back to the summit cairn and checked the

The clouds on the hills of Eifionydd lifting. **Moel Hebog, Moel yr Ogof**
and **Moel Lefn** *from the forest above Rhyd Ddu*

compass. Incredibly, I had yet again made a ridiculous navigational error. From **Moel yr Ogof**'s summit I had actually started off on the exact course I had come up on, back towards **Moel Hebog**. I just couldn't believe it.

Following the trusty old compass, I picked my way across rough, bouldery slopes and was soon atop **Moel Lefn**, the last of my daily tally of Hewitts. I followed the familiar path down into the Beddgelert Forest and contoured round the lower flanks of **Y Garn** to Rhyd Ddu and a pint in the friendly Cwellyn Arms before speeding along the water-logged road to the Snowdon Ranger Youth Hostel and a comfortable bed for the first time in what seemed like years.

Unfortunately, the warden had thought I'd appreciate having a bit of company for the night and had put me in a small dormitory full of heavily snoring French students. I only wished I was back in the old tent.

Wednesday 22nd July ~ The Nantlle Ridge

The weather forecast for the day was for sunny spells, with strong to gale force south-westerly winds increasing throughout the day. I had planned to do the four Hewitts of the Nantlle ridge starting with Y Garn, a minor top above Rhyd Ddu, but that would have meant walking into the teeth of the wind all day long, so I quickly changed my plans and decided to cross over into Cwm Pennant and start the ridge at its furthest end.

The way over into Cwm Pennant was straight forward, as I know these hills very well, having last walked this ridge in the reverse direction only six months previously. The way lies up through the woods above Llyn y Gader, and follows the path taken down from Moel Lefn the day before, as far as a junction of tracks in the forest beside a small stream. The way up Moel Lefn goes off to the left, whereas I followed a track uphill, passing a deep, quarried hole on its right side. Just before a col, known as Bwlch-y-ddwy-elor, the edge of the forest was reached and the way opened up with views down Cwm Pennant, and the rough, craggy slopes of Moel Lefn, festering in leggy heather and moss, towered over the path to the south. I passed through a gate in a tall stone wall, resplendent with lichens and bottle-green mosses, then followed the track down to some derelict mine buildings at the head of the cwm. Sheep tracks led around the open flanks of Trum y Ddysgl's long south ridge, and I was soon contouring round steep grassy slopes to gain the wide col just north-east of **Craig Cwm Silyn**. The Craig had its head firmly in the clouds, and as I climbed over the damp, greasy rocks, the rain began, only making things even damper and greasier.

At the summit three lads stopped for a chat and waffled on about 'doing a climb' until they realised that, being a climber myself, I wasn't particularly impressed by what others would no doubt have seen as insanity on such a wild day. I asked them which route they had in mind, made a few suggestions, bid them a good day and trudged off into the storm.

My energy levels seemed to have dropped a good deal as I plodded towards the base of the usually easy climb to **Mynydd Tal-y-mignedd**, and wearily, I gained height by shear will power alone. I couldn't really understand this as the last couple of days had been particularly easy, and since sending the tent home with Rachel my pack had been getting lighter and lighter each day. In fact, most of my gear had been left at the Youth Hostel for the day as I would be returning there for the night. I carried only waterproofs, map and compass, my camera and food for the day. I just felt totally drained. Perhaps it was just a consequence of six weeks on a diet largely consisting of pasta and rice. I didn't feel particularly hungry, but had started to crave for fresh fruit and vegetables, real meat rather than soya, and perhaps more than anything else, masses and masses of chocolate.

Anyway, I finally crawled out of the thick gloom to be met by an affable chap with his two young daughters. We passed the time of day and soon got round to talking about my walk. One of the girls wanted to know how many Hewitts I had climbed so far, and as I had actually lost count by that time, I had to do a quick calculation. Amazingly, I came up with the answer that **Mynydd Tal-y-mignedd**'s Jubilee-Tower-graced-summit was my 100th of the trip. We had a bit of a celebration, then I waved goodbye to my new found friends and instantly dropped out of the cloud on the ridge to **Trum y Ddysgl**. A couple of winters previously I had spent a great day traversing this ridge and had been astounded to find the northern slopes absolutely plastered with wind-blown snow packed into an almost perfect firn (see Appendix), whilst those along the southern side had been totally clear, other than the usual early morning hoar frost clinging to each blade of grass. As I walked, something similar seemed to be happening now. Great clouds were billowing up in the northern cirques above the Nantlle Valley, while those to the south at the head of Cwm Pennant were being totally cleared by the rising wind. Everything to my right was in immediate view, whilst a dank grey void lay to my left. I can only imagine that there is a peculiar weather pattern around these hills which causes this. The clouds hung like huge cornices as I walked on and up the easy slopes of **Trum y Ddysgl** with a renewed vigour.

Interesting scrambling leads the walker along the ridge to **Mynydd Drws-y-coed**, with stupendous drops to the north, but these were blocked from view as again the cloud descended, and I followed the ridge to its end at Y Garn.

A badly eroded path drops quickly towards Llyn y Gader, then joins the path into Rhyd Ddu, and so, back to the Hostel. Luckily my French friends had moved on, their place in the dorm being taken by a bloke called Richard. We spent a nice evening huddled around a feeble fire with a foreign girl-friend of his, discussing in a pleasantly sarcastic fashion the problems of each other's way of life.

Thursday 23rd July ~ Mynydd Mawr

This was meant to be a partial rest day, so I walked along the road to Betws Garmon to do a bit of shopping. Back at the Hostel I dumped this load in the kitchen, grabbed a few bits and pieces of hill gear and retraced my steps towards Rhyd Ddu.

Just short of the village a path on the right led up above the forested banks of Llyn Cwellyn, along to the east ridge of **Mynydd Mawr**. Again the cloud was low, but seemed to be thinning, and at least the wind had dropped for the time being.

I had a good old nosy around the gullies and shattered pinnacles of Craig y Bera, the impressive line of cliffs which hem in the Nantlle Valley on its north side, then scared a few sheep on the long last pull up to the summit. A huge cairn adorns the top and as seems to be the fashion amongst Welsh hills is hollowed out to provide basic shelter from the elements.

It's a sign of the times when even on relatively unfrequented summits such as this, you find coke cans, orange peel and Mars bar wrappers stuffed in among the stones of a summit cairn. Behind the cairn there was even a couple of pink tissues waving at me in the breeze. It really is pretty awful how we humans treat our beautiful, lonely places.

The cloud had decided to lift a bit so I had a decent view from the summit. The whole of Anglesey lay flattened to the north, whilst away to the west, almost at the very coast, the hills of the intriguing Rivals were silhouetted against a silvery sea whilst everything eastwards and to the south was totally blocked out.

I wandered over to the edge of Cwm Du to have a look at the unfrequented slabs, ridges and walls which fall away into the heathery bottom, then followed the edge of the cwm round to the left, eventually descending to the roadside through the fir plantation above Betws Garmon.

A familiar short plod along the road brought me back to the Snowdon Ranger Hostel for my last night here.

Friday 24th July ~ Snowdon

A dry day was promised, but it looked very much like the weatherman had been on the booze again. I made the familiar trek along the road to Rhyd Ddu as dark waves, capped by galloping white horses crashed onto the shore of Llyn Cwellyn, and high over the Snowdon range dense nimbus whipped across the summits.

I followed the Rhyd Ddu Path towards **Snowdon**, but left it to gain the col below **Yr Aran** along the disused miners' track. By the wall at the col I left my sack and headed off into the thick cloud shrouding **Yr Aran**'s pointed top. A good path led the way, and after a gentle rising traverse around Y Geuallt, a final steep climb along the east ridge had the summit cairn underfoot, whilst meadow pipits chattered merrily in the clearing mists.

Back at the rucksack it was obvious that the weather was due for a big change as the wind buffeted the clouds against the rocky walls of Cwm Llan, and quickly cleared a space revealing **Y Lliwedd** on the other side. The broad scars of the Watkin Path could be seen rising to gain the ridge from out of the cwm, and tiny, ant-like figures were slowly gaining height, heading for **Yr Wyddfa**, the very summit of Wales.

I gained height easily and quickly up and over Allt Maenderyn as the sun peeled away the last remaining wisps of cloud from around me. It looked like becoming a perfect day, with only the very top of **Snowdon** still covered.

As I walked on towards Bwlch Main, more walkers joined me from the Rhyd Ddu Path which wends a way around the rocky rim of Cwm Clogwyn with its sparkling pools and lakes, dotted like jewels in its hollow. The clouds closed in as I neared the summit, and out of the mist came the unmistakable blast of a steam train's whistle.

The summit of **Snowdon** was its usual self. A hive of milling walkers, train-tourists and others who didn't really fit into either category. At the actual summit trig pillar, I pushed a way through the crowds to touch the very top and was sharply asked to move out of the way by a young bloke and two lasses who were trying to have their photo taken. The lad explained that they'd just finished the now famous 'Three Summits Walk'—Ben Nevis, Scafell Pike and Snowdon, highest points of each country in Britain. Had they walked the distance in between each summit? I asked, and was quickly told that the idea is to drive the distance from one to the next. Of course I knew this already, but couldn't help thinking that they were making an inordinate amount of fuss for such an easily achievable objective. Thousands of people every year do the 'Three Summits', but I'd like to think they don't each make a point of shouting about it, and expecting other hill-users to grant them solitude at each summit as these three seemed to be doing.

I touched the top and went off in search of a hot dog and cup of tea. After handing over a large amount of cash for these luxury food items and trying in vain to find a table in the cafe that wasn't already taken by a large German or Dutch family, I headed back out into the cold mist and began the descent.

My way lay back towards the Bwlch Main, then cut off from the Rhyd Ddu Path and made for the Bwlch y Saethau—the pass of the arrows that separates **Snowdon** from its worthy neighbour, **Y Lliwedd**. I'd managed to lose the cloud that had seemed to be tailing me on **Snowdon**, and huge sweeps of the old 'felstone rock' now more properly called rhyolite, fell away from the summit of **Y Lliwedd** in front of me. This mighty blade of a mountain rises out of Cwm Llan on the one side and Cwm Dyli on the other, and to my mind is the real jewel of the Cambrian Mountains, the most beautiful mountain in Wales. The crags themselves rise above Llyn Llydaw in Cwm Dyli and were formed as part of the Snowdon Volcanic Series during the Ordovician Period, and are largely embedded with brilliant white streaks of quartz. It's a particularly unpopular climbing ground these days, due to the loose nature of the rock and the fact that there is little on the cliffs for today's hard men of the climbing world. I hadn't climbed on **Y Lliwedd** myself, but as I sat having a bite to eat on Bwlch y Saethau watching the glowing sun radiating off the rich red rocks I couldn't help but think that on such a glorious day, every other major crag in Snowdonia would be teeming with geared-up crag rats. There wasn't a soul on the rocks of **Y Lliwedd**. Definitely my kind of place.

Though I only had **Lliwedd**'s three summits to traverse, only the first of which is a Hewitt, before dropping down to Pen y Pass for the night, I set off up the broken ridge.

The path itself follows a line slightly to the south of the crest, but wonderfully rough and dry rock on the very rim of the cliffs looked far too inviting, and it had been far too long since I'd climbed any rock that I set about picking a route suitable for one carrying such a heavy load.

Short steps of rough, steep walls and easy-palming friction slabs led higher and higher to the top of the main peak, and it was a bit of a shame that it all had to end so soon. I sat at the summit and watched the long train of people carefully picking a way across the multi-pinnacled and dramatically serrated ridge of **Crib Goch** across the cwm, knowing that I would be up there in the morning, trying to keep my cool as hundreds of poorly-clad day trippers caused congestion on the more awkward sections of the ridge.

Moel Siabod in sunshine from just below the cloud base on Snowdon, Llyn Llydaw in the foreground

Away to the east across the deep trench of the upper Nantgwynant rose **Moel Siabod**, queen of the Moelwyns, and the only hill in that range I'd yet to climb. I'd deliberately left it out of the traverse of the other Moelwyns as it lies far to the north-east of the main chain, and is more easily bagged from Capel Curig.

At last I prised myself from my lofty perch and headed down the ridge to pick up the miners' track just above the rush-choked waters of Llyn Teryn, then on to the Youth Hostel at the top of the pass.

As the evening wore on, the sun fell slowly over the lowlands of Anglesey at the furthest reaches of sight down the Llanberis Pass, and I passed the time by scrambling and finding ever harder climbing problems on the many boulders and small outcrops which adorn the hillside above the car park at the top of the pass. A deep burgundy sky filled the long 'V' trench of the valley at my feet, as the sun finally passed out of view behind a quarried shoulder of **Elidir Fawr**.

Saturday 25th July ~ Over Crib Goch

It actually looked like being another good day, starting early as it did with vast azure skies, patched only infrequently with one or two thin lines of high cirrus.

Being a Saturday I knew the **Crib Goch** ridge would be busy, and so set off fairly early from the Hostel. Even as I rounded the slopes below point 609 metres and got my first full view of the ridge, I could see dozens of walkers ahead of me, scrambling up the broken slabs prior to gaining the ridge proper. Ah, well. I might as well take my time and enjoy it, I thought.

Across the defile of the Pass of Llanberis, the huge columnar cliffs of Dinas Cromlech towered above the road, each angular corner highlighted by the morning sun. I wondered just how many climbers would be attempting to scale the old Joe Brown classic, Cenotaph Corner. This is without a doubt the most famous rock climb in Britain and is the focal point of 'The Pass' and for climbers throughout Wales. It takes a long, square-cut corner crack in the centre of the cliff, and though not a hard climb by today's standards, is still a tough proposition for the vast majority of weekend climbers.

I soon gained the Bwlch y Moch, the point were those put off by the rising eminence of **Crib Goch** ahead can take the easier option and drop down to the south to pick up the Pig Track, traversing well below the crest of this crenallated ridge. There was no way I was going to miss out on all the fun though. Yesterday's easy scrambling on the rocks of Lliwedd, and again later that night on the boulders above the Hostel had whetted my appetite for warm, dry rock, and I took to the scrambling with zeal.

Crib Goch's *red screes and crenallated ridge*

Once on the crest, a large group of lads had chosen the worst possible place to become scared stiff, and were being coaxed into moving a bit further on by a chap who turned out to be a National Park Warden. The lads at first got a bit shirty with Bob, as he was called, but with a couple of dozen people backing up along the ridge behind him, they were soon persuaded that it was in everyone's interests for them to shift to a wider spot on the ridge. Once there, we all had the chance to whiz past, and left them to get frightened without the hindrance of an audience.

The weather by now had improved even further, although the top of **Snowdon** still cowered under a thin shawl of mist. Ahead loomed the famous pinnacles on the ridge. The normal way lies over these to the contin-uation path onto **Crib y Ddysgl**, but being a smart-arse, I managed to lead a couple of young lads down a gully on the left. A stiff climb out of the other side had the pinnacles past, although my entourage decided that prudence is the better form of valour, and climbed back out of the gully by the way they had come, and rejoined the main path.

Over the pinnacles, Bob had waited to see if I had managed to fall to my death on my short-cut. He had seen me going astray down the gully, but thought I would probably just about live to tell the tale, and so had held his tongue and left me to get myself out of the problem. As we resumed the climb up to **Crib y Ddysgl** together we had a good old natter, and he persuaded me to call in at the Snowdon café for a cup of tea. He would be hanging around **Snowdon**'s summit for most of the early afternoon, as the famous Snowdon Race was taking place that day. Apparently the record for the ascent of **Snowdon** from Llanberis, and back down again stood firmly

*A rare glimpse of **Snowdon** from Llyn Llydaw, showing the Miners Track*

at just over one hour. For the past couple of years attempts had been made by both local and foreign runners to get the time below the hour. As I was heading off along the long northern ridge of the Snowdon group, I wouldn't actually get to see the race from close quarters, and do not even now know if anyone managed this incredible time.

I popped in to the café with Bob, and soon bumped into a friend of his called Colin. Although Colin now lives in mid-Wales I couldn't believe it when it transpired that we'd both gone to the same High School in Hull, albeit years apart. It is a small world.

Back at the fingerpost above Glaslyn, where both the Miners and the Pyg Tracks join the broad ridge coming up from Llanberis, I left the crowds behind and quickly lost height along the Snowdon Ranger Path. This popular path traverses the slopes above the rim of Cwm Brwynog where the dark cliffs of Clogwyn Du'r Arddu plunge to the boulder strewn banks of Llyn Du'r Arddu. This, the 'Black Cliff of the Black Heights' or simply 'Cloggy' as every climber knows it, is the true Mecca of rock climbers in search of serious climbing on what is one of Britain's most hallowed mountain crags. Unfortunately, the path above does not give good views of the many buttresses, pinnacles and faces, and for once I would have to pass by without stopping for a climb.

Where the Snowdon Ranger Path veers off to the left on a long contour, a grassy trod climbs up to the insignificant top of **Moel Cynghorion**, my third Hewitt of the day, not including **Snowdon** of course, which was climbed and counted the day before.

From the summit, a long switch-back ridge of grassy tops sweeps round in an arc to the west, terminating at the huge cairn of **Moel Eilio**. Again this was familiar terrain to me, and the minor top of Foel Goch was soon behind me as I pushed on to the summit of **Foel Gron**.

Mynydd Mawr was casting dark shadows across Nant Betws and the long ridge of Nantlle stood silhouetted against the afternoon sun. Despite these worthy diversions of my attention, my eyes kept being drawn to the east were lay the Glyders and Carneddau. Within a week, these would also lay behind me and I would be tackling the last few miles, towards **Tal y Fan** and the end of my journey. However, a lot of rough mountain ground lay between me and **Tal y Fan**, so legs pumping away, I took in the easy southern slopes of **Moel Eilio**.

A good track led along the northern ridge to the pass at Bwlch-y-groes where, it being fairly early in the day, I unpacked the stove and got a brew-up underway, then on, eastwards to the bright lights of Llanberis and a comfortable bed at the Youth Hostel.

Sunday 26th July ~ A rest day in Llanberis

Rain, rain and yet more rain drowned the streets of Llanberis, which was fine since I was taking a rest day, but not so good seeing as the Hostel closed from ten in the morning until five in the afternoon.

I bided my time looking around the art galleries at Electric Mountain, browsing in the many shops and spent an hour or so watching the new 'Hard Grit' rock climbing video with the staff from Outside, a walkers and climbers shop near the town centre. This video really had me longing for home in a big way, as it features the hardest climbs on Pennine Gritstone, my usual climbing medium. Old favourite crags were depicted receiving first ascents of desperately, even insanely difficult climbs by all the top names in the business. Grand stuff for a wet day in Wales! I managed to pass a bit more time food shopping at Spar, before the warden would allow me back into the Hostel.

Monday 27th July ~ The Elidirs

I had a big day planned, but it immediately looked like this would be thwarted by the weather. Actual breakers were forming on Llyn Peris as I walked along the road to Nant Peris, and stinging drizzle fell from the over-cast greyness that was supposed to be a summer sky. As I took the minor road to Fron, past the camp site in Nant Peris, the weather began showing signs of changing, for the worse. The drizzle turned to huge drops, pelting me from a sullen cloud that looked like its base was only feet above my head. A cracking day for the Elidirs, I thought.

I knew the Nuttalls' book suggested ploughing straight uphill from the bridge over the Afon Dudodyn, but all I could see up there was grim slate

*The Elidirs from **Tryfan**'s North Ridge*

spoils and dankness. Instead, I opted for the better cover from the wind provided by the steep sided valley itself.

Boggy grass and long, dripping hard rushes needed to be crossed as I tried to make sense of the path shown on the map. It just didn't seem to exist, although every once in a while I came across the print of a walker's boot in the mud, urging me on.

At last the valley seemed to hem me in steeply on all sides and the stream took a sharp turn to the left, just as my map says it should do, so I plodded up the sodden slopes and emerged at the rocky col of Bwlch y Marchlyn. A perfect path headed off into the even gloomier gloom towards **Elidir Fawr**, the only 3000'er of Wales I had never climbed. The going was easy, with just the odd rocky slab and boulder underfoot, and I was soon pulling up to the summit to be greeted by the boot wearers I had been following through the mud all morning. They were a young couple who were celebrating their first successful completion of the Welsh 3000'ers. I explained my purpose, and pointed out that this summit also saw the completion of my first round of these 3000'ers, so we celebrated together.

Still the clouds refused to shift, so I bade farewell to the party-goers and bombed back along the ridge to Bwlch y Marchlyn, catching a fleeting glimpse of the Marchlyn Mawr Reservoir down on the left as I went. A rocky rib started the ascent of Mynydd Perfedd, a minor top with a huge cairn, beside which I dumped my pack and followed a compass bearing across an expanse of bouldery grass to a stile in a wall leading to **Carnedd y Filiast**'s top. This lies atop a low rocky ridge almost at the very brink of the long sweeping drop into the Nant Ffrancon down the featureless wodge of the Atlantic Slab. Of course I couldn't see anything of this due to the mist, but the sense of being at the edge of an immense void, almost a step into nothingness, was overwhelming.

I retraced the compass steps back to the pack, shouldered it and began the quick descent over shale and grass to Bwlch y Brecan, where I again met the young couple from Elidir. We again exchanged greetings and I left them behind to bag **Foel-goch**, as they began the traverse around its western flank. A well-compressed path through shaly scree led to the summit, then along, beside a fence to Bwlch y Cywion and on the long south ridge of the mountain. Only the drawn-out climb to **Y Garn**'s high summit remained, but at least the rain had switched itself off for the time being.

I had a bite to eat by the summit cairn and waited a while for the couple to join me, but the wind howled around the tops, and as it was getting colder by the minute, I began the scree-plastered descent to Llyn y Cwn.

A group of lads passed me by in the other direction, complaining about the bad weather they'd had all the way from **Tryfan** that morning, but I just smiled as the high-speed winds began to slowly lift the cloud base, then miraculously clear it altogether.

I had planned to descend the Devil's Kitchen to Idwal Cottage that night, and then go over **Glyder Fawr** and **Fach, Tryfan**, **Y Foel-Goch** and **Gallt yr Ogof** to Capel Curig the next day, but seeing as the cloud seemed to be well clear of the higher tops of the Glyderau, I decided to take the opportunity there and then, and bag them straight away.

I knew the path up **Glyder Fawr** was pretty atrocious from previous occasions, and was pleasantly surprised to find myself making short work of the screes. A local chap who was walking just in front of me, suddenly started wandering well off the path, and weaving around all over the plateau above the steeper lower slopes. When he saw how close I was to him, he hailed me, and I went over to see what his problem was. By this time the cloud had decided that it had had enough of being helpful to walkers for the day, and had set in thick around us, although I still thought the way ahead was pretty obvious and had been following the compass since gaining the plateau. The poor fellow seemed at a total loss in the mist. He urged me to go down straight away with a kind of 'you're all doomed' expression on his face. He pointed out that being local he never bothered to carry a map or compass with him in the mountains, relying more on instinct to get him out of any tight situation. I might add here that he was in fact Cornish by birth, and had lived in Bethesda for a couple of years, making him at least feel like 'a local'. He waffled on for a bit, finishing with, "So now I'm heading down, and am taking you with me." He was obviously not sure of the exact path back, as he'd managed to lose it earlier on with all that wandering about, and I certainly wasn't about to waste my time looking after this rambler. All I could do for him was put him back on the path and steer him in the right general direction, I knew that so long as he didn't wander too far to the right, he would hit the screes above Llyn y Cwn pretty soon, but that was his problem.

By this time I had begun having serious doubts about my own position, having first trotted over to speak to the chap in the first place, and then wandered around trying to find a fairly obvious path for him to follow down. There are a number of cairned paths on this plateau, and I couldn't be sure that I now stood on the same path I had been following with the compass earlier on. At least it seemed to be going roughly the right way, so I continued.

Within minutes, the rocky bluffs and spiky turrets characteristic of the Glyders main plateau loomed out of the mist. I climbed a few spears of rock looking for the highest point, and finally hit on the one that I recognised from previous visits as being the top.

I now had a positive point from which to navigate from and was much happier with my lot. Rough boulders, some pointing skywards at the most impressive angle passed me by as I made for Bwlch y Ddwy Glyder along a traversing path south of the top of Y Gribin. I noted this in particular as I knew that I would probably decide to use this as my descent from the plateau later on.

*The classic view of **Tryfan** from high on Bristly Ridge, **Glyder Fach***

Castell y Gwynt from the path to **Glyder Fawr**

Beyond Castell y Gwynt huge dripping boulders, some the size of two-storey houses but mostly only the size of buses, passed by in the mist, along with a group of D. of E. students hanging around a very puzzled looking teacher. Again I wanted to make sure I reached the very highest point of the mountain and as much from memory as good navigation I first found the famous Cantilever Stone, then doubled back 100 metres to find the short scramble to the summit of **Glyder Fach**.

I was well pleased with myself, having finished a good day's walk, then continued over two more 3000'ers in really dreich conditions just for the fun of it. I must admit to being tempted to go on to also bag **Tryfan** that night, but felt as though I might just be pushing my luck a bit too far if I did. Besides, I had been looking forward to the nice easy descent over the exposed ridge of Y Gribin since setting off up **Glyder Fawr**.

I retraced my steps past Castell y Gwynt and the D. of E. group, asking them if they were all right. The teacher just sulked and ignored me, but one of the brighter girls asked which way it was to **Glyder Fawr**. I helpfully pointed in the general direction, and watched the teacher silently take note, then confidently gather her charges and plod off on the course I'd suggested.

Down on Y Gribin I soon dropped beneath the cloud and picked up a happy middle-aged couple along the way. We chatted for a while about the wonderful hills surrounding us, each with our heads tucked firmly in the clouds, then I headed off to claim my bed at Idwal Cottage, via the climber's descent path on Gribin Facet.

Across Cwm Bochlwyd to the Elidirs from **Tryfan***'s South Peak*

Tuesday 28th July ~ More Peaks and a Cash Crisis

A nice, clear start to the day saw me striding out towards Bwlch Tryfan. I'd convinced the warden of the Hostel to let me dump my sleeping bag, stove, Gore-Tex bivvy bag and Thermarest at the Hostel until the weekend, when I would be returning to meet my old pal Andy, for the final assault on the Carneddau. For the time being, I was simply bombing over to Capel Curig to bag **Moèl Siabod** and the few smaller summits of the eastern Carneddau and would be using the Hostel in Capel as a base until my return.

I passed a couple of day-trippers and stopped for a short break at the stone wall which crosses the col. The South Peak of **Tryfan** was clear, but behind, the main summit was just a dark mass in the cloud, all discernible features being totally masked in grey. Still on familiar ground, I soon scrambled up the short South Ridge, finding more interesting ways than that suggested by the main path. At the top I made a point of jumping from Adam to Eve, the two stone bosses set perhaps two feet apart with huge, yawning drops all around which mark the highest point, just to make sure of bagging the very highest part of the mountain. Accomplishing this feat is said to make you a free-man of **Tryfan**, in which case I have earned that title more times than I can remember.

Back at Bwlch Tryfan, I picked up a contouring path known as the Miner's Track around to the long grassy ridge descending eastwards to Capel Curig. This passes over two more Hewitts, both of which were new to me, so I took the time to navigate carefully in the clinging mist. **Y Foel Goch** was dissected by the path, a rocky lump on either side, so I visited them both to make sure. The path then led through a boggy section, habituated by long-horned feral goats, towards **Gallt yr Ogof**, then strangely turned away to the south. I picked a way easily over to the summit cairn atop a little knoll of rock and grass, and followed the compass southwards to regain the path.

As I lost the height so easily gained that morning, the clouds rose above me and revealed sunny views beneath a milky sky. Looking back towards the Snowdon massif, **Y Lliwedd** could just be seen poking its head through the white pillows.

Boggy ground at Bwlch Goleuni led over and on to the drier ridge of Cefn y Capel and down to the village. The problem was that the Youth Hostel was closed for a further three hours, and I had begun to run short of money. I knew I had enough in the bank, but wasn't sure where the nearest cash machine would be. I had arranged for all these Youth Hostels to be paid for in advance (via Rachel), so at least that wasn't a problem. Only the fact that I had very little food left, and nothing to buy more with worried me.

On Cannon Rock on
***Tryfan's** North Ridge*

I thought I'd better spend these three hours wisely, so dumped my rucksack in the bike shed at the Hostel, and plodded along the road to Betws y Coed. This turned out to be further than I had imagined from previous forays down this road, although in the past these had all been by car. It probably goes without saying that the bank in Betws y Coed wouldn't accept my particular type of card, and there really was only one thing for it. I would have to break my own, self-imposed rule about not using public transport during the walk. I would have to catch a bus to somewhere larger. Where? I didn't know. I only knew that I simply had to buy more food to continue the walk. It would have been ridiculous to have been forced to stop so near to the end, for the want of a bag of provisions. I didn't feel particularly happy about my decision, but knew it had to be done. I consoled myself with the fact that my day's walk had actually finished at Capel Curig Youth Hostel, and I would be resuming the walk there in the morning. This was just an unavoidable side excursion. It wasn't as if I was actually missing out any of the hills, or using transport to get from one hill to another. This thought made me feel much better, so I asked at the Tourist Information Centre where would be a likely place to find a Nat. West. Bank. They put me on a bus to Llanrwst with only a little change left from the fare jangling in my pocket. I was pretty much penniless. I hadn't even been able to afford a return ticket, but knew that that would all sort itself out once I'd reached the bank.

There was a Nat. West. Bank in Llanrwst, but, true to form it was closed and didn't have a cash machine.

That moment started a long episode of hectic travel, all crammed into the following four hours. It kicked off with the offer of a lift back to Betws y Coed from an affable chap who turned out to be a short story writer. I explained my position, and he offered to take me as far as the dreaded Blaenau Ffestiniog where he lived, and where we both knew was a cash machine that I could use. He then went on to elaborate on his plan to help me out. I could draw out the money from Blaenau, catch a train back to Betws y Coed, and then a bus back to Capel Curig. So much for not using public transport, I thought!

The plan worked as far as Betws y Coed, where I discovered I'd missed the last bus back to Capel Curig. However, at least I had some money, so I did the necessary shopping and then began the long walk back to Capel Curig. By this time I was beginning to feel as if I'd just undertaken a much harder journey than the actual walk itself, and all for the sake of a bit of handy cash! Luckily, as I set off up the road, a D. of E. minibus driver offered me a lift back to the Youth Hostel. I knew they'd come in useful sometime.

I booked in to the Hostel with real relief, glad to be back in the much simpler world of climbing mountains.

The side excursion took about seven hours all told, involving walking about eight miles, a bus journey, a lift in an old Volvo, a train journey and a trip in a minibus. Some might say I'd do anything for money. Others know me better, and will understand that on that occasion, I really was in need!

Wednesday 29th July ~ Creigiau Gleision

By way of a change, Thor, God of Thunder and generally poor weather, decided that it would kick the day off with a spot of heavy rain.

For the next couple of days I could afford to take things easy. I still had **Moel Siabod** to climb in the Moelwyn group, but that rose from above the trees just across the road from the Hostel, and wouldn't take more than a couple of hours to bag. Behind the Hostel, to the west of the track to the Crafnant Valley, the twin tops of **Creigiau Gleision** lurked in the heather and again were within easy reach. On Friday I would be moving back to Idwal Cottage to meet Andy, and collect my things for the final assault, approaching the upper Ogwen Valley via **Pen Llithrig y Wrach** and **Pen yr**

Pen Llithrig y Wrach above the dark waters of Llyn Cowlyd

Helgi Du, another shortish day. So today, as the heavens threatened to wring the entire contents of each cloud out on my part of Snowdonia, I headed for the Snowdonia Café next door to the Hostel. I whiled away the hours, drinking coffee and reading *Jake's Thing* by Kingsley Amis, before setting off in the early afternoon for the path to Crafnant—the sun had finally seen the rain off, the views behind opened up and the day blossomed.

The path found a dry way around the boggy ground along the banks of Nant y Geuallt, before reaching the crest of the pass between Clogwyn Mawr and Clogwyn

Mannod. The main track descends from here to Blaen-y-nant, the Mynydd Climber's Club Hut above the Llyn Crafnant Reservoir, but a faint trod through the heather led westwards to the rocky crown of Crimpiau. Myriad shades of green clustered around the sylvan beauty of the valley below my feet, and countless rocky tors gave the path intermediate islands to head for in the marshy ground. Each little summit has a character and a name of its own, and each one provides a minutely adjusted view of the surrounding hills from the top before it, though each single view is sufficiently different from the others to have you stopping to savour the panorama. The whole thing is a delight.

After Crimpiau I dropped to a boggy depression, then climbed up to Craig Wen, via Bwlch Mignog and over Moel Defaid to Craiglwyn. Each one of these retains the air of an independent summit, although only the latter tops the 2000' mark, and even then by an insufficient margin to assert itself above the main top of **Creigiau Gleision**. This is the one place where size doesn't mean a thing. A good path diverts around these minor tops, but why miss out on all the fun. For a bit more effort, the most enjoyable low level ridge walk in the country is literally at your feet.

I stopped for a bite to eat just north of the main top, and was passed by a group of three walkers. They were the first I'd seen since leaving Capel Curig that morning. I let them reach the next top, known simply as **Creigiau Gleision North Top**, in an effort to get a couple of people in my photos for a change, before setting off at an ambling pace after them.

At the fence which cuts across the north ridge of the hill I turned right, down the slopes to pick up a forest track down to the Crafnant Valley. The track through the forest was easy to follow, though very boggy. At one point, half a dozen teenage girls emerged from the trees, liberally plastered with thick, oozing mud and slime, and strongly advised me to head back uphill with them to find a drier way around the dreadful lower slopes. We had a nice chat, and I managed to persuade them that I really could do with a swim through the sludge lower down. In actual fact it wasn't as bad as they had led me to believe as tree roots surfaced through most of the gunk, providing slippery stepping stones.

Down at Blaen-y-nant, the sun disappeared for a while and an odd, squally shower blew in over the mountains off the Irish Sea. As it cleared, the sun's re-emergence was quick and total, and buzzards began wheeling above in the cloudless sky. All in all I found the whole day's walk enchanting.

Back at the pass the long, rocky hump of **Moel Siabod**, my objective for the next day, rose before me and the lonely valley of the Nantygwryd stretched out to the clear horseshoe of **Snowdon**.

*The squat little summit of **Creigiau Gleison North Top** from the main top*

Thursday 30th July ~ Moel Siabod

It seemed like I was about to witness a repeat performance of yesterday's weather pattern. Blustery showers blew down from the hills, and I took up my seat in the Snowdonia Café with the last few chapters of *Jake's Thing* and an English Breakfast, as they like to call it.

By 2.30, I could delay no longer, and strode purposefully out into the wind and rain. I crossed the Afon Llugwy by the bridge near the petrol station, and took the track through the trees towards Brynengan. A public footpath led up easily above the choppy waters of the Llynau Mymbyr and climbed steadily towards the crest of **Moel Siabod**'s summit ridge. Again the rain had stopped toying with me, although the sun refused to put in an appearance at all.

Throughout the ascent the path was obvious and I soon found myself fighting a way into the wind towards the summit cairn and trig pillar. This is perched upon a rocky plinth and I used an adjacent boulder as a tripod for a photograph.

Turning my back to the wind, I hurtled down the same slopes I had just toiled up, plunging into the forest and making it back to the Hostel at exactly 5p.m. It had taken only two and a half hours to bag **Moel Siabod** and get back down. I was pretty pleased with my performance, and knew I had grown incredibly fit during the course of this walk. Any worries I may have had about the long walk I would be attempting at the weekend with Andy dissipated in a whirl of confidence. I had now completed 123 Hewitts, leaving only 14 to go, all in the Carneddau north of the A5.

Friday 31st July ~ To Idwal Cottage by Hewitts

A constant but light drizzle slurred down the window panes of Snowdonia as I pulled on my boots, shouldered my rucksack and left Capel Curig bound for Idwal Cottage. Spray from cars winding a way inland from the coast along the A5 drenched me to the skin as I plodded along the pavement, past the Pinnacle Café and on up beside the Afon Llugwy.

Just after Bron Heulog a bridleway led through over-grazed meadows, then out onto a broad, boggy plain towards the deep heather and bilberry around Bwlch Cowlyd. Dark breakers of choppy reservoir water splashed beneath the limp canopy of cloud as I took to the dismal slopes of **Pen Llithrig y Wrach**, content only to be warm and dry beneath my cloak of Gore-Tex and fleece. Even my boots, the Hillmaster Classics given to me months before by the Brasher Boot Company continued in their brave, prolonged fight against the elements to keep my feet dry. This was surprising since I had not had the chance to really take care of these at all. The leather was now almost constantly wet, and didn't seem to have dried out properly since setting foot on the lower slopes of **Garreg Lwyd** almost two months before, but being Gore-Tex lined, my feet remained toasty throughout. I had found the boots to be perfectly adequate for a summer backpacking trip, and had managed to convince a number of people that they really are the most comfortable boot currently available to the outdoor gear-buying public. As for the other stuff I'd been given before the start of the walk, I really don't think I could have been any luckier. The Saunders tent had proven its worth despite my initial worries after pitching it very poorly in the violent storm back in the Fforest Fawr which had almost ended the entire trip; the rucksack which Aiguille Alpine Equipment had been quick to donate had turned out to be about the most comfortable and robust large capacity model I had ever used; the sleeping bag I'd chosen had been sufficiently warm whilst also being very light, thanks to Weatherstop, my local retailers, and the pair of waterproof socks, the Porelle drys, had proven their worth on the odd occasion I'd stepped into a pool which was deeper than the top of my boot. Even the Ecotrekker stove, a novel idea which burns only wood and paper rather than the usual gas, meths or petrol had had its uses. I'd not wanted to carry it throughout the trip, as I knew I may not always be able to find a supply of dry twigs or heather stems to fuel it. However, for the times when Rachel came over to keep me company it was invaluable for producing large quantities of hot water faster than any other stove I've ever used. I'd even been lucky with the food, as the soups which Knorr had given were still enjoyed as a starter to most of my main meals, and on the occasional dry day when I could be bothered to get the stove out at midday, had given a welcome snack for lunch. By this time the sachets of Ovaltine Power that had been sent from Novartis Nutrition Ltd. had just about run out, and had been supplemented by regular cups of Options Chocolate Drinks. These are also by Novartis Nutrition, but were something I had neglected to ask for in my initial approach to them. I'd therefore had to buy these, but just couldn't do without my regular chocolate fix. I'll remember to ask for these as well in future!

Thoughts of my sponsors and of my stomach and food accompanied me up the pathless slopes of **Pen Llithrig y Wrach** as at last the rain abated, but cold winds kept hurling clouds around the tops and made navigation essential. A small summit cairn adorned the grassy top, and I soon started down on the 600' descent to the col at Bwlch y Tri Marchog.

The cloud hung just above the level of this col, and away to the north I could just make out the flooded waters of the Afon Porth-Llwyd swelling over its banks to engulf the flat bottom of Cwm Eigiau in the thinning mists below.

Another walker sat atop a rocky knoll eating his piece, and waved over a greeting. I waved back, then began the climb up grassy slopes to the summit of **Pen yr Helgi Du**. A cairn, perfectly formed out of eight to ten inch-long shards of rock, all pointing inwards towards the centre of the cairn like the spokes of a wheel, stood on a small flat space of ground and had me thinking I'd reached the top. But as I continued on, to gain the ridge down the north-west side, another rise led to the actual summit.

Steep rocks led by easy though wet scrambling steps down the ridge to the col above the Ffynnon Llugwy Reservoir, down in the dip to the south, and from there a good path led down pounded scree to the reservoir itself. I passed a couple of walkers, glad to be out of the windy blasts of the ridge tops, then headed on down to the Water Board access road on the southern side of the lake. A gentle descent on tarmac soon had me down on the A5 again, and speeding cars whizzed by once more, throwing caution, gravel, and oily gutter-spray, to the wind.

My way led along the road to Llyn Ogwen and so to Idwal Cottage Youth Hostel above Rhaeadr Ogwen at the head of Nant Ffrancon.

The Hostel was open, but there seemed to be nobody about. Even Andy hadn't arrived yet, so I made myself comfortable in the smoking room, it being the most comfortable room in the place, and devoured what remained of my chocolate and other snacks.

As the afternoon wore on, the cloud seemed to be lifting slightly. Outside, **Pen yr Ole Wen** started flashing more and more of its bouldery southern flank at me, revealing the route onto the tops for the morning.

At 5.30, I heard a familiar Edinburgh voice in the car park and found Andy MacNaughton unpacking his rucksack from the car. Although he's my main climbing partner both on the rocks and on snow and ice, we'd seen little of each other during the year, mainly due to my manic preparations for this trip taking up so much of my time prior to departure. I knew it would be nice to have this old friend as company for the last two days of the walk. If nothing else it would give me someone other than myself to talk to, and I must say I am surprised that in the event, I didn't actually drive Andy round the bend. I don't think I let him get a word in edgeways all weekend.

Saturday 1st August ~ Bivouacking in the Carneddau

Bright gaps above the turreted summit ridge of **Tryfan** brought a promise of better weather, although as we sorted out the last of Andy's gear in the car park, the upper slopes of **Pen yr Ole Wen**, towering up immediately from the road side, where still shrouded in heavy cloud. One thing was for sure though—we weren't going to have the mountains to ourselves that day. Already countless groups of walkers could be seen toiling up the steep slopes of our first Hewitt, vanishing into the mists, 100 metres above.

At last we were ready for the off, and we crossed the road and found a suitably slow pace for such an abrupt ascent. The path veered off up differing scree slopes, but we were quite content to pick our own line up through broken rocks and heather to the bouldery plateau before the gentle rise to the summit of **Pen yr Ole Wen**.

A swirling film of cloud blew around the summit, but as we lost the bit of height to the col at Bwlch yr Ole Wen, jagged rocks and steep grass could be seen falling away into the deep trench of Cwm Lloer to the east, its rough bottom bejewelled with the sparkling waters of the Ffynnon.

Now the steep climb was over and the terrain became much more gentle, we had the puff to chat away as we made for **Carnedd Dafydd** over the Carnedd Fach ridge. I was shocked, but not really surprised, to hear that Andy was considering packing in his job later in the year, and devoting all of his time to walking and climbing in the mountains. I knew from past experience that this is a hard decision to make, and one that few others will ever understand. As climbers we are often asked by the unknowing why we risk life and limb in search of a summit, only to turn around upon reaching our goal, and make our way back down to the bottom, having achieved absolutely nothing of worth to anyone. Perhaps the best known response is that of George Mallory when asked why he wanted to climb Everest. His answer of 'because it is there' is still often quoted by mountaineers unable to express the real meaning behind their pursuit. Better men than me have tried to solve this problem, and the fact is that no one has been able to explain the reason behind this seemingly mad activity. I always think that those who do not feel the urge to climb these mountains, or to explore vast deserts or sail tempestuous seas, will never understand the answer to the question 'Why?'. Surely if you feel passionate about something, whether it be football, music, mountaineering or whatever, the only way to live your life to the full is to devote all of your time to that pursuit. You owe it to yourself. For this reason I could fully understand Andy wanting to spend the rest of his life among mountains, rather than in the congested tedium of the city.

Talking this over, we ambled around the gloomy rim of the Black Ladders or Ysgolion Duon, the supreme winter climbing ground of Snowdonia, and followed the narrow ridge beyond to the broad slopes of **Carnedd Llewelyn**. Among the damp rocks of the summit cairn we sat for a while and rested limbs, eating and chatting all the while as more and more walkers emerged from the fastness of the cloud and sat down beside us.

Feeling fitter after this second breakfast, we carefully followed the compass north-westwards, initially over boulder and grass slopes then down a scree path to the easy climb up **Yr Elen**. A steep rise on the right nearly had us climbing up to bag this false top, but just as we stopped to ponder on this, a slight improvement in visibility picked out a higher rocky dome further north, with a solitary walker resting by the cairn.

It turned out to be a middle aged chap that we had spoken to earlier on during the long slog up **Pen yr Ole Wen**. He was in the process of bagging all the Nuttalls, but was sensibly taking a bit more time about it than I was with the Hewitts, going out on occasional weekends and the odd short holiday.

Heading back towards **Carnedd Llewelyn** we contoured around its northern slopes above the tiny Cwm Caseg with its elongated Ffynnon, then found the good path heading off for the Northern Carneddau.

Our first stop was **Foel Grach** which is easily reached via a short ascent. The refuge below the rocky summit provided a quick interlude, then we were away again, heading northwards to **Garnedd Uchaf** and better weather. We sat by the spiky rocks projecting out of the surrounding mat grass like miniature Castell y Gwynts, admiring the ever expanding views back to the higher Carnedds and across the cwm to **Yr Elen**.

As time was really pressing, with the improvement in the weather we began reconsidering our plans to descend to a bothy in the east that night. It would, after all, only entail a re-ascent to gain the ridge in the morning, whereas if the weather stayed good we could enjoy a high bivouac further along the main ridge. For the time being though, we still had the two summits of **Drosgl** and **Bera Mawr** to bag. These are out on a limb to the north-west and although they are often climbed by walkers coming from the Aber Falls in the north, they cannot really be including in an easy traverse of the main ridge from the Ogwen Valley in the south.

A faint path led over boggy grass and contoured around the rugged top of Bera Bach, a small pile of boulders on the vast plateau containing the more prominent summits of **Bera Mawr** and **Drosgl**. A vague line of cairns led up the east side of **Drosgl** to the main cairn at the summit, and which swarmed with wasps in the gathering heat of a fine afternoon. We plunged down towards the plateau again, and passed Bera Bach by on its northern flank, Andy taking a much lower line than me in an effort to find a water supply. That was to be the deciding factor in whether we would stay high that night. Without water we could neither have a drink nor cook any food, and it would be a long night with empty bellies. He found a bit of a spring at the upper reaches of the Afon Rhaeadr Bach, but I managed to convince him that there would be something further on at the head of the Afon Goch.

For such a small hill, **Bera Mawr**'s summit is a real delight. Large blocks of granite and free-standing pinnacles cluster around the highest point, and for a while we were happy to dump the sacks and spend some time working out short climbing problems on the warm rocks. We could just as easily have been on a windswept gritstone edge teeming with geared-up climbers in a popular corner of the Pennines. Alarmingly tight cracks were jammed, slabs palmed and padded until at last we thought we had better make a move towards **Foel-fras**, the last 3000'er of the day.

We picked up a vague contouring path around the head of the cwm and managed to find a not-too-clean-looking stream to fill our water bottles for the night. A sterilising tablet went into each one, and then we tackled the final slopes of our mountain.

I knew from past winter walks along the northern Carneddau that **Foel-fras** has a stone wall crossing its summit ridge, and thought that it would be a good idea to bed down behind this for the night. We each pegged out our Gore-Tex bivvy bags, threw our gear inside, then took a bearing for **Llwytmor**, our last Hewitt of the day. A wide boggy col separated the two tops, but an easy grass and bilberry-covered slope led to the cairn at the summit.

Back on **Foel-fras** we set about cooking a meal and having a few drinks. Talk turned again to our plans for the future, in much need of modification now that Andy had decided to throw in the towel at his place of work. It would be nice, we agreed, if we could organise another long trip for the following summer. My problem is, I always make far too many plans and can seldom manage to fit everything I want to do into any time I have free from my writing. Still, we know that we both have a lot of time ahead of us to achieve any long-standing ambitions in the mountains. As we talked the clouds began to fall around us once again, and kept seething in huge, grey eddies around the summit trig pillar. A couple of weary fell-runners trotted past towards **Drum**, but soon left us alone on our summit, as the cold air crept over us in the chilling atmosphere of evening.

With this in mind we turned in for the night, wriggling down into our bags with graceless abandon. We both had hooped versions of these mini-tents, which hold the fabric about eighteen inches from the groundsheet, mere inches from your face when laid on your back. The whole thing is only slightly bigger than a sleeping bag, and gives the impression that you are crawling into a coffin for the night. We lay there at just over 3000' above sea level with the doors unzipped, nattering away into the late dusk of a mid-summer's night.

Sunday 2nd August ~ The End is Reached

The final day. I knew, even as I awoke and saw the last vestiges of early morning mist dissipating in the glaring sun, that nothing could keep me from reaching **Tal y Fan** that day. Lowly **Tal y Fan**, rising amid heather and rock a mere 2000' above the lapping waters of Conwy Bay. My ultimate goal. The end of an obsession. Only the rounded dome of **Drum** stood between the pair of us and it.

We slithered out of our bags, and packed up in a haste of midge-bitten frenzy, then without any breakfast or even a drink, as we'd run out of water just prior to turning in the night before, we slipped off down the eastern flank of **Foel-fras**, alongside the wall. The grassy col of Bwlch y Gwrhyd passed by in a swelter of thirst, but a welcome breeze blew along the ridge of **Drum** and provided relief from the heat of the morning. We made to rest beside the cairn of Carnedd Penydorth-goch, the summit of **Drum**, but were, for the second time in as many days, chased away by a swarm of wasps, languishing in the rare heat of this poor summer.

A good path led down and over the minor top of Carnedd y Ddelw as the first of the morning walkers slowly began to gain the heights around us. We stuck rigidly to the broad flank heading first north-west, then north-east and down towards the Roman Road across Bwlch y Ddeufaen.

Coming up towards us I spied a familiar figure. The last time I had seen this chap had been way back in the Arans. Then he'd been alone, but today he had quite a large party with him. As we drew closer he immediately recognised me, and for the second time during the walk I stopped and chatted with Myrddyn Phillips, Nuttall bagger extraordinaire. Myrddyn again insisted on taking my photograph, and we parted after swapping addresses and hand shakes.

Sun bathers lounged around the Bwlch as the sun blasted everything dry, and we toiled wearily up the scorching heather and bilberry of Foel Lwyd, the small subsidiary top half a mile west of **Tal y Fan**.

Andy and I talked merrily of getting the thing finished and bombing off down to the pub for some much needed refreshment, but in my heart I knew that I would miss waking each morning with a quota of hills to climb, and really didn't relish the return to civilisation. I just wanted to carry on walking.

Even as we gained the final slopes of **Tal y Fan** my eyes wandered across to the Clwydian hills across the Afon Conwy, half wishing I had those to bag in the morning. Of course the other side of me was dearly wishing for it all to end. I needed a liberal supply of home comforts, and just to be able to spend time with Rachel, doing nothing but being together would be a pleasure verging on paradise.

We climbed the stone wall that runs along the crest of **Tal y Fan** via a stile, and took the last few steps to the trig pillar which stands on top. Then, as I took off my rucksack, and leaned against the pillar, I was glad it was all over. Other hills, ranges and countries could wait for other days. This walk across the spine of the Cambrian Mountains had filled a period of my life, and one that I would never forget, but my sadness at having come to the end of a dream was consoled by the fact that I knew I had chosen this as a way of life, and that this trip was only the first of many more to come. It was not, as many people had assumed, a chance in a lifetime, and never to be repeated. Sure, I probably wouldn't do the Welsh Hewitts in one trip again, wonderful as they are, but there are always the English and Irish Hewitts, the Munros or even the Alpine 4000 metre peaks. As I stood gazing across the grassy wastes of upper Afon Roe, I could see the future mountains of my life stretching out in the distance, range after range, always something more to explore, a lifetime of adventure.

We took the obligatory photos, then with hardly a word, followed the path down to the minor road near Cae-coch, where we had planned to meet Rachel, and so begin the long drive home.

300

APPENDIX 1

Hewitts in order of Height
A Logbook for Hewitt-baggers

NO.	HEIGHT'	& M	NAME /RANGE	DATE CLIMBED
1	3560'	1085m	Snowdon (Yr Wyddfa) / Snowdon	....
2	3494'	1065m	Crib y Ddysgl / Snowdon	....
3	3491'	1064m	Carnedd Llewelyn / Carneddau	....
4	3425'	1044m	Carnedd Dafydd / Carneddau	....
5	3278'	999m	Glyder Fawr / Glyders	....
6	3261'	994m	Glyder Fach / Glyders	....
7	3209'	978m	Pen yr Ole Wen / Carneddau	....
8	3202'	976m	Foel Grach / Carneddau	....
9	3156'	962m	Yr Elen / Glyders	....
10	3107'	947m	Y Garn / Glyders	....
11	3091'	942m	Foel-fras / Carneddau	....
12	3038'	926m	Garnedd Uchaf / Carneddau	....
13	3031'	924m	Elidir Fawr / Glyders	....
14	3028'	923m	Crib Goch / Snowdon	....
15	3002'	915m	Tryfan / Glyders	....
16	2969'	905m	Aran Fawddwy / Arans	....
17	2946'	898m	Y Lliwedd / Snowdon	....
18	2930'	893m	Cadair Idris / Cadair Idris	....
19	2907'	886m	Pen y Fan / Brecon Beacons	....
20	2904'	885m	Aran Benllyn / Arans	....
21	2861'	872m	Moel Siabod / Moelwyns	....
22	2861'	872m	Erw y Ddafad-ddu/ Arans	....
23	2831'	863m	Mynydd Moel/ Cadair Idris	....
24	2802'	854m	Arenig Fawr / Arenigs	....
25	2785'	849m	Llwytmor / Carneddau	....
26	2733'	833m	Pen yr Helgi Du / Carneddau	....
27	2726'	831m	Foel-goch / Glyders	....
28	2723'	830m	Cadair Berwyn / Berwyns	....
29	2713'	827m	Moel Sych / Berwyns	....
30	2694'	821m	Carnedd y Filiast / Glyders	....

31	2661'	811m	Waun Fach / Black Mountains	....
32	2661'	811m	Cyfrwy / Cadair Idris	....
33	2641'	805m	Y Foel Goch / Glyders	....
34	2631'	802m	Fan Brycheiniog / Mynydd Du	....
35	2625'	800m	Pen y Gadair Fawr / Black Mountains	....
36	2621'	799m	Pen Llithrig y Wrach / Carneddau	....
37	2608'	795m	Cribyn / Brecon Beacons	....
38	2605'	794m	Bera Maw r/ Carneddau	....
39	2595'	791m	Craig Cwm Amarch / Cadair Idris	....
40	2575'	785m	Cadair Bronwen / Berwyns	....
41	2569'	783m	Moel Hebo g/ Eifionydd	....
42	2559'	780m	Glasgwm / Arans	....
43	2526'	770m	Moelwyn Mawr / Moelwyns	....
44	2526'	770m	Drum / Carneddau	....
45	2523'	769m	Waun Rydd / Brecon Beacons	....
46	2503'	763m	Gallt yr Ogof / Glyders	....
47	2497'	761m	Fan Hi r/ Mynydd Du	....
48	2487'	758m	Drosgl / Carneddau	....
49	2480'	756m	Y Llethr / Rhinogs	....
50	2467'	752m	Plynlimon / Plynlimon	....
51	2464'	751m	Moel Llyfnant / Arenigs	....
52	2461'	750m	Diffwys / Rhinogs	....
53	2457'	749m	Bannau Sir Gaer / Mynydd Du	....
54	2451'	747m	Yr Aran / Snowdon	....
55	2431'	741m	Pen Pumlumon Arwystli / Plynlimon	....
56	2408'	734m	Rhobell Fawr / Arenigs	....
57	2408'	734m	Fan Fawr / Fforest Fawr	....
58	2408'	734m	Craig Cwm Silyn / Eifionydd	....
59	2385'	727m	Plynlimon East Top / Plynlimon	....
60	2382'	726m	Moel Eilio / Snowdon	....
61	2379'	725m	Fan Gyhirych / Fforest Fawr	....
62	2362'	720m	Rhinog Fawr / Rhinogs	....
63	2362'	720m	Pen Allt-mawr / Black Mountains.	....
64	2359'	719m	Fan y Big / Brecon Beacons	....
65	2336'	712m	Rhinog Fach / Rhinogs	....
66	2329'	710m	Moelwyn Bach / Moelwyns	....
67	2326'	709m	Trum y Ddysg / Eifionydd	....
68	2306'	703m	Black Mountain / Black Mountains	....
69	2300'	701m	Pen Cerrig-calch / Black Mountains	....

70	2290'	698m	Mynydd Mawr / Eifionydd	....
71	2290'	698m	Allt-fawr / Moelwyns	....
72	2280'	695m	Mynydd Drws-y-coed / Eifionydd	....
73	2267'	691m	Foel Wen / Berwyns	....
74	2264'	690m	Twmpa / Black Mountains	....
75	2260'	689m	Foel Hafod-fynydd / Arans	....
76	2260'	689m	Cnicht / Moelwyns	....
77	2260'	689m	Arenig Fach / Arenigs	....
78	2247'	685m	Pen y Brynfforchog / Arans	....
79	2247'	685m	Gwaun y Llwyn i/ Arans	....
80	2244'	684m	Y Garn / Plynlimon	....
81	2241'	683m	Gau Graig / Cadair Idris	....
82	2234'	681m	Mynydd Tarw / Berwyns	....
83	2228'	679m	Chwarel y Fan / Black Mountains	....
84	2224'	678m	Creigiau Gleision / Carneddau	....
85	2218'	676m	Moel Druman / Moelwyns	....
86	2211'	674m	Moel Cynghorion / Snowdon	....
87	2211'	674m	Maesglase / Dovey Hills	....
88	2205'	672m	Ysgafell Wen / Moelwyns	....
89	2201'	671m	Esgeiriau Gwynion / Arans	....
90	2198'	670m	Waun-oer / Dovey Hills	....
91	2195'	669m	Ysgafell Wen North Top / Moelwyns	....
92	2195'	669m	Carnedd y Filiast / Arenigs	....
93	2188'	667m	Tarren y Geseil / Tarrens	....
94	2188'	667m	Cyrniau Nod / Hirnants	....
95	2182'	665m	Post Gwyn / Berwyns	....
96	2175'	663m	Mynydd Llysiau / Black Mountains	....
97	2175'	663m	Fan Nedd / Fforest Fawr	....
98	2172'	662m	Dduallt / Arenigs	....
99	2169'	661m	Tyrrau Mawr / Cadair Idris	....
100	2169'	661m	Manod Mawr / Moelwyns	....
101	2165'	660m	Great Rhos / Radnor Forest	....
102	2162'	659m	Cribin Fawr / Dovey Hills	....
103	2159'	658m	Manod Mawr North Top / Moelwyns	....
104	2149'	655m	Moel yr Ogof / Eifionydd	....
105	2142'	653m	Mynydd Tal-y-mignedd / Eifionydd	....
106	2133'	650m	Black Mixen / Radnor Forest	....
107	2126'	648m	Moel-yr-hydd / Moelwyns	....
108	2126'	648m	Foel Cwm Sian Llwyd / Hirnants	....

109	2119'	646m	Pen y Boncyn Trefeilw / Hirnants	....
110	2103'	641m	Drygarn Fawr / Cwmdeuddwr Hills	....
111	2093'	638m	Moel Lefn / Eifionydd	....
112	2083'	635m	Garreg Las / Mynydd Du	....
113	2080'	634m	Tarrenhendre / Tarrens	....
114	2080'	634m	Creigiau Gleision North Top / Carneddau	....
115	2073'	632m	Fan Llia / Fforest Fawr	....
116	2067'	630m	Moel Fferna / Berwyns	....
117	2064'	629m	Y Garn / Rhinogs	....
118	2064'	629m	Foel Gron / Snowdon	....
119	2064'	629m	Fan Frynych / Fforest Fawr	....
120	2064'	629m	Craig Cerrig-gleisiad / Fforest Fawr	....
121	2054'	626m	Foel y Geifr / Hirnants	....
122	2051'	625m	Moel y Cerrig Duon / Hirnants	....
123	2044'	623m	Moel Ysgyfarnogod / Rhinogs	....
124	2044'	623m	Moel Penamnen / Moelwyns	....
125	2041'	622m	Craig-y-llyn / Cadair Idris	....
126	2037'	621m	Moel yr Henfaes / Berwyns	....
127	2034'	620m	Pen yr Allt Uchaf / Arans	....
128	2031'	619m	Gallt y Daren / Arenigs	....
129	2024'	617m	Cefn yr Ystrad / Brecon Beacons	....
130	2021'	616m	Garreg Lwyd / Mynydd Du	....
131	2014'	614m	Llechwedd Du / Arans	....
132	2011'	613m	Gorllwyn / Cwmdeuddwr Hills	....
133	2011'	613m	Foel Goch / Hirnants	....
134	2005'	611m	Foel Goch / Arenigs	....
135	2001'	610m	Tal y Fan / Carneddau	....
136	2001'	610m	Pen y Garn / Cwmdeuddwr Hills	....
137	2001'	610m	Bache Hill / Radnor Forest	....

APPENDIX 2

Equipment, Safety and Navigation

Equipment these days forms a major part of any hillwalker's appreciation of the mountains. A quick glance into any of the outdoor shops in Britain will reveal a vast array of jackets, boots, tents, stoves and literally anything that you could possibly wish for in the great outdoors. It has to be said that on the whole the main essentials for a day trip into the hills are a good pair of boots, waterproof jacket and trousers, warm jacket, hat and gloves, whistle, map and compass, food, torch and a small rucksack to carry it all in. It is beyond the scope of this book to go into detail on any particular brand of these items, but it should be borne in mind that a lot of the equipment that is sold today as being 'essential' for any hillwalker, is actually designed for use in the greater ranges of the world. Indeed it is not unusual to meet walkers attired in thousands of pounds worth of equipment in say, the Moelwyns; equipment that they would be quite comfortable in, wandering around the upper slopes of Mont Blanc. By all means buy good quality, but do not feel that you must have the most expensive items in the shop if your ambitions stretch no further than bagging the Hewitts.

If you wish to camp in the hills, a good tent and sleeping bag are essential, as well as stove and high-calorie foods. It should be remembered when buying that you will be carrying all of this equipment, and that for backpacking, weight is very important, so long as this is not detracting from the quality of the equipment used.

Generally, many of the better outdoor shops are very good at giving the right sort of advice to customers, but some are only after a quick sale of the most expensive items they stock.

The most important thing for both one day walks and longer backpacking trips is to keep all of your gear dry. Very few rucksacks are waterproof, even the most expensive ones, so a rucksack-liner, or just a thick binbag should be used inside the rucksack.

In general the subject of safety is a matter of common sense. Many hillwalkers stress the importance of leaving written word of your hillwalking intentions with a responsible party before departing for the hills, and indeed this is sensible for those new to hillwalking. However, one of the joys of hillwalking is the freedom that it provides, including the liberty to change your plans if for instance the weather improves, or you have found the going easier than expected and have time to extend your trip into the mountains. It is in circumstances such as these, that a route card can become dangerous, as any rescue team could be looking in the wrong area for you if you have modified your plans whilst on the move. Obviously if you leave a route card with someone, you must stick to it rigidly, whilst not leaving one necessitates taking extra care so as not to have an accident. This is a knotty problem that walkers and climbers the world over cannot agree on, and it should be a matter of personal choice.

On this point it is worth remembering a case in Glen Affric in Scotland where an experienced walker had headed into a bothy for a couple of days with plenty of food and equipment. However, on reaching the bothy, the weather deteriorated and he wisely decided to change his plans for long traverses in the area, and to just go out on short day trips from the bothy. He had left a route card with someone, who contacted the police on hearing of the weather changes to come. They sent in a rescue team who arrived at the bothy to find the walker's food and overnight equipment. It was obvious that he was out in the hills at the time, so they waited for him to return. That night, as the rescuers had no food, the walker was forced to share his with them, and between them they consumed the lot. The following day a helicopter arrived and persuaded the walker to be 'rescued' on the grounds that he was putting them to unnecessary worry. With his supplies now depleted, he reluctantly had to agree. Upon his return to civilisation he was much criticised by the police, the rescue team and the press for being foolhardy, when in fact he had displayed remarkable common-sense and judgement. His only mistake seems to be that of leaving a route card in the first place, thereby letting the authorities know of his plans. Without that he would have enjoyed a very pleasant few days in that wild part of the Scottish Highlands, instead of suffering an unwanted rescue.

However, all the hill ranges of Britain can be very dangerous places, and a trip into the heart of even the most mundane of groups should not be taken lightly. It is wise for every member of the team to be trained in basic first aid. It is often thought that so long as one member has some knowledge of this, the whole party will be fine. It is never considered what the result would be if that one first-aider happened to be the one involved in an accident.

If alerting the rescue services, one should dial 999 and ask the operator for the mountain rescue service, or the police, and have the following details ready:-

1) Number of casualties.
2) Precise location including grid reference.
3) Names and description of the casualties.
4) Time and nature of the accident.
5) Extent of injuries.
6) Prevailing weather conditions.

You should then remain by the telephone until a police officer or member of the rescue team arrives. If waiting with the casualty while someone else goes for help, you should make the International Distress Signal which is six blasts of a whistle, or flashes of a torch repeated after a minute. The answer to this signal from a rescuer is three blasts per minute, although it is important that if you are waiting to be rescued and hear a response, you should continue with your signal until the rescuers have positively located you.

In summer the most serious hazard to the hillwalker is bad visibility, whether caused by rain, cloud or darkness. Good navigation skills can make walking in poor visibility perfectly safe, and often it can add a bit more adventure to the day.

In winter, hillwalking is a different game altogether. While it can be much more exhilarating and enjoyable, it is also much more dangerous. The use of crampons and an ice axe should be learned before setting out, and once mastered should be practised regularly on safe slopes. Whole tomes are dedicated to the business of safe walking in winter, and it is recom- mended that you either digest one of those listed in the bibliography, or even better, book onto a winter hillwalking course with any of the Mountain Instructors that advertise regularly in the walking and climbing magazines.

A good appreciation of snow conditions is also essential, not only to minimise the risk of being avalanched, but also for the simple reason that knowing the type of snowpack to be expected can greatly enhance the chances of making a successful trip into the mountains. Thigh-deep powder snow is gruelling to walk through to say the least, whereas hard packed firn or neve, being well consolidated, are almost ice-hard and will support your weight quite comfortably, allowing you to either kick steps or simply walk on the surface with the aid of crampons.. Again, it is recommended that you take specialist advice on this subject.

Navigation is another complex subject, and no attempt is made here to explain the details. You should again consult one of the books listed in the bibliography. Although a good map can give you a greater understanding of the area you are in, giving names for things of interest on any walk, I often wonder how many people can successfully use it to navigate off the beaten track, and do it with confidence. The following tips should point you in the right direction but again, this is something that can only be fully grasped during practical sessions on the hills.

The most important navigational skill for the hillwalker is that of orientating your map. Put simply, the top of the map is always North, and the red directional arrow on your compass also points to North. It is therefore easy to line up the vertical grid lines on the map with the lines on the compass which run parallel to the North arrow. This is of course, over-simplified, as it is necessary to take into account such things as the variation between North on the map (Grid North) and that which the compass points to (Magnetic North). This varies from place to place as Magnetic North is not a constant point, actually moving around the North Pole. However, for short distances, it is enough to be able to set the map to north with the compass.

To get a rough idea about the distance between two points it is worth remembering that each grid square on an O.S. map is 1 kilometre across, but for general use you will almost certainly need to be more accurate than that. On the O.S. 1:50,000 Landranger maps (that's the pink ones) 2 centimetres on a ruler (usually on the edge of your compass) represent 1 kilometre on the ground. It therefore follows that 1cm = 500m and 1mm = 50m. If using an O.S. 1:25,000 Outdoor Leisure map (that's the yellow ones) the scale is double that of the Landranger maps. Therefore 4 centimetres represent 1 kilometre, 2cm = 500m and 1mm = 25m. These maps offer much more detail and are excellent to use but unfortunately only cover the most popular walking areas.

You can now measure distances accurately on the map, so how do you transfer your new found skills to the ground. Suppose you have arrived at a cairn that is marked on the map and are heading for a summit trig point, which you cannot see due to thick mist. You can set the map to north and so gain an idea of which direction to walk and you can also measure the distance, but there is always the chance that you may wander off the bearing slightly, perhaps due to strong winds or the steep slope to the west, you could also over-compensate for these and walk too far the other way. Now imagine how handy it would be if you could measure the distance fairly accurately on the ground as well as on the map, you would at least know when you were in the vicinity of your target. It is well worth spending an afternoon practising pacing before you need to use it for real. Measure out 100 metres on flat ground and count double paces (that's every time your left foot touches the ground). Obviously everyone has a different pace so this is something which you should establish for yourself. Pace also differs according to whether the ground is flat, up-hill or down so remember to practise on different terrain. If the measured distance from the cairn to the summit is 250m, for instance, and you know that you take 60 paces per 100m, if you follow the bearing for 150 paces you should end up pretty close to your target.

Another way of measuring distance walked is timing. The average walking speed is 5 kilometres per hour. At this speed it will take 12 minutes to walk 1 kilometre. The main disadvantage with timing is that few people can estimate their own speed accurately. I personally walk at 6 km/h, some prefer 4km/h. Also bear in mind that your speed will alter when carrying a heavy load or walking up-hill or through deep snow. You should add 1 minute for every 10 metres of ascent to your over-all tally. Generally speaking timing is less accurate than pacing over short distances though I would use timing on distances over, say 700m, as pacing long distances is tedious to say the least and detracts from the enjoyment of the walk. Again, you can measure out 1 kilometre on the ground and time yourself to see how long it takes you. Around 10 minutes is a 6 k/h pace, 12.5 is a 5k/h pace and 15 minutes is 4k/h. What is important is that you establish your own usual pace.

The next essential thing to glean from the map is whether your route will take you over hills or through a valley etc. The contours (thin continuous brown lines) depict height above sea level. Each contour represents 10 metres and, being continuous, links heights of the same altitude. It follows that if they are close together the gradient will be steep and if they are far apart this will be gradual or even negligible. Numbers are shown every so often giving the height of a particular contour, so it is easy to make out if the slope is up or down.

Navigation not only deserves much more attention than we tend to give, it can also be great fun. The next time low cloud keeps the tops covered, instead of heading straight for the cafés of Llanberis, why not make the most of your weekend, grab your map and compass and try navigating between the innumerable features on Garnedd Uchaf or Mynydd Mawr; or try following a grid line as far as possible without deviating (or trespassing!);

or why not follow a contour line. This undoubtedly will take you off the beaten track and give you a greater understanding and knowledge of our hills. Night navigation is also an excellent way of spending a starry summer evening.

APPENDIX 3

Bibliography

The following titles provide further, more detailed reading on a number of specialised subjects connected with the Welsh Hewitts.

Ashton, S. *Scrambles in Snowdonia*, Cicerone
Borrow, George *Wild Wales*, Thomas Nelson & Sons, 1862
Bridge, G. *The Mountains of England and Wales*, West Col, 1973
Brown, Joe *The Hard Years*, Penguin, 1967
Butterfield, Irvine *The High Mountains of Britain and Ireland*
Campbell and Newton *Welsh Winter Climbs*, Cicerone, 1996
Cantrell *Sarn Helen*, Cicerone
Clayton and Turnbull *The Welsh 3000' Challenges*
Climbers' Club *Rock Climbing Guides to Wales*, Climber's Club:-
    1) Gogarth (Anglesey)
    2) North Wales Limestone
    3) Ogwen and Carneddau
    4) Llanberis Pass
    5) Clogwyn Du'r Arddu
    6) Lliwedd
    7) Tremadog, Cwm Silyn and Cwellyn
    8) Lleyn Peninsula
    9) Mid Wales
    10) Pembroke
    11) Gower and South-East Wales
    12) Wye Valley
Condry, William *Exploring Wales*, Faber & Faber, 1970
Condry, William *Snowdonia National Park*, Fontana New Naturalist, 1969
Dawson, Alan *The Hewitts and Marilyns of Wales*, TACit Tables, 1997
Dawson, Alan *The Relative Hills of Britain*, Cicerone, 1992
Dean, Stephen *Hands of a Climber - A life of Colin Kirkus*, 1993
Dewey, M. *Mountain Tables*, Constable, 1995
Evans, John *The Red Kite in Wales*, Christopher Davies, 1990
Gibbings, Robert *Coming Down the Wye*, J.M. Dent and Sons, 1943
Hankinson, Alan *Geoffrey Winthrop Young*, Hodder & Stoughton, 1995
Hankinson, Alan *The Mountain Men*, 1977

Haskett Smith, W.P. *Climbing in the British Isles*, The Ernest Press, 1986

Howell, P. & Beazley, E. *The Companion Guide to South Wales*, Collins, 1977

Jones & Milburn *Welsh Rock*, Pic Publications, 1986

Jones *The Complete Guide To Snowdon*

Jones *The Lakes of North Wales*

Kirk, David *Abridged version of Pennants 'Tour in Wales'*, Carreg Gwalch, 1998

Lowe, S.C. *Llanberis Past and Present*, Odyn Copr, 1984

Milburn, Geoff *Helyg*, Climbers' Club, 1985

Moss, E. *The Two-Thousands of Wales*, Rucksack Club Journal, 1940

Nuttall, John and Anne *Mountains of England and Wales, Volume 1, Wales*, Cicerone, 1989

Pearsall, W.H. *Mountains and Moorlands,* Fontana New Naturalist, 1972

Perrin, Jim *Menlove*, The Ernest Press, 1993

Poucher, W.A. *Snowdonia Through The Lens*, Chapman & Hall, 1941

Poucher, W.A. *Snowdon Holiday*, Chapman & Hall, 1943

Poucher, W.A. *The Welsh Peaks*, Constable

Pyatt, Edward C. *Where to Climb in the British Isles*, Faber & Faber, 1960

Remfry, Paul *Castles of Radnorshire*, Logaston, 1996

Soper/Wilson/Crew *The Black Cliff*, Kaye and Ward, 1971

Strang *Brecon Beacons National Park*, HMSO, 1967

Styles, Showell *Welsh Walks and Legends*, Granada Publishing, 1979

Wilson, K. & Gilbert, R. *Classic Walks*, Diadem

Wilson, K. & Gilbert, R. *Big Walks*, Diadem, 1980

Wilson, K. & Gilbert, R. *Wild Walks*, Bâton Wicks, 1988

Wilson, Ken *Classic Rock*, Diadem

Wilson, Ken *Cold Climbs*, Diadem

Wilson, Ken *Extreme Rock*, Diadem

Wilson, Ken *Hard Rock*, Diadem

Useful instructional books include:-
Eric Langmuir *Mountaincraft and Leadership*
Kevin Walker *Mountain Navigation Techniques*
Kevin Walker *Mountain Hazards*
Kevin Walker *Wild Country Camping*
Alpine Club *Avalanche*
Barton/ Wright *A Chance in a Million*
Fyffe/ Peters *Handbook of Climbing*

APPENDIX 4

Maps

The following maps will be found necessary for detailed exploration of the Hewitts of Wales, and should be consulted both whilst enjoying this book, and out on the hills.

Ordnance Survey 'Landranger' maps (pink covers) covering the following ranges at a scale of 1:50,000 are suitable for use whilst out bagging Hewitts:-

Number 115 Snowdon and Surrounding Area:-
Carneddau, Glyders, Snowdon, Eifionydd, Moelwyns and Manods.

Number 124 Dolgellau and Surrounding Area:-
Moelwyns, Rhinogs, Arenigs, Arans, Dovey Hills, Cadair Idris, Tarrens.

Number 125 Bala & Lake Vyrnwy & Surrounding Area:-
Arenigs, Hirnants, Berwyns.

Number 135 Aberystwyth & Machynlleth:-
Tarrens, Plynlimon, Pen y Garn.

Number 147 Elan Valley and Builth Wells:-
Elan Valley Hills and Moors.

Number 148 Presteigne & Hay-on-Wye Area:-
Radnorshire Forest.

Number 161 Abergavenny & The Black Mountains:-
The Black Mountains, Cefn yr Ystrad.

Number 160 Brecon Beacons/ Bannau Brycheiniog
Mynydd Du, Fforest Fawr, Brecon Beacons, Cefn yr Ystrad.

The Ordnance Survey also publish a series of 'Outdoor Leisure' maps (yellow covers) at a scale of 1:25,000. These give far greater detail than the Landranger maps, but many find them too cumbersome for use on the hill.

They do however, provide a wealth of information and should be poured over prior to a trip into the hills. They are suitable for a more detailed exploration of any particular area.

Number 11 - Brecon Beacons - Central Area.

Number 12 - Brecon Beacons - Western Area.

Number 13 - Brecon Beacons - Eastern Area.

Number 16 - Snowdonia - Conwy Valley Area.

Number 17 - Snowdonia - Snowdon Area.

Number 18 - Snowdonia - Harlech and Bala Areas.

Number 23 - Snowdonia - Cadair Idris Area.

THE WELSH HEWITTS CLUB

The aim of The Welsh Hewitts Club is to promote the 20 groups of hills across Wales in which the 137 Hewitts lie as areas to walk, climb, or explore, whilst retaining their natural and wild environment as far as possible. As part of this it will maintain a list of those who climb all 137 summits.

Membership is open to individuals or organisations interested in promoting or encouraging the above aim. The Club receives support from The Wales Tourist Board, The Brasher Boot Company, Powys County Council and Conwy County Borough amongst others.

LAUNCH OFFER

With the Club being launched in 1999, there is an initial membership offer. Annual membership is £5 (to essentially cover cost of preparing and sending out newsletters etc.), but if you join in 1999 you may elect to take out 2 years' membership for £7.50.

To join, just complete and send the form below with a cheque or postal order for £5 or £7.50 as applicable (payable to 'The Welsh Hewitts Club') to: Graham Uney, 53 Rosedale Avenue, Southcoates Lane, Hull, HU9 2PL

Please enroll me as a founder member of the The Welsh Hewitts Club
Name:

Address:

Phone no:
I enclose a cheque/P.O. for £5 for 1 year's membership
£7.50 for 2 years' membership
(delete as appropriate)

APPENDIX 5

Useful Addresses

British Mountaineering Council,
General Secretary,
Roger Payne,
177-179 Burton Road,
Manchester.
M20 2BB

Mountain Bothy Association,
General Secretary,
Lynda Woods,
28 Duke Street,
Clackmannan.
Scotland.
FK10 4EF

Welsh Tourist Board,
Brunel House,
2 Fitz Allan Road,
Cardiff.
CF21UY

The Welsh Hewitts Club,
c/o Graham Uney,*
53 Rosedale Avenue,
Southcoates Lane,
Hull
HU9 2PL.

*The author also provides training in navigation and hillcraft throughout the mountain regions of Britain under the business name of Wild Ridge Adventure and can be contacted at the above address with regard to this.

Index

Carnedd Llewelyn	115	683644	46, 48, 50, 54, 55, 297
Carnedd y Filiast	124,125	871445	90, 264, *264*
Carnedd y Filiast	115	620627	30, 32, 284
Cefn yr Ystrad	160	086137	163, 164, 191, 195
Chwarel y Fan	161	259293	176, 204
Cnicht	115	645466	28, 64, 65, 272
Corris	124	755078	225
Corwen	125	075433	110
Craig Cerrig-gleisiad	160	960217	160, 161, 188, 189
Craig Cwm Amarch	124	710121	116, 118, 119, *119*, 228, 229
Craig Cwm Silyn	115	525502	77, 78, 79, *81*, 275
Craig-y-llyn	124	665119	124, 228 *Colour* 242/3
Creigiau Gleision North Top	115	733622	55, 58, 292, *293*
Creigiau Gleision	115	729615	49, 55, 58, 292
Crib Goch	115	624551	18, 19, 20, 21, 23, 37, 248, 279, 280, *281* *Colour* 242/3
Crib y Ddysgl	115	610551	18, 19, 20, 21, 281
Cribin Fawr	124	794153	125, 126, 244, 245
Cribyn	160	023213	168, 169, 197
Crickhowell	161	216183	177, 201, *201*, 202 *Colour* 82/3
Cwmystwyth	135	789741	139, 143
Cyfrwy	124	703133	115, 120, 121, 122, 124, 228, 229
Cynwyd	125	056411	257, 258
Cyrniau Nod	125	988279	112, 114, 253
Dduallt	124,125	810273	94, 96, 229, 235, 239, 240, 241 *Colour* 242/3
Devil's Bridge	135	740770	139, *142*, 219-20
Diffwys	124	661234	83, 84, 230, 231
Dinas Mawddwy	124	859148	97, 103, 125, 126, 243
Dolgellau	124	729177	88, 97, 115, 120, 121, 122, 125, 230, 239-40, 243 *Colour* 82/3
Dolwyddelan	115	735524	63
Drosgl	115	664679	51, 298
Drum	115	708695	53, 54, 299

Drygarn Fawr	147	862583	141, 144-6, 212, 215, 216, *217*
Elidir Fawr	115	612613	32, 33, 280, 284
Elan Village	147	934653	144
Erw y Ddafad-ddu	124,125	864233	102, 103, 248
Esgeiriau Gwynion	124,125	889236	103, 249
Fan Brycheiniog	160	825217	154, 155, 156, 186
Fan Fawr	160	969193	161, 162, 188, 189, 191, 192
Fan Frynych	160	958227	160, 161, 189
Fan Gyhirych	160	880190	157, 158, 159, 188
Fan Hir	160	830209	154, 156, 186 *Colour* 242/3
Fan Llia	160	938186	159, 160, 188, 189
Fan Nedd	160	913184	157-60, 188
Fan y Big	160	036206	169, 198, 199, 200
Ffestiniog	124	703420	267
Foel Cwm Sian Llwyd	125	995313	114, 253
Foel Goch	125	943290	112, 114, 262
Foel Goch	125	953422	89, 90, 251, *252*, 253
Foel Grach	115	688658	50, 297
Foel Gron	115	560568	8, 282
Foel Hafod-fynydd	124,125	877227	103, 249
Foel Wen	125	099334	109, 257
Foel y Geifr	125	937275	111, 112, 251, 252, *252*, 253
Foel-fras	115	696681	52, 53, 298, 299
Foel-goch	115	628611	33, 34, 285
Gallt y Daren	124	778344	94, 95, 266
Gallt yr Ogof	115	685585	30, 44, 285, 289
Garnedd Uchaf	115	687669	50, 51, 52, 297
Garreg Las	160	777203	151-5, 185
Garreg Lwyd	160	740179	151, 152, 185, 294
Gau Graig	124	744141	122, 124, 228, 229
Glasgwm	124,125	836194	97, 98, 245, 246, *246*
Glyder Fach	115	656582	30, 39, 40, 41, 285, *286*, 287
Glyder Fawr	115	642579	30, 35, 36, 37, 38, 39, 43, *49*, 285, 287, *287*

Glyntawe	160	843163	155, 184
Gorllwyn	147	917590	141, 144-6, 212, 215
Great Rhos	148	182639	148, 149, 150, 210
Gwaun y Llwyni	124,125	857204	100, *246*, 247
Hay-on-Wye	148	227422	171, 172, 206, 207
Llanberis	161,115	577604	6, 15, 281, 183
Llangynog	125	053260	254-5
Llechwedd Du	124,125	894224	103, 104
Llwytmor	115	689692	52, 53, 298
Machynlleth	135	745007	224
Maesglase	124,125	822151	125, 126, 127, 244, *244*
Manod Mawr North Top	115	727458	68, 69, 70, 271
Manod Mawr	124	723446	68, 69, *267*, 269, 270, 271
Moel Cynghorion	115	586563	6, 8, 9, 282
Moel Druman	115	671476	65, 66, 272
Moel Eilio	115	555577	6, 8, *80*, 282, 283
Moel Fferna	125	116397	110, 257, 258-9
Moel Hebog	115	565469	5, 6, 71, 72, 74, *74*, 75, 273, 274, *274*
Moel Lefn	115	553485	71, 75, 76, 77, *274*, 274
Moel Llyfnant	124,125	808351	94, 266 *Colour* 242/3
Moel Penamnen	115	716483	69, 70, 271
Moel Siabod	115	705546	23, 59, 60, *60*, 62, *63*, 64, 67, *279*, 280, 288, 293 *Colour* 242/3
Moel Sych	125	066318	106, 108, 255
Moel y Cerrig Duon	125	923241	111, 249, 251
Moel yr Henfaes	125	089369	109, 110, 257, 260
Moel yr Ogof	115	556478	75, 273, *274*
Moel Ysgyfarnogod	124	658345	x, 86, 87, 230, 233-4
Moelwyn Bach	124	660437	67, 68, 268
Moelwyn Mawr	124	658448	67, 268, 269
Moel-yr-hydd	115	672454	67, 269
Mynydd Drws-y-coed	115	548518	76, 77, 79, 276
Mynydd Llysiau	161	207279	177, 203
Mynydd Mawr	115	539546	6, 71, 77, 79, 80, 82, 276-7, 283 *Colour* 242/3
Mynydd Moel	124	727136	121, 228, 229

Tal y Fan	115	729726	49, 53, 54, 183, 264, 183, 299, 300
Tarren y Gesail	124	710059	129, 226
Tarrenhendre	135	682041	226-7
Trawsfynydd	124	707355	233-4
Trum y Ddysgl	115	544516	71, 77, 276
Tryfan	115	664593	30, 41, 42, 43, *49, 284, 285, 286, 287, 288, 288, 289, 289, 296*
Twmpa	161	224350	175, 204, 205, *205*
Tyrrau Mawr	124	677135	123, 124, 228
Waun Fach	161	215300	176, 177, 203
Waun Rydd	160	062206	169, 170, 198
Waun-oer	124	785147	125, 126, 127, 244
Y Foel Goch	115	677582	30, 43, 285, 289
Y Garn	115	630595	34, 37, *49*, 274, 285
Y Garn	124	702230	84, 87, 88, 229, 235, 237-9, *237, 238*
Y Garn	135	775851	134, 135, 136, 222
Y Llethr	124	661258	83, 84, 231
Y Lliwedd	115	622533	5, 21, 23, 24, 24, 26, 28, 277, 278, 279, 289 *Colour 242/3*
Yr Aran	115	604515	26, 27, 277 *Colour 242/3*
Yr Elen	115	673651	46, 48, 49, 297 *Colour 242/3*
Ysgafell Wen North Top	115	663485	65, 272
Ysgafell Wen	115	667481	59, 65, 272
Ystradfellte	160	930134	157